Man's Quest for Partnership

MAN'S QUEST FOR PARTNERSHIP

The anthropological foundations of ethics and religion

by

J. van Baal

1981
Van Gorcum, Assen, The Netherlands

Baal, J. van – Man's quest for partnership: the anthropological foundations of ethics and religion / by J van Baal. – Assen: Van Gorcum.

Reg., lit. rep.
ISBN 90-232-1813-2

Printed in The Netherlands by Van Gorcum, Assen

To Hilda
In gratitude

Preface

Cultural anthropology has opened our eyes to the immense variety of human reactions to divergent conditions. No one can study this variety for long without finding many of his standard opinions affected. It turned quite a number of anthropologists into fervent relativists, 'cultural relativists' as they called themselves. But relativism is not a well-considered answer to the challenge of cultural diversity. It is too rapidly given. Cultural diversity is not without its limits. There are categories of behaviour and expression, common to all mankind, which combine variety with universality. Among these are ethics and religion, and it is their universality which raises pertinent questions about human nature and the human condition to which relativism has no answer; even if it be granted that the universality of religion can be disputed.

It is common practice in anthropology to honour questions concerning the foundations of ethics and religion as first questions, common practice also to concede that for this reason they are the last to be answered. These are not questions of cultural anthropology alone, but of general anthropology. They involve the philosophical foundations of the whole discipline as well as those of the student's own worldview and attitude. Prepared to give due consideration to these questions, the anthropologist has sound reason to be reluctant to forward definite answers. They do not simply commit him as an anthropologist, but also in his personal stance with regard to questions of ethics and religion. It is only natural to take one's time before trying to answer them, and to let other tasks and commitments prevail as more urgent. Considerations of this kind certainly played a role in the author's decision to postpone the writing of this book until well after his retirement, five years ago, as professor of anthropology at the State University of Utrecht, and this notwithstanding the fact that the early foundations for this work had been laid long before in a book on the ways and motivations of religion which appeared in 1947.

The book was the fruit of my reflections during more than three years of detention in Japanese prisoner-of-war camps in Indonesia during World War II, years which taught me some lessons about human life and death which books and peace-time contacts rarely demonstrate with such clarity as the dramatic conditions of the time. The one real excuse I have that I did not take up the old thread earlier lies in the circumstance that in July 1947 I had to return to active service in the Netherlands

Indies' civil administration. There, I soon got entangled into a long series of engaging administrative and political activities which kept me extremely busy until, in 1958, I retired from a five years' governorship of (the then) Netherlands New Guinea.

During the years which followed, I had to give part of my time to the development problems of the third world, and it was but gradually that I could return to problems of pure theory. All I can say about it is that I am grateful that, at last, I have been able to finish a task which, through all these years, has weighed on my conscience as the one thing I should complete, just as I am grateful that this time I again found the firm of Van Gorcum & Company, with whom I have had a long standing association, willing to shoulder the publishing.

Still, little would have come of this book if I had not enjoyed the privilege of the critical comments of friends who kindly agreed to read important parts or even the whole of the original manuscript. That these comments induced me to a substantial deal of rewriting gives ample evidence how much they helped me to understand my own problems better. For all this I am deeply indebted to my colleagues Dr. C. F. van Parreren, professor of psychology at Utrecht University, and Dr. C. A. van Peursen, professor of philosophy at the University of Leyden, as well as to my fellow anthropologists of the Department of Cultural Anthropology of Utrecht University, Dr. W. E. A. van Beek, and Dr. A. de Ruyter. Of course they cannot be held responsible for any of the opinions expressed in this book. They have just been extremely kind to me and I thank them cordially.

I am grateful too, to Dr. P. Staples of the Faculty of Theology of the University of Utrecht for his correction of the final text and the many improvements he wrought on my English which, inevitably, is an alien's English. I am very happy that he has been willing to do this for me and, by his critical comment, made me aware of my repeated failures to express myself properly. Similar thanks are due to Mrs. Mary Schregardus for her invaluable assistance in the correction of the proofs.

But above all others I must thank my wife for her indulgence in forbearing my recluse-like habits which hardly improved when my retirement brought opportunities for a socially more gratifying way of life.

Doorn, October 1980

Contents

Part One

The Human Condition

I

Introduction
Man and Nature

1. General introduction. Man's problems with ethics and religion

Man is a product of nature, but certain peculiarities of man's behaviour impress us as inconsistent with the rationality manifest in all nature's other works and products. It is not because man enjoys a certain freedom of action; though he is supposed to have greater freedom than other animals, freedom is not a property exclusively belonging to mankind, nor is it a power which is incompatible with natural reason. What is surprising is that man uses this freedom to devise rules which annul it, and that he combines the praise and enforcement of these rules with secret or overt efforts to evade them. Similarly, there is nothing 'unnatural' or irrational in the fact that man, in his struggle for survival, fights other manifestations of nature. But it certainly amazes us that, in this struggle, he invokes the help of unknown and unknowable powers to which he ascribes a reality which reality cannot substantiate. It is to problems of this kind that this book is devoted, problems which can be summarized as follows: What is there in man, this product of the planet earth, that induces him to curtail his freedom by rules that can be described as a system of ethics, and to supplement his empirical knowledge and rational activities with an array of notions and actions concerning a non-verifiable world, which we call religion?

Ethics and religion have two traits in common. The first announces itself as an irrationality: they both attempt the impossible, ethics by obliging man to a behavioural perfection that is unattainable, religion by endeavouring to fathom the unknowable in an effort at wringing meaning from the uncertain. The one is at variance with human nature, the other is called in question by human reason. The irrationality of both finds confirmation in the proclivity of various philosophers to associate them with the *summum bonum,* the humanly unattainable highest good.

In the second place, what ethics and religion have in common is that they are culturally defined, i.e. that the substantiation of their contents is a matter of culture and thus can differ from one culture to another. Ethics and religion, then, are cultural universals; but they are this in different, and in one respect opposite, ways. Ethics are weakly developed in primitive culture; with the growth of culture the ethical rules multiply and their founding principles are made explicit. Religion finds its greatest diversity and most ardent practice in primitive culture, and tends to lose its functions

3

in modern civilization. How far this loss of functions extends is a matter of controversy, but one thing is certain: cultural diversity has a deep impact on religion as well as on ethics. The combination of universality with cultural diversity raises the problem what in both must be ascribed to culture, and what is so general that it must have its foundation in human nature or, at the very least, in the human condition. The description of the human condition is necessarily a central problem in every enquiry into the foundations of ethics and religion.

Consequently, the first part of this book is devoted to an analysis of the human condition. Beginning with human biology we proceed to a discussion of some basic features of the mind, the role of the subject, the use of symbols, and the role of cognition and affects in man's ways of life and expression. In chapter III we turn to the dialectics of the human condition which we find defined by the fact that man is a subject who must be part of his universe, and a part of his universe who must be a subject. Our hypothesis is that it is these dialectics of the human condition which lay the foundations of the contradictions inherent in the phenomena known as ethics and religion.

To test this hypothesis we turn to primitive culture. Primitive man is closer to the naked facts of the human condition than modern man, whose ways of life are complicated by the highly variegated exigencies of modern civilization. In modern man's life, the role of culture is more encompassing than in that of primitive man who faces conditions which still reflect part of the problems to which, at the dawn of primitive culture, early man was confronted. Although the study of primitive culture cannot supply us with exact data specifying the historical origins of the institutions which, in already more developed forms, direct the thought and actions of primitive people, we can certainly derive significant information from it which is relevant to the most basic problems of human existence and man's answers to them.

In Part II we concentrate on what primitive culture has to tell about the origin and development of ethics. We rarely find traces of general maxims summarizing moral ideals. What we do find are certain rules for the regulation of social conduct, and it is of some interest that with these rules it is the same as it is with rules for social behaviour everywhere: man makes them, man praises them and demands that they shall be respected, and man disobeys them as soon as it is to his advantage to do so and has reason to believe that no sanctions will follow. A more significant symptom of the limited impact of ethical rules on primitive man's ways of life is the clear tendency to restrict the recognition of moral obligations to the interaction with members of one's own society, and that these societies always are small, often even very small in size. Relations with other societies are either hostile or imbued with suspicion, and intertribal warfare is a recurrent phenomenon. In many primitive societies male aggressiveness is strongly developed, and displayed with greater openness than in modern society. Nevertheless, inside society certain rules are respected, and we find definite signs of a moral awareness which indicate that the need for partnership is a vital one, and the quest for it a motive which has a deep impact on the relations between the members of a primitive society. This implies that ethics are primarily a matter of interpersonal relations here and that their moral ends must be defined accordingly. Next to these, we find certain incipient rules for the regulation of conduct in interaction with (relative) strangers who are not considered as enemies (e.g. with regard to chance meetings and the modes of behaviour to be observed in intercommunal trade).

In Part III we turn to religion which we define as all notions and acts referring to a reality which, though it cannot be verified or falsified, is accepted by the group of believers concerned as true and as relevant to their real life and world (below: 150). Other than ethics which have proved their usefulness for the preservation of society and have grown in impact and significance with the development of culture, religion has become a subject of controversy. There are unmistakable signs that it is losing its grip on modern man. Though this need be no more than one of those temporal oscillations which, allegedly, are characteristic of certain periods of cultural transition, the fact is important enough to make allowance for the possibility that, after all, religion is not the cultural universal which it seemed to be until the beginning of the present century. Might it not then be the case that every effort to explain religion from the exigencies of the human condition is necessarily void? We must then consider the possibility that it originated from a lack of knowledge, or from a pathology of the mind.

An effort to explain religion from a lack of knowledge necessarily ends in tautology. Religion, however defined or practised, ultimately refers to the unknowable, and the existence of an unknowable is an undeniable fact which, so far, has proved itself impervious to the increase of knowledge and the perfection of our research methods. The factuality of the unknowable has hardened rather than weakened under the attacks of modern science. Religion undoubtedly has to do with a lack of knowledge but there is little in this fact that can explain the irrationalities of religion. In this respect the explanations from a pathology of the mind stand a better chance.

Such explanations find support in the many irrationalities, or even absurdities of primitive religion, and to a no less degree in a remarkable peculiarity proper to practically all the symbols of religion, those of the more developed religions included. The point is that all religions (with the possible exception of some forms of metaphysics) give shape to the unverifiable reality of which our definition speaks, in person-like symbols. All these symbols, in one form or another, refer to man's real world; that is, to the world as he experiences it. What is more, these person-like beings are all Janus-faced: alternately promising and threatening, kind and revengeful, just like the real universe to which they refer. From here to the symbols symptomatic of mental disorder is only one small step. They resemble them closely. And yet, there is one decisive difference. The symbols of the mentally sick originate in deviance from the notions and rules of the patients' society, whereas those of religion give support to the society's rules, and are recognized by its members as true or meaningful. Besides, religious believers are normal people who do not display symptoms of mental disturbance more often than others. One could not expect otherwise; until this century religion has been universal among all mankind, and what is universal is by definition normal. Of course, all this does not distract from the fact that the belief in an unverifiable reality, reified in the form of person-like beings, is – to put it mildly – a daring proposition. The fact, however, that belief in such daring propositions is so general that it must be acknowledged as normal, raises a dilemma which can only be solved by accepting that there is something in the human condition which predisposes mankind to such forms of belief. The strongly dialectic nature of the person-like religious beings indicates that this something must be an inner conflict general among all mankind. This leads us back to the dialectics of the human condition as defined above. The problem we are confronted with is to find out whether these dialectics of the human condition can supply an adequate explanation for the religious phenomenon in all its variegated forms.

This is a fairly complicated task, and this explains why Part III of this book is the most voluminous of the four. The fact, moreover, that at the end of this part we find our hypothesis vindicated, presents us with a new problem: How does modern man do without religion? We face this problem in Part IV, in combination with another one which results from our study of ethics in Part II. It is concerned with the fact that the depersonalization of human relations has led to a rather legalistic system of ethics which involves all the various aspects of modern man's life but has not the capacity to satisfy his affective needs. This void is aggravated by the circumstance that many people gave up religion as something incompatible with modern science. This raises the problem of how to find new ways for the solution of the conflicts inherent in the human condition. These conflicts persist and modern man is faced with the choice: Either to find a suitable substitute for religion, or to create such forms of religion as are compatible with a more scientific worldview, and meet the affective needs which modern culture left unfulfilled.

2. The rules of life

Our inquiry necessarily begins with the recapitulation of a number of well-known facts concerning life in general. Man is not alone on this planet. He is part of the earth's most intriguing sub-system: the world of living nature, of which man is one of the latest products. In this context man must be placed, and it is useful to give some consideration to the basic facts of biology which condition his life. We shall present them in this chapter in a seemingly haphazard way, as an introduction to the following chapters where we must enter into more detail before we can make an effort at systematizing our views in an encompassing characterization of the human condition.

The discovery that life is a matter of large protein molecules of a highly complicated structure has opened up new insights into the surprising role played by these molecules in the construction of the cell and even of the individual. Some molecules have been found capable of organizing organic matter into patterned wholes that are specific for each species separately. Each of these patterned wholes, from monocellular beings upwards, and whatever the species to which it belongs, has the capacity of self-sustenance and growth by absorbing more and more matter into its system by means of an enduring process called its metabolism. In this as well as in other activities which, together, we call its behaviour, the living whole presents itself as a more or less autonomous system which has the remarkable faculty of propagation, i.e. of producing new and more or less identical living wholes which adhere to the same standard pattern of form and behaviour that is characteristic of the species.

The term 'a more or less autonomous system' is a qualification of the individual requiring a closer specification (and limitation) of its contents. The word autonomy evokes associations with independence and free will, and that is certainly not what we have in mind. Free will is a confusing concept. It is difficult to say what a will is, let alone to define a free will. For all we know there is not much free will in a world where all things are conditioned, humanity included. What we really mean is that all living beings, whether they are mono- or multi-cellular, are individuals that can be distinguished from the surrounding world and from each other, each of them leading its own life, however much that life depends on the presence of other individuals and however strongly it might be determined by them. In this sense, even the coral-building anthozoans live their own life. All this has little to do with freedom, however conceived. It refers first and foremost to the standard behavioural pattern characteristic of a species which, in turn, is a more or less pre-ordained manner of behaving that can be defined as a standardized set of patterned reactions to stimuli. In fact, it is not because of some dubious form of freedom that we use the term autonomy in connection with the individual. It is because one of the determinants of the individual's behaviour is the constitution of the whole that we call the individual. This is most markedly so in the case of the higher organisms, those endowed with a central nervous system. With the lower organisms, and notably in the case of plants, stimulus and response may be confined to a smaller or bigger part of the organism; but even so the whole is not unaffected. In the higher organisms, the tendency predominates to react as an entity which is set apart from other similar entities. The whole is not a mere agglomerate of associated parts, it is an individual, and it reacts exactly as that individual.

There is more than sufficient reason to stress the importance of the individual in the realm of nature. Individuals of one species differ among themselves. Within the limits set by the standard patterns of form and behaviour of a species, there is a fair measure of variation in individual forms and conduct. It may be that a casual imperfection of the reproductive system caused a minor deviation from the original standard pattern, it may be a milieu-determined cause which produced a variation, but anyway every species-specific pattern has an inbuilt latitude for minor variations, some of which are genetically transmissible whereas others are not. Whatever the role of chance in the process which generates variations, this variability is an important feature, promoting the variation and development of living nature generally. The variability of the species-specific patterns of form and behaviour is sufficiently large to afford an opportunity for the sudden appearance of more drastic changes of the pattern which, as occasionally happens in the history of a species after an unknown but presumably high number of self-repetitions by propagation, result in the appearance of a viable new species.

We shall return presently to the importance of the principle of individuation for

7

the forms and development of life. First, we must pay attention to another intriguing feature of living nature, i.e. its tendency to constitute a self-sustaining system. To a great variety of species, minerals, in a form which is unaffected by influences due to life, constitute, at best, a minor part of their diet. Plants owe an important part of their food to the humus generated by the remains of dead organisms. The land-born vertebrates get all or almost all of the minerals they need by eating the plants and animals which are their regular food. Apart from fresh air, the almost exclusive contribution of uncontaminated, inanimate nature to their metabolism is water. As far as man is concerned, even household-salt is, in primitive conditions, ordinarily acquired either by eating sea-food or by consuming the ashes of certain plants drenched in salty springs. Living nature is, by and large, a self-sustaining system of interdependent species, each of which keeps itself alive by feeding or predating upon a number of others. Even plants do so for an important part of their nutrition; they thrive best on an ample supply of humus, the decayed remains of their predecessors on the territory occupied.

Life and death cooperate in a highly efficient system of interdependence made possible and necessary for both by a high fertility rate. A low fertility rate would result in the extinction of the species concerned, and in dearth for the species dependent on it for their food. Sickness, other than sickness caused by accident or dearth, is but one form of turning living beings into food, the form applied by micro-organisms in their struggle for life. Vertebrates feed more openly on their fellow creatures; if predators, by devouring them, if herbivores, by grazing. Even dead bodies are a source of food, whatever the cause of their death. In nature, the death of the one is the life of another, each serving a number of others as food.

Nevertheless, the contribution of inanimate nature to the metabolism of the living should not be underrated, certainly not that in the form of water and air. The dead organisms constitute a surplus that cannot wholly be consumed by the living. Thick layers of coal, oil and limestone bear witness to past organic life turned into inanimate matter without having been consumed by other living beings. Over time, the production of organic life is richer than can be digested by the living. It is only modern man who manages to consume more. His insatiable consumptive needs have incited him to turn to the relics of past life to cover his demands of energy.

The life of every individual of every species is finite. It is not simply a matter of the individual's destiny to serve other individuals as food: the individual is intrinsically finite. All living beings are subject to the inescapable process of aging, a surprising process because on the face of appearances it is redundant. Nature does not need senilization to clear away a surplus of individuals of any kind. If a species multiplies beyond measure, dearth will in time diminish the number of individuals until the balance has been restored. Occasionally even abortus occurs as the result of over-crowding, a phenomenon observed among various species of rodents (Ardrey 1972: 200 ff.). Yet, from a genetic point of view, senilization has its advantages. It excludes the older individuals from participation in the process of propagation and thus promotes a rapid turnover of individuals joining in the exchange of genes, a very effective way of promoting intra-species variation and, ultimately, of increasing the

8

opportunities for originating new species. The argument strongly supports the idea that evolution is a purposive process aiming at increasing variegation and perfection or, at the very least, at the production of ever more complicated forms of life. Teleological notions of this kind do not harmonize very well with those of chance and probability which are the basic concepts of the doctrine of evolution. Nevertheless, a trend towards increasing variation and perfection is unmistakably present and it would be unwise to close one's eyes to the fact that senilization has a favourable effect on genetic miscegenation because of the fear that the admittance of the fact might lure us into teleological fallacies. As far as the problem of death is concerned, senilization proves that death is an imperative necessity which, because of its favourable effect on genetic variation, may be called a function of life itself.

Senilization is a curious process also in another respect. It does not strike at life generally, but at the life of the individual. Years ago Umbgrove reminded us of the fact that "growing older is a phenomenon which disappears when a tissue is removed from the influence emanating from the living whole. Carrel demonstrated this by isolating and cultivating tissue taken from the heart of a chicken embryo; since 1912 the tissue is growing without getting old" (Umbgrove 1946: 131). The important conclusion is not that what is impossible *in vivo* can be realized *in vitro*, but that it is the individual which is subject to senilization and death, and not any part of it. It holds true even of living beings that are not necessarily subject to death, viz. the monocellular beings which propagate by cell-fission. The effect of fission is not the origination of a new individual next to the old one, but that two new individuals originate by taking the place as well as the substance of the old one which dissolves. It is not life as such that is finite, but the living individual, the organized whole. Life, death, and the individual are inseparable. What dies is the individual, not any part of it, though composing elements of a lower order (cells as well as damaged parts of tissues) may perish and be replaced.

The life of the individual shows a certain likeness to the flight of an aeroplane. Birth is its take-off, followed at the end of the trip by the inevitable landing at the airport of death. The warm-blooded vertebrates daily go through a process that in an attenuated form adumbrates the total cycle. They wake up in the morning and fall asleep at night. For all we know about sleep it is not the organism as a whole that relapses into inactivity, but exactly that part of it that we describe as the centre of the individual's conscious activities, that which in humans is called the subject. In sleep the subject is temporarily obliterated. The emphasis on individuation observed already in the phenomenon of individual variation, and in the fact that activities and reactions tend to imply the individual as a whole and not any part of it, as well as in the circumstance that death and senilization are related to the individual as such, reappears in the phenomenon of sleep which temporarily eliminates the central part of the individual's outward directed activities, the subject. In spite of all the criticism levelled in recent years at the over-emphasis of philosophers on the part played by the subject, a criticism that in some respects is well-founded, we shall have to pay further attention to the phenomenon of individuation and in particular to its centre, to that which in human beings is called alternately the subject, the ego and the self, and

9

which shall here be referred to mostly as the subject, because more than the two other terms it emphasizes the relation with consciousness.

3. The scanning subject

An outstanding characteristic of most animals is their power of locomotion. Their movements, though often predictable, invariably impress the outsider as purposive movements willed by the individual. Indeed, it is always the individual as a whole that is involved, but this does not imply that the use of the word *will* is justified. There is a suggestion of arbitrariness in the word will which is not corroborated by the possibility to predict many, if not most of these motions. This predictability is not simply a matter of animal reactions to stimuli, it also applies to normal human action. Tylor has already pointed out that we all foster and express fairly detailed expectations with regard to the reactions of our companions to events and situations to which they are going to be confronted (Tylor 1871: 4 f.). Such expectations come true so often that they constitute part of the considerations preceding almost every act of decision making in which other people are involved. Without such predictability there would not be a science of sociology. It is based on the strong conviction that, to a very important extent, human behaviour and the fortunes of human society are subject to law. To scholars inclined to associate freedom with unpredictability this implies that the freedom suggested by the behaviour of man, and *a fortiori* that by the behaviour of animals, must be rejected as deceptive. Although such an identification of freedom with unpredictability is incorrect – we shall return to this point (below: 57) – this hardly detracts from the wisdom of the conclusion that this predictability calls for a closer study of the reaction patterns structuring the behaviour of animals and man in order to trace the laws by which order and form are given to their ways of life.

A popular instrument to that end has been the stimulus-response theory of the behaviourists. However, in its older, unsophisticated forms the theory is too simple to be applied to the problems evoked by the reactions of animals to unforeseen problems*. It is not difficult, of course, to call forth a more or less fixed pattern of responses by repetitive rewards and punishments to repeatedly presented conditions; but we do not know what goes on in the central nervous system that directs these responses. Far less do we know what an animal's reactions will be to the far more variegated, often contradictory and never wholly identical stimuli presented by the vicissitudes of life outside the laboratory. Ethologists have been able to establish quite a number of behavioural patterns among animals living in freedom but even so there are numerous problems. A good instance of these problems is contained in the story of the rat referred to by Buytendijk in *Mens en Dier* (1972: 125 f).

A rat climbed a wooden case placed close to a tin half filled with water. From the case it saw a piece of meat lying on a log that stood upright in the tin close to the far side as seen from the rat's vantage point. The case was near enough to the tin to

---

* This objection cannot be raised against modern behaviourists such as Eysink, to whose work Dr. Staples kindly called my attention. Unfortunately, I have been unable to take proper cognizance of it as, by then, the present work had already been completed.

enable the rat to put its fore-legs on the tin's upper edge in an initial effort to secure the meat. To reach it the rat would have to walk along the sharp edge of the tin to its far side, an excercise from which, apparently, it shrank back. This, at least, is the conclusion of the observer who saw that the rat, after another look at the enticing meat, retreated, leaped down the case and ran straight to the other side of the tin nearest to the log with the meat on it. The animal tried in vain to climb the slippery surface of the tin. It then returned to the case and to the spot from where it had seen the meat. Again, it put its forelegs on the edge of the tin, then pulled up its whole body, and with utmost care and difficulty it proceeded slowly along the sharp edge until it had reached a point just above the log, from where it leaped down and began to consume the meat.

The animal's behaviour is instructive. In the first place, it bespeaks situational insight. The walk along the tin's edge being risky, the rat first tries another way. The spot where the animal tries to climb up the outside of the tin is exactly the one nearest to the (at that moment invisible) meat. In the second place, the rat has a good memory. When its efforts miscarry, it does not give up, but returns to the point of departure where it decides to take the risk and from where it finally succeeds in reaching the meat. We easily agree that the rat is clever, skilful, and to all appearances hungry. What we do not know is whether the rat, when it gave up its efforts at climbing up the side of the tin, was free to give up all efforts to reach the meat or was innerly compelled by hunger or greed to return to the case and act as it did. All we can say is that the rat acted rationally and effectively, more or less as a human being would do. This is by no means insignificant. After all, the rat's obstinacy can hardly be explained from innate behaviour. Walking the edge of a tin is not an act foreseen by instinct; a tin is thoroughly foreign to the animal's natural environment. More interesting still is that, in the course of the process, there were at least two moments of unpredictable decision-making; the first when the rat returned to the case, the second when it decided to try the way along the edge. Only an observer knowing everything about the rat's cunning, skill, and hunger could have made a valid prediction. Unfortunately, there is no such observer, and this lends the scene its surprising likeness to a human act of decision-making. There is an inner factor involved here which is unknowable to the outsider. No one knows what went on in the rat's head, the central nervous system which directs its actions.

A restricted unpredictability of this kind is not exceptional. It even plays a role in the activities of robots which, as man-made constructions, should be 100% predictable in their actions. And yet they are not. In his book *The Living Brain* W. Grey Walter describes an ingenious contraption constructed for the purpose of experimenting with a mobile robot equipped with two artificial 'nerve-cells', one sensitive to light, the other to touch. The machine (it had been given the provocative name of *Machina speculatrix*) had the outward shape of a tortoise. It could move in all directions, propelled by a small electric motor working on a battery inside the body of the robot. Its main equipment consisted of a rotating scanning apparatus with an electronic cell sensitive to light of moderate intensity. On its head, the tortoise had a small light which shone when the machine was standing to attention, and switched off as soon as the photocell of the scanning apparatus signalled the tortoise to move to the light that had radiated on its surface. A touch-receptor made the moving robot responsive to material objects and gradients which it met on its way to the alluring light.

The machinery was as simple as it was effective. "If placed equidistant from two equal lights M. *speculatrix* will not aim itself half-way between them, but will visit first one and then the other", thus avoiding the dilemma of Sheridan's ass (Walter 1961: 115). "The machines are fitted with a small flash lamp bulb in the head which is turned off automatically whenever the photocell receives an adequate light signal. When a mirror or white surface is encountered the reflected light from the head-lamp is sufficient to operate the circuit controlling the robot's response to light, so that the machine makes for its own reflection; but as it does so, the light is extinguished, what means that the stimulus is cut off – but removal of the stimulus restores the light, which is again seen as stimulus, and so on. The creature therefore lingers before a mirror, twittering and jugging like a clumsy Narcissus. The behaviour of a creature thus engaged with its own reflection is quite specific and on a purely empirical basis, if it were observed in an animal, might be accepted as evidence of some degree of self-awareness... Two creatures of the same type, attracted by one another's light, both extinguish the source of attraction in themselves in the act of seeking it in others. Therefore, when no other attraction is presented, a number of machines cannot escape from one another... When an external stimulus is applied to all members of such a community, they will of course see it independently and the community will break up; then, the more individuals there are the smaller the chances of anyone achieving its goal..." (ibid.: 115 f.).

In his comment, Walter points out that some of the patterns of performance "were calculable, though only as types of behaviour, in advance, [and that] some were quite unforeseen". He adds that the behaviour of the robots repeatedly suggests self-consciousness or social consciousness. "The way in which the social behaviour of the model breaks down under the influence of a competitive struggle for a common goal, imitates almost embarrassingly some of the less attractive features of animal and human society" (ibid: 116 f.).

The incalculability of the exact reactions of each machine individually must necessarily be sought in minimal differences in internal construction leading to micro-differences in reaction speed. Another factor must be time-differences in reaction to light-stimuli caused by the fortuitous position of the rotating photo-electric cell. A third factor is the state of the battery in one machine and another. There may be other factors as well, but the real point of interest is that the machine does not simply react to stimuli but that the reaction is, ultimately, co-determined by the state of the machine. In this respect M. *speculatrix* is a true model of a live organism. It is also in two other respects. In the first place, M. *speculatrix* is not a passive receptor of stimuli but actively looking for them. This is exactly what every animal does. And, finally, the robot resembles a living organism also in this respect that it signals to its surroundings what it is doing. When at rest without light it is inactive, 'sleeping'; when at rest with the light burning it is 'awake and on the lookout'; when moving with the light extinguished it is on its way to a 'prey', the 'baiting' light.

From a technical point of view, the equipment of the robot with a scanning apparatus is more or less a matter of course. As a simulation of animal behaviour it is a stroke of genius, bringing home to us that a scanning apparatus is an essential part of the mental and physiological equipment of all mobile living beings. Even a simpleton like *M. speculatrix* with no more than two neurones to command its actions, needs such a scanner. It is, in fact, no more than a simple detector, 'instructed' to look for and to report the emergence of a light of a certain quality. What other mobile beings need, Buytendijk's rat for example, is incomparably more. They must be able to locate food, enemies, dangers, congeners, and their way home, to mention only a few things. The scanning apparatus at their disposal is accordingly richer, comprising sense organs for seeing, hearing, smelling and tasting. They would be helpless, however, without supplementary equipment. The multitude of sense impressions which at any moment present themselves to the brain, must be sorted out and connected with the memory traces of earlier experiences. The animal must decide to which of the multifarious stimuli noted it will give response, and which it will ignore. In other words, it must make choices. Besides, once a choice has been made and the animal goes in pursuit of its chosen goal, its scanner cannot be switched off like that of *M. speculatrix*, it must turn round and round to warn the animal against dangers lurking on the way. However much the animal concentrates on its selected goal, it keeps in touch with its 'universe'.

All this implies that the, in itself already complicated, scanning apparatus of the animal must be supplemented with provisions enabling the animal to organize all incoming signals and impressions immediately and continually into a whole which is meaningful to it, a field, in which every new impression gets its place, changes the field, or evokes another field. How it all works we do not know, except that the arrangement of the field is probably a matter of ordering the incoming stimuli by their relative strength. For all intents and purposes this is synonymous with making choices, a term which stresses the completion of the ongoing process rather than the process itself. Ordering the field and choice making are one and the same process, and it cannot be isolated from the scanning which goes on continuously. The one and the other are almost simultaneous and we might define the scanning apparatus of the mammal with equal right as an ordering apparatus.

What has been said of the equipment of the mammal is, to a great extent at least, also applicable to the activities of what in man is called the subject, the part of the mind which directs the individual's conscious life. It is the part of the mind that is inactive when asleep. We do not know which part or parts of the brain is (are) involved. The two things which we know for certain are, first, that the electro-encephalogram of the sleeping individual differs markedly from that of the one who is awake, and also from the one who is, at best, half-awake, i.e. is passing through one of the so-called REM-periods which alternate with those of deep sleep. And in the second place we know that during sleep those parts of the brain which are connected with vital functions remain active. Inactive are the subject and consciousness

13

generally. Of particular interest are the REM-periods (periods of Rapid Eye Movements) when the sleeper is half-awake and dreams. When he wakes up, he may remember his dream; which (with an untrained person) will be quickly forgotten if he does not note it down immediately, unless it is impressive enough to occupy him more intensely during his waking state. Normally, however, the dream escapes from memory as soon as the subject, now awake, sets about his task, scanning his memory for what has to be done today, what the problems are that need his attention, and taking cognizance of what the sense organs are telling him about his actual situation. The individual has resumed his conscious life, the life of a subject. The mental activities deployed under the subject's direction shall not easily escape from memory. One of the functions of consciousness is that it stores its experiences for a shorter or longer period, during which they are available to the scanning subject who, by definition, is awake and conscious.

The scanning subject never tires from organizing its perceptions. We shall return to the theme later; but, before we take leave of it, one point must be made. If the supposition is correct that this on-going process of ordering perceptions in a meaningful field is a matter of arranging the incoming stimuli according to their relative strength*, then it is evident whence comes that strange notion of freedom that accompanies our experiences of decisions taken and of choices made, even those which were made in highly compelling situations. It is the inbuilt instruction of the apparatus ever to arrange and organize its perceptions, ever to decide between the one and the other by weighing the relative importance of the relevant brain contents against each other. This does not necessarily imply any real freedom (whatever that be); the brain contents present themselves in a rather compelling way. What it does imply is that in the process of ordering which culminates in decision making, the whole individual is involved with all his previous experiences as far as these are available in memory traces. Between the stimulus and the response stands the subject with its whole personal history and all the complexes it has internalized by accretion to itself.

4. The role of models

The individual, of whatever species, lives in a universe, and belongs to it. It is not only that, materially, the individual originates from it and returns to it. The individual exists in a never ending process of interaction with his universe. The metaphor of the subject as (inter alia) a 'scanning apparatus' again highlights the situation. The world is the individual's action field and he has no other field than this particular one. It is so with man, and it is also the case with all the higher organisms whose actions can be described as those of a subject, a choice-making self, scanning its surroundings.

Scanning the surroundings is an urgent necessity for all of them. All animals are ever on the look-out, simultaneously to find food and to avoid becoming the food of

* It will be evident that the term 'relative strength' masks a host of problems. Strength is not simply a factor of objective, measurable obtrusiveness, but also of the orientation and structure of the subject which is not a mere detector, but a self. Cf. below: 52 ff.

others. They must always be vigilant. Unfortunately, every action of the individual tends to attract the attention of others. Moving about, the animal offers itself as a prey to an occasional predator. Every animal gives itself away, just like *M. speculatrix* gives itself away, when scanning by the light on its head, and otherwise by moving. Consequently, every animal, or at least every vertebrate, needs a place of retreat where it can hide from its numerous enemies, a nest, a burrow, a cave or a lair, a place where it can sleep and relax, surrendering itself to the goodness of the earth. Although it is difficult to say why exactly the individual needs rest and sleep, we know for certain that he cannot live without them. It is a need common to all mammals. Yet, even in a well-chosen lair sleep does not pass undisturbed. The REM-periods which bring all mammals periodically on the verge of awakening have probably developed from the necessity not to sleep too long, lest an approaching enemy take the sleeper by surprise (Snyder 1966). The cave-dwellings of early man still give testimony to his need for security. His life was an uneasy one anyhow, like primitive man's still is today. His sleep is rarely undisturbed. Man is a poorly protected animal, neither very quick nor very strong, and through his nakedness cruelly exposed to the cold of the night and the never-ending pestering of all sorts of vermin. Deprived of hide and tail, he is an easy victim of all the world's blood-sucking insects. At a very early stage of his career, man's nakedness must have induced him to look for means of self-protection against predators large and small, a niche of some sort, and a fire to protect him against the cold. His more richly furred older brother of Neanderthal already had fire and we may be sure that *homo sapiens* had it too.

All animals have to be quick to perceive danger. Perception necessarily compromises between speed and correctness. Danger allows little time for inspection. A few outlines must suffice for preliminary recognition, outlines which bear the scantiest information only. If circumstances permit perception can be followed by closer observation, but even when conditions are favourable first recognition is confined to a few details only. The first impression is decisive for what follows. If it is an impression of impending danger, flight will probably cut off all efforts at closer identification. Ethologists have collected extensive information on the reactions of birds to frightening impressions. Perceiving the silhouette of a hobby (a predatory bird) ordinarily suffices to send a number of tits into hiding in the nearest shrub, even if the silhouette does not belong to any falcon or hawk but to a harmless swift whose short neck gives this swallow-species a silhouette resembling that of a bird of prey (Tinbergen 1958: 87 f., 97). Rapid reaction makes errors unavoidable. This also happens when the ominous signal is not a silhouette but a style of flying such as the spectacular nose-diving of a falcon or hawk. Occasionally, other birds, too, indulge in this kind of sweeping movements. Thus a really innocent bird like the godwit may cause panic among gulls (ibid.: 96 f). Here again the reaction is induced by what can best be described as a simplified model, i.e. an abbreviated image of a generalized standard pattern which enables the spectator to make a rapid inventory and to react accordingly.

Models of this kind are crude; they contain few details. One of the crudest is the bright red colour that arouses aggression in the male stickleback watching over its nest. In its mating season the male's inconspicuous grey colour changes into a bright red. Watching over its nest the male attacks every competitor which, naturally, announces itself by the same red colour. It is the colour which provokes the reactions. Everything red arouses anger; male sticklebacks have been observed attacking the glass of the aquarium on the sight of a red-coloured van posted in front of the window of the laboratory. More or less similarly a female stickleback will follow any crudely shaped red model which the observer pushes through the aquarium on a piece of wire (Tinbergen *in* McGaugh et al. 1966: 5 ff.).

An animal must not only be able to recognize its potential enemies, it must also be equipped to identify a prey and a congener. In both cases, more details are needed than for the recognition of a potential enemy. Fortunately, when there is no reason for immediate flight, there is always time for closer inspection. A very short time may suffice because all that matters is the recognition of a particular species. Sometimes, however, even the recognition of a congener may be fairly exacting, e.g. when one subspecies differs from a related one in a few details only. Ornithologists like Tinbergen have given much thought to the identification of the distinctive details by which a certain kind of gull distinguishes between its congeners and gulls belonging to closely related subspecies (Tinbergen 1960: 220 f.). In fact, the recognition of a congener is of no less importance than that of a prey. Among species with a poorly developed social life such recognition is a compelling necessity for propagation. Not one animal can continue to exist in a solitary state. The differentiation according to sex enforces a certain amount of socialization among congeners, even though it stimulates jealousy and fighting among sex fellows.

More exacting is the recognition of specific individuals among congeners. Mates must be able to recognize each other as well as their young or cubs. Often mates know each other from their call, from a shade of variation in the sound of its cry, a variation specific for the individual and recognized by its mate. Individual recognition can also be based on a specific smell (Schultze-Westrum 1965). Whatever the medium, the system always works and enables animals to keep up a kind of family life during the period needed to raise the young. However, the distinctive marks for recognition must be learned. Consequently, errors are possible. They need not even be minor errors. A telling case is that of the female hobby which mistook an approaching kestrel for its mate (Tinbergen 1958: 89).

Standard patterns of form and behaviour have the function that they present information to friends and enemies alike. Every act is a self-expression, and all the forms of self-expression, conscious as well as unconscious, voluntary and involuntary, are the raw materials of intra- and inter-species communication. Modern ethology has discovered that knowledge of the patterned forms of expressive behaviour (and all behaviour is expressive!) observed among interrelated species can contribute to the reconstruction of the evolutional history of the species concerned. This, in fact, is little more than another way of saying that many of these forms are at best partly species-specific. A not unimportant part of any animal's behaviour is easily inter-pretable to animals of other species, a circle which narrows down when the behaviour is more specific. In this context the studies of facial expressions among primates and humans by Van Hooff are of interest (Van Hooff 1967 and 1971). The recognition of facial expressions as indicators of certain moods need not be restricted to members of closely related species; they may give information to individuals of other species as well (cf. Jolly 1972 ch. 9). By its behaviour and movements, whether they can be classified as expressive or not, every animal gives itself away, betrays its intentions and its moods.

What is true of the higher vertebrates, and in particular of mammals, is true of man. He, too, betrays himself by his posture, his gestures and facial expression. His recognition of things and fellow beings and their intentions is, like recognition by other mammals, based on models. However, man's dealings with models are not restricted to their recognition and interpretation; he has the gift of creating new models which serve the purpose of elucidating his thoughts in his traffic with his fellow men. Illustrations in books are designed for that purpose. They have taught us that a simplified model is often more instructive and better memorizable than a good photograph. Eighteenth century travellers already illustrated their books with sketches of the silhouettes of harbours, capes and bays for the guidance of later navigators. Military observers still make use of charts with silhouettes of aeroplanes to discern enemy aircraft from allied ones. A good model is more than a reduction; it is a characterization of what in the object is important to the observer and demands his attention. A model can also be used as a means for experiment. Its reduced size and the reduction of its qualities to those of critical significance enable its designer to test the facilities of his construction by manipulation and the introduction of alternatives.

Man's power over models makes him superior to all animals, a power which manifests itself most obviously in his capability to cheat. Animals are honest; they express their intentions without being able to dissemble. The predator stalking a prey, cautiously hiding from its victim till it is near enough to attack it, cannot conceal its intentions to the casual outside observer who has not the slightest difficulty in seeing what the animal is after. The predator may conceal its body, it cannot conceal its intentions. Man can. He is a liar. Decent people like philosophers prefer to gloss over it, but it is a notorious fact that lying is man's most human gift, a gift he uses more often and more profoundly than he cares to admit. Man has the power of imagination. It helps him to see himself in a very special way. Few people succeed in being really honest to themselves about themselves. There is a lie in almost every human life. We are all inclined to pretend that we are more than we really are, primarily to ourselves. Though it must be conceded that we cannot really know ourselves, it is also true that we rarely try it honestly. We prefer to keep up a certain image about ourselves, and as long as it does not differ too much from reality, we are able to lead a moderately happy life. When we overdo it, we invariably lapse into neurosis or insanity, a curious fact that infers that, ultimately, we depend on truth and reality.

As long as lying constitutes part of an attitude which does not differ too markedly from reality, it is not a serious problem. It is implied in an approach to the world which is near enough to the truth to be acceptable. It is different when lying is not a matter of presenting a familiar personality, but is forced upon us as a dire necessity

17

because the contingence of unexpected events has turned truth into a menacing danger. I have some personal experience of such situations as a prisoner of the Japanese under conditions that made forbidden activities enticing. In a camp where all contacts with the outside world are forbidden and thus supposed to be non-existent, one must be prepared to explain the presence of a newspaper, a pound of sugar, a stolen duck or a bottle of gin, if any of such commodities is detected on the occasion of a search. An acceptable story has to be invented on the spot to explain its presence. Telling the truth would expose an outside relation to the danger of capital punishment. The Japanese were ruthless on this point. Anyhow, I will never forget the lieutenant-commander who pretended that he had found the bottle of gin, that had been discovered in his room, under a palmtree in the camp*. His problem was that he had to stick to this unconvincing story. His troubles with it are not of interest here because the Japanese, after thrashing him cruelly, failed to do what the police authorities would have done, namely to put him in custody, to leave him to his own for two or three days. It is a very effective means of confusing a culprit. If his story was a cooked one, he will almost invariably try to correct and improve it. At the end of the second day he no longer knows what he really told the police and what he hopes or wishes he told them. But the police has everything on paper and at the next session it turns out that he is lying. Desparately trying to extract himself from the inconsistencies of his stories, he gets more and more confused until, finally, he gives in and tells the truth, or gives up and wisely veils himself in a sulking silence.

It is of interest that more often than not he gives in. Logic and truth have a curious power; few people are able to resist it. It is not the effect of western education with its emphasis on the value of truth. Men and women of other cultures do not react differently; as a judge in various parts of Indonesia I found them as susceptible to the convincing power of logic and truth as anyone. And of course they are. No one has difficulty in remembering what he really did or saw, whereas the details of a cooked story are easily forgotten. To remember them they must be rehearsed and the rehearsal itself is a recurring invitation to embellish or improve the story.

This strong position of truth is only natural. Man does not merely live *in* a world, he also lives *unto* it. His whole existence is, as Merleau-Ponty pointed out, turned to his world. The formula gives a first, slight indication of what the reason is that man can lie at all. If he were as fully part of his world as other animals, he would be as honest as they. But man distances himself from his world, contemplates it from afar. At such a distance it becomes possible to imagine other worlds, slightly parallel to the real one, with other positions for the self than those actually occupied. Man is turned to his world, not immersed in it, even though materially he is part and parcel of it. And he has the curious power to give definite shape to his phantasies and desires, because he has the power of symboling, of using and making symbols.

Symbols are signs. In many respects they resemble the models operative in animal recognition. Symbols are used for denoting and designating but, other than the

* Any allusion to the moving story of Adam Bede is out of the question. Neither the lieutenant-commander nor the Japanese sergeant should be suspected of interest in the works of Tennyson or any other poet laureate instead.

models in animal recognition, they can be manipulated at will, and their forms need not show any likeness with their designata. The variety of symbols is so great and – as Cassirer demonstrated in his *Philosophy of Symbolic Forms* – their impact on human life and culture are so all-encompassing, that we devote a special chapter to a discussion of them.

II

Symbols

1. The various kinds of symbols

For all we know, the use of symbols is almost exclusively a human phenomenon. It is true that chimpanzees (cf. Jolly 1972) have been induced into making an intelligent use of a limited number of symbols presented to them by researchers. There is also evidence that chimpanzees attach a meaning to pictures. In both cases we are dealing with reactions to man-made conditions and we do not know whether symbolism plays a part of some real importance in the chimpanzees' normal way of life. It is possible that further research will lead to the conclusion that it does and that they do use symbols in their natural social interaction, but so far there is little reason to suppose that the role of such symbolism can bear comparison with that in human society. Our discussion of symbols can thus be limited to those in use among human beings. That makes it necessary to set symbols as a specific class of signs apart from the signs operative in the common forms of communication between living beings generally, the signals and symptoms by which animal and man alike perceive or communicate a thing or event.

Symptoms and signals have in common that they are situation-bound. They are perceived as part of the context in which they are encountered. The difference between the two is that the symptom conveys information that need not immediately be acted upon. It can be ignored and forgotten, or accepted as information for later use. The predator which, returning from a successful hunt, sees an antelope lying in agony, need not react to it. The next day, however, the animal may return to the spot, expecting an easy prey. To the contrary, a signal is a sign which induces an immediate response. It goes too far to say, as Leach proposed, that the signal triggers off a response (1976: 12). If we take this literally, we run the risk of excluding a wide variety of signs from the signal category which linguistic usage has always classified as such. A red light along the road-side, the referee's blast on his whistle during a soccer match, are signals, but they do not necessarily trigger off the desired response. The red light can be ignored (who is the man who never did?), the referee sometimes must blow two or three times before the players listen and stop the game. These signals are not automatically obeyed; they are simply provocative of action, and in this respect they only differ in degree with the harsh cry of the jay announcing the approach of a hawk or a hunter, which sets the singing-birds alert. They are acts which invite a response but they do not always trigger it off; even in the case of animals reaction does not follow automatically in every case.

Having excluded signals and symptoms from our discussion the question arises, whether it is expedient to use only one term, symbol, for all the remaining signs operative in human expression. Symbols are of so many kinds that classing them all in one category might lead to ambiguity and confusion rather than to clear and operational distinctions. Piaget and Leach, for example, found it desirable to differentiate between symbols and signs, the latter a term which is used here in a much wider, fully comprehensive sense. Unfortunately, each of these authors follows different ways. Piaget restricts the use of the term 'symbols' to images of representations, calling 'signs' the arbitrary, standardized signifiers of language (1962: 68). Leach, on the other hand, associates signs with metonymy and symbols with metaphors (1976: 12). To Piaget words are signs, to Leach they are symbols. Disagreement is not restricted to that between these authors. As a matter of fact, each writer on symbolism tends to classify and subdivide the various categories of human signs in his own way, that is according to the needs of his own argument. Consequently, we too shall have to find our own way. Because we have some confidence in the inner logic of language, we expect that a workable lead can be found in the answer to the question of what the common denominator is in that broad variety of signs called symbols in ordinary linguistic usage.

This usage makes mention of the symbols of science, language, art, myth, religion, dreams and neurosis; of the symbolic value of letters, hieroglyphs and icons; the symbolic content of music, a painting, a drama, or a poem. These symbols are auditory or visual; olfactory and tactile symbols occur, but are rare. Thus, the scent of burning incense has a symbolic meaning, and we have a good case of tactile symbols in the life-history of Helen Keller, the blind deafmute who was prompted to the notion of word-symbols by the recurrent scribbling of minute signs in the palm of her hand. Movements too can be symbolic; the most typical case is that of dance and ballet, in which gestures – in daily life applied as signals – can function as symbols.

There is no need to make sure that our inventory of the use of the term symbol is really exhaustive. Enough forms have been mentioned to allow us to draw at least two conclusions. The first is that symbols are associated with a really impressive variety of forms of human behaviour; the second that all these symbols refer to something which is not spontaneously intelligible from the symbol as such. Moreover, we find that there are two classes of symbols, roughly coinciding with the distinction made between signs and symbols by Piaget and many others. The first class is that of symbols which must be learned; scientific, linguistic and letter symbols (hieroglyphs included) are intelligible only to those who have gone through the long process of learning their meaning. The second class is that of symbols which are characterized by a certain closeness or likeness between signifier and signified but cannot really be understood without either a prolonged abandonment to contemplation and/or listening, or a careful analysis of their context. The symbols of art, dream and myth belong to this category. If we call the meaning of a symbol its 'message' and the

21

symbol itself a 'vehicle', then the difference between the two categories can be summarized as follows: the first category is that of messages which are clear whereas the vehicle is untransparent, the second that where the vehicle is transparent and the message is enigmatic, vague, or inexpressible by words. The contrast between the two categories is striking, and justifies the further examination which, in the following pages, shall be devoted to them, beginning with the symbols of the second category.

They are of many kinds and we turn first to those which, more than others, are the spontaneous products of the unconscious, namely the symbols of dream and neurosis. Dreams are an epiphenomenon of sleep, the symbols of neurosis the products of a disturbance of the mind caused by the repression of an inner conflict. The latter are primarily symptoms of mental disorder. These symptoms owe their symbolic value to the fact that they carry covert information on the nature and origin of the disturb-ance. A typical case is that of the girl who, every night, put her pillow apart from the erect wooden head of her bed, a puzzling rite that eventually found its explanation in the repressed wish to keep her parents (symbolized by pillow and erect wooden head) apart sexually (Freud, Vorlesungen; G.W. XI: 272 ff.). As a symptom, the act meant no more than a nonsense ritual needed to permit the girl to drop off to sleep and as such a symptom of her mental disturbance. The psycho-analytic treatment brought to light that the symptom had symbolic value, referring directly to the origin of her disorder in a repressed wish, the nature of which was easily recognizable from the act once the psychological background had been cleared up by analysis.

Dream symbols are more varied than those of neurosis. Dreaming is a normal function of the mind. Everyone dreams during certain periods of his sleep, a peculiarity which man shares with other mammals. In recent years, Freud's sup-position that dreaming protects the continuity of sleep has won increased probability. The details of the theory are of minor interest here*; for us it is important that, during these periods of near-awakening, memory traces of the experiences of the day and of problems which are more or less permanently prominent in the dreamer's mind, emerge into consciousness. They do not do this in an orderly way. The drowsy subject recognizes certain persons and situations without being able to make proper sense of them, least of all if they are concerned with deep-lying conflicts which are veiled beyond recognition. If there are no reasons to wake up, the dreamer can continue in his sleep. The contents of dreams are furtive. Even if he wakes up, he only remembers a weird configuration of persons, things and events which he is unable to organize into a really coherent pattern. Unless the dream is unusually impressive, or

* Dreaming periods are periods of near-awakening. The sleeper makes Rapid Eye Movements after which the periods are called REM-periods. On an electro-encephalogram, these periods are marked by a specific pattern. These periods return every 90 minutes. If, during such a period, there is any sign of approaching danger, the sleeper will wake up; if not, he may go on sleeping. Other mammals go through similar REM-periods during which they exhibit signs of dreaming. If anything unusual happens during a REM-period they wake up, otherwise they too may continue to sleep. The REM-period combines the purposes of security with those of sleep. Consequently, mammals are better off than birds which have to wake up periodically (Snyder 1967; cf. also R. Jones 1970: ch. IX). The theory is, as yet, far from certain. M. Jouvet (1967) reported that with cats signs of dreaming and REM-periods coincide with the state of deep sleep which, not undeservedly, he describes as paradoxal sleep.

the dreamer is trained in registering his dream experiences, the contents of the dream rapidly vanish without leaving memory traces as do events which are consciously observed or experienced. Nevertheless, some dreams are impressive enough to disquiet the mind a long time afterwards as a kind of message in a foreign language of which only a few words are recognizable.

Most dreams are visual images and they rarely speak the language of logical operations. Though notions of an intellectual nature occasionally dominate the content of dreams (Piaget refers to two cases of scientific discovery inspired by dreams; 1962: 206), dreams favour the emergence of images which are not understood by the dreamer. Nevertheless, a meaning is often implied. Many dream-images are real symbols, especially those which recur frequently or deeply impress the dreamer. A telling case is that of the young man "who was sometimes addicted to masturbation [and] regularly punished himself during the following night in dreams of which we give [two] examples: (1) He saw an Eiffel Tower reduced in size, and cut off at the level of the second storey... (2) He saw himself striking with all his might, with an enormous axe, at a python which was rearing itself in a bedroom. The head of the snake was almost cut off, and hung bleeding. The mother was hidden in the shadow of the room" (Piaget 1962: 203 f.). Piaget adds that the symbolism of the dream, though clear enough to the outsider, was obscure to the dreamer who experienced the former as a kind of childish game, the second as a nightmare.

That the dreamer fails to recognize the images of his dreams as symbols of his life problems is well in keeping with the theory of the function of the dream as a protector of sleep. The dreamer can ignore them as irrelevant nonsense. One of the dreams in the case just mentioned was experienced as childish. The second was a harder nut to crack, an indication that the emotional content of the dream's background can be more or less effectively disguised. The point has already been made by Freud who, in his *Traumdeutung*, demonstrated how thoroughly displacement can veil the conflicts and emotions behind dreams by presenting their symbols in the guise of what seemingly is just a matter of fact story. Nevertheless, the emotional background is undoubtedly there, since Freud insists that "the motive power [of the dream] is invariably a wish craving fulfilment" (quotation taken from Rapaport 1971: 161). In a similar vein, Piaget argues that there is a very close link between the symbols of the dream and imaged symbols generally (metaphors in his terminology) on the one hand, and the affective *schemas* on the other (cf. i.a. 1962: 169, 206). In contrast to the standardized verbal sign or the mathematical symbol (in Piaget's terminology also a 'sign'), the metaphor and the image do not simply express a relationship between the image and the object of reference; they also include a reference to how this relationship is experienced by the individual. His own emotional background, his personal views and feelings are involved but – and this is the most outstanding characteristic – this involvement is not made manifest. It is veiled from consciousness.

We also find this – albeit in a more limited form – in myth, a phenomenon which has much in common with dreams. Like so many dreams, a myth always contains at least one element which is virtually impossible or contradictory. Myth also speaks in

23

metaphors. Other than in dreams, these metaphors are largely transparent; but this transparency is limited fairly strictly to the etiological meaning of the myth. The affective components – which are also present – remain vague and elusive. That these components play a part is beyond doubt. In his *Mythologiques,* Lévi-Strauss emphasized the affective nature of myth by associating myth with the language of music (1964: 22 ff.; 1971: 577 ff.). And if it be conceded that myth is religious truth in story-form (Van Baal 1971: 16), one arrives at the same conclusion. One need not accept Schleiermacher's definition of religion as *Gefühl der schlechthinnigen Abhängigkeit** to agree that religion is steeped in the affective life. What demands our attention here is that the true nature of these affects is never clearly expressed: not in myth, not in dreams, and not in the symbols of neurosis. It is vaguely adumbrated in intransparent symbols, suggestive perhaps but never lucid.

Feeling or emotion has a strong impact on many systems of symbols, notably on those of works of art. The artistic element is impervious to transposition into words. The most obvious, and at the same time the most contradictory case, is that of music. The most obvious, because it is manifestly impossible to express in words what the meaning and beauty of a piece of music are. The occasional attempts to do this in concert-programmes never succeed in conveying what is essential. The superlatives, of which such texts abound, testify to the futility of every attempt at expressing the inexpressible in words. And yet, the case of music is also the most contradictory. It expresses the inexpressible, but the score presents a detailed review of every measure, note and instrument. It is all laid down in writing and gives undeniable evidence of the composer's command of the logic of music. Composing requires something like a mathematical mind; and yet, what counts is the ephemeral effect of melody and tone. Every piece of music is, essentially, a *Lied ohne Worte*** in the singing of which the listener silently joins. In Lévi-Strauss's words: listening to the performance the hearer is confronted *à des objets virtuels dont l'ombre seule est actuelle, à des approximations conscientes de vérités inéluctablement inconscientes et qui leur sont consécutives* (1964: 25)***. What turns sound into music cannot be expressed by words.

Forms of artistic expression other than music confront us, essentially, with the same problem. We can describe a painting just as we describe a photograph or a landscape, but we cannot describe what makes the painting a work of art, namely its expressiveness and its beauty. Of course, we can state that the portrait of an old woman symbolizes the beauty of advanced age; but these are empty words, incapable of conveying a notion of that particular beauty, not even a shadow of a notion. The beauty of a painting must be seen. It can only be discovered in silent contemplation, by steeping oneself in its wordless message. Some people, then, are able to describe the painting in beautiful words; but the beauty of the description is not the beauty of the painting but of the words. And here the same story repeats itself. The beauty of the

* Translation: feeling of absolute dependence.
** A song without words.
*** Translation: to virtual objects of which only the shades are actual, to conscious approximations of truths ineluctably unconscious and yet present.

poem, the drama, the novel must be enjoyed in listening or reading; it cannot be described or defined. There is no valid definition of beauty. All there is is a number of rationalizations of traits and contexts such as perfection of form (Langer 1951) or the compact arrangement of essential traits (Lévi-Strauss 1962b); but they fail, and actually do not even intend to tell us what that sensation is which we call beauty. In this respect, beauty does not differ from sensations like love and joy. They cannot be adequately described but must, rather, be experienced or symbolically expressed. The message conveyed by a work of art is not a message that can be translated into rational terms, but one that arouses a whole gamut of feelings and sentiments ranging from sorrow to joy, from horror to ecstasy, interconnected by a sensation of beauty and all one in the fact that they must be experienced rather than understood or analyzed.

A point worth special attention is that mankind has at its disposal an extremely wide variety of means to give artistic expression to its feelings: singing, playing musical instruments, painting, dance, drama, poetry, and the novelist's art of story-telling; they are all means of expression of a something that cannot be rendered by the words of everyday language*.

Nevertheless, everyday language is often instrumental in artistic expression. Language is more than a collection of symbols for concepts and the description of things and events, or a technique for the communication of rational messages. Language is certainly a convenient code for these purposes, but its use is not confined to them. Language is also used to express and arouse feelings. Apart from a rich variety of words and expressions to denote feelings, which cannot adequately be described or defined, language also has numerous words which have one or more connotations that give a certain colouring to the context in which they are used. I can note that someone gives care to someone else, but when I describe that care as motherly care I introduce a notion of tenderness. There is a difference between 'to like', 'to love' and 'to be fond of', between 'walking', 'pacing' and 'striding', and so on. Each of these words has connotations forming a more or less weak halo of shades of meaning and sentiment which make it fit for use in a specific context. This can be one of factual communication but also one which has an emotional impact. The situation decides on the choice made from the available words and expressions. An orator at a funeral will not confine himself to the lame statement that the deceased is dead now and that it is such a pity for him and everyone, more particularly for his beloved ones. He does something quite different. He paints a picture of the deceased which stirs the feelings of the audience into sincere sorrow at his passing away, into loving memory of his merits for the community at large, into true sympathy and compassion with the family. The audience is moved, and this is how it should be.

Words are a convenient medium for the communalization and expression of feelings as well as for the communication of matter of fact messages. This does not imply that the meaning of words is always clear or unambiguous. There are many

---

* The same holds true for the forms of ritual and play which have been left out of this survey because they cannot be discussed without giving previous consideration to the context to which they belong. Such consideration would seriously interrupt the present exposition which seemed all the more undesirable because we shall have occasion later on in this book to return to each of them separately.

modes of expression and some of them veil their message or confuse it rather than reveal it. Words can even be used for lying, but this is not the problem here. What is important is that words are not an infallible means for rational communication because their meaning may be ambiguous or mixed up with feelings of various kinds.

In this respect, everyday language differs profoundly from the 'language' of science which is unambiguous, clear, rational and unemotional. Its main instrument is the vast repertoire of symbols used in mathematics, physics and chemistry. These symbols are organized in formulae expressing relations between things, and relations between relations. The meaning of each of the symbols is strictly defined, often conventionalized by international agreement. Formulae are international and translingual; everyday language has no more than an auxiliary, elucidating or connecting function in the language of science. Another characteristic of this language is that it is a written language. Although it can be read aloud, the availability of a written text is essential. The written word, even that of everyday language, differs fundamentally from the spoken word. The latter is ephemeral, *einmalig* (for once), but to the written word one can return, reread the sentence and, if required, correct or improve the wording or memorize its content. The written word has an object character that is foreign to the spoken one and makes it an adequate vehicle for scientific communication. As a product of rational thought the language of science is concerned with objective knowledge, with "general expressions of relations" rather than with description (Cassirer 1944: 273). It is a language which has no place for subjective wishes or feelings; all it is and must be, is a medium for rational thought.

2. *Affect and curtailment in linguistic expression*

A rapid survey of the various categories of symbols has revealed that man has a wide variety of symbols at his disposal, and that those applied in an affective context are more diversified than the symbols for the expression of rational contents. Purely rational is only the 'language' of science, a system of symbols that is historically a newcomer to the world of symbolic expression, and a highly artificial one besides; it is primarily a written language and its origins scarcely go back more than 500 years. Everyday language, the other medium for matter of fact communication, can be used either way. It often mixes rational messages with expressions of affect.

The diversity and richness of symbols for the expression of affective contents comes rather as a surprise. Emotions and affects are always concerned with the individual and his desires and conflicts; they can hardly be as variegated as man's total universe. It is all the more surprising because the use of symbols logically implies a certain distance between the symbolizer and the symbolized. Symbols refer to matters and events which need be neither present nor real. The affective component, which saturates so many forms of symbolic expression, works in opposite direction. It betrays the personal involvement of the symbolizer in the symbolized matter. Apparently, the act of symboling tends to combine an effort at distancing with that of expressing a personal, even emotional involvement. The distancing is maximal, the personal involvement minimal in the language of science. The contrary is the case when words are used as cries serving the expression of sudden physical pain, thus degrading the symbol into a signal. In between these two extremes lies the vast field of symbolic expression, dominated by vacillating tensions between distancing and involvement.

These tensions are a first indication that all the wealth of man's vast arsenal of symbols notwithstanding, expression necessarily suffers from curtailments of various kinds, both psychological and technical. In this section we shall discuss some of those incumbent on the use of language. Language is man's most important means for symbolic expression; it is universal and also the symbol which is the most thoroughly systematized. It is desirable to begin the discussion here. Before proceeding, however, a few paragraphs should be devoted to our use of the terms 'emotion', and 'feeling' or 'affect'.

Rapaport (1971: ch. II) differentiates between emotion as "an unconscious process which mobilizes unconscious instinctual energies" (ibid.: 31), and feeling or affect as the conscious awareness of their stirrings. Although we welcome a differentiation along these lines as an appreciable contribution to clarity, two reservations need to be made. The first is that the expression 'instinctual energies' begs more questions than its use answers, but this is a problem which must be postponed to the 2nd section of the next chapter. It is different with the second reservation which must be discussed here. Feeling is a vague concept with a very wide range of meaning. To restrict its use to feelings originating from unconscious instinctual energies, is undesirable. The criterion is unwieldy in operation. There are feelings about which it is not at all certain that they originate from instinctual energies. As an example let us take moods. We do not hesitate to describe these as feelings. Merleau-Ponty (1945, ch. I) has reminded us of the fact that certain moods can be provoked by colours, an experience which I remember having seen applied many years earlier in a Rudolf Steiner clinic where the hospital-wards were painted in monocolour, green, red, and so on. Must moods thus excited be connected with instinctual drives, or should we leave their ultimate etiology to further study and experiment? Obviously, the latter.

For this and other reasons a more neutral definition which avoids questions of causality is to be preferred. To us, a feeling or affect (these terms are used as synonyms) is *the awareness of an inner state*. It is a definition which respects the vagueness of the concept without incurring the boundlessness which the terms 'feel' and 'feeling' have in everyday language where they stand for anything undefined, and can also be used for vague knowledge and surmise. Thus I can say that I *feel* that a certain expression is idiomatically incorrect. There is nothing emotional or affective in this feeling, no more than there is when, listening to a tall story, a *feeling* comes over me that the story is faked. In each of these cases the word 'feeling' refers to incomplete and thus vague knowledge, as vague as moods and affects can be. Yet, this vagueness has nothing to do with affectivity. I am not affected by it, unless I also feel annoyed. But this is quite another matter, concerned with my inner state which is repeatedly moved, affected, by impressions from within (the unconscious) and perceptions from outside.

This implies that next to the cases of vague knowledge which we discarded, there also are forms of vague knowledge which should properly be listed as feelings. Actually, they are a majority. They are even of two kinds. The first is that of the vague knowledge ensuing from marginal perception. When engaged in a discussion or in some work that demands our attention, we neglect what happens around us; a disturbing noise, bad weather, heat, otherwise exciting music, and suchlike. Yet, these facts do not pass wholly unnoticed: they contribute to constituting the mood in which we carry on our discussion or pursue our work (cf. below: 60). The second kind of vague knowledge is the result of an inner refusal or aversion to take proper cognizance of facts and events presenting or even obtruding themselves to the mind. The vagueness of the resulting knowledge is, in this case, effectuated by an incomplete act of repression, an act which itself is of an emotional nature, involving the subject's libido. This kind of vague knowledge may have long-lasting effects on the subconscious mind of the unwilling perceiver.

Affects, then, are of many kinds. The semantics of the word confirm more or less clearly, that an affect can come from anywhere, *affecting* the individual who feels disquieted, bored, annoyed, amused, moved, overcome or overwhelmed. Feelings have a quality which defies description of a precision equalling that of a description of the contents of one's room, or of the houses on the other side of the street as viewed from the front window. But, all the same, they are there. They are always there, accompanying man's every step like a shadow, a shadow which does not even budge during the night. They even creep into the mind of the mathematician who works on a difficult problem and feels pleased with the progress he makes towards an 'elegant' solution.

But to return to the problem of language. The contention that affectivity permeates human life and experience, is amply corroborated when we consult Roget's Thesaurus on the share imparted to the affective aspects of life by the vocabulary of modern English. Though the work does not pretend to be a reliable authority in matters of word classification, it is certainly not insignificant that the pocket edition devotes more than one fifth of the available space to the class of 'affections' (class VI). This is by no means insignificant if we consider that in this book all affections of a physical nature (such as pain, odour, taste) are classified in the subclass of organic matter (under class III).

The vocabulary, then, is rich; but it is not lucid. The notions rendered by the numerous terms denoting affections are ill-definable. It is easy enough to explain to anyone who never saw a table or a parallelopipedon what is meant by these words, but to explain what 'love' is or 'boredom', is an almost impossible task. Feelings – the qualities of the inner state – share this resistance against rational definition with non-spatial qualities generally. It is impossible to describe a colour, a smell, or a sound. There may be a word for each particular kind of these and if there is, that word 'describes' it better than any circumscription or definition. The difficulty is acute in conversation with foreigners. If the person addressed knows the word there is no problem; he knows what is meant. But if we must explain to a foreigner whose language has no adequate term for the specific shade of colour, sound or smell we have in mind, we must refer to something that comes nearest to it in his language, or simply produce an instance for demonstration, e.g. by referring to the correct number on an international scale of colour-shades. However, there is no such thing as a standard-scale of smells. With sounds the situation only seems to be better. A pitch can be defined by the number of the vibration frequency; but outside a laboratory this is an impossible way to solve the problem of elucidation. Moreover, pitch is only one of the elements of a sound. It says very little about that important quality known as its timbre; to specify it we must revert to such crude and unsatisfactory references as the sound of a flute, a trumpet, and so on. Besides, who is the man who can describe by words what makes the difference in sound quality between a chord in C major and that in E major? Words are a poor means for the description of non-spatial qualities. They are models which, to those who know them, are adequate means for recognition and understanding; but to know them they must first have been learned.

Learning a word implies far more than the memorization of the morpheme: the word must be filled with the experience of its proper contents to become the right vehicle for the communication of the concept, the quality or the state to which it refers. That quality or state may defy all efforts at proper definition; but the word for it finds a ready response in the hearer's intuitive knowledge; that word stands for something that is known and understood.

The learning of the meaning of words is a time consuming process. The studies made of language learning by Piaget and others, give evidence that the full content of a word is not immediately grasped. Each word is a model that eventually acquires its real content in the developmental life-history of the child. Learning to speak (as it actually is) is not the same as learning to think. Thinking is not really learned; it grows. Thinking activities develop along with the child's operational skills and experiences (cf. *inter alia* Piaget 1962). Speaking a language is only one of the skills acquired by the child. The often presumed correlation between learning to think and learning to speak is problematic. The weakness of the hypothesis that thinking depends on language is highlighted by the case of deafmutes. There is no doubt that they are able to think rationally, even though they cannot speak. And, in fact, it is not true that a normally-gifted person thinks in language. No one does. The formulation of thought in words constitutes part of a process of externalization which, admittedly, contributes substantially to the lucidity and definition of the thinking process, but is an epiphenomenon of the process rather than the process itself. Thinking involves the total content of the mind; the spoken word is but a selection from this larger whole.

Still, the influence of language on thought should not be underrated. Years ago, the linguist Whorf cogently demonstrated the influence of language on thought, both from a lexicological and from a grammatical point of view (Whorf 1941, reprinted in Parveen Adams 1972). One need not subscribe to all Whorf's conclusions to admit the fact, or to agree with the psychologist Bolton, that language "has the mysterious property... that it accomplishes the transition from the tacit to the explicit" (Bolton 1972: 207). In this transition, the function of language is a more active one. Its function is not, as it were, that of the obedient interpreter of his mute master's thought. Language selects and summarizes, it urges thought, so to say, to externalize itself, a function which can be observed in that remarkable phenomenon of inner speech which accompanies a not unimportant part of the thinking of the adult. Vygotsky's observations, in spite of their imperfections, give sufficient evidence to justify the conclusion that the process of externalization which finds its completion in speech, announces itself in isolated words and half sentences long before the thinking individual considers the desirability of disclosing his thought in speech (Vygotsky 1962).

The transition from the tacit to the explicit gives language its place in that intentionality of the human mind "which brings about the unity of the senses, of intelligence, of sensibility and motility" (Merleau-Ponty, as quoted in Bolton 1972: 225). Language, externalizing the contents of the mind, has a unifying effect on the thinking process and promotes its clarity and comprehension. This process begins long before actual externalization in overt speech takes place. Though we do not think in words, shreds of language emerge during the process. And here another problem, i.e. the problem of man and his condition, dimly arises on the horizon. Why is man *so* intent on expressing himself that even in his most secret thoughts he already anticipates on their externalization in the form of verbal communication? What urges him to express himself, more specifically to express himself by making use of words?

The question raises another, preliminary one. What does it mean to express oneself by making use of words? What does this imply? Evidently, words are models which are used to denote objects, qualities, actions and relations. If an object is denoted, the model does not denote one object specifically, but a class of objects which have specific properties in common. If the model denotes a specific quality, it is a quality which has a range of gradations; if it denotes an action or relation, it is not one specific action or relation but a whole class of actions or relations which, in each case, can be more exactly qualified. In the sentence "the tall man walks to the shop", the man can be any man but not a woman; he can be very tall but also moderately tall; he can walk fast or slowly; and the relation expressed by the term *to* can be used to introduce any direction or destination. In this case, he goes to the shop but he might just as well be going to the pub. In the verbalization of that accidental sense experience "I see a tall man walk to the shop", this operation transforms that particular man into one specific example of a class of many men, with a quality and a purpose any man or woman may have, moving about in a manner which is not even specifically human. An animal, too, can walk. The specific event, "the tall man walks to the shop", is expressed in terms of general applicability which can be used in an unlimited variety of statements. Every detail of the relevant perception is subsumed under a certain class: man, tall, walk, to, shop. As an act of ordering the details perceived, it is comparable to the intuitive ordering of sense perceptions into a field in the act of perception itself. But the linguistic ordering of the perception in words takes place on a level of more intense consciousness. In the verbalization process, what is perceived is detached from its situational context and transformed into a statement which is now at the disposal of the speaker. He or she can repeat (and elaborate) it at

30

any time and place. The perception has been turned into an item of knowledge.

Verbalization, though it does not produce or constitute knowledge, is an essential element of all knowledge. To know the names of things means to be knowledgeable about them. Names are words, and it has been pointed out that learning a word is not so much a matter of mastering a certain morpheme as of grasping and internalizing its meaning (above: 29). How much the knowing of names entails appears when we walk across the terrain at the edge of a tropical forest. Everything that grows and moves there is, to the foreign visitor, an indiscriminate mass of grasses and foliage, of trees and roots. But walk through the same terrain with a couple of competent interpreters like Conklin did in Hanunóo (Conklin 1954; cf. Lévi-Strauss 1962 b: 12 ff.) and that indiscriminate mass changes into a meaningful world of more and of less useful herbs and trees, each with a name, each with qualities which make them fit or unfit for certain specific uses. Knowing the names is identical with knowing your way there, being able to avoid dangers, to enjoy benefits: in short, to make your living. Without names this knowledge could never have been acquired and stored, let alone have been brought into some kind of order.

A name implies all the knowledge about a thing gathered by successive generations. To the native speaker, its name is the true model of the thing by which it is recognizable to all the members of the language community. It is not that, to the speaker, the name is the 'essence' of the thing. The problem of essence is beyond his ken. What counts to him is that the name is what everyone in his group calls a particular thing, and that this name includes all there is to know about it.

What the knowledge of names means in the life of man was never more dramatically demonstrated than by the life history of Helen Keller, the blind deafmute who, at the age of seven, discovered on an early morning that all things have names. The discovery not only changed her world, it also changed *her* (for comment cf. Cassirer 1944: 53ff., 169 f.). The event turned this unmanageable creature into a fully human child who – in spite of all her handicaps – set out with great determination on her way to discover her universe; a way which, in the course of years, led to a master's degree and eventually to a leading role in mobilizing world support for the handicapped.

What names and, subsequently, language did to her in a process inaugurated by a sudden discovery, it does to everyone in the course of the quiet but steady growth of language mastery. Linguistic symbols, i.e. words, enable man to order his world and his experiences in it, and to grasp it as a coherent whole. Expressing oneself in language, one subsumes the occasional and the situational under the general, and makes it available for discussion with others. This is what Merleau-Ponty had in mind when he stated that the transition from the tacit to the explicit brings about the unity of the senses, of intelligence, of sensibility and motility (above: 30). Detached from situation and sensorial immediacy, what is stated in words constitutes part of a larger world with wider horizons: the world of general concepts and notions. By translating his experiences into symbols the individual is enabled "to see beyond the end of his nose" (Van Peursen, private correspondence).

Giving names to things implies that a link is laid between man and his world, a link by which, from a distance, man participates in that world. But there is more to it than this. The name which establishes a link between a man and his world is also a link between that particular man and other men. The speaker derives that name from his social contacts with his fellow-men. All speakers belonging to a particular language community refer to the same thing by the same term and use these references primarily in their social interaction. Man may give names to things and speak about them in his statements; but these statements are addressed to his fellow-men. Fundamentally, language and its use is a matter of communication between persons. The universality of language demonstrates without any shadow of doubt that man does not live or exist in solitude, or merely as an individual, but as a member of a group. As a member of his group, however, he does not lose his individuality; there, too, he is both part of his universe and subject: and both functions combine in the act of communication.

Now we can return to our initial question: what urges man to express himself in words? It is more, surely, than just the wish to communicate with his fellow-men. Pronouncing a statement is logically preceded by a prior verbalization in silent speech, an incipient transposition of perception and experience into language categories, an act by which a person realizes himself as a subject who surveys his world from afar, formulating his participation in it. In the act of pronouncing a statement, he turns to the human part of his world, again as a subject who distances his world whilst turning himself toward it to participate in its affairs by his words. Essentially, the incipient formulation and the act of speaking (which can coincide) are both acts of self-realization, which is the inherent drive in man.

This does not mean, however, that this act of self-realization is always an easy one. Self-realization is often difficult: it must combine distancing with participation, being oneself with playing a part in a greater whole. Indeed, speaking is not an automatic process. Although a wealth of models is available for linguistic expression, we have all experienced moments when we could not produce the right word at the right moment. Repeatedly we fail to find the proper expression for conveying our feelings at the very moment when we need it most. Linguistic competence so poorly includes the ability to avail oneself of its potential facilities that successful writers or speakers are honoured as artists. The difficulties inherent in expressing oneself are implicitly admitted in the term expression: *ex*-pression, pressing out; in German: *Aus-druck*. Exertion and pressure are implied. These impediments are too general to explain them as psycho-pathologies of everyday life (Freud 1901). They must be inherent in the nature of things.

The struggle for adequate expression is aggravated by the fact that the available means for this purpose are limited. However rich a language may be, its collection of models is always finite, as is the system of rules for the combination and inflexion of these models by which they can be adapted to multiple purposes. The speakers of a language have to make do with these rules and models. If anyone feels that he needs a new model for expressing a concept not previously formulated, he must make a new derivate from an existing term, coin a composite of several terms or, as he mostly does, borrow one from another language. This is what scientists do when they wish to give shape to new ideas, or national language committees in the third world charged with developing a lexicon which is suitable for use in secondary schools where the national language has been introduced as the language of instruction. They do not make new morphemes. In spite of all the presumptuous talk about human creativity which has been generated by modern psychologists and educationalists, human creativity rarely surpasses inventivity, the ability to adapt old means to new ends.

This raises another problem. If new words are created, where do the old ones come from? A preliminary indication is provided by the fact that the few cases in which a modern lexicon is enriched with a new morpheme, that new word is usually qualified as slang. Thus the American term *oomph*, cited by Lévi-Strauss as a typical specimen of an indeterminate notion (1950: XLI), is, according to the Webster (1975), slang for sex-appeal and vigor, energy. With many other everyday words, the term has in common that it has an emotional connotation and that its author is unknown. More important in this context is the qualification 'slang': it indicates that it originated in a small, closed language community. There is no other place for words to originate than a small community. Here, people live in daily face-to-face contacts with each other. Here too, every new utterance can immediately become common property and be used from then onwards as part of the common language. It is a condition fulfilled in small-scaled primitive societies. It is significant that here, indeed, we find the greatest linguistic diversification (below: 68). These small groups are the real nurseries of language development and they produce language forms which exhibit throughout all the essential properties of language.

Among these properties is the frequently found combination of fact and feeling in descriptive terms such as was encountered in the word *oomph*. Words originate as expressions of experiences. As experiences usually affect the inner state, it is no wonder at all that the forms used to express these experiences carry the marks of the affects engendered by them.

Another, and the most essential property of all language, is order: grammatical, lexicological, and phonetical. It dominates linguistic expression in a primitive language as rigidly as in a modern one. That order is different from one language to another but the fact that there is order, is universal. Without it no language would be possible. Ordering is a basic structure of the mind (see also below: 92 f.).

3. *Affect and curtailment in other forms of expression*

Of the other forms of expression, consideration must first be given to those which use language as their medium. These are the verbal arts (poetry, drama and storytelling) and myth. Of the two, the verbal arts require less comment. In their products, intellect and affect are inextricably interwined, and it is this mixture which lends to them the power of moving the hearts of the public with a simultaneous appeal to both the intellect and the feelings. The role of the affects notwithstanding, the conscious element prevails.

Myth is different. Unlike the products of verbal art, it has no known author. It is not created for a specific purpose. It is, rather, the product of a group's engagement in

33

its members' reports of their visions and dreams (cf. below: 160 f., 165 f.). Such reports are as chaotic and incoherent as these dreams. Their ultimate form, the product of the society's sympathetic cooperation, is correspondingly strange and affect-ridden. And yet, myths have a logic and order of their own. In his *Mythologiques* Cl. Lévi-Strauss cogently demonstrated that the borrowing and transmission of mythical themes is not a matter of contingent chance but of structural rules which, to those concerned, are as unconscious as the grammatical rules of their language. Although it goes, perhaps, too far to say that these rules constitute a 'meta-grammar' (as Lévi-Strauss suggests), the existence of such rules is undeniable; as undeniable as the fact that they are unconscious.

Order is also found when we study the mythology of a particular people. A study like the one I made of Marind-anim mythology (Van Baal 1966) leads to the conclusion that this strange collection of savage stories constitutes a coherent and well-ordered whole organized on the same strict principles of dialectical opposition as those which dominate their ritual and social structure. There is 'logic' in myth just as there is 'logic' in religion in which, in spite of its affective components (above: 23 f.), intellectual considerations play an important part. They even do so in Marind-anim mythology (below: IX, 4). And, in Christian religion, they were strong enough to justify the designation of theology as 'the mother of philosophy'. Order, affect and intellect cannot be separated, even in myth and religion, a field of human activity which is deeply rooted in the unconscious.

As to the arts, painting, sculpture and music confront us with a surprising combination of affect and intellect. Although the essence of artistic expression cannot be translated into everyday language, let alone into rational considerations, the production and even the reproduction of art require a substantial investment, both of time and labour, in prolonged training in a number of difficult but perfectly rational techniques as well as a thorough study of all the relevant theory. Without for a moment belittling the affective significance of the arts, it can be stated that the impact of the intellect is considerable. Its impact on the growth and development of these art forms is eminently illustrated by the sketchbooks of Leonardo da Vinci which belong to the world's most convincing documents about these processes. However, it is not necessary to go back so far; a really baffling demonstration of the significance of the intellect in artistic expression can be found in the graphic work of Escher (Escher 1971). His etches are an abundant source of intellectual delight, a feast of cunning refinement.

There is, however, one important difference between music and the plastic arts which deserves further consideration. It is the fact that music is based on an intrinsic order of rhythm, measure and pitch, an order of a similar kind as that prevailing in language. Both are based on a systematization of differences between sounds which can be specified as follows:

	Language	Music
variations in pitch:	small	great
variations in timbre:	unimportant	important
number of sounds:	small (vowels & consonants)	almost unlimited
number of instruments:	one (human voice)	many
articulation:	by minute sound differences	by differences of many kinds

An intrinsic order of this kind cannot be found in the plastic arts. They are close to visible reality, closer also to the reality of conscious thought. Music has no tangible reality. It is elusive, and not of this world. There is celestial music, no celestial paintings. Music, then, is close to the unconscious; and it is originally based upon unconscious rules. Again: it is an indication that the notion of order has its roots in the unconscious mind of man.

Nevertheless, music makes a strong appeal upon the intellect. It is even so that the undisputed paradigm of the significance of professional expertise is presented by instrumental music. The skill required for proper performance on any musical instrument is a matter of unabated, daily exercise; and yet – it does not in itself enable the performer to do anything more or anything better than the sheer repetition of models created by the masterminds of the composers. Composing is an exceptional gift. In the *Ouverture* of the first volume of his *Mythologiques* Lévi-Strauss qualifies it as a divine gift only bestowed upon a very few isolated individuals (1964: 26). It could hardly be otherwise; apart from the specific requirements such as the right 'musical feeling', a musical ear, plus skill and imagination, the composer must have a sense of form and an almost mathematical intellect to solve the problems presented by the combination of a variety of instruments and themes. Many of these problems are technical and intellectual rather than emotional.

Approaching the problem from another angle brings us to the same conclusion. To that end, I must return to the attempt I made some years ago to trace some degree of inner consistency in the diversity of symbol-systems. For the sake of simplicity, I excluded the arts from consideration. This enabled me to arrange these systems in a scale of lucidity with, at the top, the symbols of science. They are clearly defined, unequivocal, and rational; and they excel in lucidity. The middle range is occupied by the symbols of language which can be used for the expression of contents ranging from the perfectly lucid to the utterly confused. Word-symbols can be ambiguous: most obviously so in the case of homonyms, but also because of their affective connotations. Low down on the scale of lucidity is the place for the symbols of dream and myth which can be characterized as expressions of a contradictory or confused state of mind (Van Baal 1971: 159 ff.). This scaling satisfied the purpose I then had in mind; though one difficulty obtruded which, at the time, I did not try to solve. It cannot be avoided here. The trouble is that lucidity is a quality sometimes ascribed to certain works of art, works which, by their affective nature, resist every attempt at rendering their essential traits in rational, verbal terms. What do we really mean by lucidity when we speak of the 'lucidity' of a painting by Vermeer, or the lucidity of Mozart's *Eine Kleine Nachtmusik?* What we have in mind is a particular kind of brightness and transparency, a something that refuses translation into words but is more or less of the same kind as the feeling aroused by an elegant and unexpected solution for a complicated scientific problem. This lucidity has little to do with simplicity in any case. One need only play an arrangement of it on the piano to discover that Mozart's deceptively simple composition is, far from being simple, of such a refined subtlety that it borders on cunning. Its charms appeal to the intellect in a comparable and yet in many respects different way as the intellectual excursions of most of the music by Bach. Affect and intellect are inextricably intertwined, and music, the most elusive of all art-forms, is also one of the most intellectual. Repeatedly, it is the intellectual perfection that evokes the affect.

Another aspect of all works of art is that they are not so much 'made' as 'created'. The works of art are called 'creations' because they are used as models, as standard forms which are available to others for expressing their moods and feelings or to give shape to deep-seated, affect-laden stirrings and notions. Poems are used in this way. Many are quickly forgotten, but some live on and are quoted by many members of successive generations. Other works are remembered because they represent a style which inspires others to imitation. The trend is not confined to the verbal arts; it is of particular importance in the graphic arts where 'schools' play a very obvious part and exert a far reaching influence on the general public, because their works find their way to the living quarters of thousands of people who silently submit themselves to their continuous influence by hanging them upon their walls for recurrent contemplation or just for the purpose of satisfying vague feelings of recognition and congeniality.

The most explicit case of the model function of artistic creations is again that of music, both vocal and instrumental. The song which earned itself popularity is repeated, at least for a time, by thousands and thousands of singers who find a remarkable satisfaction in meticulously reproducing the original. The religious hymn has a special place among songs; its longevity is greater than that of any other genre and even the text alone is often a source of edification or comfort. Instrumental music is almost exclusively a matter of choosing from available models, not only for the listener who makes his choice from his collection of records, but also for the performer who time and again returns to a small number of favourite compositions, even after he has mastered them by numerous repetitions. Of course, he also may improvise on his instrument; but there is a ten to one chance that what he then produces is variations on an old theme or the mixture of a couple of melodies he once heard, forgetting that he did. There is a close parallel here with language; new words are rare, new derivates or transformations are not.

Devotees are attached to 'their' music. There are compositions to which listeners return hundreds of years afterwards to express or to canalize their moods and feelings, to overcome, alternately, apathy and repressed emotions. One of the remarkable features of modern society is its attachment to old-fashioned thematic music. Some of these works have an indestructability which seems to justify the conclusion that music, being concerned with deeply-rooted sentiments, with the expression of basic affects, is less easily influenced by cultural changes than other art-forms. How could we otherwise explain the fact that classical music has retained its present strong position among so many new forms of music?

Such devotion to older forms is absent in the dance, music's partner since the days of yore. Two centuries ago dancing was a social game, something halfway between public show and elegant entertainment. We can still remember the music of minuet and gavotte; the dances are forgotten in spite of the efforts of amateur societies whose aim is to revitalize their rococo elegance and original perfection. Popular dance has subsequently developed in the opposite direction; i.e. that of gracelessness combined with complete individualization. It is no longer a social event. The dance-floor may well support hundreds of dancers, but they dance all to themselves in anonymous pairs with no obligation to the other pairs than the one which is mandatory in street traffic, i.e. the avoidance of collisions. There is no public; to every individual performer there is only the other, one's partner, to whom one adheres closely in an all-embracing grip. In recent years, even the tight tie between the two partners has been loosened; they face each other and gyrate around a common axis, unobserved by anyone, not even by the partner who, for the moment, is engaged in his on her own act, dancing out a something that is beyond description. Though we call such dancing not a form of art but one of amusement (often a subtile but always a significant distinction!), it is one of expression anyhow. However, to define what is expressed is a difficult task, requiring an elaborate analysis of the psychological and cultural framework of the performers' minds. Failing this, there is only one thing that can be held for certain, namely that it gives the performers some form of emotional satisfaction.

Similar difficulties are encountered with the role of ballet in modern society. We must, in this context, relinquish a discussion of the fact that, like music, ballet plays an important part in that baffling phenomenon of modern civilization which we call entertainment. We shall not examine either why ballet is also a prominent form of art. Only one detail is relevant here, the noteworthy circumstance that for the performance of modern ballet no expense or trouble is too much to make a good show. The choice of the music, the training of the personnel, the preparation of the appropriate lighting and decor, the imagination bestowed upon the plot or the scenario, all testifies to the inventiveness of the producers, and to the tremendous importance attributed to good performance.

This kind of ballet differs profoundly from the dance and drama of the primitive world which are poor in means, backward in techniques and rustic in their presentation. And yet, they are of a directness that goes straight to the heart. Perhaps I am prejudiced, having lived too long in that world's borderland, having stood too often in a dark corner silently watching such dances, i.e. the sometimes savage dancing in New Guinea, or refined as in Bali. But I cannot really believe that I am prejudiced. These dances, whatever they were or however they were performed, were the unfolding of feelings and intuitions which were alive in performers and spectators

37

alike. They had not been remoulded by the wish to please an anonymous public, nor by a stage-producer's conscious effort to express the preconceived meaning of the dance with greater perfection. The modern dancer (in the sense of the professionally trained ballet-dancer) does not easily reach that state of perfect abandonment to his role which, in the form of trance or demi-trance, so easily overcomes the less civilized performer who lets himself be carried away by the music, by the song, by the movement, but above all and beyond these particulars by the occasion itself which includes his whole world of meaning. After all, he is not an entertainer but a believer. And even so his self-expression is a matter of great exertion, requiring extreme devotion and concentration.

Another point of interest in the comparison of modern ballet with dance and drama in the primitive and pre-industrial world, is the prolific use made of technical perfections in staging the ballet. Artists do not hesitate to make use of new technical achievements to perfect their creations. This is not a new trend peculiar to modern art production. The artist takes an interest in new techniques everywhere. A few cases must suffice to illustrate this point. The first is a very old one, concerned with the effect of literacy on the development of poetry and drama. In a previous section we discussed the differences between the spoken and the written word and the importance of the latter for the language of science (above: 26). However, the language of science is a late product of western civilization; writing originated long before, round about the Bronze Age, probably as a development of mnemotechnic devices applied by royal stewards charged with the administration of services and levies. However that may be, among the first to apply the new expedient for other ends were the poets. Greek poetry is unthinkable without the knowledge and use of writing which enabled the poet to perfect his expression and to find his exertions rewarded by the creation of a definite text in a pure, unadulterated form available for reproduction at any time.

A second case is that of primitive sculpture. On the whole, the graphic and plastic arts are weakly developed among primitive peoples. That, nevertheless, they are and were capable of graphic expression which has artistic value even at a very early stage, is testified by the rockpaintings of contemporary Bushmen as well as by those of the early cave-dwellers in Europe. That technical obstacles must have been a major impediment to progressive development is demonstrated by a study of Asmat art published by Hoogerbrugge and Kooyman in the catalogue of an exhibition, organized by the Breda Division of the State Museum of Ethnography (December 1976). The Asmat are a swamp-dwelling people living on the South-west coast of West Irian (New Guinea), until recently notorious for headhunting and cannibalism. Till about seventy or eighty years ago, Asmat wood-carvers concentrated on the decoration of shields. About that time, they discovered that iron nails can be worked into small chisels which greatly facilitate the carving of wood. This inspired them to devote their attention anew to their crude wooden images which, until that time, had been rather inferior objects in comparison with the shields. A new period of art began to flourish, characterized by highly expressive and richly decorated images and carvings which have since attracted attention from many sides. Long before they discovered that their products had market value, they did their utmost to perfect their craft. For the sake of acquiring the indispensable nails they even raided a neighbouring district where they tore down the desks of a mission school to get hold of the nails. They were prepared to resort to radical measures to satisfy their need for better and more artistic expression!

The restrictions imposed by a rudimentary technology are most obvious in the field of instrumental music. Even drums are not found everywhere; the Australian tribes (the most backward in technical development of all mankind) had to make do with a couple of clapping sticks to accompany their singing. Stringed instruments and flutes are generally restricted to rather more advanced cultures. An older instrument is the jew's harp made of bamboo, one of the most simple means for the production of a variety of tones. However, the volume of the sound is small, and performing upon it serves the private pleasure of the one who is playing it and that of his sweetheart if he has one, rather than that of a wider audience. It was not before the discovery of metals that instrumental music could develop significantly.

In contrast, vocal music is possible to everyone. Singing is found in every culture. In Australia, it accompanies many rituals. It need not be confined to these. The Marind-anim of New Guinea had special songs for the accompaniment of their non-religious dances, and these songs were used on other occasions too. They often sang them during their journeys along the beach or when crossing the wide plains of the savannah. These songs were marvelously melodious and their sonorous, trumpet-like sound could be heard at more than a mile's distance. They sang them because of the music; the words were in a foreign language and had no meaning for them. Another, mainly secular form of songs, found among many primitive and archaic peoples, are those celebrating a special event, for instance the courage of a warrior, the achievement of a young man or, as the case may be, the failure of another. They are among the older products of music as well as of poetry.

The most elaborate forms of symbolic expression in primitive and archaic societies are those of myth and ritual. Language is well-developed everywhere, and the language used for ritual purposes is often more ceremonious than that used in everyday life. Of specific interest in this context is the immense amount of exertion bestowed on ritual. There are numerous cultures for which ritual is the heart and soul of social and economic life, to which all the daily work and effort seem to be oriented. In Australia, the older men are (were) mainly occupied with rites and their preparation. A celebration of some importance mobilizes all the members of the tribe or the village. Even in an advanced culture like that of the Balinese, rites and ceremonies take up an important part of the people's time and interest.

In this context, a form of symbolic expression must be mentioned which, although it is a matter of limited interest in modern civilization, is of specific importance in primitive culture, viz. bodily decoration. People often go to great lengths to meet the requirements relating to their ritual or their aesthetic appearance. Among these are deformations of the genitals by incision, circumcision or, in tribal Australia, even subincision; painful operations like tattooing, the filing of the incisors, and piercing large holes in the earlobes and the internasal septum, of small ones through the sides of the nose, or decoration of the body by cicatrization. Other methods are not painful but time consuming, such as dressing the hair, anointing and painting the body, and its decoration with belts, plaited rings and feathers. In pure decoration the aesthetic element is paramount. Among the Marind-anim it took hour after hour to prepare a young man for one of the grand ceremonial dances. When everything was ready, he was subjected to a final inspection by one of the older men. The old man would carefully examine him from head to foot and, if satisfied, shake his head slowly, whilst expressing his admiration in a soft whistling tone accompanied by tongue-clicking, all the time regarding the young man with honest satisfaction. And deservedly so. A traditional ceremonial dance was a spectacular performance which should really be seen for oneself in order to appreciate the splendour of the Marind-anim dance or the staging of a mythical drama, including the representation of a number of totem-ancestors.

The impersonation of totem-ancestors was also an important feature in Aranda ritual. The decoration of the performer took many hours. Down of various colours was stuck to his torso which was annointed for that purpose with human blood. Special care was given to his head-dress and to the sacred objects attached to it. The emphasis was very much on the sacred, but it would be erroneous to believe that the aesthetic did not matter. It was all in one.

It would not be difficult to cite other cases but they would add little to the conclusion which, by now, can be drawn. The first is that all forms of expression demand exertion, sometimes great exertion, and that the expression of affective contents is by no means a matter of spontaneity or intuition only, but always requires the cooperation of the intellect and the appliance of often highly intelligent techniques which must be mastered previously. The second is, that all expression depends on pre-existent models. This holds true also of ritual and body decoration. Although they are subject to change these changes rarely exceed the limits of minor innovations. When a medicine-man has a dream or vision urging him to introduce a new element into a ritual or into the traditional form of the impersonation of an ancestor, such an innovation is almost always a transformation or an elaboration of an existing form. It is the same with linguistic innovation or the ordinary artist's improvisation on his instrument. The creation of a new model is a rare event. Of course it occurs, but on closer analysis many of these new creations, new rituals included, show clear traces either of the past or of outside contacts.

Man's dependence on models is not restricted to that on forms of conscious expression. Models have been recognized also in the standard images recurrently produced in dreams (cf. Kuper 1979). Some of these are so frequent and general that they led to the hypothesis of genetic transmission, first to that of an Oedipus complex, then, more generally, to that of hereditary archetypes. Such explanations, however, are concerned with what is only a side issue, the greater frequency of the use of some images as symbols rather than others. They are unsatisfactory also in other respects. Of archetypes both Jung (1953: 205) and Eliade (1961) felt obliged to concede that the meanings associated with these archetypes are polyvalent, a polyvalence which remained unexplained. The most widely recognized of these arche-types, the Oedipus complex, does not even originate from conditions biologically determined, but from a cultural institution, the one called fatherhood. No animal knows its father; even modern man has to confess that *pater semper incertus.*

The side-step to genetics is superfluous if we start from the fact that man uses images of any description to symbolize the contents of his mind. That handful of privileged images called archetypes constitutes but a small group out of many, and the preference they enjoy ensues from their logical fitness to symbolize certain recurrent problems and issues. The father-image is an inviting one for symbolizing alarming combinations of authority and kindness (below: 90). Gallinaceous birds have a privileged position in myth and ritual among many peoples. These birds are poor flyers and as such good symbols of mediation between earth-bound man and the upperworld; they live on the same level as man and they become airborne only with difficulty. We find them associated with unusual events such as the birth of twins, but also as transmitters of divine messages in rituals of divination. Logical analyses of myth and ritual of the kind such as those contrived by Lévi-Strauss (for gallinaceous birds cf. his 1971: 481 ff.) demonstrate time and again that the symbolic use of certain images is defined by their logical associations within a given cultural context; a fact which explains the preferential use of some images over others, as well as the diversification (the polyvalence) of the meanings attached to them as symbols.

The basic problem is not that some images are more fit for symbolic use than others, but that man is so strongly given to the use of images as symbols. He does this in metaphor and myth, in poetry and the plastic arts, in dance and drama, expressing something that in one way or other is beyond words. The problem is even wider because he does the same in music, the most elusive of all forms of human expression. Whereas symbols based on images can boast a relation with observable reality which holds a tangible suggestion in what way to feel or think about the message implied, the message of music is as elusive as its rapidly fading sound. Like all the arts, music is normally played in order to be enjoyed by others, but the explanatory power of this phenomenon is small. Often, music is made for the performer's private satisfaction. Private satisfaction is an important element in all the arts. The wish to satisfy the public does not make a great poet or painter. They cannot do without what they call inspiration, an inner urge to produce their art forms the way they do.

One might suspect that this inner drive is specific to western culture. But it is not. One of the world's simplest musical instruments, the bamboo jew's harp, is hardly audible to anyone but the performer. I still remember the happy face of the boy who, all by himself, squatted on a rock playing his tiny instrument. And how much music can be an emotional reaction to a sudden experience I found out on another occasion when, after five days of slow and tiring progress through the New Guinea forest, we hit upon a small open area and saw the sun. My bearers, all plain-dwelling people, suddenly burst into a cheerful, resounding song.

The wish to express oneself, then, is general; as is the wish to express one's feelings. But why this vast array of models for expressing them? Why make it so difficult for oneself, sparing neither time nor labour to fashion and adapt them to different circumstances? If it were only to vent certain feelings, man might as well confine himself just to crying or working himself up into a tantrum in any way which comes natural to him on the spur of the moment. That is what a child does; i.e. an immature human being who has not yet reached the age at which he has learned to express himself the proper way. Why are models the proper vehicles to express oneself? Our question must be reformulated as follows: What urges man to express himself in models?

The vast array of available models and the impressive amount of work man is prepared to undertake in order to perfect the form of his self-expression confirm that self-expression is indeed a fundamental drive in man. In the next chapter (section 2), it will be argued that the self is the personalized shape of the individual's libido. But then, why this emphasis on models and more specifically that emphasis on pre-existent models? Admittedly, the creation of new models occurs, but they are the exception rather than the rule. Besides, though the creation of new models is difficult, the proper use of existing models is not easy either. We noticed that it often makes a strong demand on technical expertise.

The dominant role of existing models might be explained by hypothesizing that self-expression is always combined with the conscious or unconscious wish to communicate with others. The explanation is unsatisfactory because the role ascribed to the unconscious is an unfalsifiable assertion. Moreover, it does not find much support in observable reality. The non-professional musician does not play his instrument to communicate his moods to others. Often he feels happiest when he is alone. The artist does not paint a landscape or a face the way he does for the purpose of communicating to others how he sees that landscape or that face. He simply tries to objectify how and what he sees and nothing else. Similarly, the poet does not work on his poem until it satisfies a potential public, but until it satisfies *him*.

To fathom how and why the use of models satisfies the user we must again turn to the story of Helen Keller. The discovery that all things have names excited her; not because, by now, she could communicate with others about these objects, but because she had discovered something which laid down an unchanging relation between herself and a certain category of things: a name which covers all the objects falling in that category. A symbol – and this holds true of all symbols, not just the verbal ones – is a token by which individual things and accidental events are brought under the heading of a generalization which enables man to manipulate them as parts of a general order. That order is the order of the world of which he is a part, and he faces that order because in the act of symbolizing he has emerged from the order of sense-experience and proceeded to that of an objectifying abstraction. The transition is effectuated by an act of expression through symbols. What is in question in expression is not primarily man's relations with his fellow-men, but those with his universe. The metaphor gives shape to the poet's experience of his world, the painting to the artist's vision while considering a certain face or landscape, a melody to the performer's mood in a particular situation. The blessing of successful expression is that it gives peace to the agent's mind because it gives shape to his specific way of participating in his universe. And this is why expression is difficult. It is the result of

42

a struggle, because there is always tension between the subject and his ways of participating in, and projecting himself into, his world.

Still, this does not explain why existing models are preferred. It cannot be because creating a new model is difficult and therefore exceptional. Although this is true enough, it can hardly be the most fundamental reason. This should be sought for in the fact that the pre-existent model is itself part of the subject's world, signifying a non-self in which the self must participate at the level of abstraction in the same manner as it participated in what was signified at the level of immediate sense experience. Symbols, of whatever kind, give form and substance to man's objective universe on the level of abstract thought, and to man's manner of experiencing his world at the level of the distancing subject who contemplates his place in his universe and watches over it from afar. By embracing the right symbols he can define his place. It is only in uncommon circumstances, disclosing new vistas in his relation with his world, that the creation of new symbols is called for, a creation which demands a more subtle mind and a more thorough immersion in the various facets of that relation than are given to the average man. The ardent propagandists of an education that stimulates a child's creativity rarely fathom what they are talking about.

III

Subject and human condition

Before we proceed to a discussion of the subject and the human condition, it is necessary to make sure that it does indeed make sense to concentrate our attention primarily on the living conditions and cultural institutions of primitive man. It has already been stated that his ways of life are nearer to the naked facts of the human condition than those of modern man (above: 4). Yet, many scholars have argued that the differences between primitive and modern man are so pertinent that we can hardly consider them equals. Although such views have been refuted repeatedly, some of them are so persistent that it is not possible to ignore them. A discussion here may remove objections which might otherwise arise at a later stage in the argument.

1. The basic similarity of primitive and modern man

The survey of symbol-systems in the previous chapter gives no support to the often heard contention that the affective components of spiritual life are of greater importance in primitive culture than in modern civilization. In the latter the recent acquisition of a 'language of science' is more than compensated for by the impressive increase of the means for externalizing the affective life, such as new means for instrumental music, and new techniques for the plastic arts, including paints, etching, film, photography and light effects. Most important of all are the highly perfected means for the dissemination of 'art' products marketed by the world-wide entertainment industry. Over against primitive man's rituals and feasts, which are occasional celebrations, stands the constant flood of music and entertainment accompanying and saturating the life of modern man from morning to night. The difference between the ways of life of primitive and modern man is not a question of greater or lesser emotionality, but of a conspicuous difference in the ways of expressing it, modern man avoiding the crude irrationalities so characteristic of primitive man's magic and myth.

The explanation of these irrationalities has been a matter of controversy among anthropologists for more than a century. There were two moot points. The first is whether primitive man is intrinsically of the same nature as modern man. The second, if the latter be the case, is whether the irrationalities in the expression of primitive man's affective life and needs are a matter of socially-defined differences in mentality generally or, more specifically, of differences in religion.

Early anthropologists like Tylor and Frazer never denied that primitive man is a man like us. Yet, they called him a savage, and ascribed to him recurrent difficulties with the gift of reason which, so they felt, nature had bestowed upon him prematurely. Basing themselves on an associationist psychology long since obsolete, they hypothesized that early man had to learn from experience which associations had causal value and which were of an accidental nature. Early man had to experiment with the gift of reason, experiments which more or less of necessity led to the misconceptions underlying both the belief in, and the practice of, magic. At a somewhat later stage in the evolutionary process, these, in turn, gave way to crude efforts at explaining the mysteries of life and death on the basis of the belief in spiritual beings. A noteworthy feature of this theory is that it capitalized on defective reasoning, not on an excess of emotionality.

The reaction which, at the turn of the century, was initiated by Marett, strongly criticized the older school of thought for its rationalism and the untenability of its psychological presuppositions. It advanced important evidence that magic is somehow related to religion, and that religion is rooted in the emotions; but it did not succeed in devising a generally accepted theory to explain the origin and persistence of religion and magic. In spite of all the work done by scholars like Marett, Preusz, Lowie, Malinowski, Radin, and many others, magic in particular remained a relic of the past, resisting all efforts at its reduction to a normal human reaction to the ecological and intellectual conditions of primitive life. To a certain extent, much the same can be said of the belief in myth and ritual, but nowhere was the gap between what is psychologically normal to modern and primitive man severally, wider than in the latter's unshaken belief in magic.

More radical solutions were presented by psychologists. The interpretation of dreams and schizophrenia as states of mental regression which bring deeper layers of the mind to the surface, layers in which prominent traits of a primitive worldview prevail, automatically implied that primitive people must be viewed as immature humans. Freud's interpretation of magic as a form of the infantile omnipotence of thought, is a good instance (*Totem und Tabu*, ch. III). Others went even further. Jung's stratified model of the human mind favours the notion that primitive man's psyche lacks one or two of the layers completing the mind of modern man. Although Jung is not always clear on this point, his speculations about the racial variations of the collective unconscious support this interpretation (cf. Jung 1928: 54 note 1). Kretschmer was more outspoken. He did not shrink from such far-fetched metaphors as "the annual rings of the psyche's phylogenesis" (1926: 88). Such spatial metaphors may be very convenient – the term 'subconscious' has a well established place in our lexicon – but they do more harm than good. They find no support in the results of brain research. Besides, anatomical or physiological differences between the brain of modern man and that of primitive people have never been demonstrated empirically. Consequently, theories based on the assumption of genetic differences in brain-structure must be rejected.

This argument does not apply to theories based on the assumption of infantile regression. Their weakness lies elsewhere, viz. in the fact that such regression is a symptom of neurosis or psychosis, whereas primitive believers in the efficacy of magic do not exhibit the symptoms of asocial and deviant behaviour which accompany mental disease. Modern ethnographic research has produced abundant evidence that primitive man, far from being the halfwit of the older textbooks, is as perfectly human as modern man except in his religious beliefs and practices which continue to puzzle us.

This leads us to the second moot question: Do these religious beliefs and practices point to socially-defined differences in religion or to socially-defined differences in mentality generally? Thus formulated, the question resembles a quibble rather than a serious problem. Yet, there lies a serious problem behind it; namely: Is religion an answer to an existential human need, or is it an idiosyncrasy evoked by social or cultural conditions of a transitory nature? The presumption that religion is related to existential human needs has recurred more than once (e.g. in some of the writings of Preusz) but the point has never been seriously investigated. This is the regrettable effect of neglecting the theory of religion in the field of anthropology since the first quarter of the present century. The declining role of religion in our own civilization and the rapidly growing interest in problems of social relations and social structure diverted the attention of social scientists and historians of religion to other fields of study, and they contented themselves, when confronted with the problems of religion, with the mere elaboration of older themes or new efforts at studying religious phenomena either as reflections of social conditions, or, in more recent years, as structural variants of the ordering principles of the human mind. This does not imply that the assumption that religion is an answer to universal, existential needs can be shelved. On the contrary, we shall take the question up again in part III of this book. For the moment, however, we need only dwell on the efforts made to explain religion and, in particular, magic as the result of a specific, socially-defined mentality.

The most influential effort at explaining the irrationalities of magic and religion from a specific mentality induced by primitive man's social conditions has been that of Lévy-Bruhl. Following Durkheim, who taught that man's ways of thought are defined by his social conditions, he argued that it is not primitive man's mind or brain which differs from ours, but his mentality, i.e. the socially induced forms of his thought and behaviour. As an individual, primitive man thinks as logically as we do; the difference is in his collective representations, i.e. the social facts which are the products of a society whose members all think and react alike. It is a society without any form of specialization, in which it is the duty of every member to be like all the others, where communal ties are of a highly emotional nature, and the representations common to all originate under circumstances of a strongly emotional character such as those prevailing during initiation ceremonies, where mystic associations are more important than natural causality. The mystic participation which, in magical thinking, connects the most diverse things and events, reflects the position of the individual in a society where everyone without exception thinks and acts alike. As synthetic as this form of social life is the way of thought emanating from it. In the

46

collective representations, the law of participation prevails; it ignores the *principium contradictionis* and this way of thinking must be characterized not as illogical but as prelogical.

The theory has been largely misunderstood even by many of its adherents who, contrary to the author's intentions, interpreted the differences in mentality as differences in mind. We need not dwell upon this point. More important is that it is a weak theory anyhow. The distinction between individual and collective representations is untenable. Each representation is as individual as it is collective. For its externalization, every representation (notion) of the mind depends on models, and these models are provided by society. Every word is a product of the collectivity called society. What is worse for the theory is that Lévy-Bruhl did not support convincingly the assertion that, in the primitive world, collective representations are always mystical or prelogical. The data presented to prove this point are all of one kind: cases of mystical thinking borrowed from the field of religious thought and action. Among the hundreds, perhaps thousands even of instances of collective representations forwarded in his *Fonctions mentales dans les Sociétés inférieures* (1910) and in his later works on this subject, there is not one which is concerned with agricultural techniques, the construction of houses or canoes, or the regulation of social duties. It is evident that, in these fields, collective representations in the sense as Lévy-Bruhl had in mind, are as numerous as anywhere. In archaic societies, every tiller of foodcrops applies the techniques which his father taught him, builds houses and canoes in just the same manner as preceding generations, and observes his society's rules for social behaviour in his contacts with others. Many of these rules and techniques have been described in detail, but they are neither mystical nor prelogical. These collective representations simply follow the rules of ordinary logic. What Lévy-Bruhl really did was to give an absorbing description of the phenomenology of primitive religion (which, like all religion, is mystical) but not of primitive mentality.

This leaves us at the point where the difference between a Melanesian and a pious European farmer is reduced to the simple point that, whilst the former uses magic to protect his crop against pests and to ensure fair weather and prosperous growth, the latter, believing that an almighty God is inclined to intervene on his behalf, prays for it.

Another effort at elucidating the puzzles offered by primitive man's thinking has been undertaken by Lévi-Strauss. It is of specific interest here because the author's problem was (and is) not what, under various circumstances, man's affects and emotions do to his intellect, but how the human intellect operates under whatever circumstances. To operate at all, the intellect must dispose of knowledge. The great problem of early man was not that something was wrong or different with his intellect, but that he suffered from an immense lack of knowledge. Facing his world, that world necessarily suggested a meaning to him, but a meaning which he could neither express nor formulate. All early man could do was to produce words with a zero-value, denotations expressing the significant impression which certain phenomena in his world made on him as things with an indescribable something. Such words are like a steamed window-glass. In time, increasing knowledge will eradicate this vagueness, but as long as the blurring persists, early man struggles with notions which signify something to him without permitting him to specify its contents by a well-defined signified. It is the theme of his *Introduction à l'Oeuvre de Marcel Mauss* (1950) and his early eassays on magic, *Le Sorcier et sa Magie,* and *l'Efficacité symbolique,* both reprinted in *Anthropologie Structurale* I (1958).

In the *Introduction,* he gives two instances of words with a zero-value, the one taken from modern American slang (the word *oomph* which we discussed above, p. 33), the other from Melanesia, the word *mana.* The latter is the more significant of the two, the former being no more than an example of a denotation with a strong affective component. But *mana* refers, indeed, to an indescribable something that can be attached to the most diverse objects: persons, things , as well as to chants and incantations. Lévi-Strauss argues that it has altogether too easily been translated by supernatural potency: in reality, it is but a stopgap which is intended to fill a vacuum where knowledge is lacking. It is not necessary here to repeat the whole argument; it fails on one decisive point. The persons etc. to whom or to which mana is ascribed are not poorly known or dimly recognized, they are mostly perfectly well-known except for one thing: they have aroused the suspicion that they are more than they are, that they have something which surpasses their observable, as well-known as describable qualities. There is no question of a lack of knowledge; but, on the contrary, of the attribution of something that is more than knowledge, that belongs to the un-knowable *in se.* There is no difficulty in granting that such attributions thrive in a situation of limited knowledge but it can be denied on logical grounds that, in this concrete case, this attribution is induced by lack of knowledge of the concrete case. There is no such lack.

Similar objections must be brought against his interpretation of the magical rite for curing the sick as an attribution of meaning in a situation characterized by a lack of meaning, viz. the inconceivable sickness. This description of the situation is not fully correct. In fact, patient and public already attributed meaning to the sickness before they called in the medicine-man. That is why he is called in in the first place. His task is not to give meaning to a situation which is void of meaning, but to identify and specify that meaning. Another point is that there is no real lack of knowledge. People are well aware that something is wrong, that this something must have a cause, and that there is a chance that the situation can be ameliorated. The problem is why they attribute meaning to the situation, more specifically a super-natural meaning. Why do they not stick to the fact that, so far, the patient has bad luck, and that he either will recover or die, and that nothing can be done about it except nursing him as well as possible? This is what they actually do when a recently-born baby or a very old man or woman falls ill. Apparently, sickness with people in the prime of life is different. Then meaning is attached to the case, but that is not the automatic result of a lack of knowledge. The modern widow who mourns her deceased young husband who died of meningitis does the same when, in her grief, she complains: why should he, and only he, attract that illness? Again, I do not deny that lack of adequate knowledge is conducive to the attribution of meaning to a difficult situation, but it is not its cause. It is not even a necessary condition; the widow in mourning had no lack of knowledge and yet she suspected some meaning inherent in the event.

In a later work, *La Pensée Sauvage* (1962b), Lévi-Strauss made a more comprehensive effort at elucidating primitive man's sometimes aberrant ways of thinking. The basic idea is that primitive (savage) thought is subject to the same laws as that of modern man. The brain of primitive man is of the same structure as that of modern man, and Lévi-Strauss gives an absorbing demonstration of the fundamental role played by classification and logic order in so-called savage thought. The difference with ours is that the knowledge available to primitive man is concrete knowledge, a *science du concret*. This, in itself, cannot make a great difference, as the same holds true of much – though not all – of our knowledge, especially that which is applied in everyday life.

He makes a second distinction which is more productive. There are two ways of thinking, that of the engineer, and that of the *bricoleur*, the do-it-yourself man who makes new things from old, the remains of discarded utensils and objects which he dismantled after they broke down, storing away such parts as might be of some future use. When an engineer has to construct something he adapts his means to his design, whereas the *bricoleur* has to adapt his design to his means, i.e. to the old parts which happen to be at his disposal. In contrast to the products of the engineer, the works constructed by the *bricoleur* are charged with the reminiscence of the previous destinations and history of their constituent parts. This, applied to the *bricoleur's* way of thinking, implies that his concepts are not as matter-of-fact as they should be; something of the past, a human dimension is clinging to them. What that human dimension is, the author does not explain, but we probably do not err seriously if we associate this concept with the meaning imputed by the medicine-man and his patient to the sickness the former is about to cure by a rite. There is more in this presentation of facts which reminds of the earlier essays. The engineer is a rich man who can acquire all the means he needs, whilst the *bricoleur* is poor and must therefore make do with what is at his disposal. A good instance is that of myth. To explain his world primitive man has to make use of older mythical concepts and stories which he borrows from the past or from his neighbours and adapts to his own conditions. The engineer is rich in concepts, the *bricoleur* poor.

However, the book does not refer to the formulations presented in his earlier essays. It does not even make clear whether the *bricoleur's* way of thinking coincides with the *science du concret*, nor whether the engineer's way of thinking is limited to the members of modern society. In fact, the difference between the two ways of thinking is blurred by the author's assurance that the *bricoleur,* too, contributes to the increase of knowledge and the progress of culture. Indeed, such possibility is implied in the concept. The *bricoleur,* too, is a constructor who must devote much time to logical thinking though, at times, he may be swayed by his sentiments. Only one thing is made clear and this is that, in his pursuit of the arts, modern man still thinks as a *bricoleur.* If primitive man must be identified with the *bricoleur*, the problem remains: What is the difference between certain aspects of his thinking and that of the engineer? In what respect does the man who made the first spearthrower, or the one who constructed the first bellows, differ from an engineer and the latter's way of thought? Of course, this overlapping suits the author's purpose to emphasize that, in principle, there is no difference between the thinking processes in modern and in early man. One can agree with this and still wish to get an answer to the question why the *bricoleur* sometimes thinks in terms which are of the kind applied by the engineer, and then again lapses into representations and notions of a highly unscientific nature. Or, to put it more generally, why does man sometimes think as an engineer, and sometimes as a *bricoleur*?

There are reasons, in fact, why Lévi-Strauss does not answer this question. But, before we try to specify his reasons, it is pertinent to point out that he himself raised the problem in the first chapter of his book. There he posed the question how it is possible that the brilliant technical development which was initiated with the Neolithic Age came to a standstill with the Iron Age. He never gave an explicit answer to this question. One can guess that it is because all the inventions made were made by the *bricoleur* in man, but this is not a very satisfactory answer because it does not explain the halt in progress after the Iron Age. Nevertheless, there is a simple answer. It was recently given by Dr. de Ruyter in an as yet unpublished paper. He points out that, at the end of the Iron Age, the archaic engineer (or *bricoleur*?) had made all the progress that possibly could be made on the basis of a *science du concret*. For further progress he needed other intellectual tools than concrete knowledge can provide: to wit, intellectual symbols for proper designing, computing and measuring. Though, at the time, the art of writing had already been developed, writing alone could not solve the problems of measurement, quantification, and mathematics that hampered the engineer's progress. Script halted at the written form of the spoken word. This certainly contributed to its clarity and acuity, but it did not tell how to solve even such a simple problem as the computation of the area of a piece of land. There is hardly a more persuasive document for demonstrating the immense difficulties of such simple problems than the *Rhind* papyrus, an Egyptian instruction for surveyors dating back to some time between the 18th and the 15th century B.C. (Newman 1956, I: 170). The techniques applied were ingenious, very ingenious even, but so hopelessly awkward that it was impossible to make headway. Although Greek mathematicians later offered solutions for some of the mathematical problems, no great progress could be made before the discovery of the numeral zero had opened up new methods leading to the solution of simple arithmetical problems. To fathom the scope of these problems, one need only try to perform an addition or a multiplication sum in Roman numerals.

Intellectual progress, then, is a matter of intellectual tools, just as we found that artistic progress is a matter of technical tools. But all this does not bring us any nearer to the solution of the problems posed by magic, primitive ritual and myth, phenomena which cannot be explained from a lack of knowledge alone. Lévi-Strauss cannot help us on this point and, as has already been suggested, there is a good reason for this. It is not really his problem. His central problem is the grammar of human thought, the laws ruling the processes of thinking. He has made an important contribution to our knowledge of it by demonstrating that, even in processes such as myth, which impress us as perfectly unruly, certain rules are always followed. To achieve this he methodically studied the forms of thought by concentrating on the results of the thinking processes. He did not ask *why* people thought this and that, but *how* they thought this and that. Perhaps it can best be expressed in German: what he analysed were *nicht die Gedanken, sondern das Gedachte*, not the thoughts, but what had been thought. He did not ask primarily for motivations, but for the final results. It is for this reason that his interest in the affects is limited to their results in final forms of expression, for this reason too that he eliminates the subject, the ego, from his considerations. He wishes to learn from the result of the process, not from what drives it. The latter is our problem. We wish to find out why people think this way or that, and in this context the subject, the ego, necessarily stands central. One cannot study man and ignore that he is a subject even though, for purposes like Lévi-Strauss's, it can be useful to abstract from it. The importance of his writings for us in the present work is that they have supplied us with new data to confirm that, basically, there is no difference between modern man and primitive man. In essence, we all are alike, and with this certainty in mind we can return to our enquiry into the human condition. To that end it is desirable to turn first to the nature and function of the subject.

2. The subject

The subject is elusive. We know other persons, some of them even intimately, but we never know anyone so well that we can know his or her ego. We may have opinions about it, but we never really know it. In fact, no one even knows his own ego. Of course, everyone knows or can know how he presents himself to others, but in thinking about this ego, the ego thought of is not the same as the ego thinking about the ego which presents itself. Turning his attention to his secret desires and his own intimate behaviour, he can again draw a picture of himself, but again this is not his ego. His ego is at that moment his soul-searching ego. And so on *ad infinitum*. The ego always steps aside, is the onlooker, the contemplator, not the one who is looked at or contemplated. All we can say about our own ego is that it has varying dimensions. When, playing tennis, I smash the ball, my ego is my whole body. When I fall and hurt my knee, I stop to examine my knee. Now, part of my body is an object; I, ego, inspect the wound and I suffer pain.

The elusiveness of the ego has engaged the attention of philosophers from Aristotle and St. Augustine to Kant, Witgenstein, and the phenomenologists. Contemporary philosophers describe the ego or subject as the individual's orientation towards his universe, as a potency or direction in the individual's interaction with the world of which he is a part (Van Peursen 1966 ch. 11). If this is translated into the language of psychology, then the subject must, if not identified, at least be associated with the centrifugal mental energy, the libido, which sways the individual's mind and actions.

The conclusion opens up new ways. It extricates our notion of the human psyche from the unsatisfactory view that it is ruled by blind, instinctual drives which follow their own bent. It is a view which, on the one hand, makes man the slave of his own emotions and drives and, on the other, fails to appreciate the organized order of the mind. We know that the mind orders its perceptions, that it creates order in language and other complicated forms of expression, so why should there not be order in the mind as a whole?

If the subject itself is the moving principle prompting the individual's actions, even the heart and core of them, then the subject must be far more than what, in chapter I (p. 13 f.) was compared to a scanning apparatus with inbuilt mechanisms for ordering the incoming stimuli. Of course, the subject is this too; the simile of a 'scanner' is a perfect metaphor for the subject's restless activity. It is always active, scanning, unless sleep has 'switched off' the motor. Nevertheless, even the best-equipped and most-perfected scanning device is but a receptor, dependent upon the impulses caught on its rotating shield. The subject, as depicted by philosophy, is far more; it includes and directs the productive energy of the mind. It makes choices and decides on the ways consciously to be followed in order to achieve certain ends, but it is itself part of the unconscious. It is unknowable, but it channels the unconscious energy denoted as libido, instincts, or drives.

This raises important problems. Is the subject, in principle, the accidental sum-total constituted by equally accidental drives, generated by accidental variations in hormonic production, or is all this combined with the results of choices made by the subject in the course of its personal history which were so important that the subject accreted them as it were to itself? Apparently the latter; there is more continuity in the subject's decisions and choices than can be explained from a never-constant hormone production or the activity of so-called instinctual drives.

Instinctual drives is, in fact, an objectionable term. Modern ethologists avoid its use and speak instead of innate behaviour. They claim that, among mammals, behaviour is never innate purely and simply but amplified and detailed by learning processes (Jolly 1972 ch. 8). If the latter is true of mammals generally, it is certainly true of man. The extreme length of the latter's juvenile state is an indication that he has much to learn. Born in a perfectly helpless state, in a phase of his ontogenesis which other mammals pass in the maternal womb, man has more to learn than any other living creature. Even perception, the ordering and combining of incoming percepts in a field, must be learned. Only gradually does the baby learn to recognize faces, its mother's face first, those of others afterwards. If the ordering of the perceptions in a field is an unconscious process, this does not mean that the performance is innate. Innate is only the capacity; all the rest must be learned as, in a subsequent stage of development, the infant learns to master a language and to follow all the rules of grammar, lexicon and phonemics without knowing anything about rules at all. Without ever becoming conscious of these rules, the child handles them unconsciously and more and more perfectly. We learn from the child that the unconscious is more than a collection of innate laws for the operation of the brain; it also includes all the automatisms resulting from learning processes, in particular early learning processes. The wide compass of these automatisms becomes apparent when we compare the results of a child's language learning to those of language learning at a later age. Technically, the latter is a quite different process, and it takes many years to acquire mastery in that later language, that is, to speak it without giving ever a second thought to grammar, lexicon or phonemics. Personally, I never acquired that mastery in any foreign language that I speak with some fluency.

Here the question arises as to what the difference is between these early acquired automatisms and the equally unconscious, so-called instinctual drives. Can these drives, too, be automatisms acquired through the interaction between the young individual and his universe? The answer is that they are different anyway because of their strongly emotional content. They are charged with energy. The standard expression is that the individual is carried away by his drives, that he is swayed by his passions. Perhaps it would be more correct to say that it is the energy by which the subject sways the individual, but even if this conjecture be true, it says nothing about the origin of these passions and drives. Is it possible that they are transformations of the mental energy by which the subject turns to its world, and that these transformations acquired their specific forms and contents during the early years of the individual?

Of one thing we can be certain: that the mental energy by which the subject turns to its world is innate. Turning to their world is what all living beings do. They are always scanning it. They move about in their universe, displaying species-specific forms of behaviour to satisfy their species-specific needs. The patterns of that behaviour are not necessarily innate. Mammals need a period of learning in order to acquire the behavioural patterns necessary for self-preservation. With many of them, a period varying between a couple of months and a year suffices to develop the hereditary traits into fully-adapted patterns of species-specific behaviour. Most of these patterns are concerned with the acquisition of food, a few only with social contacts with congeners. With humans this is different. Not only is the period of learning incomparably longer, but patterns for independent food acquisition are not developed before the child is six years old, usually even much later. For food acquisition, and for all its daily needs generally, the infant depends upon older congeners, in the first place its mother. The first patterns of behaviour developed by the infant are patterns of social behaviour. The acquisition may cause a considerable deal of frustration. A notorious instance is the case of toilet training. Anthropologists paid much attention to this item of early education in peasant and primitive societies; they soon found out that on this point archaic living conditions offer better opportunities for considerate treatment of the infant than the modern bourgeois family home. Of more considerable importance is the infant's dependence on his human environment. He quickly learns to expect comfort and food from it, also that he can attract attention by crying, that occasional tantrums may lead to special attention and comfort. That the child develops habits is evident, but do these habits really lead to long-lasting patterns of behaviour and even to the fixation of deeply emotional drives and passions?

Yet, child psychologists insist that infant experiences have a long-lasting influence on character formation, even to the extent that the early conditioning of the child is an important contribution to cultural continuity. A whole school of anthropologists, from E. Sapir and Ruth Benedict, Margaret Mead and A. Kardiner down to the Whitings and H. Geertz and many others, have been engaged in the study of the impact of early education on cultural personality to the effect that, today, the significance of early education for the establishment of lasting attitudes and patterns of cultural behaviour is an accepted fact. Whence this perpetuity? Can we deny that, maturing, the child grows into a different person from what it was when it was dependent?

At this point, two interesting phenomena demand our attention. The first is that of infantile amnesia (cf. Rapaport 1971: 155 f.). What anyone remembers of his infant years is next to nothing. And yet, these infant experiences have not been lost. Psycho-analysis has demonstrated that awesome or frustrating infant experiences constitute the basis of many neurotic deviations in adult life. What is more – and this is the second relevant phenomenon – infant experiences play a decisive part in dreams. Freud explicitly states: *Das Träumen ist ein Stück des überwundenen Kinder-seelenlebens* (his italics; 1930: 387). And again: *Das Träumen sei im ganzen ein Stück Regression zu den frühesten Verhältnissen des Träumers, ein Wiedererleben seiner Kindheit, der in ihr herrschend gewesenen Triebregungen und verfügbar gewesenen Ausdrucksweisen* (ibid.: 375)*.

It is evident that infantile experience has not been lost but has been incorporated almost *in toto* in the unconscious. The first question which arises is: Why in this period? Why do we remember later experiences without great difficulty, and not these earlier ones? Must it be concluded that the tendency to repression is stronger at an early age than later in life? It would be difficult to explain this. A more realistic answer seems to be that, at this age, repression is much easier. The period of infantile amnesia comes to an end roundabout the time that language-mastery is completed. Language-mastery implies more than just an ability, a technique. The capability to externalize experiences in symbolic form includes the capability to objectify experiences in conscious models. Objectivation implies distance, and with infants this distance is small. Their experience is more direct, is lived through with abandonment, without afterthought or side-reflections. This makes it possible that desires and expectations developed during this period become incorporated in the subject's unconscious attitude, the unconscious *projet de vie* (plan for life; Sartre 1943) which programs its choices, and channels the mental energy into the drives and passions which reveal themselves in the subject's later life. The child, lacking the power of distancing itself from its experiences, a power that grows in the process of language-mastery, identifies itself with its experiences, its desires and its wish-fulfilments. What suits its desires is accepted, what thwarts them rejected.

This rejection by the subject of untoward experiences is what Freud called the 'censor'. Rapaport (1971: 169) defined the censor as "the function preventing the emergence to consciousness of an unconscious idea which, if it became conscious,

---

* Translation, borrowed from Brill, Modern Library edition 1950, pp. 421 and 404: Dreaming is a fragment of the superseded psychic life of the child. – And: Dreaming is on the whole an act of regression to the earliest relationships of the dreamer, a resuscitation of his childhood, of the impulses which were then dominant and the modes of expression which were then available.

would give rise to a conflict", a somewhat contradictory manner of saying (ideas cannot really be unconscious!) that the subject is unable to inspect the basic motivations which, together, constitute its unconscious *projet de vie,* the self as the concrete manifestation of the libido.

However, what is natural with the child who is unable to objectify its world, leads to conflicts in the life of the adult. The latter's increased power of objectivation as reflected in complete language-mastery, implies that the distance between the subject and its world has widened. The adult subject is aware that his universe is more than simply a field for his self-realization. The adult has discovered that his universe makes demands on him to which he has to adapt himself. The growth of conscious awareness makes repression more difficult. Not every frustrating experience can be repressed. The individual has to deal with these and, distancing himself from his world, must find ways and means to realize his *self* as a personality capable of conscious interaction. He becomes aware of himself as a self confronted by the awareness of others. In this awareness, distancing deepens. Logically, there is no greater distance than that between subject and object.

Distancing his world, the subject can rely on a long and fairly exact memory of previous experiences. These memories have one thing in common and that is the subject itself. All these experiences and adventures are those of the subject itself; the ego who went through them and was moulded by them into the self that the subject actually is. What happened an hour ago is as much an experience of the subject as the event of forty years ago of which it reminded him. The subject of today and that of forty years ago are the same, invariably identical in spite of whatever happened and changed the individual's views in the course of all these years. The subject is the one point of permanence in all human experience, the point along which all its experiences flow and to which all its memories return. Even if the subject is aware of changes in its own views and attitudes, it is still itself, incorporating these changes into itself.

Over against the permanence of the self, everything else is 'other' and, in a certain way, accidental. The opposition of subject and object necessarily carries the opposition between 'me' and 'not-me', between 'self' and 'other'. The forms and contents of that 'not-me' change, continually bringing up new aspects and events, but the subject remains identical with himself, is unique vis-à-vis all the other subjects and all the world surrounding him. No one can stand in his place, not in the sense that anyone is irreplaceable in society, but in the sense that no one has the experience and the views which he has. Subjects are not interchangeable; they are separate units, each with its own way of being in and acting to its world, in other words, with its own way of arranging the relations between itself and its universe. The subject, though turned to the universe to which it belongs, though constituting part of the universe in which it must realize itself, is self-centered. Self-awareness is a movement away from the world, necessary to enable the subject to condense its relations to its world into one compact whole, the personality that presents itself to its universe and communicates with it.

The personality is the self which is displayed over against others, but also the self which conceals itself from them too. As a unique and self-centered movement away from the world, the subject has its secret, its inner considerations, the total whole of its experiences and desires. Some of these are of the kind to be known by others, some are shameful, others so subtle that they, too, had better be hidden. The secret of the self is well-guarded. Part of it is not and cannot even be guessed by the subject itself but this is hardly of concern here. The subject consciously, and, in the long run more or less automatically, conceals part of itself to others, showing itself only (or at least trying to do so) as it wishes to be seen. The individual who is like an open book to others would turn himself into an object which can be manipulated. He must be a subject. The dialectics of being a movement away from the world as well as a movement towards the world (which was stressed earlier in this section) must result in a compromise. This compromise is the *persona*, the mask which the subject turns to its world, presenting itself, as the case may be, as the strong man, the kind man, the politician, or the rogue, according to its preferences; that is, all along the line the subject prefers to think of itself.

This *persona* is the social personality that, with moderate success, plays up to its image. It is not the only role it plays. Every social relation is found to be combined with culturally defined forms of expected behaviour. Not every social role suits the social personality, but the social psychologists have taught us that, usually, each role has its culturally permitted margins of variation which allow the individual to adapt the playing of his social roles to his social personality and to the role-set associated with his position in society. As a social personality always is a more or less successful adaptation to the ideal cultural personality, this adaptation need not give great difficulties, at least not often.

All the same, it is through the *persona* as well as through the cultural role that the lie enters into the individual's life as the mediator between the secret of the self and the reality of his universe. Pursuing his desires, the individual must often distort both the reality of that universe and that of his self. Man is not situation-bound, and he can imagine things as other than they are. Usually, this is not altogether too difficult. The mask of the *persona* lends a certain automatism to role-playing. Under such circumstances, lying is not difficult, simply a matter of consistent role-playing. It differs widely from that in more uncommon situations such as those mentioned on p. 17 f., situations which do not suite the *persona* or any other better known role, but in which danger forces the individual to tell lies. That is a difficult kind of lying and it can happen that then the mask must be dropped. At other times, it is easier. Everyone learns to accept a certain amount of constraint and insincerity. They are inherent in every act of role-playing and constitute a part of the social personality. Some find their way with ease, either because they are better adapted to the exigencies of their world, or because they are better liars. Only the saint is really sincere. One of them might have been Socrates. He had a *daimonion* – apparently his conscience – who warned him what to do (Van Dijk 1949). The conscience of ordinary people only tells them what not to do.

Two questions remain, the first of which is concerned with the persistence of the unconscious drives and desires of the subject which were constituted in infancy. We noted that infant experiences have an enduring influence on character formation as is only logical with dispositions rooted in the unconscious. Yet, it is inconceivable that later experiences could have no influence at all on these unconscious dispositions. The subject is immersed in a never-ending flood of experiences, many of them neutral, some shocking and frustrating, and some liberating and satisfactory. Although a pattern of unconscious motivations has been set, it is impossible that these later experiences do not affect that pattern. If they never did, psycho-analytic therapy would be perfectly useless. It is in the belief that it exerts an influence that the therapy is applied. There can be and will be change, though it will always be difficult.

Our second question is quite different: Is the freedom of the subject an illusion? Has it any real freedom at all? On the face of it, very little indeed. The subject's freedom is restricted by the limited number of possible choices, by the subject's dependence on its universe, and by the nature of the subject itself. Each of these limitations must be discussed separately.

The fact that human reactions to situations and events are, to a not unimportant extent, predictable, is often advanced as proof of man's bondage. Within certain limits, rightly so. Nevertheless, we may not extend the statement until freedom is identified with unpredictability of behaviour. If that were true, the margin between freedom and craziness would be frightfully small. Freedom has nothing to do with a random selection of one out of the numerous mathematically possible answers to a problem of choice. The point was brought forward a few years ago by Van Beek in a discussion of Burling's attack on the ethno-scientists who, according to Burling, had greatly underestimated the multiplicity of alternative solutions to problems of componential analysis (Burling 1964). Van Beek cogently pointed out that these alternatives, mathematically numerous, are factually restricted to just such a few possibilities as the chess-player has who must repel the attack of his adversary. His choice is not made at random; he has to repel the attack and to that end only one or two out of the hundreds of mathematically possible answers are worth considering (Van Beek 1973: 64). The same is true of all human situations. Decision-making is a matter of choice but the choice itself is usually limited to two or three alternatives which can stand the standards of operational feasibility. Freedom of choice differs widely from random selection.

The second limitation of the subject's freedom is its dependence on its universe. To a certain extent it constitutes part of that universe. The subject can only realize itself in that universe and nowhere else. If he emigrates it is only to find another universe on which he depends, in which he must act, playing the roles which that universe prescribes, or bear the consequences of their neglect. The realization of any man's freedom is restricted to the choices presented to him by his universe. As a matter of fact, it is approximately the same limitation as the one discussed in the preceding paragraph. There is, however, this difference that the influence of the universe also affects the subject itself. To a large extent, the subject is a product of his universe. It defines his physical circumstances, his language, his culture and everything that his education gave him.

This leads us to the third limitation, that of the nature of the subject itself. In the course of its personal history it has accreted certain preferences and automatisms to itself, conscious as well as unconscious, which together constitute its answer to the conditions under which it developed, but also define the forms of its future actions, of its desires, interests, expectations and fears. The self has what Sartre called a *projet de vie*, which is presented to the outside world as a personality (above: 56). The latter is the more or less stable form by which the subject partakes in the social life of its universe, but this very stability implies that the subject has sacrificed its freedom. It lost it in part to the *persona*, the mask behind which the individual meets his congeners, in part to the conscious and unconscious desires and fears which constitute the secret of the self.

All that remains of man's freedom is the necessity to make choices and the intuitive knowledge that he must and even does make them. Unfortunately, they rarely ever are free choices: Whereas the form has remained, the material freedom has evaporated. The alternatives from which a choice must be made are differently weighed by the subject's own preferences, and the rational considerations bestowed on their pros an cons have the character of rationalizations and justifications rather than of independent judgement. Does this imply that freedom is an illusion? On the face of it yes, but fundamentally it is different. The relentless activity of the scanning apparatus which the subject is, whether he likes it or not, never stops confronting him with facts which compel him to make choices. Most of these choices are made rather automatically, as logical sequences to the way in which man is accustomed to order the field of his perceptions. Yet, more and more new facts and impressions appear on the screen, ever anew pressing him to new choices and – what is more – to reflection on earlier choices. In this scanner, man has a thorn in the flesh reminding him again and again of the necessity to make himself free. He knows that he could have decided otherwise than he did. Freedom is not a property of man but a faculty which can be developed; a task, not a gift.

Here, however, we touch a point which cannot properly be discussed at this stage of our enquiry. We will return to it at the end of Part II. For the present, we confine ourselves to a general statement concerning the concept of freedom. Too often, freedom is identified with arbitrariness, with acting in conformity with one's preferences. It is evident from the foregoing that this can hardly be freedom. The subject who follows the dictates of his secret preferences sacrifices his freedom to a self which originated from the subject's reactions to his own personal history, i.e. to his past and to decisions consciously or unconsciously taken in that past. Real freedom is the faculty to act against one's preferences and one's past without being forced or induced by outside pressure or compulsion to do so.

3. Part and subject. The human condition

Man confronts his world. As a subject, he distances his world more thoroughly and explicitly than any other animal. Yet, he is necessarily also part of his universe. He belongs to it, and it is of considerable interest that nature contrived to balance man's ego-centred and world-opposing tendencies by uncommonly powerful gifts for communication and a strong inner motivation for sociality.

Man's gifts for communication have been discussed in chapter II. There is no more comprehensive medium for communication than speech, and the copious development of language in even the most primitive communities affirms that living in relatively small groups must have been universal from early times. This inclination toward sociality is strongly supported by an uncommon capacity for sex. Sexually, man is more privileged than any of the other mammals. Even the anthropoid apes have not, like he, the capacity for sexual activity at every day and hour of their mature life. There is no rutting season for *homo sapiens*. For males and females the opportunity for sexual gratification is always there, and an impulse near at hand. There is little reason for frustration because nature has kindly arranged for the procreation of males and females in approximately equal numbers. When nature played a trick on man and delivered him to the attacks of every insect which bites and all the vermin which sucks his blood by depriving him of hide and tail, it recompensed him for his nakedness with a highly stimulating extension of the erogenous zones of the body which contributes substantially to his capacity for enjoying the delights of sex. The naked ape (Morris 1967) may suffer from the cold, but this very inconvenience drives him all the more eagerly towards a mate in order to enjoy both warmth and delight. This over-capacity for sex is an ever-recurrent reason for seeking the company of congeners, preferably of the other sex but, if need be, also of the same.

Besides, the subject in man may distance its world, but it also incorporates the libido which is turned towards it. It is man's nature to be active (Gehlen 1961: 48f) and this activity can only be realized in the universe which the subject confronts. In action, this confrontation rapidly assumes more benign forms; distancing becomes minimal and opposing his world is transformed into togetherness as soon as man actively participates in his world by working. A man who constructs something, e.g. a new bow or a drum, stands in a continuous dialogue with the object of his work. Not in the sense that he talks to it (though occasionally he may indulge in inner speech), but rather in the sense that from moment to moment he is engrossed in the successive details which are taking shape under his hands. Now and then he lifts the object to examine what progress he has made, and to see what he must do next. When at last he sees that the work is good, he is happy; happy both with himself and with the thing he has made. That thing is, logically, part of his world; but, emotionally, it is also part of himself. The process is similar to that which the gardener goes through in the succession of clearing, fencing, planting, weeding, and finally harvesting his field. The gardener's action is interaction with his world in an atmosphere of togetherness, of belonging together.

Man's belonging to his world cogently manifests itself in the fact that his behaviour is subject to rules, the more compelling of which are unconscious: such as those of logic and language. Easier disobeyed are the conscious rules for the regulation of his social behaviour, but the fact that it is man himself who devises these

59

rules everywhere and always, demonstrates how important rules are to him. On their behalf he sacrifices his freedom, a point particularly evident in the universality of rules restricting his freedom of sexual indulgence (cf. Lévi-Strauss 1967, Introduction).

The close ties between man and his world also appear from the study of human perception. A man who is actively engaged, his attention focussed on what he is doing to the point of neglecting all what happens around him, still perceives what is going on in his vicinity. Without consciously noticing these side-perceptions, they nevertheless are registered. The worker ignores the cold and the wind, as well as the voices of others who are at work at some distance, and yet they have an effect on him. He feels annoyed by the cold, reassured by the near presence of others. Without being guided or directed by the subject, the 'scanning apparatus' goes on turning around. The senses keep the individual in touch with his surroundings. They act as sentinels on the one hand, as active lines of communication on the other. Their effects on the subject need not be more than a dim feeling, a mood, but they ensure that he feels safe, annoyed, or happy, all as the case may be. The senses perceive far more than is consciously registered by the subject. Merleau-Ponty's *Phénoménologie de la Perception* (1945) is, on this point, a rich source of information.

Though feelings may warn man of what is going on around him, the primary function of the affects is that they keep him informed about his own inner state. If he is at work, feelings warn him that he is becoming fatigued or in danger of over-straining himself. They also mirror his relations with his work and his world generally. If he meets with unexpected difficulties, he feels vexed or discouraged; if all goes well and his work progresses satisfactorily, he feels happy. When the latter is the case, he is at peace with his world, at home in it as a functioning part. To feel at home in and with one's world is a really good thing, the essence of human happiness. Unfortunately, it does not last.

Man is not always actively engaged with his universe. There are also hours of rest, hours of contemplation. They may be used to make new plans or to consider difficulties which have arisen. One of the topics which easily turn up, is one's own situation in the world. At that moment, uncertainty arises. Man is never really certain about his position in his universe. He does not know whether pests will spare his crop or what the weather will do, nor does he know what others will do, or how they really feel about him. He is well aware that his relations with his world are not harmonious. They cannot be. The desires which gave shape to the constitution of his inner self are rarely fully realistic; the self tends to design a universe which differs from the real universe. The drive of his libido for self-realization brings man into conflict with his world, and as soon as he indulges into contemplating his place in his world and what that world can do to him, uncertainty necessarily worries him. He may suppress his worries but this is rarely ever successful. Repressed anxiety will return in symbolic form. Instead, he may turn to adequate action which can take away the particular source of his worries; or, at least, reduce these feelings of anxiety so that life again becomes bearable. Man's relation with his universe need not be one of perfect harmony or happiness to be viable. All the same, the effect of action is limited. At best it can obviate a particular difficulty, a specific source of anxiety. Against general uncertainty – and most uncertainty is of that kind – action is powerless.

More expedient against uncertainty and anxiety, both specific and general, is ritual action: prayer, sacrifice, magic, or whatever. Unfortunately, there is one proviso. To be effective, the agent must be a faithful believer.

A third way to overcome uncertainty and the attendant feelings of worry and distress, is by expressing these feelings. It has already been noted (above: 42) that this is not done by crying like a child, working oneself up into a tantrum, but by venting these feelings by means of any of the models which the individual's culture makes available. He can use language forms and depict his woes in no uncertain terms, presenting himself as a sorrowful part of a woeful world. He can turn to music and play a melody on his instrument which expresses his mood, or listen to a record that gives voice to his feelings. If he is an artist, he can try to express his feelings in a new work of art that may have the value of a new model. Or perhaps he simply weeps, evoking the compassion of others. Whatever he does, expression does not take away the source of his worries and uncertainty; rather, it gives them a shape which represents a certain mode of carrying on with one's world, of bearing its adversities. It is possible to project oneself as a suffering part of one's world and find a certain satisfaction in it. One need not have a happy relation with one's world to feel a part of it.

Still, uncertainty is thematic in everyone's life, and it is not always easy to find a form of expressing one's trouble which is sufficiently adequate to characterize the complainer's felt relation with his world. Uncertainty is not only concerned with one's world, but also with one's self, with all that is vaguely known to be wrong with it. It is this uncertainty which is the deepest source of the difficulties frustrating expression. Lucid expression can be redeeming, a blessing. It opens new vistas to the world which then appears in a new and more acceptable shape. But how should man give lucid symbolic form to an inner uncertainty which, by nature, is confusion itself? If thus confused, he is almost by necessity thrown back on images as confused as the feelings which worry him. The cathartic effect of such expression is open to doubt. The individual who fails to express his feelings in symbols which can reconcile him with his world, and finds no comfort in either religion or pragmatic action, is in real distress. In the contemplation of his situation his world even stops being a hostile world. As long as that world was hostile it could be fought, but if the individual has given up the idea of fighting and finds all other ways to come to terms with his world closed, that world has lost its meaning. Meaning implies a relation, and when every relation breaks down all that remains is a subject who has no access to his world. In this situation even Heidegger's characterization of man as a *grundsuchende Ungegrundheit* (an unfoundedness in search of its foundation) is too optimistic. He has stopped seeking. What has remained is pure distance, and the inner state of such an individual is necessarily that of alienation.

Complete alienation is rarely reached. The subject is not only a distancing subject but also a libido turned to its universe and it usually finds some way to return to it. Yet, the effort sometimes miscarries and then complete alienation takes possession of him. The only way to express full alienation in an ultimate effort to address one's world is suicide. It is relatively rare, but it happens. And of course it happens. When all is said and done, there is no logical proof that either life or the universe have a meaning. Man's position is ek-static. He can step aside and look at his universe and his self from afar to question their meaning. When he does this while feelings of alienation prevail, there is little that can stop him on the way of doubt. The fundamental truths which, in happier days, constituted the ground of his faith in the meaning of his universe, rapidly lose their power of conviction. The ultimate ground for accepting a truth is its self-evidence. Nothing can be self-evident in the state of alienation. The inner state, the feeling of alienation, denies that there is any truth or meaning in the universe.

Some pretend that the main reason for despair and ensuing alienation is the certainty of death and that, consequently, the fear of death is the prime mover behind man's efforts at creating cultural forms which permit him a satisfactory and reasonably secure way of life. Thus, fairly recently, the late Ernest Becker in his book *The Denial of Death* (1973). This is very doubtful. Man's attitudes toward death are more variegated, even in European history, than Becker guessed. They are not necessarily characterized by intense fear (cf. Ariès, *l'Homme devant la Mort*, 1977). The significance of the fact that in many languages real fear is denoted as 'deadly' fear, is easily overrated. All it means is that the fear of death is treated as a model, a paradigm, for fear in general. It does not imply that, of all fears, that of death is the worst. This is denied by fact. Time and again, we find people prepared to die for a cause, for the sake of the nation, of freedom, of revenge, of religion, or whatever is valued as dearer than life. Innumerable are the young men who sacrificed their young lives for such a cause. There are also the martyrs to think of; the Christian calendar has a day of the year devoted to the memory of each or several of them at a time. Nor should we forget the suicides. Often suicide is a last effort to function in the world of the living; for example, to give the blame to one's relatives whose heartless behaviour drove the poor self-murderer into death! Death certainly is a problem, but life is often a worse one. Perhaps it is more correct to say that death is only one of the problems of life.

Life itself arouses fear. One of my earliest recollections is that of myself as a small, sick boy sobbing not for fear of death, but for fear of eternal life, a state of bliss admittedly, but one which can never, never end. Since then, well over sixty years have passed, some of which were not uneventful, and I still feel that the boy was right. Life can be frightening and disheartening.

One might object that all this is true but that alienation is a purely western phenomenon which cannot occur among primitive people for the simple reason that their capacity for abstract thought has been insufficiently developed to measure the full depth of their forlornness. Yet, I have seen primitive Papuans die in jail, showing no other symptoms of ailment than those of shock, exactly the same as those of a man who dies because he knows himself to be the victim of sorcery. I still reproach myself in one case which I could – and should – have foreseen (Van Baal 1972: 95-101). Furthermore, suicide is not uncommon among primitives, either in New Guinea or in other parts of the world (for a beautifully described case cf. Malinowski 1926: 77f.). It may be rare in aboriginal Australia (R. M. & C. H. Berndt 1964: 386f.) but it is certainly not in Melanesia. Real despair is a repeatedly stated cause for suicide among women in the New Guinea Highlands (M. Strathern 1972). The life of man is hard everywhere and not everyone who is steeped in distress finds his way back to participation in his universe.

We must sum up. Man is happiest when he is actively engaged in doing something in his universe which is positively valued by him and the members of his group; in other words when, as a subject, he acts as a real part of his universe. We still have to answer the question whether he can be part of his universe without being a subject. The answer is a simple 'no'. It is man's nature to be active. He is always a subject who cannot refuse or omit to be what he is without turning himself into what he is not, namely an object. Anyone who tries, may expect to be instantly called to order by his fellow-men. There is no choice: man is a subject who has to act as a part, who is a part of his universe that must act as a subject.

Such is the human condition, the source of ever recurrent uncertainty and conflicts. Its duality repeats itself in the subject which directs itself to its universe as its field of action, and away from it to consider it from afar or to contest it. The subject, assuming the shape of a self, incorporates the driving force of the libido. It is out for self-realization which brings it into conflict with its universe, in particular with the human part of it. In the process of growing up the individual has learned to depend primarily on other humans for the fulfilment of his daily needs (above: 53), and all his later life is spent in the company of other men. His relations with the members of his society are contradictory: on the one hand, he tries to use them as instruments for his self-realization; on the other hand, he desires to be recognized and treated as their partner. A compromise is necessary, a compromise that can only be reached by submitting one's behaviour to certain rules. What is at issue here is not that man devises rules for his conduct. He always does; the framing of rules comes as natural to man as the inclination toward deviant behaviour. Our problem here is more specific, namely to find out what in the rules for social conduct the general principle is that can combine the self-realization of the individual with that partnership in the society of men which is the condition for human happiness, i.e. with a minimum of inner and outer conflicts. To this problem Part II is devoted.

Even so, inner conflicts remain. Partnership in society is never perfect. There are also the individual's difficulties with his universe at large to consider. Inner uncertainty is thematic in human life, an uncertainty which threatens man with alienation. This is man's second major problem. We found that three ways stand open to counteract the dangers of uncertainty and alienation, to wit: pragmatic action, religion, and (artistic) self-expression. Of the three, the first is only effective in cases of uncertainty which have a specific cause. It does not work against general uncertainty, the uncertainty caused by the opacity and contrariety of the human condition as such. Against general uncertainty the available means are either religion or self-expression. The effectiveness of religion depends on faith in its relevance and in its truth, that of self-expression is inversely proportionate to the increase of uncertainty. In Part III the analysis of the religion of primitive man gives ample opportunity to discuss the grounds of man's faith in religion and the comforts he derives from it. This discussion shall be continued in Part IV where we pay attention to the possibility of finding a remedy for the ailments of uncertainty and alienation in the consolations of art and the diversions of play before we conclude with a general assessment of the role of both ethics and religion in the life of modern man.

Part Two

The Social Life of
Primitive Man

The social life of mankind is subject to a great variety of rules which are culturally defined. The problem of the present part of this enquiry is twofold. In the first place, we have to find out whether the variety of these rules can be reduced to one or two fundamental principles which, if observed, guarantee the combination of a maximum opportunity for self-realization with maximal partnership in any given human society. In the second place, we must examine whether such fundamental principles, in case we find them poorly observed in practice, can nevertheless be recognized as proper to the human condition because their neglect leads to efforts at self-justification or evokes other symptoms of a bad conscience.

To introduce these problems we first turn to the social conditions of early man's life and to the institutions characteristic of primitive society. We then consider the studies which have been made of the effects of such general principles as reciprocity and authority in situations of equality and inequality, of organized power and togetherness. They lead us straight to our first problem, the interrelation between these institutionalized forms of behaviour and the human condition, and to the moral law which can be derived from it. We then come to our second problem, that of the impact of the moral law on the conscience of man.

IV

The Social Conditions of Early Man's Life

1. The human band and its economy

Current notions regarding the social life of early man are based on inferences derived alternately from what is known about human and primate physiology and ethology generally, from ethnographic descriptions of primitive societies, from the scant information produced by the spade of the prehistorian, and from preconceived notions on human life originating from philosophy, religion, and ethnocentric prejudice. Under these circumstances, we must try, at every step, to explicate what we really know and what the foundations are of the inferences we feel justified in making.

With early man we mean *homo sapiens*, not any of the prehistoric *hominidae*. We refrain from speculations on a single or multiple origin of *homo sapiens*. The racial variation of the genus is not of an order of divergency justifying the supposition of important differences in the forms of life of early man. All his descendents, whatever their race, speak a well-developed language, have rules for the regulation of their sexual and social conduct, and dispose of a wide variety of religious practices and representations. The similarities – somatic and cultural – are more impressive than the differences.

We do not know for certain how mankind originated. It must be taken for granted that it happened in a tropical climate; man's nakedness is a strong argument for this assumption. Furthermore, he certainly did not originate in a void. Man's hominid ancestors already knew how to use stones and sticks as implements, and from prehistoric evidence we know that his precursors, "the ancient men who inhabited the Old World from 500,000 years ago to the middle of the last glaciation... used fire and made complicated tools according to clearly defined traditions" (S. L. Washburn, 1960; *in* R. F. Thompson 1976: 11). On this ground it can be assumed that early *homo sapiens* made use of fire, sticks, and stones. He needed them badly because his natural equipment was poor. He was naked and ill-protected against cold and vermin. He had no natural weapons of his own. His teeth and mouth were small, and the muscles of his neck and jaws too weak to allow the use of his mouth as a weapon. He had no hoofs to kick nor horns to butt with. To defend himself, he had to rely on the artificial weapons which his wit devised. This, together with the fact that he was a biped and a man like us, is about all that is known for certain. Everything else is a matter of inference.

The first inference that can be made is that he lived in groups. It is a safe one. Man everywhere has the exceptional gift of language, and language presupposes group life. Whether the earlier hominids already had some form of language and how language further developed is not known, but it is a valid assumption that this took place in small groups. A language can only develop in a group within which all members live in daily face-to-face contacts with each other. A new morpheme has no chance of being accepted in a larger group. It cannot be by accident that practically all our new words are derivates (above: 33). A new morpheme must be accepted and recognized by all the members of the group. The enormous diversity of languages among primitive peoples of the same stock who live in small, isolated groups, corroborates this view. In the first half of the present century, the process of linguistic diversification was still going on in isolated parts of the world. I remember that in 1937 I once came in contact with a very small group of people in the lowlands of southern New Guinea. The group counted some 13 individuals and they pretended that they had a language of their own, different from those of surrounding tribes. Unfortunately, I had at the time neither the opportunity nor the means for further research, but I know for certain that language groups of something between 60 and 200 speakers were not wholly exceptional in these parts.

It is difficult to give a more detailed estimate of the medium size of the early human band. Parallels with the life of savannah-dwelling primates suggest round about one hundred as an absolute maximum, dependent on ecological conditions and the opportunities for shifting habitat. In view of man's rather diversified dietical needs and that of a shelter which must not be constructed anew every two or three days, some sixty people would not be a bad estimate. Even so, they would have to shift their residence every two or three months. Of course, the number is purely hypothetical, but the assumption gives some substance to what such a primeval group may have looked like. In view of the high rate of child mortality (some 50%) about 40 to 45% of the group must have been juveniles, i.e. 24-27 individuals. This means that there were 16-18 men and as many women of 18 years and older. It also implies that each woman (out of 18 three of four may have been above child-bearing age) had to produce at least four children because half of these children would have died before reaching maturity. Probably conditions were even worse but we will leave it at this. Child mortality was so high that we may assume that the women were inclined to postpone weaning as long as possible, a phenomenon widely observed in contemporary primitive societies. The Australian experience is that these women tried to spread successive pregnancies over a number of years. It is not impossible that a similar trend prevailed in early society. How they managed can be left undecided. The one thing certain is that early man's life was difficult.

One of his main problems was how to keep alive. What was his food? Modern physical anthropologists have few doubts on this point. Prehistoric finds provide evidence that early man ate animals and shell-food. Consequently, early man is described as a hunter and/or fisher. This is what Washburn suggests (op. cit.) and what is strongly emphasized by the anthropologists Tiger and Fox (1972). The latter even assert that "we are wired for hunting", suggesting that our genetic inheritance is defined by the hunting past of early man. If that be true, then it must be assumed that in early times both males and females were hunters. If not, the statement excludes women from contributing to the composition of the genes pool of their offspring, a standpoint scientifically untenable, and – today – socially a challenge. Yet, if this be conceded, the assumption is still untenable. It contends that early man was a carnivore. If that were true, he can hardly have been *homo sapiens* who, today, is omnivorous. There is only one exception to this rule, the Eskimo, a people living under wholly exceptional physical conditions. Their case is one of extreme adaptation to highly frustrating conditions and has no paradigmatic value.

Neither has the fact that traces of vegetable food are blatantly absent in prehistoric sites. One could not expect otherwise. Who believes that, even under favourable conditions, a tuber or fruit leaves observable traces over a period of between 40 000 and 50 000 years? There is good reason to probe deeper into this matter and to enquire whether – under normal conditions – man ever tried to subsist on animal food alone. An argument might be derived from the fact that among primitive peoples meat and fish are usually more highly appreciated than vegetable food. Many are fond of them. Yet, the Australian aborigenes who describe themselves as hunters and meat-eaters, do not subsist on meat alone. Though there is plenty of game, the observations made by Meggitt among the Walbiri (Meggitt 1957) and by Mountford *et alii* in Arn-hemland (1960) supply evidence that up to 70% of the caloric value of their food derives from vegetable food and that, at times, they even prefer it to more animal food. Detailed records of primitive peoples' daily intake of food are rare. Equally scanty is our knowledge of the daily fare of pastoral nomads who – until recently – boasted that they lived off their herds and flocks. Yet, we know that everywhere they either lived in a kind of symbiosis with corn-growing tribes, or had their womenfolk do the necessary planting and collecting. The fact that in most parts of the world animal food is prestigeous food leads to an over-emphasis by native informants on its significance for the daily diet. Up till World War II ethnographers rarely tried to check native communications on this point. Indeed, there is hardly a more dis-couraging and time-consuming work than the precise recording of a family's daily intake of food, a circumstance which has an unpleasantly limiting effect on our knowledge of the daily diet of people living under really archaic conditions. Yet, what we do know allows one to conclude that the vegetable part of the daily intake rarely fell far under 50% of the total caloric value. The Australian case is a strong one. Even though these data, too, are limited, they are detailed and reliable, which is more than can be said of the numerous reports based on hearsay. Besides, they tally well with my experience among the Marind-anim of New Guinea. At the time I visited them regularly (1936-1938) they had no lack of either fish or game; and yet vegetable food constituted the main part of their food (sago, coconuts, tubers). Consequently, the assumption that the ratio between man's animal and vegetable food oscillates round about equal shares with a wide margin of variation mostly in favour of vegetable food, is a sound one, a conclusion which must be taken account of in our picture of early man's life.

We can be sure, then, that early man, like the Australian aborigines, collected fruits, seeds, leaves, roots, and probably tubers. He certainly was capable of cracking nuts and grinding hard seeds, and it is a fair guess that he made use of fire and heated stones to make them more palatable if necessary. There can hardly be any doubt that he also made use of fire to roast the game he captured. Yet, there is one problem. How did he know which vegetables were edible and which not? Fruits, seeds and leaves cannot have given important problems. It is just a matter of trying out in small quantities. Moreover, in part early man could rely on the experience of his proto-human ancestors. Roots, e.g., need not have caused great difficulties. We know, that "ground-living monkeys dig out roots for food" (Washburn, op. cit.: 15). With tubers, however, it is different. They constitute a quite substantial part of the menu of primitive peoples, in spite of the fact that some of these are highly poisonous when not previously processed. Everywhere primitive peoples have developed techniques to render them harmless by mashing or grinding them, and either washing the pulp or exposing the flour to the sun to remove the cyanide. How did they find this out, and discover it all over again when their migratory habits brought them into a new habitat with all its new varieties? Fortunately, man is an inquisitive animal and every time hunger or a new habitat induced him to try unfamiliar roots or tubers, he must have followed more or less similar procedures as we did when, in 1945, we were starving of hunger in our last prison camp in the mountains of central Celebes (Sulawesi), so far away from anywhere that the Japanese means of transport failed to provision the camp to more than roundabout 50% of our earlier frugal rations in the lowlands. The area abounded with mushrooms which were all unknown to us. The problem of their edibility was solved by volunteers who first tried one and, if all went well, three. When, after a couple of hours, they had no complaints, the food was cooked and distributed. It is highly improbable that early man ever acted like the man in our camp who found a tuber of an unidentified kind and, wishing to keep it all for himself, ate it and died within eight hours. Our first ancestors must have experimented time and again with new foods, trying titbits, or mashing them and exposing them to sun or water, to find ways to make use of them.

Initially, the vegetable part of man's diet must have been less variegated than it has become in later days, a situation which repeated itself every time he entered upon a new habitat. He may have found compensation in an abundance of game every time he came into a new area but this can never have lasted for long. Moreover, he really wished to eat vegetable food as well, being omnivorous by nature. Animal food may have had a more prominent part in his diet than it had later in that of the Australian aborigines, but it is out of the question that it predominated to such an extent that we can characterize early man simply as a hunter. He was both a hunter and a collector.

This raises the socially relevant question: Who did the hunting and who the collecting? Did each individual, whether male or female, hunt and collect for his own or, in the case of the females, for her and her dependent offspring, or was there some division of labour, the males specializing in hunting, the women in collecting? There is every reason to raise the question because some scholars tend to find a paradigm of early man's life in the social life of contemporary chimpanzees. The latter live in bands in which the males keep more or less on their own. Something resembling a marriage bond is unknown. Each female takes care of her dependent offspring and forages for her own and for her baby, helping an older child or two when necessary. The birth of a new baby does not prevent the mother from pursuing her normal economic activities. She carries the baby, which clings to her fur, with her, during the first two months supporting the young with one hand whenever there is danger that it might fall (Jolly 1972: 224).

The human baby is far more helpless. His mother has no fur and if she had, he would be unable to cling to it. The baby is born in a stage of development which the young of an ape passes in its mother's womb. If the human mother does not carry the baby in her arm – which she cannot possibly do all day – the baby must be laid down in a safe place. Even so, she cannot go too far away because the baby must be fed every few hours. Not before the baby is a few months old can the mother carry it with her in a piece of tree bark or a carrying bag, the latter a contraption which demands a fairly advanced technique of preparing and knotting fibres, and must be of later date. However that may be, carrying the baby with her she can do all the collecting she wishes (she can always put down the tree bark with the baby for a few minutes) but serious hunting is out of the question. Moreover, the baby is not the only child which she has to look after. Maturing takes many years and before the age of about eight years a child is incapable of doing substantial foraging on its own, or of accompanying its seniors on distant foraging expeditions without making itself a nuisance. Until that age, a child is a source of recurring anxiety for its mother. Insufficiently experienced to heed the dangers of the jungle, too weak to follow the men on their hunts and too noisy and indisciplined to be welcomed on an occasion which demands silence and ordered interaction, the child must be controlled by its mother who, if she has a baby and a toddler of 4 or 5 years, cannot go far from camp anyway. In the early days of mankind, when predators were more numerous, this was also the area of relative safety; an important point not so much for the women who will have preferred to go in one another's company, as for the children who, by nature, tend to stray off into the bush, where they may fall a prey to a panther or any other predator which is roaming about.

This implies that women with children (the majority) are compelled to specialize in collecting. This collecting need not be, and actually never is, restricted to the collecting of vegetable food, and always includes the collecting of shell-food, insects, and all the small fry and the occasional game which happens to come their way and can be mastered without too much exertion. It also implies that the women take care of the children until these are at least eight years old, and probably beyond that age. The food which has been collected cannot be consumed on the spot but must be prepared, both for herself and for the children. This must happen in camp. A camp is necessary anyway as a result of man's social needs. There must be a shelter for himself and even more for the children and, above all, for that indispensable commodity, a fire which may not go out. Here the mother prepares the food for herself and her children, an arduous task which includes the cracking of nuts, the scraping of roots, the peeling and roasting of tubers and any other food which she has acquired on that day, and it is only logical that she does the same with the food which the older children bring in. With all this there is enough to do to keep a mother busy. It is not enough that she feeds the family, the children must also be taught how to behave, and to cooperate in the assembling of food, firewood and water, or the supervision of a toddler who, for some time, must be left to the care of a senior child.

In one respect the meals, which are the products of the mother's efforts, are deficient. That is on the point of animal food. Although she collects shell-food and insects, there is practically no meat among it. This must be provided for by the other half of the community, the males who, so far, were ignored in our discussion because their contribution to the household economy is restricted to just this and the produce of their fishing.

It is thinkable, of course, that in early human society the males managed for themselves, just like the females, and that next to hunting they also collected such vegetable food as they needed for a palatable meal which each male prepared for himself on his own fire. But the human male does not return to camp in the afternoon because he expects to find a fire there, but because he expects to find a female. There is a decisive difference between the social life of *homo sapiens* and that of, say, chimpanzees. Female chimpanzees are sexually available only once in two years for a two weeks period, a period far too short for the development of fixed behavioural patterns of sexual relations (cf. Jolly 1972: chs. 10-13). Human females are different; they can be sexually aroused all the year round. Besides, man's nakedness provided him with additional capacities for erotic delight (above: 59). Man is oversexed and the willingness to indulge in sexual intercourse is present in both sexes. Coming home carrying the spoils of their hunting with them, the men expect to find a sexual partner. They find women waiting for them who are eager to have a share in the game they have captured, and prepared to let them have an equivalent part of the vegetable and other food that they have collected. Game is a tasty food worthy of compensation in kind. In principle the homecoming of the two sexes can be schematized as a barter of game for vegetable food followed by a pairing off of the sexes for intercourse.

This interaction between the sexes has two important consequences. The first is the institutionalization of roles. If the women are willing to exchange the spoils of their collecting for those of the males' hunting, why should the latter bother to do any substantial collecting for themselves? The sexual division of labour is one of the earliest assets of human society.

The second consequence is a definite trend toward the institutionalization of fixed pairs. Difficulties need not arise as long as there are equal numbers of mature males and females but this is a situation which rarely lasts for long. Females refuse copulation shortly before and after parturition. They are temporarily excluded from sexual intercourse. Worse is that there are rarely equal numbers. Every death disturbs the balance. Under these circumstances, a preference for fixed partners may easily develop. After all, it is something to know that a partner is waiting on homecoming. It is always better than queuing up in anticipation of who is available. And this is

72

where difficulties arise. Some males (and females) are dominant, others stand back in the social hierarchy. Children are growing up and new males and females are forthcoming, expecting a place in the social order. We must scrutinize the relations of males and females in more detail before we can give an answer to the question of how human society solved its most pressing problems.

2. Male and female in early society

Before we proceed, we must dispose of a couple of scientific myths which, by their wide spread and authority, hamper a realistic assessment of the potentials of males and females in early human society. The first of these myths is that of the father of the primeval horde who owned and sired all the women of the horde and chased his sons when, maturing, they tried to interfere with his sexual monopoly. The task imputed to the father is humanly impossible. He had to provide game for all his women and children, and every female with the sexual satisfaction she needed. The latter may have gorged him with vegetable food but it is out of the question that he could reciprocate their careful attentions with a satisfactory amount of meat and sexual gratification for each. How does anyone think that he could defend this crowd against the attacks of jealous bachelors who kept up secret relations with his frustrated women? Some psycho-analysts like Roheim (1930) must have had a subconscious inkling of the untenability of their assumptions. They reverently write Primeval Father with initial capitals. Deservedly so, the primeval father who managed to live with such a ménage until his sons had come of age was really a superman, a god!

A second myth deserves more serious attention. It is that of the women's need for male protection. Protection against what? Predators? If we assume that the males are the hunters (as we feel is imperative) then it is simple logic that the males do the chasing of predators to protect the surroundings of the camp. Yet, this does not mean that the women, when they go out to do the necessary collecting, need a bodyguard to protect them against wild animals. The other males would soon suspect the guards of taking advantage of this opportunity for obtaining sexual privileges. Besides, the women do not need such protection if they go out together. They are perfectly capable of defending themselves against an occasional predator that happens to cross their path. The physical power and skill of a female are not much less than those of a male. The females may be a bit smaller than the males, but the differences in body stature and weight between the races are greater than those between the sexes of the same race. The natural weapons of men and women are equally underdeveloped among all races. To defend himself against predators, man has to rely on his intellect, on his ability to construct and to handle artificial weapons in his encounters with dangerous brutes; and in respect of intellect there is no difference between male and female. On the really decisive point, male and female are equal and there is no truth in the assumption that, normally, the females need the males to defend them against an occasional brute.

Yet, men and women alike claim that women (and children) must be protected by the men. As far as the children are concerned, there is no problem; but with regard to

73

the women there can only be one enemy against whom they must be protected, and that is other human males. It is not the weakness or incapacity of the women that makes their defence a necessity, but the aggressiveness of the males. The males must protect the females against the dangers which they and their sex-fellows themselves evoke. This leads us to a problem of great importance, that of the aggressiveness of the human male.

The impact of male aggressiveness on primitive social life should not be underrated. Although the small size of primitive societies can be explained as the inevitable outcome of a gathering and hunting economy, the always more or less tense and often rather hostile relations between these societies are anything but an economic necessity. The frequent occurrence of this harmful, sometimes even fateful trend, justifies the suspicion that aggressiveness has corroborated to keep these societies undersized, restricting the observance of the self-devised rules for social intercourse to the regular relations with a minimal number of congeners. With these things in mind, it is small wonder that the circumstance that it is always the males who are the fighters (at least in fights for the purpose of killing) has given rise to the assumption that this male aggressiveness is the rudiment of an innate drive, a trait man inherited from his animal ancestors.

In the mating season, these ancestors used to fight their congeners for access to the females. With the disappearance of a mating-season, the seasonal restrictions on aggressivity disappeared too, and fighting could be generalized and thus reinforce the aggressivity inspired by territorial drives or by competition for food. Modern ethologists hold the view that the great anthropoid apes, in spite of their mainly vegetarian diet, fight and kill monkeys which visit their territory because these monkeys (which feed on the same fruits as they do) are competitors (personal information from Dr. H. D. Rijksen). In the case of mankind, amongst whom women are important producers, the need for food coincides with that for women. The defence of the territory against competitors and fighting for the possession of women thus constitute mutually reinforcing motives for a continuous state of war between neighbouring human groups. In conformity with this pattern, the widespread custom that successful warriors are hailed by their womenfolk on their home-coming, can be explained as a vestige of innate female preferences for the best fighting male.

Such theories, however, find little support in ethnographic fact. Although in a war one or two women may occasionally be captured by force, the normal way of acquiring a marriage partner is by negotiations and not by violence. Besides, primitive peoples do not always live in conflict with their neighbours. Although they distrust them, they often try to keep up peaceful relations, at the same time waging their wars far beyond the borders of adjacent tribes. Such wars are allegedly motivated by lust for revenge, for loot, or for capturing women and children. More often than not, however, the real motive is the warriors' wish to distinguish themselves and to be admired for their prowess and courage. The Marind-anim in the southern lowlands of New Guinea were of this kind. Their headhunting expeditions were directed at tribes at a distance of up to a hundred miles, people with whom they rarely, if ever, had any contacts. Evidently, they killed for the lust of killing, but they said that they did it because they wanted names for their children who were called after the heads they had taken (Van Baal 1966: 676, 696 ff.). The irrationality of this kind of warfare is striking. Yet, it is dubious whether, in this respect, the Marind-anim really constituted an exception. All one can say is that, in their case, the irrationality of warfare was exceptionally obvious. After all, even in modern society rationally motivated wars might well be a minority, whatever the rationalizations forwarded by those concerned.

The human male is more aggressive than any other mammal. Other animals fight congeners when confronted with a situation which induces them to fight, but the human male repeatedly creates situations enabling him to fight. Men fight primarily for self-assertion, to prove their prowess and to enhance their status in the group. This makes it difficult to accept the ethologist's hypothesis that human aggressiveness follows inherited patterns. This aggressiveness (or more precisely: this excess of aggresiveness) must be culturally defined. Not in every culture are fighting and warfare matters of recurrent indulgence for all males. Our own, western history knows long periods in which fighting and bloodshed were the task of specialists, of a noble warrior class, the rank and file of the peasants and townsmen keeping aloof. In primitive society, warring is more endemic than in many more developed cultures. The question arises what the reasons can be for this sex-specific, increased aggressivity among peoples of simple culture? For an answer we must return to the conditions defining the early ways of life of each of the sexes severally.

Let us first of all see what the reasons *cannot* be. It is certainly not that males are more courageous than females. In primitive society, women are often more plucky than men. They have the courage to let themselves be married out, often to a distant settlement, far away from their relatives. One cannot read accounts such as those by Marilyn Strathern (1972) and Father Hylkema (1974) without being impressed by the nerve and self-confidence of the girls who set out on an unknown and often fairly gloomy future in a village that is almost or wholly foreign to them with a husband they have hardly ever met before their marriage.

Neither can the reason of the more moderate behaviour of the women be sought in the fact that, innately, women are less aggressive than men. Women can and often do act aggressively. There is only this difference with male aggressivity that they do not go to the excess of purposively killing their congeners. In other words, women are as aggressive as any of the mammals. They all have conflicts among themselves, but it is only the human male who developed the custom of deliberately killing congeners. Women may fight among themselves or even with men, using sticks (and abuse) as weapons, but they are not bent upon killing, and certainly do not equip war expeditions, though they occasionally will accompany their males and, if cannibalism be the custom, partake with relish in a cannibal meal following a successful battle.

The difference between men and women is primarily one of a wholly different life style, a life style which has to do with the procreative function of the women. It is not simply that it is the women who bear children but that, by nature, they have been equipped with special glands for nurturing a baby during the first one or two years of its life, and that the baby's suckling gives the young mother a sense of physical well-being. Her physiological make-up enables a woman to bestow effective care on her baby, and it is only natural that this capacity for care-giving has been culturally developed into a regular habit which extends over the years until the time that a child can take care of itself. In every human society, primitive as well as modern, we find that the female child is so educated as to prepare her for the successful performance of a mother role. In primitive society this is done by charging the girl from an early age onwards with the supervision of a younger sibling (or cousin) and with household chores of all sorts, in modern society by inciting girls to play with dolls. Everywhere girls are conditioned to become mothers (M. Mead 1949; Van Baal 1975: ch. III).

The result, still observable in primitive society, is that a woman and her children constitute a closely-knit unit. Growing up, the children more and more do some foraging of their own, but the mother continues to prepare the meals. A daughter will often assist her mother in food-collecting, but a boy tends to associate with the men. Yet, as long as he has not passed the age of adolescence, he may be expected to bring part of the spoils of his hunting to his mother who provides him with vegetable food and prepares the game which he brought her. A son is a valuable asset. Surprisingly often, we find that the ties between mother and son are more affectionate than those between mother and daughter. Though the reverse (strong ties between mother and daughter) is certainly not an exception, the son is often seen as a kind of husband substitute who, when the latter is dead or the marriage dissolved, will clear and fence his mother's garden, as a Papuan mother told Hylkema (1974: 202 f.). And in a society of hunters, the son is the child who can provide the mother with the kind of food which neither she nor her daughter can make available, namely game. But we need not insist too much on this point. Far more important in this context is that, on maturing, every boy in whatever society, is fully accustomed to the fact that there is a woman who cares for him. He is so accustomed to it that in many societies he cannot properly manage without that care.

By now we can draw up the balance sheet of the economy of the early human band with, on the one hand, the mature females and, on the other, the fullgrown males. The women, collecting vegetables, insects, small fry, and shell-food, produce at least 50% and more often up to 70% of the calory value of the daily diet, the men the highly prized game and some fish which rarely amounts to more than one third of the nutritional value required for keeping up the family. Besides, the women produce children and give care to them. They are the society's care-givers who prepare the food, nurture the children and nurse the sick. They are divided into a number of units, families consisting of a mother, her children and a befriended male, her husband. Each woman is busily engaged in caring for her own family. She has a specific aim to live for.

On the other hand, there are the males, the hunters. They bring in one third of the daily diet, and that is about all. The labour bestowed by them on the construction of huts for shelter is negligible. They have nothing further to care for in particular. We pictured their daily home-coming as that of a bunch of males, loaded with game and longing for vegetable food and sexual intercourse (above: 72). The picture is somewhat dramatized but the essentials tally with the facts. Every male has learned as a boy to rely on the good cares of a woman, his mother to whom, growing older, he brought game and who went on to provide him with prepared food, the greater part of which she had herself collected. The assumption that the males on their home-coming bartered, as it were, their game for vegetable food, is not unfounded. It is what every male learned as a boy. The point which, in this phase of our discussion, needs attention is not how each man finds an exchange partner who also will be a sexual partner, but the fact that the function of the males is insignificant when compared to that of the women. They produce one third of the food stuff and are otherwise cared for, whereas the women provide two thirds of the food, make and raise children, and give care to everybody. The males have little to live and to work for in particular. Their hunting task is a pleasurable one, and that is practically all that is expected of them. They are the spoilt loafers of the group. Loafers, because in these early days game was sufficiently plentiful to fill the bags of the males in no more than half a day's work.

This picture of early man deviates from the romantic views so long cherished by the scientific world which imagined early man as the heroic male who, after having fought sabre-toothed tigers and other terrible brutes, returned triumphantly towards evening to his cave dwelling where his wife and children hungrily awaited their protector's return from his daring expedition into a murderous world. Yet, our picture certainly is more realistic. Later in this book (ch. IX), discussing primitive man's religion, we shall have occasion to dwell on the important part taken in it by fertility cults. These cults are, predominantly, a male affair by which the men arrogate the blessings of fertility as, primarily, the result of their ritual exertions. No one can study these cults without being impressed by the obtruding conclusion that the men were jealous of their women's procreative powers and functions and were, sub-consciously, altogether too well aware of their own insignificance. And rightly so. The men had nothing to care for and nothing to be proud of. They either had to find compensation in ritual performance, or to become morose and aggressive.

Male aggressivity found an additional stimulus in the specific nature of their group, the society of males. The role of the male in family life, insignificant in early society, was destined to remain of secondary importance for long afterwards. For all we know of the life of primitive man, it is evident that, however much he is honoured or feared as a *pater familias*, he is a relative outsider to his own family. He is often absent and his contributions to the proper well-being of the family are clearly secondary to those of his wife. The better part of the time and activities of every male is passed in the company of other males, the men of the group who, like himself, have a minor share in the household tasks of their families. The men, instead, go out hunting together, celebrate rituals together, or join each other in mischief of any kind. Whereas for the women the primary social group is the family, this is for the men the local society of males. There is a clear difference between these two types of social groups. They have in common that they serve certain ends which for both regard the well-being of the group's members. However, in the smaller unit, the family, the woman has a well defined and undisputed function. She is the care-giver of the unit and there is no doubt about her position. With the society of the males this is different. The society has its functions in the protection of the group, the performance of rituals, in hunting and fishing, and in keeping the group together; but the function of each of the males in these activities is highly variable. Some are leaders, others followers; some are honoured, a few are tolerated or at the command of everyone who ranks higher in the esteem of the group's members. In a society of males, the only way for an individual to achieve really satisfactory self-realization is by competing with the other males for the appreciation and respect of the group as a whole. Competition is an essential trait of male group life, and a second but certainly not a lesser impetus for nursing aggressive feelings.

In the context of early man's life, it is enticing to think first of all of competition for women. Numbers of males and females are rarely even, and if they ever are, they are easily unbalanced every time a woman dies or a young man or woman comes to maturity and desires a mate. But the members of early society were not free to indulge in competition for the available women. Such competition necessarily leads to internal conflicts which end in bloodshed or manslaughter and, consequently, in fission of the group. Early man must have found out at a very early date that group-life demands an equitable distribution of the available women as a precondition for the persistence of the group.

The only form of competition compatible with group-life is that for status positions. It is a question of ranking higher or lower in the appreciation and respect of the group's members. A higher rank must be earned by specific merits for the common good, for example as a good hunter, a brave warrior or as a performer or innovator of ritual. Among these, warfare and ritual rank higher than hunting, at least under the conditions of early man's life when game was sufficiently abundant to enable every man to fill his own bag.

Warfare was certainly the most obvious way for a young man to acquire merit. Warfare is more than just a chosen opportunity (as it is, too) to vent the aggressive feelings resulting from an unsatisfactory way of life, more even than a good opportunity to show one's worth and to realize oneself as a proper male. Warfare has a positive effect on the solidarity of the group's males among themselves, an important point as they have to submit themselves to so much self-restraint in their competition for women. A war-raid combines the urgent need for male solidarity with an opportunity for every man to distinguish himself as a brave man, braver than any of his fellows. The hero is the man who helps and protects his comrades, and kills more enemies than any of the others.

Aggressivity thus becomes a self-perpetuating evil which has its own rewards. Warfare being directed at outsiders, it promotes the solidarity of the males of the group, instills the fiction that they protect the society as a whole against the attacks of other groups, and awards the daring individual with honours. When, in the course of history, the males succeed in improving their self-esteem by making themselves important as the performers of rituals and as co-producers of food by gardening, warfare remains a favourite opportunity for any young man to promote his social status. The competition inside the society of males is strong enough to inspire aggressive feelings among them. Besides, every boy is encouraged to be aggressive by his whole education; warfare and prowess are social virtues which contribute to the security and glory of the society. The dangers of war are the cement of the solidarity of a society's members.

The ideology of the hero and the glorification of war as a proper means for the unfolding and development of male virtues have persisted until recent times. We find a good specimen of it in the Old Testament: "And it came to pass... when David was returned from the slaughter of the Philistine, that the women came out of all cities of Israel, singing and dancing to meet king Saul,... And the women answered one another as they played, and said, Saul hath slain his thousands and David his ten thousands. And Saul was very wroth, and the saying displeased him" (1 Sam. 18: 6-8). The men do the fighting, the women applaud, and every man feels sure that he is somebody, that he has his worth. And competition goes on without seriously endangering the solidarity of the group. Primitive society knows many examples of this kind.

For a full picture of the significance of warfare in the social life of primitive man, one should see the film *Dead Birds* made by R. Gardner of Harvard University. It gives a breath-taking illustration of a battle between two Papuan villages in the Eastern highlands of what now is West Irian. The warring parties halt at some distance from each other at a place previously agreed upon. Their ranks are open and widely dispersed. They shout insults at each other. Now and then a champion leaves the ranks, runs forward to launch his spear, then retreats to the safety of the ranks. The scene is something halfway between a battle and a tournament, but it is all in deadly earnest. The warriors will not stop before one or two men have been killed on either side. The film (I wish to insist on this point) was not made under my administration. A few years earlier I paid a short visit to the then brandnew government station in the area. In the afternoon I saw the boys of 10 to 12 years old fighting each other with mock-spears made out of banana-stalks, one would say really harmless substitutes. Yet, two of them were wounded. The boys fought with so much zest and abandonment that I thought it necessary to renew my instruction to the Assistant District Officer in charge not to extend his administrative offices beyond a three miles zone from the airfield for as long as it was still under construction to make it fit for DC3 aircraft. I had seen enough to persuade me of the truth of the rumours that these people glorified in warfare and prowess.

There are, of course, other ways for a man to win distinction than by warfare. He can become a medicine man or a prophet. However, the results of such action are never as tangible as those of the warrior whose success and prowess can be measured by the number of people he has killed. Besides, the appearance of such functionaries is a matter of later development. War, with its attractions of quick glory and status improvement, hardly makes demands on cultural progress or social development. All that is needed is that there are at least two organized groups, one to be fought and one to identify oneself with, i.e. the one in which glory is earned. The immediate effect of war is that it makes the solidarity of a group's male members a must. Yet, in a club in which prowess is a valued virtue and aggressive behaviour of the younger members encouraged, conflicts arise easily. The bigger the group the greater the probability of conflict; this probability increases quadratically with the size of the group (Van Bruinessen 1978: 448 note 1). The consequences are that the size of the group is restricted to a minimum, thus increasing simultaneously the number of hostile groups, the opportunities to fight, and the necessity to maintain in-group solidarity.

All this agrees fairly well with our initial supposition that these early human bands will have counted little more than sixty souls, two dozen children and, on an average, 18 men and 18 women of various age. It is possible now to say something more of its inner structure. The males form a compact unit, bent on avoiding conflicts among themselves. The females, however, are divided into as many separate units as there are women with children, some 15 of such units in all plus a couple of older women whose children have already reached the age of maturity. With the possible exception of the latter, each of these women is interested primarily in the small unit dependent on her personal cares. Besides, each woman may have one special friend among the males who is her exchange partner in the daily barter of game against vegetables.

Of these exchange partners, we will have more to say presently. For the moment, we must concentrate on the males. It is evident that they are in a power position and can act as a pressure group. They form a unit which has common interests to look after, such as the defence of the group against outsiders, and the maintenance of viable relations within the group at large. Although the women may pursue their collecting activities in one another's company, each of them collects for her own unit, occasionally helping an other woman who is sick or otherwise indisposed. They do not form a collectivity like the males. They have no common interests to defend; they only have to look after their family, a duty which keeps them fully occupied. The group as a whole, the society as such, is a male affair. Fighting, as well as an important part of their hunting, is done by the men collectively, by coordinated action. Hunting collectively is more than hunting in one another's company; it is action in concert in which every individual has a part to play. It is only the males who act as a whole and for the whole.

We argued (above: 78) that one of the basic interests of the males is that the relations with the females do not lead to conflicts between them. It is not only a question of the barter of vegetable food against game, it is above all a question of finding a sexual partner each time they come home. Sexual relations are of an intimate and emotional nature, and frustration on this point can lead to jealousy and conflict. Theoretically, it is possible that the men leave the finding of a partner to chance and adopt the rule that whoever comes first has first choice of a partner for the night. This might work, provided that the women are willing to comply; but this is far from certain. They may have certain preferences, and so may have some of the males. Conflicts can only be avoided if every male and female has a regular partner with whom they know themselves to be welcome.

Besides, having a partner serves other needs than those of food and sex alone. There is the human condition to think of. Man is a lonely animal, always in need of affective ties. During the day, when everyone is at work or loiters in the company of others, the affective needs may slumber; but the nights are lonely, fearsome even if there is not someone close by who says: how good that you are here, and with a simple caress confirms togetherness. The loneliness of the subject and his uncertainty about his world are so fundamental that nobody, either man or woman, can dispense with the recurrent confirmation of his belonging to his world. The deep silence of the night in the tropical forest, now and then interrupted by some unidentifiable sound, has an uncanny power of throwing the waking individual back on his loneliness. There can be no doubt that the adolescent's craving for a partner is a very essential human phenomenon that dates back to the dawn of humanity. There is no ground to suppose that early youth lacked the capacity of falling in love. But, within such a small group, a young man's falling in love with a certain girl can never be an affair between the lovers alone. It may very well be that another man desires the girl too, has waited longer for a partner, or claims precedence because of his merits. The society as a whole is involved because internal peace depends on an equitable distribution of the available women. Women are not only the objects of the men's desires, but also of their worries about the solidarity of the group.

Some might object here that we over-emphasize the emotional needs involved in choosing a partner of the other sex. Admitting the needs for sex and food, they might argue that the emotional needs cannot be very strong because so many primitive peoples segregate men from women and children during the night, the men passing the night in separate men's houses. However, we find these men's houses mainly among horticulturalists. Here, husband and wife cultivate their gardens together. In the morning the two go to their gardens and find there opportunity for sexual intercourse. In societies of hunters and collectors men and women go different ways at daybreak, the men going one way to hunt, the women another to collect; the men avoiding coming into the vicinity of the women so that they are not suspected of adulterous intents. To hunters, the night is the most favourable time for sexual intercourse.

Others will argue that the average size of the primeval group must have been smaller than the 60 as assumed here. This number implies that each group consisted of some 15 to 18 mature males, a number too high for a workable hunting pack. The argument is correct; eight or nine men would be a more suitable number. Yet, it is uncomfortably low for self-defence, and we have to consider the possibility that one group consisted of two or even more separate hunting-packs, each foraging and managing for itself and even living in different camps, but allied to each other by ties of friendship. However strong the aggressive tendencies of the males may be, they cannot eliminate their social needs. They need partners with whom to discuss experiences. From this point of view a society of less than 60 individuals is hardly viable.

In such a society the community of males is paramount. One of its recurring problems is that of the distribution of the available women, because the solidarity of the community of males depends on, for every member, acceptable decisions concerning this distribution. As long as numbers are equal and there are as many mature males as females, there need not be problems. Even a surplus of women need not give problems. Some older men might be given a second wife to assist his aging mate. Trouble arises as soon as there are less women than men. The obvious solution is either polyandry or an attempt to rob a woman from another group, the latter a matter of violence of course, but not contrary to the permanent state of war reigning between groups. The smaller the groups, the greater the chances of an unequal distribution of numbers, and the more certain the escalation of conflicts between groups. These are circumstances under which the word of Tylor becomes true that early man had only one choice, that between marrying out or being killed out (Tylor, 1889). It is good enough for the men to prove their mettle in successful warfare, but there comes a point at which the dangers and the troubles exceed the profits. That point is reached fairly soon when the enemies live nearby and attacks become frequent. Then it becomes worth while to consider the possibility of giving a woman away rather than being killed for her. For the woman concerned, it does not make much difference because she will be taken anyway, probably with some of her sisters and cousins; for the men it is a matter of life or death pure and simple.

From distributing the available women between the members of the group to distributing them between several groups is only one step. No more is needed than the promise that any girl coming of age will be available to a member of one of the other participating groups, whether that group be a friendly hunting-pack or an originally hostile band. Once the groups have decided to make their maturing women available to one another, the main reason for internal conflicts has been removed. Everyone can be happy with such a solution. The men because, apart from eliminating a source of dissension, the alliance allows of a more even distribution of the women by the increase of the society's numbers, and gives greater security because of the superior size of its fighting force. Even the girls can be satisfied. Because life has become more secure, the chances of abduction by foreign warriors to a hostile tribe have lessened considerably. Though forced to leave her group of origin, a girl need not travel far to meet a mate. She goes to people with whom relations exist on terms approximating friendship, and she can keep up fairly regular contacts with her own family. Besides, she is young and at an age that she wishes to create a family unit all of her own; she may well wish to escape her mother's daily supervision. Boys can realize their longing for self-fulfilment by participating in adventurous hunting expeditions and war raids, girls by letting themselves be married out to another group.

The arrangement does not put an end to every form of warfare. The men would not have liked that. It simply turns war from an ever recurrent and unbearable trouble into an event of more or less periodic occurrence, an event which has great social significance for the participants in the alliance. War unites them in a common body of allies and friends in which everyone can feel reassured and encouraged by the number and quality of his friends.

3. The social context of the marriage institution

The rule that each group shall make available its maturing women to members of another cooperating group implies the institutionalization of marriage by exogamy.

This 'alliance model' of marriage (a term introduced by Lévi-Strauss; cf. 1945, 1967) offers a suitable foundation for the further analysis of the implications of the institution. However, acceptance of the model implies that, originally at least, virilocal marriage must have been the rule, a rule which necessarily leads to patrilineal descent. What then about the matrilineate and the occurrence of uxorilocal marriage? According to Murdock, the two are interrelated; the matrilineate being the result of uxorilocal marriage (1949). If this is true, it must be assumed that primeval human society knew a second, alternative form of social organization.

But it is not necessary to change our ideas on early human marriage. It can be demonstrated that the matrilineate, far from being the result of uxorilocal marriage or a survival from a promiscuous age, is a logical consequence of virilocal marriage. The consequence need not be materialized, but it always is potentially present in every society in which virilocal marriage prevails. The marriage of a girl into another group establishes an alliance between the groups concerned. The factuality of this alliance is reflected in the widely spread custom known as the avunculate, the institutionalized relation between a mother's brother and his sister's children which obliges the uncle to act as the children's protector, helper, or mentor, all as the case may be. The avunculate is strongest developed among strictly patrilineal, virilocally marrying peoples. The studies by Radcliffe-Brown (1924) and Lévi-Strauss (1945) have given evidence that the institution is not a survival of an earlier matrilineate, but the unmistakable symptom of an alliance between two related families.

The *raison d'être* of the avunculate can be approached from two angles. The one is to consider the brother's cares for his sister's children as a recognition of his indebtedness to his sister (Van Baal 1975 ch. II). The substantial gift (usually denoted by the misleading term brideprice) which was rendered to the bride's father or brother by her husband and his kinsfolk, enables the bride's brother to acquire a wife for himself. The brother – who acts on behalf of his kinsfolk when the father is old or dead – is also the recipient of the gifts presented by his sister's husband on such occasions as the sister's giving birth to a child. For as long as the sister's marriage lasts, the alliance is a source of useful and often profitable relations to the brother, and he redeems his indebtedness to her by paying attention to and being friendly towards her children.

The other approach starts from the point of view that the girl who is given away as a bride, constitutes a lasting link between the two families, as, in fact, she does. This implies that by becoming a member of her husband's kin she does not stop being one of her family of origin. She is a member of both, in-between, as Marilyn Strathern characterized it (1972). The children which she bears her husband are not simply the children of his kingroup, they all have a special link with their mother's family who recognize and treat them as a sort of external members of their group who are entitled to their protection and kindness.

The two approaches are complementary. Both lead to the conclusion that a child, growing up in a society where virilocal marriage is the rule, has specific links with its mother's group. In terms of descent this means that from early age onwards the child learns to discern between relatives belonging to its own patriline, and relatives belonging to the mother's group, relatives with whom the child is related matrilaterally. Whether this will lead to an institutionalization of the matriline is a matter of circumstances. If the mothers' brothers play a role in the arrangement of the marriages of their sisters' children there is a chance that the matriline will be made explicit. There is a bigger chance when sisters' children, on reaching the age of adolescence, make it a custom to stay for a shorter or longer period with their mothers' kinsfolk. It becomes an institution when the sons settle there permanently and thus give precedence to the matriline over the patriline.

The circumstances which promote or impede such processes of social change are not important here. The main point is that every boy has a mother's brother who himself is a sister's son to his own mother's brother, so that the discovery of a matriline can never be a problem. The matriline is always present and has always a function, a function which can be of lesser or greater importance. How it can win precedence is a matter of conjecture and we would be led far astray if we tried to make an inventory of the more concrete possibilities. Yet, there are a few points to be kept in mind. The first of these is that brother and sister are often attached to each other by strong ties of affection (for an example cf. Burridge 1969: 105 f.). The second is that brother-sister incest is by no means unknown in the primitive world (cf. Malinowski 1927; Whiting, 1941). It could hardly be otherwise. Brother and sister grow up together, and the wide spread of the avunculate is but another proof of the significance of their affection, even though such affections do not always afford effective means to protect a sister against harsh treatment by her husband and his folk. The facts as such give sufficient reason to assume that a decision to hand over a girl to a foreigner can evoke strong protests from the side of her brother, in some cases also from that of her father who need not be the lesser of his son in compassion with the girl. If such protests do not stand alone, a compromise is called for, for example one by which the parties agree that the children born from the girl's marriage will, at adolescence, be returned to their mother's group. Her husband would thus have the benefit of the girl's cares and labour for as long as she is not beyond middle age, and the girl would have the guarantee that by that time she may return to her group of origin to take up residence with her son. It is not unthinkable that arrangements to that effect were already made by some fairly early societies.

The origin of uxorilocal (or matrilocal) marriage is a more complicated problem. Actually, the forms of uxorilocal marriage are so diverse that their denotation by a single term adds to confusion rather than to a clear understanding of the implications. These forms range from the restless habits of the visiting husband whose main residence is not with his wife, as among the Minangkabau, to simply crossing the dancing place of the village as among the Shavante (Maybury-Lewis 1967), where a young man takes up residence with his parents-in-law as a badgered underling to end up, after a number of years, as the master of the house. None of these forms seems compatible with the conditions of early man's life, and we must assume that the institution is the outcome of later developments of a historical, that is accidental, nature.

More conclusive than the examination of always dubious conjectures is the fact

84

that, whatever line of descent be given precedence, it is always the men who ultimately take the decisions. They are dominant. They did not gain this dominance when, in a dim past, they introduced the rule of exogamy. Although this rule certainly increased their powers by opening up new opportunities for arranging alliances and for disposing of their girls, they were already dominant when they decided upon exogamy. Being united in an encompassing solidarity, they constituted an effective power group from the very beginning. From the earliest times, it was the males who decided on peace and war, on matters of camp sites and migrations, and began to fill their spare time (they had lots of it) with the performance of the first rituals. These rituals would place additional power in the hands of their progeny, the men of primitive society.

In matters of marriage arrangement the men have the choice between two mutually exclusive ways of materializing their dominance; i.e. that of the patrilineate with virilocal marriage, and that of the matrilineate with viri-avunculocal or uxorilocal marriage*. The former gives them dominance over their wives and children, the latter over their sisters and sisters' children. Where the latter is combined with uxorilocal marriage (what in such case coincides with matrilocality) the women are usually better off than their virilocally married sisters. They have vested rights which are protected by their brothers who, in agricultural societies, till the family land. All husbands are visiting husbands (at least theoretically) who go to their wives in the afternoon to pass the night with them. For the rest of the day they keep an eye on their sisters and particularly on their sisters' children who are their legal heirs. They have authority over these children, not the fathers who are their children's friends rather than their disciplinarians. The system protects the women from the excesses of male supremacy which sometimes go combined with virilocal marriage in patrilineal societies. Yet, it strictly limits a woman's freedom to give proper shape to her own family life. It is not so much that she remains under the authority of her brother who often stays with his own family, but that she has to bear her mother's enduring tutelage. The old woman is always there to keep a strict eye on her.

In patrilineal societies, the women's lot can be hard. It often is so among Papuan Highlanders, such as those described by Marilyn Strathern in her book *Women in Between*. Many of these women marry into a community which is partly or wholly foreign to them. They are received with distrust. In these war-ridden societies, they are suspected of secretly favouring their society of origin at the expense of the one into which they have married. A woman must prove her worth, both as a spouse and as a mother, before she is really trusted. This can take a long time; too long sometimes for women who are partners in a polygynous household. To them, building up a relation of confidence with her husband is more difficult than it is for women who

---

* Viri-avunculocal: the man stays with his *avunculus*, his mother's brother; uxorilocal: he stays with his wife. Other possibilities for post-marital residence such as ambilateral choice and neolocal marriage must remain undiscussed. They emerged later in history as, in the present writer's opinion, did uxorilocal and avunculocal marriage.

have contracted a monogamous marriage. Quarrels with co-wives and other misfortunes frequently lead to suicide.

Hylkema, describing a fairly closely related, Nalum speaking society in more personal detail (Hylkema 1974), points to the fact that men and women live in two different worlds. To the men, the female sex is a mystery as is well borne out by what they believe to be the cause of menstruation: an opossum and an eel run up and down the woman's uterus, carrying a piece of sugarcane with them which causes the bleeding. The symbolism is obvious, as obvious as the distrustful wavering of the men with regard to women. This does not mean that there are no happy marriages in this society. There are a few cases of unions which are harmonious over time. There are far more which begin happily and finally deteriorate. Nalum girls have greater freedom than those of Mt. Hagen described by Mrs. Strathern. A girl can take herself the initiative to choose a husband, though she risks heavy conflicts with her prospective mother-in-law. Once the marriage is contracted she tries to keep her young husband exclusively for herself. Charmed by her devotion, the young man may agree to build a house apart from the settlement where he can pass day and night with her alone. It will not last for longer than a few years at best. The men's house community always succeeds in persuading the young man to return to the settlement and to resume his place in the men's house. Over the years, the men's house becomes more and more important in his life. More and more frequently he passes the night in the men's house, visiting his wife's house only to take his meals. In the course of time, even this may stop. He takes his meals in the men's house and in the end the marriage quietly dies out, the woman taking up residence with one of her sons where she can still make herself useful, the man depending for his meals on a daughter-in-law. Socially, he becomes a nobody, tolerated by his sons who do not even bother to consult him on their plans. What is of interest here is that the wife, though originating from elsewhere, has a more lasting position than the husband. She is a mother of sons and has become identified with the group. She has proved her worth.

Such women are entitled to give an opinion on matters of concern to all. They just walk into the circle of leading males or enter the men's house to tell them frankly what is on their minds, or to scold them for their highhandedness and recklessness, and not without success. Thus, a few years ago, Kapauku women of the Wissel Lakes (another society of Papuan mountaineers) stopped a rebellion against the Indonesian government. The older women told the men to stop this nonsense, and the men meekly followed (personal communication by F. Hylkema). Old women enjoy similar prerogatives with regard to secret rituals. From many corners of the primitive world, we hear that old women may be consulted on the preparation of great celebrations. They know what it is all about, and will instruct the younger women how to behave and to cooperate when and where their assistance is needed. This does not imply that such older women have equal rights with the men. Sometimes the latter demur and complain that they cannot stop these women because, having passed the menopause, they can no longer be considered impure. They feel that they have no power over them rather than that these old women have a legal claim to such a position.

86

One wonders why the women acquiesce so generally and so excessively to male domination. If ever they decided to resist collectively against the outrageous claims of the men and denied them their co-operation, the men would be in a very difficult position. The women can exist for longer without the men's meat than the latter without the women's cares and their daily contributions to their meals. Of course, the men might try to beat the women into obedience, but if it really came to fighting it is not at all certain who would win. These women are not weaklings. Accustomed to long working hours they are better trained than the physically stronger males. But we need not speculate upon what might happen, because the women do not offer organized common resistance. They restrict themselves to canalizing their wishes with regard to public affairs through influencing their husbands and brothers, and not by open action. Why?

The ethologist's answer might be that male dominance is a rather general rule among mammals. It is not without significance that with many species the common gesture of submission, even for a male, is that of offering oneself for copulation. Submission to male dominance thus would be the result of an innate behavioural pattern. However, even if this is true, then the problem arises as to how it is possible that this dominance can be so successfully assailed and progressively reduced in modern western society where more and more women take leading positions and public functions formerly strictly reserved for the males. Moreover, the explanation of social facts from innate behavioural patterns is, scientifically, dubious. One should first of all investigate the social conditions leading to male dominance. The forms and extent of this dominance are culturally so divergent that these social conditions must have precedence.

The fact that the decline of male dominance in western society coincides with the decrease of the importance of child bearing and the drastic simplification of household tasks by mechanization points the way to a more conclusive answer to our question. In primitive society childbearing is a very important task for a woman. It is also a necessity, an *insurance* for her old age. She must bear many children to be sure that, when she is a widowed or divorced old woman, she will have at least one son or son-in-law who will give her game or clear her garden-site. Child mortality is high and marriages do not last for ever. A good illustration of a woman's need for sons is the often heard saying of a Nalum mother to her recently born baby son: "Don't weep, my dear, I am going to give you my breast. When you are grown up and my husband an old man, you will fence in my garden". To a baby girl she speaks differently: "Come, my dear, I am going to give you my breast. Yet, I will welcome the day on which they marry you off to a distant valley" (Hylkema 1974: 202 f.).

A woman concentrates on her family. She has things and humans to care for. In the first years of her marriage, the husband is the focus of her attentions. He is the first object of the predisposition to care-giving resulting from her early education. Gradually, the children take more and more of her time and devotion. She lives for them and finds happiness in her care-giving. She does not bother about all the things the men do. The men have plenty of leisure time; they fill their hours with hunting, talking, rituals and fighting. All the while a woman takes care of the food and the interests of her family, including those of her husband. It is the focus of her life and this focus also defines the limits of her complaisance to male domination. There is one thing no husband ever will think of: to take away any of the food a woman has collected or harvested from her garden without her consent. The husband has a right to food; but he cannot just take it away, for it will be given to him anyway. Everywhere in the primitive world the right of a woman to dispose of her private property and of the things produced by herself, is respected. In one way or another it is even respected in societies where the lot of women is hard and sometimes almost unbearable. In quite a number of peasant societies in which the social position of women is rather low, women play a not inconsiderable part in internal trade. Often their financial position is more secure than that of their husbands. The many mammie-wagons one passes on the West African roads prove that these female traders are not necessarily small pedlars; they often transport substantial loads of goods with them when they travel from one market to another. Their prosperity arouses the envy of the men and it may happen that these try to have a share in their earnings (cf. Nadel, *A Black Byzantium*) but all the same these women manage to maintain a fair degree of independence.

Female traders are not a specifically African phenomenon. They are found in many peasant societies. Bali is a case in point. At certain times of the year, when there is no work to do in the ricefields, the visitor can see scores of men quietly squatting alongside the road, each with one or two baskets with a fighting cock. Every now and then a cock is taken from its basket to be caressed and compared with another man's bird. Farther down the road one finds a market where thrifty and hard working women are busily engaged in earning the money which their loitering husbands will occasionally try to borrow to finance their betting on cock fights. These women may have a financial hold on their husbands. Yet, all this hardly improves their social position. The fact that she is a woman, marks her as inferior. In Hindu-Bali society every individual is the product of his previous incarnations. To be reborn as a woman is the effect of a sinful life in the past. The women are excluded from public affairs. These are matters organized and invented by the males, and women have no say in them. Society at large is a society of males.

Society at large and the household meet each other in the husband. The household being primarily a responsibility of the wife, one might expect that husband and wife are here more or less equals. As sexual partners they are almost necessarily equals of each other. Their common interest in their children is another reason for seeing them as equal partners. The fact that a husband has to respect his wife's property and her rights on the produce she planted or collected, is a further reason for characterizing spouses as partners with, up to an extent, equal rights. The reality, however, is different. The husband is a male, a member of society, and the reflection of its glory and authority dwells upon him. The husband has authority and he is entitled to make certain demands on his wife. This is typically the case with food. Though the husband has to respect his wife's rights and property, he may claim that his wife prepare and give him his food in time, and if she fails he has the right to beat her. This, at least, is the case in aboriginal Australia and New Guinea. One could explain this right to chastise a negligent wife from the fact that the economic relation between husband and wife is based upon barter; the husband brings in game, a prestigeous food, the wife the more plentiful food which she collected or brought from the garden. Yet, the situation is more complicated than this. The Australian hunter does not give the choiciest parts of the game which he captured to his wife, but to her father or brother, in other words to the men who made her available to him. In the transaction of game against vegetable food the wife is not party but instrument; as Lévi-Strauss said, the object in the transactions between groups of men. We must conclude from it that the rights a woman has, the rights which her husband must respect, are derived rights, rights of the group which married her out and which will defend them if they are violated by her husband. And perhaps this is the deepest motive for a woman to desire a son. A son gives her a status of her own in a society of males.

Marriage relations would be unbearable if their ramifications were confined to their legal aspects. A marriage is either more, or it is dissolved. There are also sexual intimacy and comradeship, and neither of the two can be defined in terms of legal rights or unequal positions. They create the comforting relation which can be defined as togetherness. It is the heart and core of family life, the fruit of co-operation in matters of common interest. One might object that the opportunity for such co-operation is small among the Australian tribes with their sharp division of labour between men and women, and that is has a better chance among primitive horticulturalists like the Papuans. Yet, this opinion on the Australian way of life is not quite justified. In times of dearth – and they are frequent enough in these parts – the group spreads, dividing into units of one or two families. It is on such occasions that husband and wife are more together than ever and, for their survival, thrown back utterly on their comradeship. They form a more harmonious pair than the legal position suggests.

It is the wife who, by her care-giving functions, contributes to the internal family relations the better part of their contents of togetherness and comradeship. The husband's position is ambivalent. He lives in two worlds, and his main interests are with the society at large, i.e. with the community of males. To him, this is the world that counts, the world of intertribal friendships and conflicts, of ceremonial barter and festive celebrations arranged to promote the status of the feastgivers, of religious speculation and the observance of rituals for the benefit and the fertility of the total community. This does not change when the introduction of horticulture presents new opportunities to the men for making themselves useful and for enlarging their share in the production of food. One might expect that they appreciate that, by now, they can cooperate with their wives in the construction of gardens and the growing of crops, tasks which unite them in a common effort. It may be that they do but, coming home from a day of work in the garden, the men more often than not disappear into the men's house, there to pass the rest of the day and frequently the night as well. They feel that their proper place is among the men. They fear to be mocked as hen-pecked if they did otherwise.

In Melanesia the male trend to segregate takes the form of living in men's houses. Elsewhere, one often finds the more mitigated form of meeting-halls. A special form is that of the polygynous family in Africa. Here, the husband usually has a hut all for himself like each of his wives who all dwell within the same compound. In turn each of the wives passes the night with her husband (at least, this is as it should be). The distance between the man and his wives is clearly made explicit by this arrangement.

A man's heart, unlike that of a woman, is at best only partly with his family. He is predominantly a member of the community of males which constitutes and directs the society as a whole. As an encompassing and organized whole it is authority incarnate. Every male is a co-bearer of this authority, but the one bears more of it than the other. Between the males there is competition for power, i.e. for the wielding of authority. Whereas the size and prosperity of a man's family of procreation are co-determinants of his status in the males' world of authority and power, his participation in this world in its turn affects his position in his family. That position is ambiguous; he always stands with one leg outside his family. The family is not merely an end to him as it is to his wife, it is also a means. Within the family, he represents authority; not the authority derived from the family as a unit, but the ultimate authority derived from the community of males. He shares the authority derived from the family with his wife who, more than the husband, acts as the disciplinarian of the children. It is an authority of low degree, subject to that of the father as a male. As a member of the family, the father's role is ambiguous. On the one hand, he belongs to a group in which togetherness and comradeship prevail, on the other hand he represents outside authority and command. It is this inherent ambiguity which engenders tensions between husband and wife and defines the father's relations with his children. It is only natural that fatherhood has become a universal symbol of a combination of loving care with distance, authority and constraint.

We must leave it at this. We have come across positions of equality and inequality, and relations of togetherness and competition, of power and conflicts, of subordination and authority, as well as of friendship and hostility. We also found that these relations and the interaction ensuing from them, are subject to certain rules. Man always devises rules, even though he sometimes experiences them as frustrating. These rules may remain implicit, unconscious, but often they are made explicit and consciously formulated. But whatever they are, and how much they may vary from place to place and from situation to situation, they are not products of pure arbitrariness. Certain general principles are of universal occurrence, principles inherent in the two basic positions which any human being holds in his interaction with others, those of equality and inequality. For a relationship of equality the leading principle is that of reciprocity, for one of inequality that of subordination to authority. It is to an analysis of these two principles that we must turn now, beginning with that of reciprocity which has been for many years an important topic of discussion among anthropologists.

V

RECIPROCITY

1. Introduction

Reciprocity means doing or rendering something in return for goods received, for services paid, or evils inflicted (Van Baal 1975: 11). Presupposed is an exchange, primarily one in which the contributions made by each of the parties concerned are of approximate equivalence. The first to demonstrate the significance of reciprocity for the various forms of social interaction in primitive society was Malinowski who devoted his *Argonauts of the Western Pacific* (1922) and *Crime and Custom in Savage Society* (1926) to their description. In the same period (1923/24) M. Mauss published his *Essai sur le Don*, a study inspired by the Durkheimian problem of the moral obligation imposed by contract, and devoted to the remarkable fact that an act, seemingly so free and unobliging as that of receiving or presenting a gift, entails the obligation of giving a return-gift, an obligation which, in western society, is not protected by law but nevertheless there, like everywhere, meticulously obeyed by the parties involved.

Later research brought abundant evidence of the universality of reciprocity as a general principle, but also of recurrent infringements of it, in particular in the practice of gift-exchange. Here, the balance of exchange, vaguely but unmistakably implied in the concept of reciprocity, is subject to exceptions. Mauss himself paid specific attention to the fact that people of superior status are obliged to give more than those who are inferior. The lesser, who reciprocates the gift of a superior by a present of equal or higher value, acts insolently. He does not know his place. Later, M. Sahlins (1965) pointed out that reciprocity, apart from sometimes being unbalanced, can also be muddled. It is in the case of the give-and-take going on between members of such small and closely knit groups as family units. He suggested that muddled and unbalanced reciprocity have the function of keeping the participants in such trans-actions under an obligation to each other. Perfect balance, he argued, exhausts the obligations which the parties have to one another, and thus may exhaust the relationship as well.

Sahlins here accepts reciprocity as a given, a binding obligation acknowledged by all mankind (see also Sahlins 1968). He does not try to give an explanation as, many years earlier, Mauss had done in his discussion of the gift. Mauss founded his explanation mainly on the Maori statement that a substantial gift has a *hau*, an innate supernatural power, which urges the receiver to reciprocate lest the *hau* of the object make him ill or kill him. Apparently, the given object is not just a thing: something, emanating from the giver, travels along with it. Although the comment has the virtue that it emphasizes the personal element in the exchange of gifts, it cannot possibly explain the universal validity of the obligation to reciprocate. Lévi-Strauss was right when he noted that Mauss's explanation is but a native theory by which the Maori explain to themselves the force of the obligation to give a countergift, not a scientific theory which exposes causal relationships (Lévi-Strauss 1950: XXXIX). In his *Structures élémentaires* (1949) the latter has suggested another explanation of its universality: reciprocity is a structure of the human mind.

It is expedient to examine this explanation in more detail. We find it in a curious passage (p. 98 of the 1967 edition of the book) following the statement that in kinship and dual organization certain fundamental structures of the human mind are involved which he specifies as follows:

> The mental structures which we believe can be demonstrated to be universal are three in number. "They are: the claim of the Rule as a Rule; the notion of reciprocity considered as the most immediate form under which the opposition between the I and the Thou can be integrated; finally, the synthetic character of the Gift, that is the fact that the agreed transfer of a value from one individual to another changes the two into partners, and adds a new quality to the value transferred".

One of the merits of the exposition is the clear distinction made between reciprocity and gift. The description of the effect of gift-exchange on giver, receiver, and the transferred object itself, is of a penetrating acuity and highlights more than anything the specific social value of the gift. Nevertheless, as an explanation the exposition is unsatisfactory. If the gift must be called a structure of the mind, it is a structure which in part ensues from the structure called reciprocity. Gifts must, ordinarily, be reciprocated. In other words, these structures are not of the same level. If they are fundamental, one at least is more fundamental than the other.

Doubt on the fundamental nature of these structures also arises with regard to reciprocity and the claim of the rule. To begin with the latter: the statement refers to the obligation to respect rules, but fails to mention the conspicuous fact that in all his activities man is not only subject to rules, but acts as a producer of rules, conscious as well as unconscious ones. The real, fundamental thing is not the claim made by rules, but the ordering activity of the mind which more rightly deserves to be called a fundamental structure. Unconsciously, man orders his perceptions into a field; i.e. an activity which, ultimately, is identical with choice making, the subject's most distinctive function (above: 13). Ordering also underlies the unconscious rules of language, rules which man not only unconsciously follows in the practice of speech, but also rules which he, equally unconsciously, created in the course of time. In the preceding chapters, it was pointed out that order also underlies myth and man's systems of classification, as well as the expression of his feelings in music. Equally fundamental is the order of logic. The rules of logic as developed by philosophers from Aristoteles to Beth are not rules of correct reasoning imposed on human thinking by logicians, but rules which logicians made explicit from human reason. Man followed them long before they were formulated. More than the rules of language with their wide variation of systems, those of logic are uniform and of universal validity. Yet, they cannot be classed as laws automatically obeyed, but must be conceived as rules or norms. They can be ignored or misinterpreted and it can take quite a time before a transgression is diagnosed, but ultimately man accedes to them and accepts their outcome.

Ordering, then, is that basic activity of the mind from which the unconscious and conscious rules followed and occasionally disobeyed by man are but derivates which give content to this ordering activity. The activity as such is really a structure in the sense as once defined by Lévi-Strauss himself in his comment on the unconscious: "l'inconscient est toujours vide; ou, plus exactement, il est aussi étranger aux images que l'estomac aux aliments qui le traversent. Organe d'une fonction spécifique, il se borne à imposer des lois structurales, qui épuisent sa réalité, à des éléments inarticulés qui proviennent d'ailleurs" (1958: 224 f.)*.

When taking these things to heart, one cannot possibly call reciprocity a structure, certainly not a fundamental structure. Reciprocity is itself a rule, one which presupposes the structure of ordering and can be defined as the effect of this structure on the exigencies of man's social intercourse with his congeners, just as logical and linguistic rules are the effect of ordering on his forms of thinking and linguistic expression. Yet, reciprocity is more than just one rule amongst many rules. One of the main principles of ordering is that of ordering by way of bipolarity. Bipolarity is characteristic of reciprocity. It confronts the I with the other in a dual opposition of balance. Reciprocity being a clear case of binarity, it is no wonder that it is universal, and lays a foundation to quite a variety of dependent rules which, by their specificity and concreteness, give reason to call reciprocity a principle rather than a rule. A second reason to call reciprocity a principle lies in the fact that it refers directly to yet another basic condition of the human mind that, with equal right as man's ordering activity, deserves to be called a fundamental structure: i.e. the fact that man is a subject who must be part of his universe, and a part of that universe which must be a subject. The principle of reciprocity is a direct consequence of this structural condition. Reciprocity is not, as Lévi-Strauss asserts, the form under which the opposition between the I and the Thou can be integrated, but the form under which the I can be part of its universe and still be a subject.

Reciprocity is a principle, and the various ways in which the principle is applied are defined by the situations, positions, and specific purposes of the interacting persons. At least four main types of reciprocal action (there are more of them but they can eventually be classed under these headings) can be discerned: trade, gift-exchange, the give-and-take characteristic of the interaction between members of small, closely knit social units, and the exchange inherent in crime and punishment, wrongs and

* Translation (borrowed from the one by Jacobson and Schoepf): The unconscious is always empty – or, more accurately, it is as alien to mental images as is the stomach to the foods which pass through it. As the organ of a specific function, the unconscious merely imposes structural laws upon inarticulated elements which originate elsewhere – impulses, emotions, representations and memories.

revenge. In all these the principle of reciprocity plays a role. They shall be examined in the following sections. The data and analysis are borrowed from my essay on *Reciprocity* (Van Baal 1975) from which the presentation differs in this respect that I found it expedient to deal with the give-and-take within small groups as a separate category.

2. Reciprocity in the exchange of goods and services

a Trade is the simplest form of exchange of goods and services (which in this context can be considered as goods). Every trade transaction is a transaction between two parties. We speak of parties and not of persons (though persons they are) because a trade relation is not primarily a personal relation. The transacting persons can be and often are strangers to each other. They are not interested in one another's person, but in one another's goods. All they need for trading is an opportunity to meet each other in peace, a condition fulfilled by the institution called the 'market'. Here, hostilities are forbidden and the carrying of weapons is not allowed. Only two functions count: those of buyer and seller, and their respective positions are those of equals.

The market is a product of more advanced culture, that of peasant society. In more primitive societies, people often avail themselves of the opportunity presented by a feast or ceremony to meet relative strangers who came from far to attend the occasion. They often bring some goods with them for barter. At a feast, hostilities are forbidden; this is a chosen opportunity to negotiate with people who under other circumstances cannot be trusted. Trading in the form of barter is an epiphenomenon of such feasts; it is performed more or less at the outskirts, and unofficially. Yet, a ceremony can also be arranged for the purpose of creating an opportunity for trade. A typical case is that of the Trobriand *kula*-expedition as described by Malinowski and later commented upon by Uberoi (cf. Van Baal 1975: 39 ff.).

A kula-expedition culminates in a festive ceremony which takes place on the arrival of the expedition at its place of destination, a village on a distant island. Officially, its main feature is the exchange of valuable gifts between guests and hosts, a celebration which is quickly followed by elaborate trading activities. Such an expedition carries a wide variety of merchandise, and the hosts retain a similar variety of local products in readiness. Trading is not allowed between kula-partners; they are considered to be friends, and friends exchange gifts. Friends do not bargain, let alone haggle with each other like people do who do not know each other too well. Such people are the traders. They are more or less strangers to one another and they behave accordingly, negotiating and bargaining persistently on the price to be paid. Elsewhere (ibid.) I have argued that the kula must be seen as an over-developed form of a wide-spread institution, that of trade-friends. It is the institutionalized friendship between men of different societies or tribes who exchange presents among themselves, guarantee each other's safety, and help one another to find the trade-relations or articles they need. It is not the friends who trade with one another; they either trade on behalf of their friends, or introduce them to a trade-party.

There is good reason for this. The essential technique of trading is that of bargaining, and bargaining is a mild form of aggression performed without any soft-heartedness on either side. The market in archaic societies has no fixed prices; these are an invention of modern retail economy. In modern society, bargaining still takes place on the stock exchange. It is a matter of hard negotiations in which occasional friendships do not count. Such friendships as may occur between traders are rigidly excluded from interfering with their trade transactions. Business is business. In primitive society, where personal relations are of prime importance for the maintenance of the social fabric, people do not take the risk of letting them be affected by the aggressive negotiations associated with trade. Friends give presents to each other but they do not trade among themselves.

A typical feature of all trade is that traders negotiate with each other as equals. Differences in rank or status need not be ignored (a customer of high rank will be addressed in the language forms obtaining to his status) but they do not affect the process or, if they influence it at all, they do so to the benefit of the party of inferior status. A person of high rank may avoid visiting an eastern market where his status is known, for fear of being overcharged. He sends a servant instead.

The functional equality of the trading parties materializes in the freedom each has to break off negotiations. No one is obliged to sell or to buy. There is only one binding obligation: to pay as soon as an agreement has been reached. Where trade takes the form of barter, payment follows automatically by the exchange of the relevant goods. In principle, postponement of delivery is not excluded, but it is infrequent. This changes when money enters the scene, but even then credit is not readily given. A stranger has no credit unless an acceptable bailsman makes himself answerable for him. In societies lacking a well organized judiciary willing and capable to compel a debtor to pay his due, credit facilities necessarily remain restricted to a minimum. There is, in principle, no personal tie between buyer and seller. They can be strangers to one another, persons who are inclined to deny their moral obligations to each other because they belong to different societies.

The functional equality of the traders and their freedom to ignore any obligations except those of delivering and paying for the goods as agreed, has the effect that the balance of reciprocity is as perfect as humanly possible. Bargaining goes on until both parties agree that their respective offers are in balance. This does not exclude the possibility that one of the parties complains that his bargain was poor. A market may be lively or poor, i.e. the goods offered for sale may be much or little desired at the time of the transaction, and their price accordingly high or low. The balance of trade is a function of the scarcity or abundance of the goods offered for sale. This balance can be affected by monopoly situations created by manipulation or crop failure. Yet, the price fluctuations ensuing from monopoly positions do not differ in principle from those caused by the always irregular supply. In fact, the so-called monopoly-situation is but an aggravated form of the market situation as such. All ownership of goods constitutes by its relative exclusivity a form of monopoly, and bargaining can be defined as a weighing against each other of the worth of the respective monopolies implied in the transaction. If the price offered to the seller for his goods does not satisfy him, he is free to decline the offer and to try to find a more eager buyer who is willing to pay a price which comes closer to his demands. The bigger the market, i.e. the greater the number of competing buyers and sellers (which implies that the relevant monopoly positions are weaker) the better the system works. The right of every participant to decline an offer and withdraw his goods from the market guarantees the setting of prices which are commonly accepted as the true image of the balance of trade. This is expressed in the saying that they are the outcome of the market mechanism.

The term 'market mechanism' implies that trade is an impersonal technique for effecting the exchange of goods. Yet, it is persons who trade, and it sometimes happens that traders develop personal friendships which induce them to trade with the one rather than with the other. Nevertheless, this does not prevent them from hard negotiating: if the friendship has an influence, it is at best marginal. A clearer case of the interference of personal relationships in trade behaviour is that of the shopkeeper, one or two blocks down the street where we live. It happens that we feel faintly obliged to favour his shop though for some goods his prices are higher than those asked in the big super-market nearby. What induces us can be our appreciation of his personal services and helpfulness, or our moral disapproval of the way small shopkeepers are eliminated from business by the merciless competition of the big concerns. Yet, the effect of such personal considerations is small and even virtually negligible. After all, every buyer is free to go wherever he wishes. A trade transaction does not bind the parties to negotiate with each other in future. In principle every trade relation is exhausted by the trade transaction ensuing from it. Trade is a matter of goods, not of persons, and it is good practice not to let personal relations interfere with business.

This impersonal character of trade is not a matter of modern development; it is typical of trade throughout. Trading can be accomplished without persons meeting each other. This is not an invention of modern post-order firms, it is a fact almost as old as trade itself. That trade is a matter of goods and not of persons is cogently demonstrated by the procedures customary in that curious form of primitive trade known as 'silent trade'. It is a form of trade which, in different parts of the world, developed between parties who are unequal and normally hostile to one another, to wit a tribe of inferior forest dwellers on the one hand, and on the other a group of superior agriculturalists occupying the edge of the adjacent plain. The agriculturalists need certain products of the forest such as rattan, resins, and ivory. The bush people in turn need ironware and tobacco. At certain times of the year, the bush people draw near and deposit their products at a place where the farmers will notice them. The latter then bring their merchandise which they put next to the products of the forest dwellers. It is the price they are willing to pay. When they have retired the bush-people return and, if satisfied, take the merchandise with them, leaving their products to their counterpart. If not, they do the reverse. The whole transaction is completed without any personal contact at all between the parties concerned. They never meet.

b Gift-exchange differs profoundly from trade. In gift-exchange there is no bargaining for a return-gift; the return-gift is expected but not specified. In trade a bid can be declined, but a gift cannot be refused. In trade reciprocity is always balanced; in gift-exchange the balance between gift and return-gift is subject to exceptions. A trade transaction does not bind the interacting persons to anything but paying their debts, but a gift-exchange turns the participants into partners, friends. Finally, a trader has no obligation to sell his goods, but to a responsible member of society there are many occasions when he knows it his duty to give certain goods away. The two points the exchange of gifts has in common with the exchange called trade is the object of the transaction, the goods and services exchanged, and (but this under limiting conditions) the observance of the principle of reciprocity. Each of the points here mentioned requires some comment.

There is no bargaining in gift-exchange. Of course, anyone can ask for a gift and specify his desires. But it cannot be done on the occasion of presenting a gift to somebody else. Then to tell the recipient that a return-gift is expected, let alone to specify one's expectations, is bad form. The Trobrianders condemn it as degrading a *kula* transaction to the level of trade pure and simple, and they are right. The rule which forbids bargaining is a general one. Yet, there is one exception to it which, surprisingly, is fairly general. The ceremonial gift-exchange on the occasion of a marriage often is preceded by extensive haggling between the prospective inter-marrying families. This is what earns the marriage gift made by the bridegroom the name of 'brideprice'. There is sound reason for such negotiations. A marriage introduces or seals a lasting relation, an alliance between two families. The scope and contents of this alliance are too important to be left to chance. Complaints afterwards must be precluded; they can spoil the alliance. Once agreement has been reached, everything is done to present the transaction of the subsequent dealings as a gift-exchange. It is combined with elaborate ceremony, something perfectly foreign to a sales transaction. And, indeed, it is not. The transaction initiates a binding relation between the parties, one of an intimate, lasting and very specific nature. The buyer of a cow does not call the seller his father-in-law, as the bridegroom does the man to whom his family paid a brideprice.

Ceremony is a typical feature of every formal gift-exchange. It accompanies the presentation of both gift and return-gift. The two rarely coincide. In contrast to trade, there always is a fair measure of credit in gift-exchange. Non-ceremonial gift-giving is of a different nature. Most of it falls under the pattern of the give-and-take between the closely related members of the small group. Such a relation permits asking for specified gifts, a liberty which can also be taken by personal friends. In the absence of such relations, asking for gifts is called begging and falls under the heading of charity, an obligation of the rich to which we return later.

A gift cannot be refused without giving offence. In fact, it is never done, not even in modern society, except when the recipient suspects a bribe, a payment which has the form of a gift but has the purpose of acquiring illegal or otherwise undue services. A bribe is not a real gift. The fact that a real gift cannot be refused without giving offence is an indication that something personal is involved. Indeed, a gift is a token of appreciation of the recipient's person. It is given to please him, and the giver takes account of the recipient's status and special circumstances. The gift presented to a bride on the occasion of her marriage differs from the present offered to a feast-giver on the occasion of a celebration; and this, in turn, from the contribution made to a friendly family when there is a funeral.

The occasional disbalance between gift and return-gift is primarily a matter of social positions. A rich man who gives away a present must give a larger one than a poor man; if he did not he would be mean. Those who claim that they are rich must prove it by being generous. The poor man, offering a return-present to a rich one, should not try to equal the latter's initial gift, far less to surpass it in magnificence. If he did do so he would deny the difference in social status between them; in other words, deny the specific status of the recipient. That is not the way to please the recipient. Gifts that do not reflect the respective statuses of giver and recipient are not proper gifts but weapons in a fight for prestige as happened to be the case in some forms of the Kwakiutl *potlatch* (below: 100). Normally, gifts are presented not to vex but to please.

This is confirmed when we consider the goods given as presents. If the exchange is informal the presents consist of (prepared) food and delicacies, in other words, something palatable to the receiver. On formal occasions the preferred objects of transfer are valuables. It is the nature of these valuables which is of specific interest. More often than not they are objects of little practical value. The most expensive valuables are ornaments. This does not merely hold true of modern, western jewellery, it also holds for the shell ornaments, the pearls and the beads used by primitive people all over the world to adorn themselves on ceremonial occasions. Why are they valued so much higher than practical things, and why are they the most favoured objects in gift-exchange in each and every society? Obviously, because there is no more appropriate means to please a recipient than the material expression of appreciation of his person. There is no more adequate means to that end than an ornament which has the function of enhancing the beauty of his person.

"A gift-exchange turns the participants into partners, friends", we wrote on p. 97, quoting Lévi-Strauss. Is this not an over-appreciation of the effect of the gift? True, giving a present is a kindness, an obliging kindness even, but must it have the lasting effect which Lévi-Strauss ascribes to it (above: 92)? Did not Sahlins argue that such a simple and in itself friendly act as perfect reciprocation can exhaust the relationship (ibid.: 91)?

A closer examination of the meaning which a gift has for a recipient can take away doubts on this point. Gifts are vehicles carrying the giver's recognition of the recipient's position and his actual circumstances, as well as the giver's appreciation of his counterpart's person. This is not insignificant in a society based primarily on networks of interpersonal relations. To every member of such a society, his personal position in it defines his well-being. Unfortunately, the human condition is such that no one can ever be fully sure of that position, of the place he has in the appreciations of his fellow-men. Esteem and popularity are fragile properties; no one enjoys these as a durable good. The message of the properly presented gift assures the recipient that everything is all right with his position, that he is recognized and appreciated, and the gift does not do so by mere words which easily melt into thin air, but by the tangible

98

factuality of a durable good. Taking away the recipient's inner apprehensions and his uncertainty, the gift necessarily arouses feelings of togetherness and of belonging together. The message conveyed by the gift is exactly what, according to Joseph Pieper in his unsurpassed essay on love, is the fundamental essence of all love: *Wie gut dasz es dich gibt. Wie wunderbar dasz du da bist* (Pieper 1962. Translation: How good that you exist. How wonderful that you are here).

Who could refuse a gift? It would be a denial of one's own partnership in one's universe as well as of that of the giver in it. Nobody is so sure of himself that he could do this. In fact, the gift is a 'godsend', calling for reciprocation which cements the relationship established by the initial gift. The reciprocation is essential. The recipient's appreciation of the gift's message must be expressed in an equivalent return-gift lest doubt arise on his feelings of togetherness. It would be an expression of contempt if a return-gift were not forthcoming. And this is why the reciprocity incumbent on gift-exchange rarely needs protection by the law*. It is well-protected by deep feelings of togetherness and affection on the one hand, by the mechanisms defining social status on the other.

One need not fear that such reciprocity ever exhausts the relationship between giver and recipient like payment in full does in trade. What Sahlins overlooked is the fact that the completed exchange cemented a new relationship, that of belonging together as friends, and that such a relationship involves a lasting obligation to confirm that friendship by acts of mutual help and renewed gift-exchange.

Finally, we must comment on the obligation to give. In modern society, the duty to give does not bear heavily on one's budget. This does not mean that substantial gifts are not given; but that, if given, they are an expedient means to lower the rate of one's income tax rather than an instrument for creating enduring social relations. Giving is of secondary importance in a society in which business relations prevail over personal relations. Primitive society is different. Because of its small scale, face-to-face relations (that is personal relations) necessarily prevail. Business relations (trade relations) are few or non-existent; trading is done with relative strangers. Trade-friends always are foreigners. In such a society, the ownership of goods is not an end in itself; goods are a means for the maintenance of social relations, or the improvement of one's social position (status). A man cannot keep his goods all to himself without losing status; failing to use his goods for social interaction, he isolates himself from his society. He is mean and of little social use. Besides, he does not lose much if he shares his riches with others. Most goods are perishable goods: food, game, and, to a certain extent, also livestock. In the absence of a market, he can hardly do otherwise than dispose of such goods on behalf of the improvement of his social status. Thus, the successful hunter will distribute the greater part of his catch. Certain parts go to his in-laws, other to his own kinsfolk or to people to whom he is indebted. In time, he will be rewarded; but he can scarcely expect that the reward balances his

* Here again marriage gifts are an exception. Their size having been established by negotiations, they are not vehicles of the givers' appreciation of the recipient's person, but of their appreciation of him and his group as partners in an alliance to which the recipient contributes the basic ingredient, viz. his daughter.

gifts, certainly not if he is an uncommonly skilful hunter. His greatest reward is his fame as a generous hunter.

Similarly, in less primitive conditions, a rich man (a chief, e.g.) will give a feast when a suitable opportunity presents itself, such as the final mortuary feast in honour of his deceased father. A big sacrifice is celebrated where scores of cattle are killed and their meat distributed. What else can he do with his cattle in a society which has no access to the world market, where local wealth cannot be exchanged for anything else than one or two other items of local wealth*? Part of the meat goes to relatives and friendly headmen to whom he is under special obligations. Another part goes to the commoners who, on this occasion, are rewarded for the services rendered and the tribute paid by them in previous years. The balance of reciprocity can hardly be exact. The main point is that the commoners can say: the chief cares for us. A chief must, at times, be generous; certainly where food and cattle are concerned. With unperishable goods (valuables), the rich can be more reticent. They are too precious to be given away on other than formal occasions which are practically always occasions where the rich meet their equals, the leading men of other but related groups. All the same, these valuables too must circulate; they must be used to keep up social relations. This is what they are for. An owner of valuables is not expected to be tardy in the *kula*, the intertribal exchange of the Trobriand people. Valuables must serve the social good.

This leads us to the essence of giving. It is not reciprocity or the anticipation of profit. It is presenting oneself as a partner and doing that in recognition of both one's own and one's partner's social position.

This is why some forms of *potlatch* are a misuse of real gift-exchange, in particular those in which gift-exchange has adopted the distinct features of a contest. Although self-assertion and rivalry are often combined with feasts celebrating a ceremonial exchange of gifts between otherwise loosely related groups, this rivalry has too easily been considered as the real core of the matter. We owe this in part to Mauss who introduced the Kwakiutl word *potlatch* as a generic term for this type of 'total' celebration. What he could not and did not know was that the opulent potlatch celebrations as described by Boas, were products of a period of rapid cultural change during which an impressive increase of all sorts of wealth coincided with a serious decrease of population and a concentration of formerly distant tribal groups round the centres of external trade (Van den Brink 1974). In this situation, potlatch celebrations offered an effective means for reshuffling the traditional power positions. The new rich could manifest their superiority by surpassing the old in magnificence. Such celebrations, however, during which gift-exchange ultimately gave way to the destruction of their wealth by the givers, were a non-violent form of warfare rather than a way of consolidating friendship between otherwise competing groups and chiefs. They are certainly not paradigmatic for exchange celebrations, not even for the

* Today, all this has changed. Everywhere in the world people can bring their produce to the market and get money to buy themselves any of the western goods their money will pay for. However much it is, it will hardly ever suffice to cover their desires. Modern wealth is too immensely variegated. All the same, it has changed the socio-economic conditions so considerably that much of what is described here belongs to the past.

more traditional forms of Kwakiutl potlatch which did not involve such extremes.

Yet, that such aberrations are not really exceptional is borne out by the connotation which the word 'gift' has in German and in Dutch, viz. that of poison, a combination to which Mauss called our attention. Gift-exchange is a so important phenomenon in archaic society that it easily invites misuse. Earlier in this chapter we came across another form of misuse, the bribe. The opportunity to enhance one's status by exalted generosity is an even more inviting form. These aberrant forms, however, have only become feasible because gift-exchange is a most expedient means for the advancement of social relations and the promotion of social solidarity. Properly executed, it confirms the participants in their respective places in society by honouring existing social differences, and it makes life acceptable to the lonely individual who is made aware that he is recognized as a member, a partner. The important effect of the gift is that on the recipient's inner state, the feeling of togetherness which it generates by the recognition of his social position. He is confirmed in his partnership.

c The give-and-take that typifies interaction between the members of small groups is informal by nature, an informality which extends even to the composition of the group. It is not confined to the nuclear family. Often the group is an extended family consisting of a couple of closely related nuclear families, one or two surviving parents and a widowed uncle or aunt. These give-and-take relations even extend beyond the compound occupied by the group and include one or more neighbouring families, a solitary relative living all on his own, or a personal friend. Informal and ill-defined as the group may be, it is always restricted to people who maintain really close and daily-renewed face-to-face relations with one another, people who in their mutual contacts feel at home with each other, an expression that indicates an awareness of belonging together.

As a collective, the small group is, primarily, a co-operative unit. What counts is the daily exchange of services, each member contributing to the common good in proportion to his abilities. No one is supposed to do more than this. The children, the sick and the aged are cared for without complaint. The group protects and supports its members and is, in general, tolerant of their defects and weaknesses. Within the group, there is no question of formal exchange of contributions, but of pooling resources and services, and of redistributing the spoils by someone who has authority in the group. Members of the group can make a present of certain things to one another as gifts, but not by the way of formal gift-giving. Seemingly an exception is the gift-exchange attendant on ceremonial occasions which include participation by relatives from outside, such as the celebration of the passages phasing a child's growing up, like a first ceremonial hair-cut, giving a child its first armlet, piercing its earlobes, a boy's circumcision or his formal entrance into the men's house community. However, the gift-exchange which goes with such a celebration is a matter between the leading members of the host- and the guest groups rather than between members of the small group among themselves. Formal gift-giving inside the small group is practically limited to the exchange of birthday- and christmas presents in modern society where, for reasons to be discussed in part IV, festive gift-exchange lost its significance for the maintenance of the social fabric and was restricted almost exclusively to the confines of the family group (below: 290).

The attitude of the members of a small group towards one another is qualified by tolerance. They bear each other's peculiarities with equanimity, though not *ad infinitum.* Lingering sickness or protracted infirmity in old age can become too burdensome to the group. If there is no hope of recovery, the sufferer, in some societies, may be killed or abandoned; more often than not with his own consent. It would lead too far if we tried to quote cases, and we confine our comment to the remark that such savage cruelty has a parallel in the undue prolongation of the suffering of the incurable sick in many modern hospitals.

Of greater importance are the exceptions to the rule of tolerance caused by a member's failure to fulfil his duties. The least that is expected of anyone, weak or not, is that he shows a willingness to co-operate. When doubts arise with regard to a member's good intentions, the first reaction is to remind the offender of his or her duties in terms of reciprocal obligations. In the daily practice of the small group's life, the principle of reciprocity may appear to be muddled because nobody feels the need of keeping an account of every member's contributions, but this does not mean that the principle is not valid. It is held in reserve to be put forward as soon as doubt arises about anyone's willingness to adhere to the rule as the guiding principle of interaction.

On such occasions, serious conflicts can arise. A study of the casuistics of such conflicts would be instructive, but lead us far beyond the limits set to a simple inventory of leading traits. One of the latter is that the margins of tolerance appear to be narrowest in the relations between husband and wife. If a wife fails to prepare her husband's food, the latter may beat her with a stick or a piece of firewood; if a husband is lazy or too exacting, the wife may run off. It is of interest that, whatever the rule of marriage residence, one of the pair is by origin an outsider, at least if we except the case of patrilateral parallel cousin marriage. Conflicts between parents and children, between siblings, or with close friends and aged relatives who belong to the small group are not unknown, of course. In fact, they are not even an exception. The main difference is that they are rarely as violent as those between husband and wife, conflicts which more easily result in the group's lasting dissolution than conflicts between those who are born members of the group. The latter, too, may end in fission of the group. Conflicts between brothers often do. Yet, such conflicts rarely lead to lasting hostility. If the group breaks up, it does not usually lead to such a complete rupture of relations between the dissenting groups as a divorce does. Parents, siblings and close relatives generally have things in common which husband and wife have not: prolonged co-habitation since early infancy, the sharing of experiences through a series of years, and a common network of family relations. Parents, children and siblings have a great part of their social identity in common. They belong more together than husband and wife. They are a unit by virtue of their origin, whereas husband and wife must try to constitute one.

The devotion of the members to their group and to each other can be conveniently

102

described as an identification of the subject with the group of which he is a part, a qualification which tallies with Sahlin's characterization of their interaction as the solidary extreme. It can also be seen as a fulfilment of the requirement, incumbent on everyone, to act as part of his universe when acting as a subject.

Yet, such a description is rather an over-simplification of the case. It is rather dubious to say that the members of the small group are motivated to act toward each other as they do by identifying themselves with the group as such. Give-and-take behaviour is not limited to the family unit, but extends to more remote relatives, friends, and neighbours, some of whom are simultaneously members of other small groups. Besides, such an extension to others is selective. One neighbour or relative is included, another is not although, formally, he is equally close. In fact, those selected are helped and help in turn because they like each other.

It is not really different inside the family. A father taking care of a sick son, a mother nursing a baby, do not do this because the children belong to their family but because they feel compassion for them. They may, in a way, identify themselves with their offspring, but what actually motivates them is feelings of affection. Their impact should not be underrated. Primitive people go to great lengths to express such feelings when a member of the family dies. They indulge in heart-rending wailing. The expression of their sorrow may be stimulated by the social conditions which prevail locally, but there would be nothing to express with such vehemence without underlying feelings of affection. There is little point in trying to reduce these feelings to an identification either of the subject with the group, or of the beloved with the ego. They are just sad, bitterly sad. Similarly, the daily social interaction of a close, face-to-face nature arouses awareness of togetherness and belonging, feelings of affection which motivate the interactors to mitigate the application of the rule of reciprocity to one dictating reciprocal intents and feelings rather than reciprocal contributions. The participants take one another's well-being to heart and rejoice that the others are there; that they exist. The affections they feel for each other constitute the group rather than that these affections follow from the consideration that each of them is a member of that group. To a certain extent the group is an abstraction, the members never are. They are real, living persons who interact. They do not always do it harmoniously, far from it, but without certain feelings of affection nothing would come of it. They must feel at home with each other. A feeling, being the awareness of an inner state, affirms a reality which otherwise might be doubted.

3. Reciprocity in the exchange of injury. Conclusion

The previous pages may have conjured up an over-flattering picture of primitive society. Concentrating on positive phenomena like trade, barter, gift-exchange and the solidarity of the small group, little attention has been paid to egoism, jealousy, hatred and violence which, in primitive society, are of as frequent occurrence as anywhere. Wrongs occur, and they provoke reactions.

Every wrong is an injury. The most drastic form of wrong is that which adds insult to injury, because every injury is in itself already an insult. Injury is the factual denial of the victim's rights and position, it ignores the fact that the victim is part of society. The injury touches him at the most sensitive spot of his self-experience, his partnership in his social universe. Consequently, every injury provokes violent emotional reactions which seemingly upset the balance of reciprocity. If one feels that strict reciprocity can be effected by repairing the material damage caused by the injury, then indeed the exigence of a punishment, i.e. the infliction of an additional harm, necessarily seems excessive. But it is not merely the material damage which must be compensated; the insult too must be balanced and this can only be realized by the infliction of a harm called punishment. It is the administration of a punishment that makes reciprocity properly balanced.

In practice, however, judicial reciprocity is rarely so well balanced as the theory pretends, and the careful adjusting of the punishment to the gravity of the crime suggests. In spite of the minute specifications of the kind and maximal duration of the punishments laid down in penal codes, the administration of penal law repeatedly infringes the balance of reciprocity. We must go deeper into this and we turn first of all to the punishment of crime in primitive society.

In contrast to modern society, the judiciary of primitive society is at best weakly developed. Sometimes a judiciary is woefully absent, in other cases powerless and for the implementation of its verdicts dependent upon public opinion and the unsteady balance of local power relations. E. A. Hoebel's *Primitive Law* is a revealing document on this point. It demonstrates that the notion of crime in the sense of an act provoking correctional intervention by an independent authority, is widely lacking. In primitive society there are only torts, not crimes. The injured party must itself take the initiative to obtain justice; if a judiciary is lacking by taking the law into its own hands (which easily leads to revenge pure and simple) or, if there is one, by publicly denouncing the culprit and claiming his punishment by the authority concerned. This authority is not an independent judge. He may be related to either party; and, even if he is not, this does not imply that he is free in his decisions. To be a judge is only one of his functions which, in their entirety, focus on his duty to take the internal peace of the community at heart. The system need not work out as badly as it seems to us, but it certainly burdens the parties concerned with greater responsibility for intra-group relations than a modern citizen is ever expected to shoulder.

A closer examination of the administration of justice in primitive society gives ample evidence that legal security here is minimal, and that crimes can be committed without anyone lifting even a finger. A man who kills his father or his brother may go unpunished because there is no one interested or aggrieved deeply enough to denounce him and shoulder the responsibilities and troubles inherent in the role of an accuser. Outsiders may take the crime to be a family affair in which it is not up to them to interfere, and the members of the family may agree to abstain from action in order to prevent further dissensions.

Another possibility is that a man may be killed by a member of a group which is superior in power to his own. The injured party, who would not hesitate to take revenge if powers were more or less equal, will probably abandon the plan to retaliate openly, and resort either to sorcery or to accept some form of arbitration leading to the payment of an indemnity, i.e. 'weregeld'. Payment of weregeld does not necessarily remove bad feelings (it rarely does) but it has the virtue of making relations tolerable, and in spite of its inadequacy it is of frequent occurrence. The rule of an eye for an eye and a tooth for a tooth is not such a hard law in primitive society as is often thought. It is a good formulation of the ideal of balanced reciprocity, but not of what actually happens.

What really happens can, perhaps, be best illustrated by what occurs when an Australian aborigine commits adultery with another man's wife (R. & C. Berndt 1964: 293 f.; Meggitt 1962: 101; Spencer & Gillen 1927: II 467 f.). If the offended husband catches the offenders in the very act he may kill both of them on the spot. Similarly, if the two have decided to elope and happen to be overtaken by the husband and his party, they may pay with their lives. But if they manage to escape – as they usually do – an arrangement is by no means excluded. In secret, negotiations are opened and after a year or so they may be allowed to return after accepting punishment. In a public meeting, the male culprit must meet the offended husband and listen in silence to all the abuse which it pleases the latter to heap upon him. Then follows an uneven duel. The defendant is only allowed the use of a shield. He may not retaliate while the accuser throws his spears at him; he may only try to ward them off. Once the plaintiff has managed to draw blood (preferably by hitting the defendant in a thigh, but if the latter has bad luck the result may be far worse) the ordeal is over. In the meantime, the woman has been given a severe thrashing by her own relatives. The adulterous pair is now permitted to rejoin the group as husband and wife. The woman does not return to her former husband who, by now, may have found a more congenial substitute. The point of interest for us is that, in the case of taking the wrongdoers in the act, the injured party has the right to kill them. It is a right of clearly unbalanced reciprocity provoked by the strongly emotional impact the discovery has on the offended husband. However, once feelings have cooled down, a more appropriate arrangement becomes possible provided that the wrongdoers are willing to atone for their crime. In the arrangement, the offended husband finds his rights publicly recognized by the community which grants him the privilege to abuse and to harm his opponent. Though his wife is not restored to him, he finds satisfaction in the thrashing dealt out to her by her own relatives.

The important point is the atonement. Another case, borrowed from Amerindian ethnography, has been beautifully described by Hoebel (1954: 151 f.). Two Cheyenne youngsters, ignoring the explicit prohibition of the chief, rode out to attack a herd of bison. They were overtaken, their horses shot, their rifles broken, and they themselves were severely whipped. Subsequently, they had to appear before the chief who rebuked them rigorously for ignoring his commands. They listened in silence. What happened then is noteworthy. The chief inquired who had spare horses and rifles. Shortly after this, the boys received new rifles and horses and were readmitted to the band.

Here again the essential point is the atonement, the acceptance of a deserved harm. It restores them to membership of the group. Reciprocity (a harm for a harm) is evident, but this reciprocity is not balanced. The former husband did not have his wife returned to him, the harm done by the youngsters (startling the bison which might take another direction) is not annulled, the weregeld does not restore the slain relative to life. There is reciprocity but it is incomplete, just as incomplete as it is in modern society which punishes a homicide with imprisonment.

Of course, in modern society, a murderer can be sentenced to death. But apart from the fact that this rarely happens, is so-called capital punishment really a punishment? The consequences are in any case basically different from those of other forms of punishment. Capital punishment does not lead the culprit back to society, but ousts him for ever. He is eliminated. Besides, in contrast to a normal punishment which begins with its 'execution', capital punishment ends with it. And even if the execution is preceded by torture (a stiffening of the punishment not uncommon in Europe until well into the eighteenth century) the capital punishment as such is a deliverance rather than a chastisement. In fact, capital punishment is not a punishment at all. It is a revenge, an act of war directed against a person whose behaviour classed him as an enemy of the society and thus has to be treated as an enemy by killing him. The difference between punishment and revenge is parallel to that between chastisement and war. War and revenge deny the presence of social ties; the criminal does not (or no longer) belong to the society and must be annihilated as an enemy. On the contrary, the punished criminal is considered as a member of society who went astray, and must be led back to proper behaviour by atonement.

Revenge and punishment have in common that they reciprocate a harm with a harm. In the case of revenge, the reciprocity implied is often evenly balanced but if it is not, the balance is to the detriment of the wrongdoer. In the case of punishment, the reciprocity is rarely well-balanced and the imbalance is to the wrongdoer's advantage. In revenge, the overtones of hurt feelings easily lead to excess; there is a parallel here with the gift-exchange between persons of different rank. A blow must be reciprocated with a superior blow to turn the victim of the first blow into the superior of his adversary.

Punishment is more complicated. Here, too, feelings play a role. The criminal is a fellow-member of the society; he erred and must be brought back to social acceptance by correction and atonement. But there is more to it than just this; punishment is administered not by the victim of the crime but by the society concerned. The original victim can have a role in it as in the case of the Australian adulterers, but society as a whole intervenes and superintends. Preferably, the punishment is dealt out by an authority, the chief or the community at large, and in the case of a transgression inside the family by one of its leading members, usually a parent. This implies that the crime is not only a matter for the individuals concerned, but for the group as a whole. The group, represented by its leader, arranges a settlement which restores the victim of the crime to his status and gives the criminal the opportunity to be re-accepted as a member of the group by his atonement. The rule of reciprocity is maintained but not allowed to attain full balance. The effect of the rule is mitigated for the sake of social peace. Hurt feelings are granted recognition but they are not allowed to flare up; they are calmed down to the extent that atonement can lead to reconciliation.

106

In this context, it is of specific interest that truly balanced reciprocity, though rarely found in the administration of criminal law, is the hard and fast rule in that of civil law. In a civil lawsuit, no attention is paid to feelings. They are ignored. The whole process is focussed on the material consequences of the conflict, on rights and benefits or on the damage caused by a tort. These consequences are carefully weighed and the balance defined which the contending parties must make good. The civil lawsuit is closely parallel to a trade transaction. In both the ideal of balanced reciprocity reigns supreme. They are matters of goods, not of persons.

Conclusion. Balanced reciprocity is a hard and fast rule for all interhuman conduct but the balance suffers infringements when the interactors occupy unequal social positions. In trade this is never the case; the interactors are persons interested in goods and as such they are equals. In other forms of exchange, social positions count more heavily. If they differ markedly, the difference affects the balance of reciprocity. Infringements are to the benefit of the one in the inferior position. In gift-exchange the rich must give more than the poor; in the give-and-take in small groups the strong and the capable bear the burden of caring for the weak and the sick; in punishment the culprit accepts an inferior position by atonement and is thus allowed to pay back for his crime less severely than he ought.

In all this, the social good takes precedence over the rigidity of the rule, not by denying social differences but by making them explicit in a manner which binds social superiority to socially superior acts of generosity, helpfulness, and forgivingness. The rich, the powerful and the expert find recognition by bearing their burdens in conformity with their pretentions. By thus adapting the balance of reciprocity to the unbalance of social conditions, participants find themselves consolidated in their positions as partners in the total social fabric, each in a position of his own, which, be it high or low, enables him to feel at home in a world in which togetherness prevails. Social scientists feel inclined to attribute all this to the social mechanism ruled by the principle of reciprocity. By putting it this way, one fundamental fact is overlooked, viz. that there is no mechanism. What there is in social reality is persons, persons who enter into relations with one another by deeds which, as carriers of intent, engender feelings of social solidarity and mutual acceptance.

If, at this point, our summary stopped, our picture of archaic society would be unduly flattered. Of the four forms of exchange here discussed, trade, gift-exchange, give-and-take, and the punishment of crime, only two are connected with workaday life, namely the hard negotiations which make for balance in trade, and the informal give-and-take which is restricted to members of closely knit units. Gift-exchange and the administration of justice belong to the world of ceremony, to the great occasions which language rightly typifies as holidays (holy-days). The benevolence incorporated in the gift, the mercy combined with a redeeming punishment, are not daily events but rare opportunities for adjusting and repairing social relations damaged in the course of daily life by, respectively, thoughtlessness and crime. Human beings are not always kind to each other. It is true that, as a subject, man must be part of his universe; but it is equally true that the subject is constantly at war with his universe, trying to make it part of himself instead of making himself part of his universe.

VI

Authority and Power

1. Authority

The term authority refers to legal or rightful power. Authority is attributed to laws and rules; to governments and institutions disposing of administrative and executive powers; positions of power and persons occupying them; to certain opinions and to persons of scientific or moral eminence. They are all treated with respect; their statements and decisions invite esteem and obedience. Authorities, whether institutions or persons, are superior to ordinary people. An authority-relation is a relation of inequality, one in which the superior can command and the inferior has to obey. The earliest interhuman relationship in the life of every man and woman is of that kind, viz. one in which they are submitted to the authority of their parents; first to their mother, later also to their father. It is only natural that this is so; children being perfectly dependent on their parents' care for many years, it could not be otherwise. Yet, this dependency comes to an end upon reaching maturity. The relation with the parents changes; but, ordinarily, the child continues to pay respect to his parents and to follow the rules and laws which they taught him to obey. He does so, it is said, by the force of habit. It is a weak explanation (the force of habit is small anyhow) and it certainly does not explain the fact that, after reaching maturity, the young man or woman persists in accepting a position of inferiority towards so many other people than the own parents, paying respect to them and obeying their commands. Why do they? Why do they give support to these unequal relations by accepting them? We have to examine the implications of the phenomenon of authority.

The core concept is that of legal or rightful power. Power, in this context, means primarily "the opportunity a person has to restrict the behavioural alternatives of other persons or groups" (Van Doorn & Lammers 1964: 66). However, what is the meaning of the qualifications 'legal' and 'rightful'? They are not synonyms; the word 'rightful' carries more personal conviction than the term 'legal'. When we say that a power is rightful we mean that, in our eyes, the power is just and equitable, or fully competent to decide in the matter under discussion. Our personal agreement gives unconditional support to a rightful authority. This is not necessarily the case when we state that the power is legal. It is no more than a statement of fact affirming the juridical validity of a law or rule, or the formal competence of the official person to decide in certain matters. The statement does not say that we, personally, agree with the law and accept it as just, nor that the legally competent official is materially competent. We may be of the opinion that he is a bungler, a criticism which, in a democratic society, we need not suppress. Of course, it is also possible that the legal power is perfectly rightful, but this happy coincidence is not included in the term legal.

The judgement 'rightful' implies the speaker's support. In this, rightful is more than legal but, sociologically, legal has a wider impact than rightful. The latter qualification is, after all, no more than a personal judgement, whereas the use of the term legal implies the recognition by a social group of the competence of the authority and the validity of the rule. The word legal refers to the *leges* of the society, that is to its accepted rules. Legal competence is a competence founded on the rules of the society concerned. The point is important because rules have such a wide impact on human life. In the previous chapter (p. 92 f.), it was argued that man's passion for making rules originates from the ordering activity of the mind. Unconsciously and consciously man devises and follows rules. Sometimes he also breaks or amends them, in particular when conscious rules are concerned. When he breaks a rule two things can happen. Either he disobeys because he feels that his private desires are more important than any rule, or he excuses himself by appealing to another rule. If the first is the case, he is well aware that he is in the wrong. He can ignore this, but it can also give him a guilty conscience, or, more probably, raise the need to have an excuse ready, which leads him to the second solution, that of self-justification on the ground of other rules.

The transgressor's frequent inclination to justify his aberrant behaviour suggests that rules have a peculiar power over man. Is there some such thing as an inner trend to respect rules? Man more often obeys the rules than he disobeys them. In view of the ease by which man obeys the unconscious rules of his language and classification schemes, one might think of some innate bent to respect rules, the effect of the ordering activity of the mind which (above: 93) we recognized as a real structure. This, however, would be most unlikely. Conscious rules are objects of thought, objects also of deliberate amendment or initiative. Why should man pay special respect to rules which he helped devise himself, of which he is himself a co-author? Certainly not because of his own share in their introduction or persistence, far less because of some innate bent towards obedience, but because the real author of the rules is not any individual but the society at large, the authority which really counts because it represents all the moral and material power that can be mobilized.

Society is the ultimate legislator as far as rules are concerned, and the claims it makes on respect for these rules is extended to all those who must supervise their observance. "Social authority may be defined as the right, vested in a certain person or persons by the consensus of a society to make decisions, issue orders and apply sanctions in matters affecting other members of the society" (quotation from J. Beattie by G. Balandier, 1972: 40). At the back of laws and rules, of authorities and supervisors stands society, the human part of any man's universe as conceived by him.

The respect paid to rules and authorities is founded on man's respect for his universe, the supreme power man must submit to, preferably as a participating part and, if not, as the vanquished in a lost battle. The legality of a rule or authority implies a claim on the respect of every member of the society concerned and this claim is made by the society itself; the qualification 'rightful' makes similar claims but has no other backing than that of the individual unless it goes combined with that of legality. Rightful is a praise, legality a fact.

The term 'legality' refers to law, and this raises an in this context relevant problem, that of the universality of the difference between rule and law. Every law is a rule, but not every rule is a law, i.e. a rule the observance of which is sanctioned by an authority. Do primitive societies know laws? Early anthropologists believed that these societies are custom-ridden, which makes the distinction between rule and law senseless, because it implies that primitive people invariably adhere to their customs. We now know that this opinion is as unfounded as the even earlier view that primitive people are wholly lawless. Yet, difficulties remain. The rules of a primitive society are rarely formulated clearly and, even if they are formulated and have the form of a law (because a sanction is attached to transgression) it is often done in a manner which makes it practically certain that the law will seldom be applied. A good example is that of the frequently given assurance that theft, adultery, or the violation of the rules of exogamy are always punished by death. That this rarely happens is not amazing, but the fact that repeatedly nothing happens at all, raises doubt about the actual presence of an authority who maintains the law. It was noted earlier that in primitive society the judiciary is weakly organized: so weakly that even the murder of a father or brother can go unpunished (above: 104). In other cases, a homicide can start a feud between two sub-groups without any authority being available to stop it. In feuding, there is no question of punishment but of revenge; a feud leads to acts of war, not to a legal prosecution.

The problem has been taken up by Leopold Pospisil who, in a couple of articles (1956, 1967), since then followed by a more comprehensive study (1971), turned to a careful and detailed analysis of the relevant facts. He argues that we should not base our studies of primitive law on the absence or presence of abstract rules such as those formulated by informants when interrogated by ethnographers interested in law and punishment, but on what actually happens in case of a conflict. If the conflict is submitted for a decision to the group as a whole or to the acknowledged leaders of the group, then the decision given must be considered as a law, at least if the two parties accept it and the group agrees. Law is not a matter of abstract rules but of how to behave or to decide in concrete situations. It is not general formulations that are important, but concrete decisions. They are, or become, law if they meet the following four criteria, each of which is essential for the constitution of a law: the criterion of authority, that of intention of universal application, the criterion of *obligatio*, and that of sanction.

Pospisil's definition of authority is pragmatic: "authority is manifested when an individual (or a group) possesses an influence that causes the majority of the members of the group to conform to his decisions" (1956: 748). What is decisive is "that the decision or the advice of the authority is followed by the rest of the members of the group" (ibid.: 749).

The second criterion is that the decision must have normative value. The principle upon which it is implicitly or explicitly based, will also be followed in future. More often than not, this principle coincides with some existing custom or rule; in which case the decision simply confirms its continuous validity. There is no problem about its legitimacy, as can arise when the authority's decision introduces a new principle for solving a moot problem. It all depends upon the group's willingness to accept the decision, a willingness which soon makes itself manifest in the implementation of the decision and afterwards in the appeal which occasional litigants make to it. If the new principle meets with approval, it soon becomes integrated into the society's culture as a customary law. If not, there is a good chance that later conflicts will lead to decisions based on more conservative principles.

The third criterion states that the decision must refer to an *obligatio*, i.e. to a duty of the one and a right of the other party. Without it, there could be neither a reason for conflict nor a reasonable ground for a decision. The *obligatio* is the form about which the parties dissent. Finally, there is the sanction as the last essential criterion of law. Sanction can have many forms, ranging from admonition to the compulsory repair of damage, and from derision and shaming of the culprit to his corporeal punishment. The application of the sanction is, normally, a public affair on the occasion of which the group lines up against the culprit, signifying that the infringed rule is not an invention of the authority, but a rule of the group which gives support to the authority.

In Pospisil's views not every rule is a law. There are transgressions which are never punished, either because the rule is a so-called dead law or rule, one which has lost its validity in the eyes of the group, or because for some reason or other the authority does not think it necessary to intervene. A custom which never led to an authority's intervention becomes law when an authority enforces its observance by a sanction and rules that, from now on, this sanction shall be applied.

In this pragmatic concept of law, there is no room for criteria of an idealistic nature, such as the juridical norm of equity. This does not mean that the principle is ignored. It can be largely respected, but equity is not a necessary condition for the constitution of law. Even a shockingly unjust decision (to us at any rate) can be law, also in the sense of accepted *ius*, provided the decision answers the four criteria of authority, intention of universal application, *obligatio*, and sanction.

The advantage of this concept of law lies in its most immediate consequence, i.e. the recognition that every organized group has its own law or laws. In the case elaborately described by Pospisil, that of the Kapauku of (what is now) West Irian, these groups are: the nuclear family, the sub-lineage, the lineage, and the confederation. The most encompassing group is the confederation, the smallest the nuclear family. In all of these we find at least one person who is recognized as an authority, not a formal authority usually, but a man whose advice is sought and whose decisions tend to be followed, be it with occasional exceptions. In his comment (1971: 343) Pospisil writes:

111

"The essential feature of law ... is the fact that the adjudicating authority who passes a decision has to have power over both parties to the dispute or, in other words, he must possess jurisdiction over both litigants. In sociological terms this means that ... the parties to the dispute as well as the authority have to belong to the same social group ... In this sense, then, law is an intragroup phenomenon ... Law is not floating around in an unstructured way in a society. Furthermore, it belongs only to functioning, politically united groups. As a consequence a society segmented into politically *independent* lineages cannot and does not have an overall legal system. In this sense there is no law of the Nuer or Kapauku. That, however, does not mean that there is no law within these tribes ... As a matter of fact there are as many legal systems in segmented or other types of societies as there are functioning groups".

An intriguing feature of the Kapauku authority-system is the hierarchy of its constituents: family heads, sublineage heads, lineage heads, headman of the confederation. Superficially, it looks like a well ordered system of ever more inclusive levels of authority. However, an authority of higher level has no say in matters which regard one of lower level. Kapauku adjudication does not recognize the right of appeal; a lineage headman cannot overrule a decision of a sublineage headman of his lineage. There is only jurisdiction in the first instance, of a family head over his wives and children, of a sublineage head over members of the sublineage who belong to different families, of the lineage head over litigants belonging to different sublineages of the lineage. Even the headman of the confederacy can only mediate in conflicts between members of his own (sub)lineage, or conflicts between members of different lineages which constitute part of the confederacy.

The hierarchy of the authorities includes a minimum of subordination. This is reflected in the actual practice of adjudication. A verdict given by an authority is not a decision which the headman, having heard the litigants and their witnesses, communicates in the form of an order which has to be obeyed, but the final result of an often heated discussion between headman, parties and public during which the headman tries to persuade both the public and the parties involved of the merits of his proposal. It is important that it be accepted by both parties. If not, the conflict will linger on, as the headman's powers to impose his will are small. His position is not based on formal appointment but on his prominence among the members of his group, because of his wealth, his power of oratory, and, occasionally, his prowess in war or his knowledge of magic. Most important of all is his wealth. It enables him to gather a small number of faithful retainers who are indebted to him, e.g. because he assisted them to collect a bride-price. Even so, he cannot afford to deviate too far from the expectations of either his fellows or his followers. Such a following, which a man can acquire by means of his wealth, is not a very stable one. To be really sure of his retainers he must be generous, and generosity and the accumulation of wealth are difficult bedfellows. This sets fairly strict limits to a leader's powers, also to those of the headman of a confederacy who must be a really wealthy man, and a prominent personality besides.

The most effective support to a headman's authority is his ability to organize a pig-feast. Only the really wealthy can. If he succeeds, it is proof of the confidence he inspires. The feast itself is a curious mixture of a market and a ritual. It attracts and temporarily unites people from nearby and from far beyond the borders of the confederacy. In the normally frugal life of the Kapauku, the feast is a rare climax of prosperity and well-being which has important religious undertones which, so far, have not received the attention they deserve (Hylkema, unpublished fieldnotes).

In segmented societies, politically organized comprehensive units are limited in scope. Among Papuan highlanders like the Kapauku they (i.e. the confederacies) rarely exceed some 3000 in number, and it is a fair guess that this also holds true for segmented societies in Africa, such as the Nuer. More encompassing societies need a more effective organization, one in which the various parts have special tasks, if not in daily life then at least on the occasion of the celebration of rituals. Rituals combine various functions in societies with a subsistence economy. They enable people who otherwise hardly ever meet each other, to come together and to co-operate in some common task. The rituals lay a basis for broader contacts than those ensuing from a restricted amount of internal trade and occasional intermarriage between groups. Among the Kapauku, pig-feasts have an electrifying effect; they are the talk of the day during all the long months of preparation in a wide area. More primitive societies like those in Australia combine the celebration of ritual with the establishment or renewal of connubial ties between local clans. The leaders of these clans are often re-incarnations of divine ancestors; they act leading parts in the rituals, combining worldly authority with religious power.

The unifying role of ritual is not confined to primitive society. In peasant societies like those of North Lombok and South Celebes in Indonesia the great rituals constitute the rare occasions on which the outsider can observe the total society functioning; he can see the many functionaries from all over the county acting in their proper place in the total social fabric (cf. i.a. Van Baal 1941). Here also, the worldly leaders play an important part in ritual. Their authority is backed up by their specific relations with the world of the ancestors and gods.

In a similar vein Balandier summarizes the connections between leadership and religion in Africa. The relevant statement concludes with a broad generalization of the religious implications of power in human history everywhere (1972: 99 f.):

> "The lineage or clan 'chief' is the point of contact between the real clan (or lineage), formed by the living, and the idealized clan (or lineage), the repository of ultimate values, symbolized by the totality of the ancestors: it is he who transmits the words of the ancestors to the living and those of the living to the ancestors. The overlapping of the sacred and the political is already, in such cases, incontestable. In modern secularized societies it is still evident; power is never completely emptied of its religious content, which is reduced, inconspicuous, but non the less present. If, when civil society was established, the state and the church were originally one, as Herbert Spencer claims in his *Principles of Sociology*, the state always preserves some of the characteristics of the church, even at the end of a long process of secularization. It is the nature of power to maintain, either in an overt or in a masked form, a political religion. This fact explains Luc de Heusch's brilliant, and apparently paradoxical, formula: 'Political science derives from the comparative history of religions' (1962)".

The passage is of particular interest because Balandier is a leading authority in the field of political anthropology, a discipline for which power and authority are core concepts. Equally illuminating is the following quotation from his work (ibid.: 109 f.):

113

"The relation established between the king and *each* of his subjects is regulated by the principle of authority, opposition to which is equivalent to a sacrilege; the relation established between the king and the *totality* of his subjects is seen in terms of the complementary dualism. It is reminiscent of a formula of ancient China. 'The prince is *yang*, the multitude *yin*'. The sacred and the political together contribute to the preservation of the established order; their respective dialectics are similar to that which constitutes that order – and together they reflect that which is proper to any system, real or theoretical. What men revere through the guardians of the sacred and the depositaries of power is the possibility of constituting an organized totality, a culture and a society".

The origin and foundation of man's respect for authority could not have been expressed more lucidly than here by Balandier. It is not because of the authority's physical power, but because he represents the order of the society and the order of the universe as a whole. Rules are the essence of the universe. The authority who supervises their observance, is rules incarnate. The English language very appropriately calls him a ruler. Rules are man's guides in his intercourse with his universe; the ruler imposes and maintains them. Rules are the exigencies of the universe. They must be respected and the homage paid to them is reflected in the homage paid to the ruler, the authority who is the symbol of the society's power and will.

Seemingly, the conclusion is evident. Still, it raises a question: can a universe or society really have such authority that the subject – always experiencing itself as other than its world – feels innerly obliged to subordinate himself to it? The supernatural qualities attendant on authority hold a clear indication that man's respect for the society's organized will and its rules is not a matter of his recognition of its superior power, but of his respect for an authority which transcends society, the universe, and the subject alike.

2. Power

The term power denotes the faculty or capability to do something. For anything we do we need power: physical power, economic power, financial power, technical, intellectual, political power, or whatsoever. It depends upon what we wish to do. To walk we need the power of walking; to give a beggar a shilling the financial power of one shilling's worth, and so on. For every form of self-realization the individual needs the power required. So does a group or a society. In the preceding section we discussed the power of authority. It is the power derived from the recognition that, as a power, it is legal or rightful, backed up by the rule which expresses the will of a society. We shall have to return to this form of power presently but we must first pay attention to the implications of power generally.

Power is a highly contradictory attribute that can be used in many ways: legally and illegally, to further the interests of society and to promote those of one's own at the expense of others. Seemingly, within the limits of his power, a person can do as he likes. This is a misconception which overlooks that every form of power has an impact on the social life of a group, represents a position in the universe of its members. No possessor of a power which has social relevance can really be part of his universe and ignore the obligation to use that power in such a way as may be expected of a partner.

In our discussion of the rules of gift-exchange, we came across the case of the rich who are obliged to give more than the poor. Like *noblesse oblige*, so power obliges its owner to use it in a socially approved manner. Not that the owner always does, but it is certainly what he should do. In primitive society, the eminent huntsman shares his bag with others. He is also the one who is called upon to bring down the dangerous predator that infects the vicinity of the village. Similarly, the renowned warrior is invited to lead the war-party. The wealthy man who still has a store of food when all go hungry, has to share at least part of it with the less privileged. Negligence of such obligations recoils on the powerful's own head. The wealthy Kapauku man who is not generous has small influence and will never become a headman. He is a miser and forfeits respect.

In modern society, the same trend can be noticed. The rich are more heavily taxed than the poor, and the wealthy are supposed to contribute more substantially to charity than the average citizen. The higher a person's position in the hierarchy of power, the more is expected of him, and the greater are his obligations. The point is of interest because it implies that the obligations incumbent on power increase with the opportunity to misuse it for selfish ends. It is worth while following the dialectics of power in more detail.

Purely personal power is limited in scope. It is only the power of the individual over against that of other individuals: his physical power, his wit or knowledge in competition with that of others. It does not reach far. Power cannot become really redoubtable unless it be backed up by society by being recognized as legal, as being invested with the authority of the accepted rule. The powers of legally approved wealth, of ascribed authority or acquired managerial position can be tremendous and a permanent temptation to the incumbent to use them for selfish ends. The most impressive case is that of wealth. In a period during which society recognized every form of property as a natural, inalienable right of its proprietor to dispose of at will, the owners of wealth got the opportunity to develop that specific form of wealth management which we call 'capitalism'. Based on the false assumption of ultimate harmony between self-interest and societal interest, it turned economy into a purely impersonal mechanism of which only those could profit who already owned money, or held a position in the machinery of its management. We have learned since that the contents of proprietary rights are not defined by nature but by society, and can be limited accordingly. In contemporary society, enterprise is no longer free. Its socio-economic importance is too great to allow owners to deal with their factories at will. Their rights have been curtailed severely as, in fact, the rights of ownership generally. In this country I have the right to plant as many trees in my garden as I like, but I am not allowed to cut any without being licensed by the town authority. Even the ownership of a tree implies a responsibility vis-à-vis society.

The power inherent in wealth has decreased; but that of the managers has become more important. Their power, however, is challenged by the power of the managers of the unions, and both parties are repeatedly confronted by the power of the government which tries to control their activities by means of a steadily growing number of government officials with managerial powers. Formally, the final word in societal

115

control is with the electorate, a circumstance which places – again formally – great power in the hands of an anonymous mass. In practice, it is the opinion makers who exert a decisive influence; they control the mass media about which no one can say whether they follow or make public opinion. We need not take sides here in the dispute concerning the role of the media in opinion making. The one thing that is relevant in this context, is the dominant role of organized public opinion in the ongoing struggle between the managers of competing parties and interests. Its dominance confirms that everyone in power can expect to be called upon sooner or later to account for the use made of that power.

Power is a responsibility, and it can always be contested. It is most evident in the case of political power. Even in the extreme case of power vested in the person of an absolute monarch who is the recognized symbol of the power of the country under his rule, the monarch's power is far from absolute. Norbert Elias's analysis of the real power exerted by the most successful absolute monarch of European history, Louis XIV, has cogently demonstrated that his real power resulted from his personal ability to utilize his position to balance the powers and interests of competing power groups in 17th century France (*Die höfische Gesellschaft*, 1969b). Being the symbol of the country's power marks a power position, but the contents of that power position and its actual effect on the management of the country depend upon the way that position is used in the contest of conflicting powers on a lower level. It is the privilege of kings that, as symbols of their societies' greatness, they may show their power. That is the advantage they have on lower authorities who must always avoid provoking the jealousy of their rivals. However, to reap full profit of this advantage the monarch must not only be a skilful person; he also needs the backing of public opinion if, as a monarch, he should be more than a symbol.

In a non-European context I once saw this demonstrated on the occasion of a great traditional ceremony in the former princedom of Bayan (North Lombok, Indonesia). Representatives of all the villages in the district poured in to pay their respects to the heirs of the former princes, the district chief and his older brother who acted as a kind of high priest. Among these guests were the headmen of Sesait, a big village which held special allegiance to a competing princely family, that of Bayan West, the feastgivers on this occasion being the House of Bayan East, the one more prominent in rank. I had been informed that for all practical purposes the district chief (being of Bayan East) had very little authority over Sesait. On this occasion however, the Sesait people quite willingly and humbly paid him their respects, recognizing him as their overlord. The chief was honoured as a symbol but as far as they were concerned, he was not supposed to go beyond this. Conversely, the extremely limited power of a constitutional king who is rarely allowed to be more than a symbol pure and simple, can acquire important practical content in times of distress. So the story goes that during the years when the Dutch government took refuge in England because the Germans had invaded the Low Countries, there was only one man among the members of Her Majesty's government, and this one man was Queen Wilhelmina herself. Her leadership was effective because, more than her ministers, she represented national unity, the one thing which counts in a war which, temporarily, obliterates party differences. In moments of crisis, the king's symbolic power can suddenly be actualized as real power, provided the king has the necessary abilities. The queen had them.

A constitutional description of a king's powers (like those of a president) seldom mentions its limitations. He is called the supreme commander of the army and the navy, he appoints and dismisses his ministers at will, judgements are administered in his name, and so on, though everyone knows that his hands are firmly tied by both law and convention. What the constitution says is only true in as far as he acts as the symbol of his country's unity. As such he is the embodiment of the country's rules. This is why he is called a ruler, preferably a ruler by the grace of God. As the representative of the social universe, he is closely associated with the supernatural. And yet, whether his actual power is great or mostly imaginary, whether the picture presented of his power be inflated or not, during the rites celebrating his investment with power, the coronation rites, he is always reminded of the fact that he also has duties. It is the standard pattern of every coronation ceremony in Western Europe. Also in the African rites cited by Balandier (1972) as well as in the Eurasian and Pacific rites commented on by Hocart (1941), the explicit recital of the king's duties is a recurring theme. The king swears that he promises his people equity and protection. Since the days of old, mankind has been aware that power implies a responsibility, and that a king, like a universe, is not only redoubtable but also a bringer of good.

To a certain extent, coronation rites are misleading. The fact that the incumbent ruler promises his people protection and equity, and that the representatives of the latter swear him their allegiance, suggests some sort of a contract between the ruler and the ruled. Is, indeed, the relation between the ruler and the ruled the result of a primeval social contract? The theory of the social contract has played an important role in European history. It was re-introduced into modern political philosophy by Théodore de Bèze, Calvin's successor in Geneva (Halbwachs 1943: Introduction), and it had the merit that it salved the by Calvinism affected consciences of, first, the members of the Provincial States of the Netherlands who, in 1581, decided to abjure their Spanish monarch, and some sixty years later those of Cromwell and his Ironsides when they took up arms against King Charles I. The theory has been further developed in later years; I need only mention the names of Hobbes, Locke and Rousseau. Yet, the theory finds no support in the coronation procedure. It is true that, in its initial phase, the procedure suggests an interaction between two parties who meet each other as equals, one the prospective king, the other the prospective subjects. However, at the moment the agreement is sealed by oaths, the sworn relation which invests the one with power and commits the others to enduring obedience and respect, is made irrevocable and irreversible by ritual acts which turn the prince into the divinely elected one who, from now on, reigns by divine grace. The king is changed into the *Lord's* annointed, not the *people's* annointed. If there was a contract it is, from now on, a contract between the king and God whose annointed he is. There is no longer any question of equality, and if the king fails to live up to his part of the agreement it is open to question whether the people have the right to

117

reject the king. A third party has been introduced to the so-called contract, and that third party is God who gave his blessing. We know from history that rebellion weighs heavily on the consciences of subjects who cherish a grudge against their king, even if they have a well-founded reason to feel injured. The doctrine of the social contract is an excuse for rebellion rather than an explanation of the obedience due to the king. This obedience is based not on contract or oath, but on the fact that the king is the ruler, i.e. the rule incarnate and as such invested with all the authority of society itself, an authority identified with that of the universe, or even with that of the ruler of the universe.

The authority of the universe is reflected in the authority ascribed to the king, and not only in that of the king but – to a minor but by no means negligible degree – in that of all those whose position is, in one way or another, seen as an inevitable part of the world order. In a stratified society the order of the universe guarantees the authority of all who, by birth, belong to the upper class.

Such a society was that of medieval Europe. Norbert Elias in his *Über den Prozesz der Zivilisation* (1969a) has drawn a frightening picture of the unruly violence characterizing the early phases of its history, a violence which subsided only very, very gradually and could not be reduced to acceptable limits before the emergence of strong and well organized states created law and order inside their boundaries. I must refrain from a discussion of his theory concerning the role of the displacement of affects in the process of civilization. I must make fairly strict reservations on this point, but the theory is not at issue here. All that counts is the author's description of the origin and persistence of a warrior class which, for centuries, kept Europe in turmoil. It is a description which presents power as primarily physical power that can only be limited by other physical power, a point of view seemingly realistic, and yet partial. It ignores the fact that power is limited from within, and we have to enter into a somewhat broader discussion of the dialectics involved in power and the protection which it promises as an excuse for wielding it, an excuse meant to justify violence as a noble warrior class's contribution to law and order.

The invasion of Western Europe by Germanic tribes of all sorts had crushed the Roman Empire. It brought a class of warlords to power who were seeking a territory of their own for each of them. Part of his territory each overlord divided among his captains as heritable fiefs. These dukes and counts did the same to reward their barons. Once the ultimate limits to further conquests had been reached, and the opportunities for opening up new land had become scarce because of demographic growth, younger sons saw the way to acquiring a fief of their own blocked. Yet, they did not give up their fighting habits, and everywhere the lords and barons fought each other for more territory, a process which resulted in the survival of the strongest and, finally, in the emergence of a small number of states in which, after many vicissitudes, the kings succeeded in gaining the upperhand and established civil law and order.

Subject to this warrior class was a large population of commoners, mostly the descendents of the early inhabitants of the country, for a smaller part the offspring of the men who once constituted the rank and file of the invaders' armies. From these lower strata of society the lords and barons recruited the manpower for their fighting

118

forces, but a large majority refrained from participation in military exploits. They were the peasants, artisans and traders who, together, served the economy of the territory. The artisans and traders, concentrated in the towns, managed to break away from their overlords' interference in their daily affairs. They established stratified communities of their own. Less fortunate were the peasants. They remained at the beck and call of the local lords who (albeit within the limits of certain rules) were entitled to the peasants' services and tithes. The question is how the warlords managed to maintain their authority over that large majority of commoners? In other words: how did they succeed in getting this social stratification with its inequity and violence accepted as part of an unalterable world order?

The answer is that, in the history of mankind, prolonged periods of peace are the exception rather than the rule. Migrating tribes have been roaming the Eurasian and African continents from time immemorial. The relative peace enjoyed inside the Roman Empire was merely an episode interrupting a long history of violence which rarely ever knew a lack of men willing to make fighting their *métier*. Yet, even a warrior culture is never without its men of peace. No society can endure without them: the warriors need them more than ever, for their food, their clothes, the building of their fortresses and the forging of their arms, in short for everything. They even need them for the sheer fact of their domination. There is no dominance without those who are dominated. But they also need the dominated to support them in times of war. The problem of the warriors was how to combine domination with workable relations that endure in danger and adversities. They needed their vanquished.

There is an age-old, time-honoured model for solving this problem: the self-confirming lie that the strong protect the weak. We have come across it already when discussing the division of labour between the sexes (above: 73 f.). The males do the protecting, fighting and hunting, the females concentrate on planting, collecting, care-giving and child-bearing. Just as the protection provided by the males to the females is nothing more than a protection against the violence of their own kind, so is the protection offered by the rulers and patrons to their protégés a protection against their own kind and manners. They protect them against the dangers provoked by their own aggressive behaviour and bellicosity. The parallel does not stop here. Not only is there a whole lore glorifying masculine virtues (they are all concerned with fighting) as noble virtues, but hunting, the one useful occupation of the primitive male, is up to the present day a noble sport. The commoners who partake in it are commoners who have made headway on the social ladder and can be classified as potential nobility. The lower class hunter is, more often than not, a poacher. The nobles of European history perpetuate the role and pretentions of the primitive male.

The fiction of protection – and it is not even always a fiction: often it is hard necessity – has made deep inroads everywhere in the world. It did in the world-wide system of patronage. It also did in the political notions of medieval and 16th and 17th century West-Europeans. Confining myself to the history of the Low Countries: one cannot read the account of the succession of noble houses holding supreme power over the various counties and duchies without being struck by the fact that the towns and the people generally showed themselves little interested in the origin or linguistic affinity of a new ruler. All they wished of a new lord, whether he were of native, French, German or Austrian extraction, was that he protected them against enemy invasions and that he was willing to vindicate the privileges of the towns. What they minded was the new lord's power to guarantee law and order; personal affection apparently played no role.

The need for protection plays an important part even in the 16th century. Having abjured their Spanish monarch in 1581 (after no less than 23 years of rebellion!) the States General of the United Provinces offer sovereignty to the Prince of Orange who declines, because he feels unable really to protect them. They then offer it to France, to the Duke of Anjou, who makes such a mess of it that soon after the sovereignty is offered to England. Again, it does not last for long. In 1589, after the failure of the reign of Queen Elizabeth's representative, Lord Leicester, the States finally – and unwillingly – decide to do what they should have done in 1581, and take the sovereignty into their own hands. They never regretted it. Yet, their desire for a protector was certainly not a specifically Dutch notion of what a sovereign should be. More than sixty years later Cromwell assumed the title of Lord Protector.

Behind the unwillingness to assume sovereignty lies the notion that sovereignty is associated with military functions and that commoners, though well prepared to fight if need be, are called to more peaceful occupations. We find the ideal of the commoners explicitly formulated in the Confession of Faith drafted by Guido de Bray and afterwards adopted by the reformed churches of the Low Countries and France. Its 36th article charges governments with the task of punishing the wicked and of protecting the good, and demands of the latter their prayers for the government "so that we may lead a quiet and secure life in all godliness and virtue".

Some might prefer to explain this final statement as a reaction to the endless wars and turmoil which scourged late 16th century Europe. It certainly is, but this should not make anyone blind to the fact that all through history the commoners, in particular the townspeople, have looked upon war and defence as a task which primarily fell to the noble class. In as far as they craved for political power, it was always local power they coveted, not territorial expansion. The two republics Europe counted before the end of the 18th century, the Netherlands and the Swiss confederacy, never tried to extend their boundaries, something by which princes, perpetuating an old tradition, were invariably tempted.

This wariness to assume and accumulate power is not a really uncommon feature. Of course, political power is a desirable good. It is a tempting opportunity for self-realization. Few people today realize how much effort it takes. Politicians are the hardest working people in the world. Having some personal experience of political life, I have had the opportunity to note what is at stake and how disappointing the prizes are that can be won. Former generations were more willing to leave the power contest to others and to prefer a limited measure of injury to the drudgery of politics and the dangers of military life. It is a kind of wisdom sometimes found even in primitive societies which are so often devoted to aggressiveness and warfare. A good case is that of the Arapesh of New Guinea as described by Margaret Mead (1935;

1936/59). Here, the men are averse to positions of leadership. From among the boys they select a few who seem more assertive than the rest, and they encourage them to become 'big men'. Another case is that of the Zuñi (Ruth Benedict 1934). A third that of the Tarascans described by Van Zantwijk (1967). Their notables, when elected to act as functionaries at the annual festival, are flattered, but realistic enough to call their office a burden and to describe themselves as burden bearers.

However, we should not lay too much emphasis on these more or less exceptional cases. We are dealing with the fiction of protection. A far more general form of it is the widely spread institution of patronage. It is found all over the world. It prevailed in medieval Europe as it does, in fact, in all stratified societies. The system is highly unpopular today. Many social scientists are allergic to it. It is small wonder, because the more detailed descriptions of its implications derive from times and situations when the system was already in decay. With the diversification of wealth and the increasing absenteism of landlords the position of the dependent clients necessarily deteriorated. Personal ties between master and client weakened, and the temptation to exploit tenants increased with the opportunity to spend money on luxury at home or a second household and the extravagancies of a courtier's life in a distant town. In times when luxury was scarce and the articles of wealth available contributed little to its owner's personal comfort, a patron had little reason to embitter his clients' lives with extravagant demands. Moreover, if he was not a really big lord, he knew his clients personally. He had grown up with them when a child, and had learned all the ramifications of their ways of life. The accounts of early medieval peasant life probably give a more negative picture of a client's life conditions than is actually warranted. Granting the fact that these were times of unsurpassed savagery (barbarians are more cruel than primitives!) there were limits to a baron's highhandedness. A client could always try to abscond; and the loss of clients necessarily weakened the master's power. Besides, he had to depend on them in his numerous conflicts with other lords. There is no reason to doubt the veracity of the reports recounting the cruelties committed by barbarious barons and the sufferings they inflicted upon their poor clients; but there is every reason to remember that in times when writing is scarce, written accounts do not primarily describe what is common, but what is extraordinary. When all is said and done, a master has to rely on his clients and this reliance can be enforced only in fairly exceptional cases.

In this context, it is not without interest what Mousnier writes on the relations between master and client in 17th century France, a time when the decay of the system had already set in and abuses may be expected to have increased:

"Often the manor constitutes a truly human community, the squire keeping up relations with his people which are founded on the protection-loyalty model. True, one easily finds cases of brutality or cruelty by abuse of power. In the Basse Auvergne some of the squires are tyrants, brutes... In Bretagne the poor lower nobles, men who reside in thatched manors which hardly differ from farm houses, men also who rarely join the army, have a reputation for idleness, inebriety and brutality. Apparently, the stick played a prominent part in their relations with their tenants. Yet, more numerous are, in Bretagne, in Normandy, in the Auverge, in the Limousin, the instances of squires who behave as family chiefs, as heads of the community, as protectors. There are many cases of squires who invite footmen or maid-servants recruited from the rank and file of their tenants, to stand as godfathers and godmothers at the baptism of their infants. Squires act as co-signatories of the marriage contracts of the villagers, are godfathers of their infants, and participate in the village feasts. They have a great influence in the affairs of the villages and local communities in their domains. Sheriffs, aldermen, mayors and notable inhabitants solicit their advice and more often than not follow the squire's lead. The squire takes action in difficulties with the functionaries of the treasury and with bailiffs, interferes against soldiers and military collectors of the *tailles* [a tax], against military troops passing the area, against the armed bands which another gentleman in his district has dispatched to loot, to take vengeance or to restore his prestige, outrages occurring even in the midst of the 18th century. In his castle or fortified manor, the squire gives shelter to his farmers and their cattle. He arms his attendants and the servants of his house, his *familia*; he assists his tributaries in arming themselves, gives orders to shoot at aggressors with arquebusses or matchlocks and, if need be, he turns to a counter-offensive. In times of dearth, it is his duty to give support to his peasants, and quite often he acquits himself of this duty effectively. All these activities are aspects of the traditional seignorial life which have left fewer traces in the archives than disputes on leases and the conditions of tenancy, but they are aspects which should be studied more systematically" (Mousnier 1974: 410).

We conclude that the system of patronage in 17th century France did not differ significantly from that elsewhere as, for instance, in Indonesia and New Guinea in colonial times. Here, in my role of administrator, I noticed repeatedly that the so severely condemned pattern of colonial paternalism is solicited by an attitude of filialism.

Everywhere filialism is the traditional attitude. The local lord is invited to decide when important decisions are at issue. This does not mean that he is free to proceed without consulting the villagers; they wish to be heard but they are ready to leave the final decision to their lord. At times, even slaves can hold important positions as advisers. In pre-capitalist societies, slavery never reached that apex of cruelty which was the rule on North- and Latin American plantations. In the small sized communities of peasant society, the relations between patron and client are necessarily of a more personal nature; the patron is a father figure rather than a commander. He is the man who has relations well beyond the boundaries of the local community, the man who is responsible for inter-community contacts. Although he is in a position which allows him to assert his will and to act against the desires of his clients, he cannot go too far, lest his clients leave him. Customary law in Bali recognized the villagers' right of resistance against an unjust and tyrannical chief and to have him replaced by a more agreeable one (Korn 1932: 289, 340).

The system of patronage is typical of stratified societies all over the world. The transition to a market economy leads to its deterioration for the reasons mentioned on p. 121. Yet, it takes a long time before the system collapses. The habit of letting the lord make the important decisions, and that of seeking his advice in matters which are beyond the ordinary peasant's horizon, persists for a much longer time than is in the peasants' own interest. Even when they change masters, they remain true to the established pattern. Chasing their one-time masters – as they did in the colonial revolutions all over the world – they follow their new political leaders with equal faithfulness as they once did the old. During the years of the Indonesian revolution, I noticed with amazement that the demeanour of some union leaders vis-à-vis the members of their union closely resembled that of the old feudal lords with regard to their clients.

Sometimes, the people's attachment to their traditional leaders constitutes a serious brake on the process of change. Recently, Van Bruinessen described such a case in his *Agha, Shaikh and State,* a study of the social and political organization of Kurdistan (1978). There too, when new, more progressive leaders are accepted, the old attitude of unquestioning loyalty to the master persists. One of the distressing phenomena of political history is that the great revolutions, whatever else they achieved, rarely resulted in a real change in the power system. The French revolution brought an emperor to the king's empty throne, and the Russian revolution replaced the czar and his boyars by a party secretary and his apparatchik. Today, before our very eyes, we can see the history of the Latin American revolution repeating itself. There, round about 1820, a local élite stepped into the shoes of the metropolitan government and perpetuated its colonial-style rule. The same now happens with slight variations in almost all the new states which, since the late 1940's, have gained independence.

What persists is the attitude of reliance on authority and of respect of its power, an attitude promoted by a type of early education which discourages the taking of responsibility and teaches the child to accept guidance by others. The point of interest here is that the respect of power goes hand in hand with an aversion to taking responsibility, a negative way of confirming our view that power and responsibility belong together. A power position is always a position in a universe, a fact which favours the chances that it be given a place in a religious world order of which, more intensely than of the universe as such, people expect the good life even when they bow to its wrath. One of the disadvantages of the association of power positions with a religious world order is that it tends to sanctify the inequities of the existing power system as proofs of divine wrath instead of taking them for what they are: culpable failures in responsibility. Even if they blame the authority, people do not easily rise to resistance. They abide until a leader arises who announces himself as a rightful substitute, or succeeds in persuading the people that the prevailing system of authority runs counter to the true order of the universe. In the first case, a rebellion brings a change of personnel but leaves the system intact, in the second case, revolution follows which does not confine itself to changing the personnel, but also introduces a new system. We noted already that the new system tends to resemble the old one more closely than its leaders pretend.

We come now to the final question: What is the conclusion which, with regard to ethics, can be drawn from this long exposition of man's troubles with authority? In the first place, that an authority who constitutes part of the recognized order of the social universe must be obeyed, and that in actual practice this duty is widely respected. In the second place, that the recognized order of the social universe is prone to controversy, because either the authority itself disturbs this order, or because social change turns the order into a matter of dispute. Man's attitude vis-à-vis his universe is always ambiguous. On the one hand he is subject to that universe and can be regarded as its product; on the other hand, his universe is also his field of action and subject to the changes wrought by man's initiative. Consequently, the rule of obedience is subject to exceptions, primarily exceptions determined by changing notions relating to the rules dictated by the social universe. A specification of these exceptions is not necessary here. It can only lead to casuistry. Our concern is not casuistry but the explanation of universal rules for social behaviour and their effect on the social life of mankind. A critical appraisal of this effect is required before proceeding to our final task; i.e. to inquire into the possibility that these rules converge in a moral law incumbent upon all mankind. The fact that power involves responsibility, holds a promise.

VII

The Moral Law

1. Social reality and the moral law

In the previous chapters consideration has been given to a small number of generally acknowledged rules for social behaviour which, in combination, must have a beneficent effect on social life; the principle of reciprocity, that of respect of authority, and the rule that power imposes a responsibility as well as an obligation, the obligation to give and to do more and better than the powerless. The universality of these principles is consistent with the view taken here, that, as a subject, each individual must be part of his universe and that, as a part of that universe, he must be (and act as) a subject.

Unfortunately, the universality of these principles does not imply that the rules ensuing from them are duly observed or wholeheartedly recognized in practice. The rules express an 'ought' rather than a state of affairs. Social reality deviates widely from the rules which society acclaims. Hostilities, injury, and violence repeatedly poison human relationships. Worst of all, many socially-accepted rules and customs run counter to the principle of the recognition of everyone's right on social partnership, the principle implied in the application of the three general rules or principles already discussed. Power positions have been misused to create social rules for the protection of power positions rather than for the protection of the powerless. Very early in history, the males already created rules which are discriminatory and often even humiliating to females. Later, they proceeded to create rules discriminating between classes of men. One case is that of the introduction of castes which condemn certain groups to impurity and abasement from generation to generation. Another is that which makes the good life a matter of scarce money. Deviations are so numerous and diverse that the suspicion arises that these so called principles are vague ideals, the figments of a worried mind, rather than fundamental and universal norms for social behaviour.

Our doubts increase when we turn to the works of those anthropologists who specialized in the study of ethical behaviour. In contrast to Durkheim, who also was interested in ethics (but subordinated this interest to his account of the forces which hold a society together) these students of ethics until recently preached ethical relativism. The first to tread his path was E. Westermarck, the author of a voluminous work on the ethics of primitive man, *The Origin and Development of the Moral Ideas* 1906/08) and of a more philosophical book entitled *Ethical Relativity* (1932).

We will not deal here with the evidence presented of the great diversity of ethical rules, a diversity which is readily conceded; but with the theory behind it, a theory which effectively prevents the author from ever finding any conformity in the muddle of diversity. Ethics are, to Westermarck, a matter of retributive feelings of approval, controlled and verified by a so-called 'impartial spectator', a character in whom we recognize the impersonation of the gossip about town, and introduced to philosophy more than a century earlier by Adam Smith in his *Theory of Moral Sentiments* (1759). Modern anthropologists would describe this spectator as the 'generalized other'. The theory boils down to the idea that the good is what people say is good, that this differs from culture to culture and that, for unexplained reasons, every culture has to be respected.

Westermarck's choice for philosophical guidance is, to say the least, surprising. The *Theory of Moral Sentiments* is a sanctimonious book in which the reader has great difficulty in recognizing the hand of the author of that later masterwork, *The Wealth of Nations* (1776). Unlike Smith, Westermarck did not become wiser over the years. In 1932 he is still applauding the *Moral Sentiments*, that confusing monument of an astonishing sentimentalism which, for more than a century, had helped the rich to justify their neglect of the poor. *Ethical Relativism* is a weak book. Westermarck had, by that time, become a professor of philosophy, but he ignores Kant's refutation of A. Smith, just as he ignores the work of Freud and of M. Mauss. The basic problems of morality are consistently evaded. Confounding variability with relativity, the un-deniable fact of variability is presented as definite proof of cultural and ethical relativity. The reference to cultural relativism is the one point where the book is abreast with the times.

In those years, cultural relativism was a favourite theory among American anthropologists. It held the view "that man's every word and deed is determined by his culture" (Tennekes 1971: 7) because it is from his culture that everyone derives his standards for judgement. This truism is then treated as a sufficient ground for the conclusion that these judgements must be respected, a conclusion which compromises the validity of both logic and ethics as the judges of the truth of the opinions, and of the intrinsic value of the moral standards which it has pleased the adepts of any culture to adopt as guidelines for their beliefs and behaviour. But Herskovits, the main champion of the theory, had no hesitations on this point:

> "In every case where criteria to evaluate the ways of different peoples have been proposed, in no matter of what aspect of culture, the question has at once posed itself: 'Whose standards?' The force of the enculturative experience channels all judgments. In fact, the need for a cultural relativistic point of view has become apparent because of the realization that there is no way to play this game of making judgments across cultures except with loaded dice" (Herskovits 1958: 270).

In spite of the severe criticism which it aroused (I mention only Bidney, 1953; Redfield, 1953; and more recently Tennekes) the theory had a long life. It is also found in A. Macbeath's book *Experiments in Living* (1952). The work can be described as an ethics of self-expression. Every culture is the expression of a way of life, adopted as an ideal by all. "An idea is morally good not because considered in isolation it seems to be so, but because in fits into, and is expression of the spirit of this way of life"

(1952: 102). Evidently, the way of life is sacrosanct, like culture is in Herskovits's relativism.

The main weakness of this theory lies in the fact that it is man who produces culture (which is not denied) and that, nevertheless, man himself is in everything and at every point defined and shaped by his culture. It is the problem of the chicken and the egg in its most defiant form; and, when consequently pursued, essentially a denial of the possibility of cultural change. It is evident that, as a theory, cultural relativism is not persuasive. If, in practice, ethics are as variable as relativism pretends, what is true then of such rules as those of reciprocity, the respect for authority and the obligations of power?

Ethical rules, however, are not as variable as is often pretended; variations may be extremely numerous, but the margins of variation are fairly rigidly limited. In 1955, in a study noteworthy for its cogent critique of cultural relativism, K. E. Read pointed out that the wide difference between the ethical system of a Papuan tribe and that of modern Christian thought "does not imply the absence of a moral sense or anything we can recognize as an objective standard ... but does indicate a difference in the degree to which the principles underlying right behaviour are abstracted from the social context and related to a generalized concept of the good and of obligation" (Read 1955: 282). And, a few years later, in their *Anthropology and Ethics* (1959), Mary and Abraham Edel presented evidence of an impressive amount of conformity in the variety of moral codes, a conformity which gainsays the relativists' identification of variability with relativity. There could not be such conformity inside variation if there were not something in the minds of men which urges them to analogous reactions in diverging situations. The conformity noted by the Edels suggests that there are certain general principles for human interaction which are common to all mankind. Yet, mankind so often sins against these principles, even up to the extent of devising unjust rules, that one wonders whether they really have their ultimate basis in the human condition and not in matters of convenience or of the logics of power relations.

In view of the strong position held by the subject as the embodiment of a libido which is bent upon self-realization, it would not be surprising if, after all, we found that the rules to which man condescends to submit his conduct, are more a matter of convenience inside a system of power distribution than of inner necessity. Numerous scholars hold the view that the most commanding of all inner necessities is that of egoism, and that power itself is the most persuasive of all arguments. And yet, this is at best a half truth about power. Many people shun power for fear of taking responsibility. Besides, power obliges its incumbent to use it to the advantage of society. He may ignore the obligation in daily life, but he will not fail to live up to it on public and ceremonial occasions by demonstrating his generosity. Though it is true that this generosity enhances his glory and strengthens his position, it is equally true that it costs him dear. And it is a significant fact that on such public occasions social control is strong enough to encroach the balance of reciprocity by reverting the privilege of the rich and the powerful into a temporal disadvantage at the benefit of the poor.

127

The fact that such a reversion of positions is effectuated on public occasions, demonstrates how and what the general public thinks of the obligations incumbent on power; however, that the powerful occasionally comply with these expectations and exigencies, does not prove that they share the public's views and see generosity as a duty. The fact that the rich can use generosity as a means to support their social status, adversely affects the value that can be attached to it. Public generosity easily deteriorates into an instrument for the support of power, giving additional reason to doubt that the noble "general principles for human interaction ... common to all mankind" to which we referred, are the blessed outcome of the human condition. There is ample ground for the suspicion that they are either "matters of convenience or of the logics of power relations".

Yet, these noble principles must have originated somewhere. As ideals of human behaviour, they are too patently universal to be the products of a childish imagination which, for no obvious reason at all, believes in the reality of some such thing as human virtue or compassion. There must be something in the reality of human life and society that evokes this idealism. And, indeed, there is. What is more, it has its ground in the logically and historically most primitive form of social life, in the closely knit family unit, the small group bound by kinship and friendship. It was noted (above: 101 ff.) that in this group no member is supposed to contribute more to the unit's common good than is proportionate to his abilities. In the group formalities do not count for much. What counts is good intentions, and for as long as these are evident, the group can ignore the rule of reciprocity in the daily interaction of its members. Commensality and the readiness to mutual help prevail over the dictates of egoism and self-interest.

It would be wrong to pretend that life in the small group complies with all the ideals of frictionless communality. It does not. Family life knows dissensions everywhere. Adverse customs such as a strict segregation of the sexes may keep the families divided. Yet, where this is the case during the night (as in Melanesia), husband and wife will meet in the privacy of their gardens during the day, where segregation prevails during the daytime (Australia) they will associate during the night. This does not prevent occasional conflicts, nor does it exclude the possibility that relations suffer severely from the daily round and common task; but, in spite of all its recurrent insufficiencies, the small group is a strong and reliable unit, the place where its members feel at home. This becomes apparent when extraneous conflicts arise and the group is threatened by outsiders. Then its members suddenly wake up to togetherness and solidarity. Side by side they defend each other against their assailants. They even do so when they know that the conflict has been elicited by a wrong committed by one of themselves. In conflict, solidarity prevails over reason. This kind of reaction tallies with the fact that in daily life the stronger members of the group are inclined to let the needs of the weak prevail over their private desires.

Is this solidarity simply a matter of self-identification with the group? Just an extension of the ego and its feelings? In a way, yes; but not in the way usually intended, i.e. that of the incorporation of the interests of the others into those of the I. On the contrary, this solidarity is the expression of the individual's partnership in the group, of the self-realization of the subject as a part. The subject does not submit the group to its own ends, but submits the self to the ends of the group. Admittedly, such submission is by no means complete, but the tendency is evident. It is a community where good intents count for more than achievement, above all a community in which the members feel at home with one another. This is by no means insignificant. Of all the affects, that of feeling at home is one of the most rewarding as well as one of the most indispensable. This feeling implies two things, the first of which is the inner certainty of one's own partnership in the group. The second is that of being free to be oneself, i.e. free to express oneself, and free to behave just as one likes, the latter under the understanding that the use of this freedom does not importune other members of the group. Feeling at home thus combines the certainty of being a part with the opportunity to be a subject, a self. This certainty the individual member derives from the circumstance that he is always welcome with the other members of the group. Their mutual relations can be briefly summarized as follows: they welcome each other as partners in their common group.

To be welcome in a common social universe is what every single soul is looking for, what everyone wishes to be; not only in his family, but also in his society at large. It is everyone's desire to find the security of the small private circle extended to the full fabric of his social relations. The feasibility of such an extension is confirmed by occasional deeds of generosity which, whatever the private motives of the benefactor, give substance to the feeling that human interaction should always be based on benevolence and mutual aid. The limited – and admittedly incomplete – realization of full partnership inside the small circle of friends and kin is, in spite of its deficiencies, a hard fact. It sets a model, a model which confirms for all mankind that such partnership should be the fundamental rule for all social interaction and behaviour, a rule which might be formulated as the command to welcome the other – any other – as a partner to one's universe. We hold the view that this command is the essence of the moral law, and lays the foundation for all ethics. In the following sections we have to examine the limitations as well as the ultimate validity of this law. Here, we must first of all examine the implications of this formula of the essence of ethics.

This formula of the moral law is consonant with our analysis of the human condition. If man is a subject who must be a part of his universe, and a part of his universe who must be a subject, then the command to welcome the other to one's universe is the logically consistent answer to the human condition. It takes this condition seriously, and meets its exigencies to the full.

Besides, this formula has two important advantages over other efforts at summarizing the essence of ethics. In the first place, it includes a positive evaluation of the affective aspects of human life and thus avoids the legalism of Kant's categorical imperative, the command always thus to act that the maxim directing your will can at all time be validated as a principle of universal legislation (Kant 1920: 39). And in the second place this formula, without neglecting the affective needs, avoids the exaggeration implied in the often advocated ideal of self-denial, a demand that is as impossible as it is unnatural. Man is and must be a self; to deny the self cannot serve any useful purpose. When, as a part of and a partner in his universe, man must subject his self to the exigencies of that universe, he must do so as a self, a subject. Man's partnership in his universe does not turn him into an object, an *automaton* mechanically functioning in the wheelwork of his universe, but implies a dialogue, a direct communication between the self and the agents of his universe.

On the other hand, this formulation of the moral law is anything but intrinsically new. In essence, it is but a rewording of what Joseph Pieper advanced in his erudite and realistic essay on love (1972). For Pieper, love is the essence of all morality. It is saying to the other: *Wie gut dasz es dich gibt, wie wunderbar dasz du da bist*; 'how good that you exist, how wonderful that you are here'. The saying addresses the other as one of us, as received as a partner.

Pieper argues that the act of giving love, of bringing happiness to others, has its reward in itself; it engenders a deep feeling of happiness in the giver. On this ground, he concludes that, in a way, self-love is the true model of all love. However, this true self-love is narrowly prescribed. He does this by quoting a sentence borrowed from Bernard de Clairvaux; "True love does not calculate, and yet simultaneously receives its reward; it can only receive its reward because it does not calculate . . . Who, loving, only wishes the rejoicing of love, receives the joy of love. But he who, loving, seeks other things than love alone, he loses both love and the rejoicing of love all at the same time" (Pieper 1972: 137). The argument, though borrowed from medieval, intuitive psychology, is of interest. It confirms that mankind has always known that there is happiness in goodness, in affectionate communication with one's fellow-men. Essentially, it is the same as saying that man finds happiness in his partnership with others, in obeying the command to welcome his fellow-man to his universe.

However, happiness is a tricky concept. It is of two kinds. There is also happiness in realizing the pursuits of the self, in successes of self-realization; and these pursuits easily run counter to the precepts of ethics. To aver that this is not true happiness, is nonsense. All that can be said against it, is that it does not promote the happiness of others and eventually may lead to disaster. In fact, it is a serious warning against recommending personal happiness as a reliable motivation for social action. Eudemonistic ethics involves a misleading theory. For every form of happiness a price must be paid. For the happiness of self-realization the price is isolation and social disapproval, for that ensuing from loyalty to the moral law the necessity to give up certain pursuits dictated by the wish for self-realization, or, more exactly, the necessity to revise the secret desires of the self. Ethical behaviour is poorly served by the belief that it brings happiness. The reward that it brings is the certainty of full partnership in one's universe.

2. *The limitations of the moral law and the foundation of minimal ethics*

The moral law is a principle which must be applied to relations in a human universe. These relations are variegated. Welcoming the other to one's universe does not imply the duty to adopt him as a son (the term son would quickly lose its meaning by overcrowding the family!) but the duty to welcome him in his proper right and place. A universe has many possible places, some nearby, and far more at greater distance. These distances are intrinsically part of the universe, and cannot be ignored with impunity. Of course, it may happen that an unforeseen encounter with a perfect stranger evokes a relationship of affection. The classical case is that of the Good Samaritan. Such encounters, however, are rare. Even if we admit that this rarity is, in part at least, a matter of the small number of Good Samaritans rather than of a scarcity of people in distress, the fact remains that such encounters are not daily routine and do not make part of that multitude of relations which one by one have their proper place in every man's daily experience of his universe. Societies have rules for these relations, and these rules are of different kinds. This is also the case in primitive society in which every one knows everyone else personally and, consequently, the moral law with its immediate appeal to the other one's person (to be welcomed is an affect-laded concept!) seems more readily applicable than anywhere.

In primitive society, the principle that relations inside a human universe are of varying intimacy, is reflected in the differences which the rules make for social intercourse between persons belonging to the same or to different small units, and between persons of the same or different age, sex and status. Social distance has a conspicuous influence on the various manners of complying with the moral law. Where social nearness is greatest, in the small unit constituted by close family and friends, interaction is informal and follows the rules of give-and-take as described on p. 128 f. and discussed on p. 101 f. Here, mutual help and friendliness are a matter of course (at least normally). If members of different units wish to display friendliness and comradeship, different procedures are followed, in particular those of such a more formal exchange of food or gifts as described on p. 99 f. Different again is the interaction between people of status, the big men of the society, and members of lower rank. The latter display a moderate deference to these leaders, and an equally moderate willingness to follow their directives. The authority of these leaders is limited in scope, and so is the respect they enjoy. All the same, big men are expected to be generous and to protect the rights of ordinary people, not every day of course, but when occasions arise. The relation between a big man and the ordinary ones can be characterized as one of moderately disbalanced reciprocity. On the whole, the big men give more and the small ones do more.

A certain willingness to welcome the other as a partner in one's universe can be observed in all these different forms of interaction. It even is found when a gross violation of the rules has deeply disturbed good relations, and the culprit shows signs that he is willing to atone for his crime. If that be the case, he may get off with a relatively light punishment and eventually be reintegrated as a partner in the society (ibid.: 105).

The gradations in these different modes of adherence to the moral law are evident. Formality increases with social distance, and with increasing formality the opportunities for interaction of this kind rapidly decrease in number. A formal exchange of prepared food or small gifts is of relatively rare occurrence. It is an occasion for bridging gaps between the interactors which have been allowed to

131

become too wide, and as such it is a correction of inadequate social behaviour rather than a means for its perfection. If all were well, the exchange would hardly be necessary. The small family unit does not need formal exchange for the promotion of mutual relations of a truly cordial nature. They thrive on good intentions and informality. Nevertheless, all these acts of formal gift-exchange are performed on a person-to-person basis, meant to confirm or establish partnership between the participants and to express the appreciation of one another's social status and situation. As such they comply with the moral law though, at the same time, they are symptoms of insufficient obedience to its precepts in daily life. The main merit of formal gift-exchange is that it restores moral well-being.

Unfortunately, the practice of gift-exchange is necessarily confined to relatively small societies, societies in which all members know each other personally. They do not exceed some one and a half thousand people in number. All others are either relative or real strangers, relative strangers if the society is more populous and includes people who do not know each other personally, real strangers if they belong to different societies. At times, contacts between strangers occur, in primitive society more or less exceptionally, in modern society daily. What are the rules for carrying on with strangers of either category, and have such rules any connection with the exigencies ensuing from the moral law?

Before tackling this question a closer examination of the concept of the stranger is called for. It has already been noted that strangers are of different kinds. There also are strangers who are identified with enemies and, on this ground, denied a place in the social universe. At this point we are confronted by our first problem: is any man's social universe confined to his own society? On logical grounds the proposition can be defended that enemies, too, make part of anyone's universe. Man's universe includes enemies of many kinds: bad weather, earthquakes, microbes, pests, predators, and hostile congeners. They all constitute part of it, just like the good things such as good weather, food, and friends. A universe is by nature ambiguous, alternately hostile and friendly. However, as enemies, like microbes, pests and predators, must be fought, a concept of social universe which includes both enemies and friends necessarily leads to confusion. It is more convenient to restrict it to that part of the congeners in one's universe with whom interaction other than warfare is possible and either occasionally or regularly realized. Even so we are left with a rich variety of strangers.

In the primitive world all strangers are suspect. Moreover, the word stranger has a wide denotation here. Related groups are often looked upon as comparative strangers. Though they know every member personally and occasionally exchange gifts between them, the groups do not trust each other well enough to exclude suspicions of witchcraft and sorcery. The Baktaman (below: 209) are a case in point. Mutual relations and social interaction are based on a fiction of friendship, on an 'as if', rather than on genuinely friendly feelings. Not all primitive societies are of the kind in which even fairly close relatives are suspected of attempts at sorcery and witchcraft, but they are not an exception either. And it is fairly common to mistrust guests from distant villages invited to attend the celebration of a local ceremony. Usually, such guests are more or less distant relatives. Outwardly respected and always warmly welcomed, their doings are closely observed, lest they find an opportunity for secret mischief. It is evident that the people concerned are well aware that this is not as it should be. They go to great lengths to conceal their misgivings and, exchanging presents with them, do all they can to maintain good relations. There is quite a lot of hypocrisy in all this. Though deplorable, it is good to remember that hypocrisy lends an important support to morality everywhere. Hypocrisy never tires of preaching the rules of true morality.

A perfectly different category is that of the real strangers, people who, in the primitive world, are met with accidentally when they are on their way to an unknown destination. The journey such strangers make is not without peril. There is always a chance that they will encounter hostility. Yet, in spite of the frequently told stories about strangers killed in cold blood, such events are pretty rare. In most parts, it is customary to greet strangers by enquiring where they come from and what their destination is. The exchange of information which follows easily leads to a talk and often to the discovery that the strangers are relatives of relatives or friends. An invitation to pass the night in the village may follow, and occasionally the encounter leads to a more or less formalized friendship with a distant village, a useful connection for extending trade relations. Peaceful relations always are an appreciable good which, for reasons of practical rather than moral considerations, should not be recklessly jeopardized. Interest often supports morality.

Much the same can be said of trade relations. In primitive society, traders are relative strangers to one another. Friends exchange gifts and are instrumental in finding trade relations for their friends, but they do not trade together (above: 94 f.). A close, personal relation should not be exposed to a negotiation technique which tends to ignore the personal element. We noted that traders are not interested in one another's persons but in one another's wares. Further, that they always meet as equals. The rule of trade is one of strict reciprocity, combined with honesty and civility.

For as long as trade is confined to direct barter, the observation of the rules of trade is warranted. Difficulties arise when one of the parties does not dispose of the commodity sought after by his counterpart in the quantity needed to balance the goods offered by the latter. Then credit is needed, but credit cannot readily be given to a stranger who, almost by definition, cannot be trusted. In such a case, the transaction must be annulled, unless a bailsman turns up, or the debtor is such a regular trader that he can be expected to deliver his due in time. If the latter is the case, he is more of a nominal stranger than a real one. He has a standing interest in maintaining his trade relation. Yet, such traders are rare. Moreover, precisely the fact that it serves the debtor's trade interests to meet his obligations, explains why credit is but reluctantly given, if it be given at all. Trade interests are interests in goods, and it can quite well serve these interests to cheat by omitting to pay the creditor. There is all the difference between the binding force of reciprocity in trade and that in the exchange of gifts. In the latter, reciprocity serves the satisfaction of a serious need, that of establishing and confirming partnership in a wider universe (above: 99), whereas in the former it simply leads to a loss of goods. As long as a debtor cannot be summoned by an independent judge and compelled to pay his due, credit giving is risky. In the primitive world, trade is transacted on the outskirts of society, at the margins of the social universe where moral obligations are weak or corrupted by competing interests.

Though weak and badly in need of protection by a judiciary, the rules of trade are universally recognized as valid. The debtor who cheats is invariably liable to scorn and revenge. The mere fact that the rules are universally valid raises a problem. Have these rules anything to do with the moral law as previously formulated, or should we suppose that there are two systems of ethics, one for interaction with the insiders of a society, and one for dealings with outsiders? To answer this question we have to turn to modern society. It is of a type which can be characterized as a society of people who are relative strangers to each other. In societies of this type, trade (and contract) fulfil a very important function, a circumstance which encourages us to turn first of all to the rules of trade in the modern world.

A point of great importance is that here trade follows the same rules as in primitive society. There is only one exception: friends are allowed to trade with each other. It is an exception of small consequence. The rule that business is business, is maintained and the impact of friendship on the outcome of the negotiations negligible. Of far greater importance is the presence of a strong judiciary and an elaborate legislation. The combination of the two gives immense support to the proper fulfilment of the contractual obligations of trade and business, and has contributed substantially to the growth of trade and the development of credit facilities. In this context, it is of some importance to note that the legislator never gave such protection to the obligations ensuing from gift-exchange. Apparently (and not without reason) the notion prevails that these strong, moral obligations protect themselves.

Trade and the management of contractual obligations are not the only instances of impersonal, businesslike interaction in modern society. The same trend permeates the products of legislation. In the eyes of the law all persons are equal, just as in trade. Obligations are formulated in a matter-of-fact way; the law does not inquire whether these obligations affect the one harder than the other. The law is impersonal, as impersonal as many of the modern forms and rules for social behaviour. Although I may have an occasional talk with the grocer or baker whom I meet every two or three days, this does not lead to paying each other social calls. We do not participate in one another's lives. Nor, for that matter, with our doctor or our lawyer. Although, to them, we have to report many details of a strictly personal character, we avoid unnecessary intimacies. Besides, doctor and lawyer are not interested in us personally, but in our medical and legal problems. A certain distance is maintained, a distance which protects the interacting parties from getting involved in one another's more personal affairs. It is bad form to ignore that distance. When some stranger asks me where a particular street is, and I know my way about town, I shall certainly tell him, but I shall never ask him what he wishes to do there. That is his affair and not mine.

The moral rule demanding such conduct is that to respect the person of the other by not unnecessarily or uninvitedly intruding upon his freedom or privacy. It is a very general rule; it applies to chance meetings and social intercourse generally as well as to

134

trade and business contacts. Even in primitive society, its application is not confined to trade and chance meetings with strangers. It is the rule of conduct in all cases where two or more individuals co-operate on behalf of some common end. Besides, it is the easiest rule to follow in dealings with fellow-tribesmen who are not closely related. We noted that relations between different units of one and the same society are often not as cordial as they should be. Periodically, formal exchanges of gifts must repair the damage done to these relationships by, alternately, neglect and polite but stand-offish behaviour; two forms of conduct which go hand in hand with the increase of social distance.

The principle of respect is more generally applied in modern society which has adopted it as the founding principle of its legislation. Treating all persons as equals, the laws refrain as much as is socially justifiable from intervention in their private affairs. It is a highly important principle which gives substance to the supposition, put forward on p. 134, that there seem to exist two divergent systems of ethics. If this be true, the question obtrudes, how are the two interrelated?

The two principles, i.e. that of respect and that of welcoming to partnership, have more in common than might appear at first sight. Both treat the other person seriously, the first by respecting his wish to remain aloof, the second by satisfying his longing for communication and partnership. The interconnection between the two principles reaches even further than this. It is not possible to welcome the other as a partner to one's universe without respecting his person. This implies that the principle to respect the other one's person is the more general of the two. This, in turn, raises the problem of which of the two is the more fundamental; the principle of respect as the more general one, or that of partnership as the more encompassing one? Although one might be inclined to give pride of place to the more general one, the principle of respect, there is sound reason for doubt on this point. We are up to the curious fact that the rules based on, or derived from the principle of respect need protection by the law and enforcement by an independent judiciary, whereas those based on the principle of sharing partnership can do without such protection. Up to a point, the latter have their reward in themselves. Besides, the rules of law are precisely formulated and consistently applied. Far more than those implied in sharing partnership. It is possible to formulate rules for all sorts of business relations and matter-of-fact transactions. It is not feasible, however, to formulate rules for how to welcome another as a partner to one's universe. The command is of a too personal and encroaching nature to allow such satisfactory categorization of cases and circumstances in specific rules, as is characteristic of legislation.

There is every reason, then, to go deeper into this question. One of the first things we note is that the effect of legal rules is always limited in scope, confined to the realization of certain material ends. Even the most humane products of legislation are unable to enforce the satisfaction of man's deepest needs. An enlightening case is that of the elaborate legislation protecting the poor and the destitute in the modern welfare state. They are well provided for in hunger and sickness, in unemployment and old age, in misfortune and desertion. And yet, this care leaves them unsatisfied at the most relevant point, viz. their partnership in society. The victims are cared for not

135

as specific persons, but as cases foreseen in article x, paragraph y of this or that law. Excluded from participation in productive, social life, they stand aside from society, the easy victims of that loneliness which, in spite of progressive legislation, is nowhere so acute and so widely spread as in the big cities. Loneliness is the natural ailment of a society which resembles a market rather than a community. Legislation is unable to cure this. This can only be achieved by persons who welcome the destitute and the lonely to their own universe. To be respected as a person has by no means the same satisfaction as it has to be welcomed as a partner. Bearing this in mind, one finds reason to consider the possibility that the principle of respect is but a derivate of that of sharing partnership, an attenuated form adapted to the reduced role of the personal element in the highly diversified interaction typifying a modern society.

However, there are other possibilities to be considered. One of these is the idea that the principle of respect, requiring balanced reciprocity, honesty and civility, is just a consciously, at the very least more or less intentionally devised principle for the purpose of creating workable relations with and between comparative strangers. The supposition is a strong one because all the rules based on this principle are conscious rules. Why should not the principle itself be based upon pure reason, on the conscious consideration of the obvious truth that the advancement of social interaction and the growth of the social body are best served by rational rules based on equality and equity, as comprised in the principle of respect? Considerations of this kind can be found already in various readings of the doctrine of the social contract.

The theory that the principle of respect and the obligations ensuing from it are the products of reason finds support in the fact that these obligations are sanctioned by penalties in case of offence. Reason is rarely strong enough to enforce obedience to a law when its application runs counter to private interests. When this happens, the individual who feels his interests are jeopardized, will undoubtedly raise rational objections against the law. It is never difficult to find them. Modern laws are the products of legislation. They have gone through a long process of discussion which led to their ultimate forms, forms in which some objections raised by opponents have been allowed, whereas others have been ignored. The objector who finds his interests harmed by a law never has difficulty in proving to his private satisfaction that the law is wrong and conflicts with the principles of equity and reason. When, nevertheless, he obeys the law, is this from fear of punishment?

In some cases, certainly. In matters of drafting one's annual income tax return the apprehension of the tax-collector's sometimes very effective methods of inspection is often a strong argument in favour of honesty. Yet, fear of punishment is by no means the sole argument for obedience in cases where the law provokes an individual's objections or indignation. If it were only fear of punishment which prevents objectors from disobedience, offences would be far more numerous than they actually are. Obedience is supported by all sorts of rational and quasi-rational considerations which all converge upon the point that adherence to the law is a moral duty. The same holds true where contractual obligations are concerned as in trade and business. Meeting them is sometimes difficult or even onerous, but an important argument for honest fulfilment is always a moral one. It is a duty.

136

The individual objector's reasons for accepting loyalty to law and contract as a duty are various. It may be because everyone sees it that way; if he is a philosopher because it is the command of practical reason, the social contract, or some other general principle; if he is religious because it is the Divine Command or the revealed Will of God. Mankind, in starting from so many different points of view, could not converge so universally upon the point of loyalty to law and contract as a moral duty, if there were not a reality behind it. This leads us back to an earlier observation on the subject of rules generally. Man cannot live without rules. When rules are lacking he makes them. In that context, we concluded that rules represent man's (social) universe. Though he often clashes with that universe, man cannot escape from the ultimate recognition of its authority (above: 93, 109-114). This implies that the authority behind the law, and behind loyalty to it as a moral duty, is man's social universe. Can we maintain that this holds true also for modern man?

There are reasons to contest this. The core of modern man's social universe is the nation state, and the nation state does not, today, enjoy all the respect which is due to the symbolic centre of the social universe. Up to a point this must be ascribed to the fact that the nation has yielded a not unimportant part of its sovereign rights to international organizations. To progressive thinkers the nation is an already, more or less, obsolete concept. Considering the many obstacles on the way leading to sub-stantial internationalization, such views seem a bit rash, though they find support in the fact that any social universe has always exceeded the boundaries of the nation state by far. However, when, today, the nation state and its rules and laws are frankly and intensively criticized, this is more immediately due to the circumstance that the latter are conscious rules which are broadly rationalized and thus invite discussion and criticism, than a matter of intrinsic resistance against the state's authority. When a real crisis turns up and imminent danger threatens the nation, the sceptical attitude rapidly vanishes. Being in danger, the nation's significance is rediscovered, and overnight the sceptic of yesterday is found willing to fight and to risk his life. He has no difficulty with identifying himself with the nation. Without questioning the legal authority's wisdom, the average citizen, normally a regular objector, simply obeys though he knows that it may cost him his life. Behind modern man's alternately recalcitrant and sloppy manners of law-abidance lies his mostly unconscious allegiance to the nation state which induces him to a more faithful obedience to its laws than his frank criticism might make an outsider expect. The emotional significance of the nation state and its impact on action go deeper than, in our sophistication, most of us care to admit.

The fact has been convincingly demonstrated by the history of the decolonization process. I have argued elsewhere (Van Baal, 1976a) that it was not caused primarily by colonial oppression, but originated as the inescapable product of what can be called the colonial state, the colony organized like a state in the making. For its realization, the colonial state needed a fair amount of native personnel. In the course of their career, which carried them from one corner of the colony to another, these native servants gradually discovered that their original tribal identity more and more lost its interest. With increasing acuity, they felt themselves citizens of that much larger community constituted by all that lives inside the boundaries of the colony. What became important to them was not that they were Aryans or Dravidians, but that they were Indians; not that by origin they were Javanese, Buginese or Ambonnese, but that they were Indonesians; etc. To realize that new identity they started a fight, risking their lives and their newly acquired wealth. They fought it with so much violence that everywhere they won and created new nation states. That these new states suffered from many of the defects of the old colonial state, plus a few new ones besides, did not bother them. The critic who, addressing a United Nations meeting, stated that "own government is better than good government", hit the nail on the head. Whether for better of worse, the nation state gives form and substance to a people's social universe. That is why, rebellions and coups notwithstanding, the new nation states are, like the old ones, respected, and their laws and rules obeyed to a much greater extent than mismanagement or the persistence of tribalism made outsiders expect.

Although the reality of the nation state as the embodiment of the core of man's social universe is still formidable, the extension of that universe beyond the boundaries of the state is progressively taking shape in new and more, eventually all encompassing forms of political organization. A world community of all mankind is no longer a vague chimera. It has already acquired an incipient form of organization, weak perhaps and still lacking of executive power, but real enough to give substance to great expectations of further development. Such expectations are not new. Philosophers cherished them long before. They were well aware that man's real universe exceeds his organized social universe by far, and rejected the confinement of the social universe to the boundaries set by the nation state. One of these was Immanuel Kant, whose formulation of the categorical imperative (always to act in conformity to maxims fit to be accepted as principles of universal legislation) refers clearly to the idea of mankind as a social reality. While ignoring the state Kant did not ignore the reality of the social universe; he extended it, rather, to its proper horizon: i.e. mankind. The social universe is implicated in the term universal legislation.

However, all these arguments which emphasize the significance of man's *social* universe, are defective on one point. They ignore the obvious fact that man must not merely respect his *social* universe, but his universe generally. It has a great deal of authority over him and imposes its rules upon him. If, in recent years, one thing has dawned upon all of us, it is the necessity to respect nature and the life of nature. It is not a new duty of course: it has always existed, but it is the consequences of our trespasses that have us made conscious of its strict validity. It is the authority of our universe that demands to respect all its parts. They are under the protection of the universe's higher authority.

We can now return to our initial problem, that of the connections between the principles of sharing partnership and of respect. It is evident now that the latter is the more general, the former the more inclusive one. The principle of respect aims at leaving the two interacting parties intact and apart, each respected as a fellow-part by the other, which implies that each must be polite and honest. They interact not because they have a specific interest in one another's person, but because they have an interest in some common, extra-personal end which defines the need and nature of their interaction. The paradigmatic model of this type of interaction is the trade transaction. The rules incumbent upon the behaviour of the participants are those which have to be observed by traders. We call these rules *minimal ethics,* in contra-distinction to those to be followed by those who seek partnership. The latter will also respect each other because respect is obligatory in every interaction. But they will do more than just this: they will welcome each other to their personal universe. These rules are more encompassing, but obedience to them is more rewarding. This complex of rules we called the moral law. We might also call them *natural ethics* because they lead to that type of togetherness which fulfils man's need for partnership in his world. Obedience to natural ethics has its reward in itself and needs no protection by law, whereas the fulfilment of minimal ethics, the embodiment of the exigencies of an authoritative universe, must be enforced by the sanctions which are wielded by those who represent the ultimate authority that formulated and promulgated the rules.

All the same, business relations may lead to situations calling for the observance of the moral law. This happens each time that, during the transaction, one of the participants' need for partnership becomes apparent. This is certainly not an excep-tion. It frequently occurs in the relations between employer and employee. Does, in such case, the obedience to the moral law do away with social distance and enjoin interactors to brotherly care as often as such a situation presents itself? It certainly does not do away with social distance. Such distance is a reality and can never be ignored. It makes an inalienable part of every situation in which partnership has to be realized, and defines the character of this partnership. The care and sympathy bestowed by the master on the employee, differ considerably from those given to the latter by his wife. It is a matter of course that the duty to welcome the other to one's universe is more easily and more profoundly realized where social distance is minimal than where it is wide. Where distance is small, opportunities for actualizing part-nership are optimal as well as permanent. Where distance is great, the opportunities are scarcer and of a more occasional nature. Yet, the duty to heed the person of the other and to treat him and welcome him as a partner is always there, whenever a person presents himself as in quest for partnership.

In modern society, such persons often go by unnoticed. Altogether too often all attention is focussed on the various tasks which must be realized, so that the persons who co-operate in their execution hardly are noticed. We have no time for them, and (apart from an occasional office-party, or an exchange of drinks in the pub), our society does not dispose of the means to make good for this neglect of personal needs by organizing ceremonies of formal gift-exchange, the answer which primitive society has in reserve to repair such deficiency. As a result, this lack of interest in others has serious consequences for modern society. The need for realized partnership is more acute than ever. We noted in passing that loneliness is a common ailment of our society, a point on which we have more to say in Part IV. There can, in reason, be no doubt about the duty to offer more and better partnership than we actually do. The one question which remains and which we have to examine in the next section, is the question whether the moral law is sufficiently well founded in the human condition to accept it as a law incumbent upon all mankind.

3. The effect and significance of the moral conscience

In the preceding sections it was argued that the moral law and the rules of minimal ethics are the logical consequences of the human condition. We found the contention confirmed in the universal occurrence of rules and ideals which give concrete form to the inherent principles of sharing partnership with, and of respect for, the person of the other. However, we also had to mention the socially accepted rules which run counter to these principles, rules discriminating against women to the advantage of men, rules discriminating between pure and impure castes, and rules which perpetuate the poverty of the poor (above: 125). The occurrence of such immoral rules is something far worse than the frequent transgression of moral ones. Offences against rules are a normal consequence of the human condition which is contradictory by nature. It includes a self that, in spite of its perpetuous quest for partnership, is also the embodiment of a libido which is striving for self-realization and the satisfaction of its selfish desires.

Immoral rules are quite another matter. Instead of calling the unruly self to order, they do not merely condone immoral behaviour, but prescribe it, animating the self to satisfy the egoistic ends of the self. The presence of such rules, not occasionally but in practically every society, necessarily constitutes a flat denial of the universal validity of the moral law, unless it can be proved that these unrighteous rules provoke reactions of discomfort, not primarily among the victims of these rules, but specifically among those who reap the benefit of the privileges unduly granted them by these rules. As possible symptoms of such discomfort one may think of religious beliefs bearing the marks of a bad conscience, of rationalizations forwarded to justify these rules, and of actions to revise them undertaken by those who enjoy unrighteous privileges. In fact, such symptoms are surprisingly numerous. In the following pages, a selected number of cases are examined which all testify that there is, indeed, some such thing as a natural moral conscience which warns man that there is something wrong with rules which enable him to satisfy his desires at the expense of others who are denied the respect and partnership due to them as members of society.

A moral conscience of this kind differs profoundly from that which engenders the remorse of the drunk or the thief. They have sinned against well-established rules, and their remorse is the natural reaction to offences against enculturated and internalized rules which, by education, have been integrated into their moral consciousness. In the case of what we called a natural moral conscience, there is no question of a reaction against a breach of a rule but, reversely, against the application of a cultural rule. The reaction, running counter to the cultural precept, gives proof of an awareness of a moral rule which is independent of the dictates of culture. It cannot possibly originate from culture, and thus must have its foundation in the human condition itself. To this fact – which has wider implications than the corroboration of the views

140

expounded in the previous sections – we shall return after having expounded a number of relevant cases, borrowed from a wide variety of cultures.

One of the most widely spread rules which discriminate against women in primitive societies is that which excludes them from participation in ritual. Most of these rituals are fertility cults in which the men arrogate female functions. It was argued (above: 77) that these arrogations suggest a reaction of the males against the unsatisfactory position of their sex when compared to that of the women. The Australian culture area abounds with a rich variety of such cults. Thus, the Aranda hold the view that pregnancy is not caused by sexual intercourse but by a germ of life which a divine ancestor shot into the woman's abdomen. It is the task of the men to stimulate these ancestors by ritual celebrations to increase their fertilizing activities. In a later chapter (below: 173 f.) evidence is presented that the Aranda are not really ignorant of the function of the sexual act. All the same, the men do the women a favour by ritually promoting their fertility. It is the males' contribution to the persistence of the tribe, a contribution they can make because they dispose of the relevant secret knowledge which only they can apply. The excluded women ought to be grateful for it.

Are the men really unaware that they are treating their women meanly? Of the Aranda, I know of no signs of moral anguish on this point, but this does not mean that they were non-existent. A renewed analysis of the extensive and highly scattered ethnographic data might bring them to light. This is all the more probable because such evidence is clearly present among the more northern tribes. In Arnhem Land, the men are well-aware that they are in the wrong. The view that the celebrations of the males are a usurpation of female rights finds overt expression in the myth of the Djanggawul Sisters, the founding myth of their most important ritual (Warner 1958; R. Berndt 1952):

> "The sisters are real culture-heroes; they give shape to the landscape, they produce the (phallic!) ritual implements, they initiate the ritual, and they give birth to many boys and girls. There is also a brother, but his role is a minor one, although not really unimportant. One day the men, headed by the brother, take possession of the ritual implements and start the ritual whilst the sisters are fishing. These are soon aware of it, but cannot interfere because they know the secret power of the sacred songs and fear to do anything about it. The older sister is the first to realize the consequences of what happened; resigning in her fate she states:
> 'Men can do it now, they can look after it. We can spend our time collecting bush foods for them ... We know everything. We have really lost nothing, for we remember it all, and we let them have that small part. For aren't we still sacred, even if we have lost the bags [with sacred implements]? Haven't we still our uteri?' (Berndt 1952: 40 f.). The younger sister agrees. Together, the sisters are paragons of maturity. Yet, it is the men who tell the myth, tacitly admitting that the women, as superior mothers, let them, the boys, have their way" (Van Baal 1975: 121).

And the boys go their way after this confession of their inferiority, finding justification in the divine precedent which settled things for ever and ever.

An analysis of the mythology and the ritual of the Marind-anim of the South coast of West Irian (below: ch. IX, 4 and ch. X) gives more, equally interesting evidence.

Their case is complicated, however, by institutionalized homosexuality which is more highly valued in their culture than heterosexuality. Homosexuality is associated with the superior moiety which has authority over the great, cosmic initiation rituals, heterosexuality with the inferior moiety which presides over headhunting, the celebration of feasts and matters connected with black magic. There is no question here of any pretended ignorance of the physical effect of the sexual act. They know all about it and they are deeply convinced that no pregnancy can lead to a successful birth unless the men do their utmost to promote the woman's fertility: by collectively copulating with her first, by daily and long perpetuated sexual intercourse with her husband – who must 'feed' the foetus – afterwards. The collective act of impregnation, involving intercourse in rapid succession with some ten to fifteen men, is a ritual act denoted as *dom bombari*, a bad rite, bad in the sense of reprehensible. The term does not refer to the fairly obvious fact that the act gives small satisfaction to the participants, but to the to them revolting truth that as proud homosexuals they have to submit to heterosexual intercourse. Heterosexual intercourse is dangerous, a belief substantiated by a fair number of castration myths. Impregnating the women is a duty, an act of self-sacrifice on the part of the men.

Strangely enough, the central deity of the great cosmic ritual is a female, sometimes represented as a mother, then again as the terrible Excrement Woman. Although, at the end of the ritual, she is symbolically killed, ultimately, she is triumphant. The ritual following a successful headhunt – always a statutory sequel to the great ritual – gives proper evidence of her ultimate superiority (below: 176-178). Marind-anim behaviour is ambiguous from beginning to end. One would have expected that their married life is a greater failure than anywhere, and yet marriages are more stable here than among the non-homosexual Mountain Papuans. Sexually, the life of the women must have been unsatisfactory (Van Baal 1966: 950) but socially they enjoyed better treatment than the women of the neighbouring tribes. They were admitted to participate in the great cosmic initiation ritual, and even encouraged to play minor roles in the festive impersonation of the divine ancestors. It also happened that, sometimes, the men arranged a feast for the women to have a big ceremonial dance all of their own, because the men felt that they owed their women a treat (ibid. 859). Although the men could find plenty of self-justification in their notions concerning the male contributions to their women's fertility, the fact that they thereby wronged their wives did not escape them.

With neighbouring tribes, a vague realization of the unjustice done to their women can be overheard in their myths on the origin of the bullroarer, the ritual instrument used to chase the women away when the men set out to celebrate their secret rites. The bullroarer was originally discovered by a woman, or produced from her genitals (Van Baal 1963: 205).

The conclusive force of these few cases is, numerically, limited. Materially, they give sufficient evidence that among peoples where the position of women is decidedly low and their ritual incompetence an article of belief, the notion that there is something wrong about it does not pass by unnoticed and assumes institutionalized forms of self-justification in daily life, and of feelings of guilt in myth. This is not insignificant when we remember that the underlying motive is the male protest against female superiority. The men must prove their worth and justify themselves by their ritual activities. Though they have a reason which is psychologically sound, they are aware of some collective guilt. Almost inaudibly, the moral law makes itself heard.

Comparable cases can be collected from elsewhere. It is not feasible to describe them all in full, and I just raise them in question form. Thus, why do the Mountain Papuans of the Mt. Hagen area represent the goddess of their fertility cult as a young and beautiful woman without genitals? (cf. A. J. Strathern, 1970). And, turning now to the Hellenic era, why are Cybele and the rather formidable mother-goddesses derived from her always depicted sitting on a lion? (Vermaseren 1970). May we hypothesize that the cruel self-castration practices connected with these mystery cults are expressions of a guilt complex due to some collective sin? I refrain from giving an answer. Questions of this kind arise repeatedly once one's interest has been aroused.

When considering the question of castes, the first case one comes across is that of the belief in *karma*. This belief adroitly combines two contradictory ends: the urgent necessity to do, even to be, good, and the explanation of all human suffering as the well-deserved wages of sins committed during a previous existence. No one is undeservedly born a woman or a streetsweeper. No one has a right of protest. The excuse is perfect, and yet there is a vague realization that there is something wrong with the ill treatment befalling these one-time sinners. In spite of their previous sins, it is virtue to have compassion upon the poor and to alleviate their sufferings by deeds of charity.

Similar views have been held by the Christian Church. She shielded the persistence of social woes by explaining them as the wages of sin or as the result of God's inscrutable decree who, in his wisdom, thus bade the rich and the wicked an opportunity to expiate their sins or to increase their merits by liberal acts of charity. In later times, comparable considerations have increased the missionary zeal of Christians in colonizing countries. It is hardly by accident that missionary activities have not been confined to the propagation of faith, but also excelled in the dissemination of education and medical care well before metropolitan governments, adopting a more lenient policy, accepted these and other tasks as proper fields of government care.

It has not always been the Church who gave the lead in actions for improving the situation of the poor and the destitute. The great revolutionary movements aiming at social progress and the elevation of the lower classes found their precursors and many of their leaders among members of the ruling classes who had little to win and much to lose from the abolition of their prerogatives. Such names come to mind as those of Montesqieu and Lafayette in France, of Tolstoi in Russia, to mention only a few out of many. In this same context, mention should be made of F. Engels who was a well-to-do industrial, and of Karl Marx, a relative of the founders of the Philips concern, who married a Baroness Von Westphalen. It is amazing how often one finds members of the ruling classes in the front ranks of those who fought against them. Studying history in more detail, we repeatedly meet with people who sacrificed the interests of their class to the dictates of their social conscience.

A comparable case is that of the weak resistance offered by the metropolitan powers against the independence movements in the colonies under their administration. In spite of the Cold War, the decolonization process would not have passed off so quickly and universally if, at the home-front of the metropolitan states, public opinion had not condemned colonization as something wrong. Time and again we come across the voice of conscience as a power initiating political developments.

This voice of conscience is neither a strong, nor always a reliable one. More often than not, it is smothered in rationalizations of all sorts, devised to justify unrighteous rules or to minimize their harm. Yet, the voice is there, and the pains everywhere taken to silence it confirm more convincingly than anything else that the protests of conscience are by no means exceptions but a recurrent phenomenon. As, in all these cases, that voice of conscience cannot possibly be the result of education or enculturation, it testifies to the fact that man is not only a libidinous being bent upon self-realization at the expense of his universe, but also a part of his universe which longs to be received as a partner in that universe, a partnership that can only be achieved by choosing the narrow path of the moral law.

It is a truth which no one can earnestly deny, but also a truth which the loud claims of the unsatiable desires of the self easily repress. How shall man hear this truth? The self, "in the course of its personal history . . ., has accreted certain preferences and automatisms to itself, conscious as well as unconscious, which together . . . define the forms of its future actions, of its desires, interests, expectations, and fears", we wrote on p. 58. And we added that the self sacrificed its freedom "in part to the persona . . ., in part to the conscious and unconscious desires and fears which constitute the self" (ibid.). What can induce man to listen to the voice of his inner, natural conscience?

The answer is obvious: his moral conscience itself. It is always there and, though its voice is weak, it speaks. In any human life there are always moments when it is heard. The scanning apparatus of the mind invariably discovers it. The apparatus can be turned away from it, but the experience does not pass by unnoticed. It demands making a choice, that between obliterating it or listening to it. And choice implies freedom. Discussing the rather depressing subject of human freedom we wrote: "Real freedom is the faculty to act against one's preferences and one's past without being forced or induced by outside pressure or compulsion to do so" (above: 58). Man has few opportunities to realize this freedom. The one real opportunity presented to him by his inexorable scanning apparatus is that of his natural conscience, the inner awareness that he must take his partnership in his universe seriously. No one knew this better than Heidegger who concluded: *Existieren, das heiszt Gewissen haben wollen* (1927). Indeed, to exist in its full sense means to *will* to have a moral conscience!

What does this mean? Simply, that "freedom is a task, not a gift" (above: 58). The last word in ethics is the duty to make oneself free to give the still small voice of conscience the opportunity not only to be heard (it is always there) but also to be considered. Only then does the subject really act as a part of his universe, the part of his universe as really a subject. Does this imply happiness? Although in one place (p. 63) I quoted the quest for happiness as man's most obvious motive for action, without raising even one word of doubt, I am far from certain that this really is true. And if it be true (which I do not exclude) I feel strongly inclined to deny its legitimacy. The pursuit of happiness involves all the dangers of hedonism (cf. above: 130). Besides, those who really try to obey the command of the moral law invariably discover their failures rather than their virtue, their guilt more than their goodness. All that can be said of the rewards of the effort to follow the moral law is that it leads to a fuller realization of humanity.

Like freedom, complete humanity is not a gift, but a task. This brings us to the point where the emphasis on the nature of this task necessarily must be reversed. All the time we have stressed the desirability, the necessity even, that the subject act as part of its universe, thus giving primacy to the universe. Having come to the end of our enquiries into the implications of this duty, we discover that the subject, in order to comply with the exigences of full partnership, must first become a subject in the most rigorous sense of the word, namely a free subject, i.e. a subject which has freed itself from the fetters forged by the self.

Postscript: The view that immoral rules cannot permanently suppress the voice of man's moral conscience, is not new. It was presented already by Victor Turner who, in *The ritual Process* (1969), opposed *communitas* as anti-structure to the rules of society as incorporated in its structure. That Turner's use of the term structure differs profoundly from that in the present work, is not important. Important is that, approaching the facts of ethics from a totally different angle, Turner arrived at the same conclusions as I did. There are moments and situations in which man gives in to his moral conscience which, far from being a philosophical construct, is the existential reality on which humanity and the ultimate good are founded.

Part Three

The Religion of
Primitive Man

VIII

The World of Primitive Man
and its Provocations

1. Introduction

In the previous part of this book we examined facts, the rules of social behaviour and the forms which it takes. In the present part, our primary concern is not facts but symbols, in particular symbols referring to an unfalsifiable reality which man believes to have an impact on his universe and on the daily events marking its course. In the introduction to chapter I it was pointed out that these symbols resemble those produced by the mentally sick, from which they differ in three respects: that they are the products of minds otherwise normal, that they give support to the accepted rules of the society concerned, and that they are of such universal occurrence that we are obliged to accept religion (the field of these symbols) as a normal human phenomenon. Yet, doubts arise on two points; the one is the apparent incompatibility of some forms of primitive religion with the dictates of reason, the other the circumstance that since the beginning of the present century large sections of the modern world reject every form of religious belief, and do so without overtly showing traces of greater unhappiness or disquietude than found among those who pretend to draw comfort from such belief.

The disputed position of religion and the forms in which it appears in the modern world will be taken up in part IV. Here, we shall confine our enquiry to the forms of religion in societies in which religious belief is accepted as obvious. The central problem of this enquiry is whether the various forms of religion, the allegedly absurd forms of primitive religion included, can be acknowledged as logical answers of the human condition to the exigencies and pressures of man's universe in varying stages of his societal and scientific (cultural) development. If the answer is positive, and even myth and magic become intelligible as normal human reactions to the conditions under which they occur, the conclusion seems justified that our formulation of the human condition has important heuristic value. However, if this is so, it then must be conceded that religion, in spite of its absurdities, has to be regarded as a normal phenomenon, a conclusion which has implications for the problems of non-religion to be faced in Part IV.

The extreme variation of religious beliefs and behaviour obliges us more often than once to enter into greater detail than we did in the previous chapters. Albeit that even so our expositions will be parsimonious, we cannot refrain from returning to a subject already summarily discussed in Part II: the conditions of primitive man's life. Some of these conditions have a wider impact than the qualification primitive suggests.

Before we set out to discuss primitive man's experience of his world, it is desirable to give some additional comment on the compass covered by the definition of religion presented in chapter I, viz. *all notions and acts referring to a reality which, though it cannot be verified or falsified, is accepted by the group of believers concerned as true and as relevant to their real life and world* (p.5). The wording has the twofold advantage that it avoids a delimitation of the subject matter in terms derived from western philosophy or theology, and that it forwards an easily identifiable feature as the basic characteristic of religion, namely the belief in an unverifiable reality which has an impact on the visible world.

Some will object that the definition is too wide because it implies the recognition that magic and a significant part of metaphysics are forms of religion. This is undoubtedly true, but it can only raise objections if the essence of religion is sought in feelings of dependence or the service of socially beneficent ends. Such views, respectable in themselves, are founded in philosophical (or theological) prejudice rather than in a delimitation of the field of phenomena by external characteristics. In fact, the supposition that magic and religion are radically opposed has been a rich source of controversies which, in the end, resulted in a confusing compromise: i.e. the acceptance of the contradictory term 'magico-religious' in which magic usually stands for deplorable error and selfishness, and religion for approved piety. These are value-judgements which are not in place in matters of categorization. For a broader treatment of the issue I may refer to my book *Symbols for Communication* (1971: 5 ff.; ch. IV; 263 ff.). Here, two simple remarks must suffice. The first is that there is nothing against using the term magic for certain forms of religion, in particular for rites aiming at the realization of concrete ends. The second is that, once it is tried to delimitate the field of religion, no one can ignore so conspicuous, significant and universal a feature as the acceptance of a non-verifiable reality that has controlling power of and over the visible world. It is by no means insignificant that people put faith in such a reality. Man is so well equipped with means for acquiring adequate knowledge of his world that this appeal to unknowable powers both to explain and to solve his difficulties impresses us as contradictory rather than as a logical answer to his problems. Nevertheless, this absurdity has been a cultural universal until the beginning of the present century, and one has to face the fact that religion is an 'absurdity' which is 'normal'. Such an absurdity is worth studying not in one or two, but in all its facets, whether they fall inside or outside the scope of what our own cultural tradition has taught us about what is typical of religion. For this reason, the scholarly speculations of the metaphysicians deserve as much to be included in our concept of religion as the controversial notions and acts of the magician. What counts is that they all have one basic trait in common: i.e. the presupposition of a powerful and yet unverifiable reality.

What is excluded from the field of religion are the imageries of the mentally sick.

150

Although their symbolism displays striking parallels with that of primitive and exotic religion, its etiology differs. The symbols produced by mental disease are the products of individuals who deviate from their societies' notions and norms both in thought and behaviour (above: 5), whereas the religious symbols express feelings and notions which are the common property of all the society's or its religious sub-groups' members. It cannot be said of the symbols of the mentally sick what can indeed be said of religious symbolism: that they constitute part of an absurdity which is normal and that, in each case, they are accepted by the group of believers (a group which may count its numbers in millions) as supreme wisdom and an infallible compass for their behaviour.

In contrast to those who reject our definition as too wide, there are also scholars who will condemn it as too narrow. Trying to safeguard religion as a universal, they define the phenomenon in terms of ultimate concern. Thus, among others, Baird who, following Tillich, identified the two in the formula "religion is ultimate concern" (1971: 18). Every effort at specificity and identifiability of the religious phenomenon has been abandoned here. There are people whom I suspect of finding their ultimate concern in their stamp collection, but I cannot prove it, as little as I have certainty that the preacher who earns his living by disseminating a religious creed, has that belief as his ultimate concern. What a definition must give is a clear and identifiable delimitation of the field of thought and action which a term covers. Ultimate concern does not do this.

More attractive is the definition given by Geertz (1966: 4): "a system of symbols which acts to establish powerful, pervasive and long lasting moods and motivations in men by formulating conceptions of a general order with such an aura of factuality that the moods and motivations seem uniquely realistic". But the definition fails to inform us that the means to establish these moods and motivations are uniquely *un*realistic and always controversial. Besides, it neglects the ominous fact that the widely spread custom of speaking of religion as a belief, is symptomatic of doubt rather than of trust. The term 'belief', whether its use be justified or not (for elaborate criticism see Needham 1972) has a strong connotation of uncertainty. I never heard the point so well made as by the teacher who reprimanded a boy for beginning his answer to a pertinent question by the words 'I believe', with the cross-tempered remark: 'Believing you do in church, in class you must know'. Religion may be described as the supreme good, but there is much uncertainty about it. There is no point in making religion seem more respectable by concealing the dubiety which, so often, seems proper to it.

2. Uncertainty and the notion of intent

Early man's life must have been very much like that of primitive peoples until recent years: hard, devoid of all the securities which, through the ages, progressing culture has devised to protect man against the vicissitudes of life. He had to make do with the edibles that, on his wanderings, he happened to come across. If he had bad luck, he had to come home empty-handed. Unless a camp-fellow had caught a piece of big game – always a stroke of good luck followed by a distribution of meat – he and his family had to make do that night with the tubers and fruits, possibly supplemented with some grubs and shell food, which his wife had brought home. This might suffice; matters would be worse if the wife, too, had encountered some form of misfortune. She might, a few days earlier, have hurt her foot and thus been compelled to do her collecting in the vicinity of the camp where good food is scarce, thus forcing her to content herself with substitutes of inferior nutritional value or poor taste. In times of plenty, she would have little difficulty in borrowing some food from one of the other women or to find a 'sister' prepared to do some collecting on her behalf, but all this is far from simple during a period of scarcity when every man and woman must do the utmost to find sufficient food for the family. There is no baker or butcher round the corner, and everyone is supposed to take care of his own family first. Borrowing is not impossible, but it is not encouraged; it should not be done too often.

Periods of scarcity are a recurrent affliction. A rainy period of long duration causes the tubers to rot in the ground. Fruits do not ripen properly, and part of the country may be inundated. This, in turn, makes fishing unrewarding because the fish spread all over the inundated areas. The incessant rains prevent the men from organizing hunting expeditions into the more remote areas. It is a time of malaise generally; the weather is chilly, sometimes even cold. The fires burn low because the wood is wet, and, during the night, everyone is pestered by the now numerous mosquitoes. They have nothing to cover their naked bodies, and, more often than during other seasons, they wake up in the course of the night to stir up a half-dead fire, the only source of comfort under a leaking shelter.

Prolonged drought has other consequences, but does not make it any the better. The ethnographic reports on the natives of Central Australia and the Bushmen give extensive information on the sufferings caused by lack of water and a failing food-supply. Dispersing in small groups of one or two families the people try their luck in more remote areas. It is not necessary to enter into details; the main point is that this way of life is full of uncertainty; an uncertainty which always strikes at vital needs.

This uncertainty is aggravated by the dangers of warfare and sickness, among which those of sickness are the worst. Primitive man's life is not the healthy life tourists imagine it to be. It is all very well to go about naked when the sun shines, but it is unpleasant when it rains, and definitely trying during a cold night. They often suffer from colds and rheumatic afflictions. Against infectious disease they are powerless. Of course, the sick will stay in camp and be taken care of by their families. Yet, it all depends whether the patients can rest themselves till they are really better. If there are many sick or local scarcity of food urges the group to move to another camp, they may be obliged to partake in food collecting or to set out on a long trip well before they have recovered properly. Wounds are treated poorly; they often hurt their bare feet and legs and carry on with an inflamed wound or a sore leg until its worsening condition compels them to stay in camp. Although death takes its heaviest toll among babies and infants, so that only the fittest survive, mature men and women rarely live into old age. To them, fifty years is really old.

We do not dwell on the dangers caused by predators, venomous snakes and insects. They are real enough, but small when compared to those of warfare. There is always the chance of a sudden raid by enemies who, at the crack of dawn, assault the camp to kill its inmates. The danger is not always imminent but during at least one season of the year they feel worried that some such thing may happen.

Uncertainty, then, was thematic in early man's life. It is also in that of primitive man, in that of horticulturalists and in that of many peasant populations. It is not the kind of uncertainty modern man suffers from during his lifetime. It is worse. Some threat is always there, and it is always directed at really vital needs and security. The experience all these peoples have of nature is one of utter whimsicality. Of course, there are good times when people delight in prosperity and enjoy nature's bounties, but such times never last long enough and one never knows what will happen next. The question is: How will people react to such uncertainty?

The answer is that they will experience it as a threat, just as they experience prosperity as goodness or kindness. Included in it is a notion of intent, the vague sensation that the threat is not an impersonal danger but a menace directed against me personally, the prosperity not a casual boon but a kindness smiling at me – again – personally. It is not the kind of intentionality Merleau-Ponty had in mind when he characterized man's relation with his world as being-to-the-world (*être au monde*) but that psychological reaction to events of vital importance which was elaborately commented on by Bergson in the second chapter of *Les deux Sources de la Morale et de la Religion* (1932). This kind of reaction is of universal occurrence and to understand its significance it is convenient first to examine its impact on modern man who is less inclined than anyone to attach meaning to such reactions.

To introduce the subject we follow Bergson by turning first to a clear case reported by a professional psychologist whose acumen is beyond reasonable doubt, viz. William James. James was near San Francisco when, in 1906, the town was destroyed by an earthquake. Before he came to Stanford University as visiting professor, a friend had warned him that he should not be surprised if an earthquake spoiled his sojourn. As a matter of fact it did, though, thanks to his friend's warning and his personal good luck, to a fairly limited extent only. His comment runs as follows:

> "First, I personified the earthquake as a permanent individual entity. It was *the* earthquake of my friend B's augury, which had been lying low and holding itself back during all the intervening months, in order, on that lustrous April morning, to invade my room, and energize the more intensely and triumphantly. It came, moreover, directly to *me*. It stole in behind my back, and once inside my room, had me all to itself, and could manifest itself convincingly. Animus and intent were never more present in any human action, nor did any human activity ever more definitely point back to a living agent as its source and origin.
>
> All whom I consulted on the point agreed to this feature of their experience. "It expressed intention", "It was bent on destruction", "It wanted to show its power", or what not. To me, it wanted simply to manifest the full meaning of its *name*. But what was this "It"? To some, apparently, a vague demonic power; to me an individualized being, B's earthquake, namely" (James 1912: 212 f.; cf. also Bergson 1932: 161 f.).

To James, the earthquake, having a name, had lost the overpowering terror which it

153

inspired to others. He recognized it as someone he knew about, who now had come to show himself and his meaning to him. To others, the earthquake did not show its meaning, but its intention to destroy; it was vicious, more foreign and terrifying to them than it was to William James. But to all of them, including James, the intentionality of the event was evident. He and all those he interrogated had felt addressed as by a personal being.

Similar experiences are made by modern people who go through a fatal accident which strongly affects their lives. A man or woman whose child is killed in a traffic accident may lament: 'Why, of all things, did we let the child go? Why had he to be just there at that fateful moment? Why?' Some complain: 'Why should this happen to the poor child, so young, so full of vigour'? And others: 'Why should this befall to me'? "It does not matter so much what anyone says. What matters is that he feels addressed, as if some power had intentionally staged the casualty" (Van Baal 1971: 229).

Fateful events carry a message. The English language has the expression 'an act of God' for such events. It expresses how people feel about it, namely as an affliction sent by a superior power. In danger, Fate reigns superior. During World War II we once hid in an open trench against an air-attack. One of us complained that the trench gave little protection. He was told that, if his name stood on a shell-splinter, he was lost anyway. A cold comfort, of course, but it worked; he held his tongue. A few seconds later the bombs were coming down. I had the frightening sensation that one was hurrying down straight towards me.

When it is all over, one speaks of such experiences as 'as-ifs'. We reject them as imagination. It is easy enough for those who escape with a fright, but the parents of the dead child may have continued brooding over the accident for years on end. So may the widow of p. 48 have done who refused to be reconciled with the fact that her late husband caught meningitis. In fact, the suspicion that events carry a hidden meaning or an intent is, even in our culture, more frequent and more general than we care to admit. It befalls us even on the occasion of such a common-place event as missing the bus. If the bus 'which is always late!' is exactly on time 'that one day' when we happen to be less than half a minute late, we feel it as a case of intentional badgering. 'Of course, such a thing had to pass just me!'

We feel 'addressed' in many ways, even by pleasant events. If the weather is fine on the day we had chosen for a holiday, we say (and feel) that the weather is kind to us. We may also feel addressed by a landscape or a work of art, but we refuse to react to such experiences. Sometimes we reject them as childish, at other times we explain them as merely psychological. The latter is what the staunch rationalist does who catches himself in the act of touching wood in reaction to an optimistic prediction. Degrading it to something psychological, he divests the experience of its meaning. The only persons permitted by us to elaborate on feelings of intent are poets. They personalize the intents, and their works are appreciated as well produced artistically and as psychologically meaningful. We agree that the poet has a marvellous way of saying and feeling things, but the intentionality expressed in the poem is not regarded

154

as a sign which should be taken seriously, as a directive for action. It is beautiful imagination, and that is all.

Nevertheless, we indulge daily in all sorts of personalizations which express an intention of some sort. In their weakest form, they are characterized more by a certain caprice of language than by the expression of a real experience. So we speak of the sun that shines brightly, of the storm lashing the tree-tops, approve of the big tree which proudly spreads its branches, and of the old house that displays its glory in the evening sun. Or we listen to the ringing bells that call the faithful to church. To us it is poetic language or just a manner of speaking, just as we say that the rain gushes down and that the ivy climbs the wall. We refuse to attach a meaning to it, because it is just how you say things. Language happens to be that way. This is all true, but all the same it is a poor argument. If language happens to be that way there must be a reason that it so happens.

One reason is certainly the notion of intent accompanying certain events which require an exertion from us. It is brought home to us if we consent to remember how, yesterday morning when we left home in a hurry, we addressed the ignition of our car which 'refused' to work. Or what, on another occasion, we said of (and to!) the rusty nail which we tried in vain to extract from the wall because it did not 'will' to come out. How we addressed car and nail does not matter so much as the fact that we did it in terms of the same order as those directed to the boy who kicked his football right through our front window. We personalized the car and the nail because we experienced their immutability as a resistance against our determined efforts, as a will resisting our will, in other words, an 'intent'.

The experience is not confined to anger-arousing events. When a heavy table must be pushed aside we say to ourselves 'come along boy', words which we explain as an effort at encouraging ourselves, but all the same words which are directed to the table. On other occasions we caress an object of art or an old book that we like, just as we caress a dog or a cat. The semi-personalization of inanimate objects is a frequent occurrence. We explain it in psychological terms because we refuse to attribute meaning to these manifestations of experienced intentionality. The question is: Do other people do the same?

They certainly do not. There is a vast amount of ethnographic information which confirms that primitive people and pre-industrial people in general have the same experience as we have, namely that events sometimes carry some such thing as an intent. However, being less learned than we are, they do not try to explain it away. Though they will not do this in each and every case, they are inclined to attach a meaning to a perceived intent, for example by interpreting it as an omen or warning. A matter of a prelogical mentality? Or just one of attributing meaning to the universal fact that man is inclined to interpret his world in anthropomorphic terms? It is by no means insignificant that in any language the terms denoting inanimate objects if presented as grammatical subjects, are simultaneously presented as the logical subjects of actions which lend them a certain similarity with living beings.

But we need not enter into theoretical speculations on the human trend toward anthropomorphism. Primitive man's life is a life of great uncertainty combined with

155

little knowledge. His universe confronts him with an unpredictable alternation of abundance and dearth, prosperity and famine, life and death. He necessarily experiences it as whimsical and unreliable, threatening him on vital points of subsistence and survival with far greater frequency than it does modern man. More often than the latter, primitive man has reason to experience events as intentional, as carrying a hidden message of some sort.

Yet, to have a feeling that there is some sort of a meaning or intent behind disturbing events is one thing, to give it content or shape is another. We rarely try it, discarding the experience as imagination. But primitive man broods on it and finds ways to give it manageable shape. How can he? What is there in his way of life that promotes it? This must be examined in the next section.

3. Silence, relaxation, and receptivity to dreams and visions

In primitive man's life there is little in the way of entertainment, of things which turn his thoughts to brighter prospects than his daily worries and toil. He is almost permanently confronted with these worries. Life in nature is life in silence, a silence of a magnitude which is wholly unknown to modern man. To the latter, silence is part of his entertainment, or a cure for his afflicted nerves. As entertainment, it is part of the holiday which he enjoys; he sings its praise in lyrical terms. Of course he does; he need not enjoy its blessings a minute longer than is agreeable to him. There is always a transistor radio ready at hand to banish silence as soon as it has satisfied the tourist's wishes. The patient who must recover from the stresses of urban life does not differ from the tourist anyway. As a medicine, silence must be swallowed like any other medicine in small, pre-calculated portions. This silence, which can be ordered and rejected at will, is not the silence which primitive man has to deal with. To him, silence is not a servant or a cure, but a master. His whole life is enveloped in silence and he can only ward it off by talking, singing or drumming. He must exert himself to escape its reign, and no one can do this for long.

This silence, though oppressive and almost tangible, is never an absolute silence. Every now and then it is broken by the snapping of a twig, the rustle of a falling leaf, the cry of a bird, the hissing of a snake or simply the soughing of the wind in the tree-tops. Most of these sounds are eminently familiar to primitive man, but sometimes he hears one that carries an unclear message inviting more attentive listening. One never knows what is behind it. If nothing happens, the routine silence returns. One must have lived long and close enough with that silence to realize what it means. The trouble with lasting silence is that it speaks; it leaves the individual all alone by himself, with nothing to listen to but the voice of his heart, which is the true voice of silence. Such silence is powerful; it is always there, the ever present backdrop of primitive man's existence.

With few exceptions, primitive people dislike being alone. They prefer to go out in the company of others. This does not mean that they wish or try to talk all the time. They certainly do not. What they need is the opportunity to break the silence by a few words every time it becomes oppressive. I was told of two young men in South New

Guinea who came home late, after darkness had fallen. Not far from the village, something happened which frightened them. They immediately started singing, an act which they rationalized as a means to ward off the spirits that were haunting them. It is evident that, psychologically, they chased away a silence which had become oppressive through actualizing their inner fears.

The surest way to lay the disturbing effects of silence is, without doubt, by doing things which demand the individual's close and uninterrupted attention. When actively engaged, silence is not noticed. Such engagement of the mind is certainly not exceptional, but in primitive society it is not the rule either. With regard to activity, the ways of life of primitive man differ markedly from ours, and the influence of this second difference between the primitive and the modern world cannot easily be overrated. Actually, one of the first things striking the ethnographer's attention is that these people can relax by doing nothing in particular, by just sitting down, their hands resting in their lap, quietly listening to the murmur of a nearby brook or the cooing of a dove without apparently thinking of anything in particular. One might comment that, at times, the language of silence can be kind, but that is not the point here. What really matters is that primitive people have a remarkable faculty to enjoy doing nothing in particular. It is something we cannot achieve; even our children do not succeed.

The difference between western children and children from primitive and peasant communities was never brought more cogently home to me than during the frequent travels by coaster or motor-schooner which I made during my early years in Indonesia and New Guinea. Often, we had native children on board, mostly with, sometimes without parents or guardians. They never gave trouble. They squatted quietly somewhere or stood gazing at something happening on board or on the nearby shore. But western children were different. The first hours after embarking they were neither heard nor seen; they were looking around everywhere on board. But then, when scarcely half a day had passed, they turned up to ask their parents: 'Mummy, Dad, what shall I do now?' A question which returned every hour or two for as long as the trip lasted. It is evident that they felt that they should do something; they were explicit about it. Curiously enough, their parents never said: 'But child, why should you do anything at all?' Logically, it would have been the right answer: Why should anyone do anything at all if his food and drink are provided for? It is the answer the children never got from their harassed parents. When the children turned up they found their parents, too, doing something: reading, playing bridge, or talking local politics. To them, doing things was as natural as to their children. A racial difference? Certainly not. It is simply the outcome of the early conditioning of parents and children alike. I may quote here what, in 1969, I wrote for a symposium on educational problems in developing countries (CESO, 1969b: 38 ff.):

"The difference between the way children are brought up in western countries and the way they are educated in less complex societies is wider and goes deeper than the differences in religion, important as they are, would lead us to suppose. A sense for periodicity and order is instilled into the western child from birth. Within a few weeks after his birth the child has got used to a regular schedule of feeding, sleeping and crying. He is given toys from the moment his tiny fingers are capable of grasping them. Playing with these toys is not left to the child's own initiative; all the members of the family cooperate to teach him how to play properly. Everything is done to arouse his interest, and as the child grows older his parents and other grown-ups try to explain all sorts of things to him. He is encouraged to ask questions because that is the way to learn. And rightly so, for a great deal of knowledge is needed in our man-made world with its tremendous variety of inanimate objects. Yet, when the child asks questions about 'that young lady staying with Mr. Jones' we do not give him an answer and try to divert his attention to his toys. We set great store by the truth, but the truth about people is not meant for young children.

The directed playing with toys and the encouragement of provocative questions both serve a purpose. We want a child to do something. An older boy who lazes about, playing with the cat for hours on end, invariably gets on his father's nerves. 'For goodness' sake go and do something. I don't care what, just do something!' Basically, the father's exhortation does not make sense. Why should the child do something? Why shouldn't he learn the art of doing nothing? Yet, we don't want him to do nothing and neither, really, does the child. Children, too, think that they should be up and doing... etc.

The conditions under which children grow up in a developing country are widely different. Of course, the children in these countries also receive a home education, but it is an education directed towards other aims and values. Toys are relatively rare and undiversified, and playing does not constitute part of the child's training. The socialization of the child is the primary aim of home-education; the child must be oriented towards people, not to things. Despite an upbringing that seems permissive, the child learns to behave himself. One of the habits he is soon taught to drop is the asking of questions. Asking questions is not proper vis-à-vis older people, nor is it with regard to animals or inanimate objects... It is in keeping with this view, however, that the child usually has the opportunity to listen. Children may be present at almost all occasions, provided they keep quiet. The truth about people is not kept from them. People, i.e. the several individuals of the community, are important. At an early age the children learn the forms of differential behaviour with respect to specific relatives, such as a mother's brother or a father's sister. And rightly so: in a community with few goods, little money, and no shops, personal relations are of prime importance to all who are in need of anything. These relations must be carefully cultivated".

The conclusion is that from a very early age children in primitive communities are not encouraged to busy themselves, but to keep quiet and to listen. All that is expected of them in the way of activity is that they shall lend a hand in household chares, but in this respect parents usually are very permissive.

All this has a deep impact on our present problem, that of primitive man's intercourse with silence. He is exposed to it in a way which makes him extra receptive to its messages, that is, to the messages of his worried heart. The habit of sitting down without busying oneself with anything in particular – there is not always work to do – favours a state of mind which is only slightly above that of a light slumber, a state during which the subject slackens its control and the subconscious has a better chance to draw near to the threshold of consciousness. This state is closely akin to that of the medium in parapsychological experiments. He must keep his mind blank, i.e. he must think of nothing in particular in order to become more receptive to the stirrings of his subconscious. To modern people, conditioned from early youth to be perpetually active, this is an almost impossible task. They are always engaged with something. With primitive man this is different; in moments of leisure he easily surrenders to a state of absent-mindedness which facilitates the emergence of the reactions of the subconscious to his worries. Left alone to the company of an unrelenting silence, he is an easy victim to the phantoms of his most fundamental disquietude, the uncertainties of his life which are inspired by his universe, the spender of everything that is good and bad in his life. He fears that world, and yet he belongs to it and loves it. We argued that he cannot miss feeling addressed by the notions of intent suggested by its whims, whims which decide on life and death, on hunger and abundance. Theoretically, he can reject these feelings as he can reject his dreams and visions as mere imagination. But can he really?

Apart from the fact that he need not know the concept of imagination, he suffers from a serious lack of reliable knowledge concerning the natural processes accountable for good and bad weather, for plenty and dearth, for sickness and health. The notion of natural law is foreign to him. Law implies rule and regularity; to a great extent his experience of nature runs counter to these. The nature he knows is whimsical. The notion that there is something of an intention behind it is, to him, the only indication and hope that there is something better and wiser at the back of this all than pure chance, than cold indifference on the part of his universe. It can also be put another way: the apprehended intentionality is his only possible opportunity to get a grip on an unresponsive and seemingly inimical nature by which he can associate with it, and feel himself something like a partner and not the ostracized victim of its apathetic unconcern. The apprehended intention is the one and only lever which makes contact with it. Unfortunately, it is too vague, too fleeting to do anything with it. It suggests some mystery, but it is a mystery void of content. It must take a form of some sort to meet his need for communication, for penetrating into what is at the back of it. To that end, it must clothe the mystery in a shape tangible enough to accommodate approach, and strange enough to incorporate its mystery. Such forms cannot be conceived; mystery cannot be thought out but must be experienced. One must chance upon such forms. Man meets them in rare, extraordinary experiences which stand apart from reality, in the weird and unexpected phantoms called hallucinations, visions, or dreams. What is more, he seizes upon them to wrench a meaning from them.

Many anthropologists think that primitive man's preoccupation with dreams is more or less a matter of course. Following Tylor, they take the view that primitive people have no reason to distrust dreams because they have never been taught that dreams are empty. The argument is considerably weaker than it seems at first appearance. Dreaming is a normal function of the mind, the ineluctable companion of sleeping. Dreams are so numerous and, besides, so elusive, that one must have a sound reason not to neglect them, not to consider them empty. Indeed, primitive people do not attach meaning to every dream. Even they differentiate between important dreams and insignificant ones, between 'big' and 'little' dreams. Only the more impressive ones are taken as signs and turned into objects of meditation and speculation. Still, in this respect, primitives differ significantly from people who have been taught to ignore their dreams. For this interest in dreams they have a sound reason. They are confronted by a universe that has a lack of meaning to them. It suggests meaning by revealing itself as a world full of intent, and it debars mankind from communication and partnership by shrouding its meaning in mystery. Man's universe necessarily remains unreliable, inscrutable and whimsical for as long as no

159

meaning can be attached to the intentions which are suspected behind it. The arresting dream, the conspicuous hallucination and vision promise an opening which gives entrance to the secret behind the mystery in which the universe veils itself. This is why they get so much attention and become objects of meditation and scrutiny.

Arresting dreams are discussed and examined in the community of the men on their relevance and significance. What counts is whether the other men, too, feel addressed by a certain dream as a meaningful revelation of the world's mystery. This will only be the case if the dream refers to a problem or situation that is common to all the members of the group, at the very least to a situation or event that could befall any of them. In other words, it must express something of the tension between man and his universe, a universe that is experienced as both hostile and inviting, inimical and generous. The dream must also point a way out, a condition which will often be fulfilled because there is always a close connection between a dream and an unfulfilled desire.

A significant dream, then, is a dream which gives content to the mystery of the world and man's desire to get in touch with that world, to communicate with it by penetrating into the secret surmised behind its indifference and inscrutability. To have significance a dream need not have all-encompassing, cosmic implications. It can be concerned with very simple things, though things which are connected with difficulties or problems common to all. To give substance to these rather generalizing considerations, let us take a few hypothetical cases: one of a hallucination, and two of dreams.

The first is, in as far as its implications for the group as a whole are concerned, a border case. A man comes home with the story that, walking through the bush, he had an encounter with a large boar. He pointed his spear at the animal which suddenly changed into a man holding a large tuber in his hands who then disappeared. Near the place where he stood, the hunter discovered quite a number of wild yams well provided with sizable tubers. The story is puzzling. It must have a meaning but what? It certainly cannot be that, in future, boars should no longer be killed. They feed on tubers and, in this respect, are competitors of man. The most probable answer is that the man who had the encounter should refrain from hunting boars and that, as long as he does, he will be more lucky than others in finding tubers. There is something between him, tubers, and boars.

More conclusive is the following, equally hypothetical case. A man fell from a tree and broke his neck. The next night his brother dreams that he is following him on his way through the bush. He sees him climbing a big tree, trying to catch an opossum hiding between the leaves. Suddenly the oppossum leaps forward; it has a human face, a face which he recognizes as that of a man from a distant camp group. The next day the dream is discussed. We do not know whether early man already disposed of more or less detailed notions of sorcery or witchcraft; but, one thing is certain: such a dream is a contribution to their development. The man seen in the dream is under serious suspicion anyhow.

Of more lasting consequence might be the following dream which a man had during a period when game was scarce. In his dream, he is loitering near a well, far away in the bush. A giant emerges from the water, half·man, half animal, his torso covered with a thick hide of curly hairs. The dreamer wishes to fly but the giant orders him to stay and to look closely at what is going to happen. To the man's surprise he suddenly realizes that he must address the giant as grandfather. Then the giant squats down. He lets his whole body quiver so violently that drops of water fly from his hide on all sides. The moment they touch the ground, the droplets change into bandicoots and wallabies. At that moment, the dreamer wakes up. He tells the men what he has dreamt. They listen in silence. It is almost certain that, after a while, one of the older men says: 'tell it once more', thus intimating that the story has significance to him.

The story is a hypothetical one and I shall not try to imagine what the men did with the story. It would be an altogether too cheap trick of fortune telling because three elements in it have been taken from Aranda ritual and myth: the well, the covered torso, and the quivering; they all belong to a ritual promoting the fertility of a totem species (below: 172 f.). Yet, it is not improbable that these rituals have their origin in dreams of this kind. We know for certain that many rituals have their origin in dreams or visions. We have ample information on the first beginnings of new cults in North America, Melanesia and Africa. Most of these cults are prophetic cults. One of the earliest accounts is that by Mooney of the Ghost Dance religion (1896) in the United States. Descriptions of the history of many other cults have since followed, both from America and elsewhere. Well-known are the Melanesian cargo-cults and, to a somewhat lesser degree, the anti-witchcraft movements in Africa. All these cults invariably begin with an impressive dream or vision. It is tempting to conclude that the first cults also originated from dreams. Yet, this is logically inadmissible. All these new cults originated in cultures which already had rituals and cults, which disposed of an elaborate arsenal of models telling how to react to impressive dreams. Early man was in a less favourable position. He had no models; he had to create them. No one can tell with certainty how he created them. It would be rash to conclude that he immediately started dramatizing the dream like the one in question. It is even improbable that he did. It is more likely that nothing happened until one or more other men had had similar dreams. The one thing which counts is that dreams confirm the surmise, aroused by the experienced feeling of a hidden intent, that behind the silent universe lies a secret which embodies all in one both the willingness and the unwillingness of nature to satisfy the wants of man, and that, if man could communicate with that secret, it would be all the better. Then man could find himself a place in it as a participant, perhaps even as a partner.

It is pointless to hypothesize in detail about how early man developed his rites and religious representations. All we can do is to study the outcome, the religion of primitive man. A survey of its main features, viz. of myth and ritual, magic, sorcery and witchcraft, of animism, taboo, and sacrifice and prayer must decide upon the correctness of our supposition that it is man's need for communication, for becoming a partner in his universe, which is the driving force behind that intriguing complex of contradictory belief and behaviour that we call religion. One thing, however, is known for certain: that, to feel at ease, man must feel at home in his universe.

IX

Myth and Ritual

1. Introduction; some general observations

There are close relations between myth and ritual, but these relations are anything but uniform. Many myths do not refer to any ritual action at all. All they have to do with ritual is that they may be recited in the course of ritual celebrations or that their recitation as such must be considered as a ritual act. In such cases, the relation between myth and ritual is thin; sometimes so thin that it can be ignored. Other myths, however, give an explication or justification of certain rituals. Most rituals are connected with such a founding myth which can be looked upon as its charter. Whereas there are many myths which do not refer to a ritual, there are few rituals which are not associated with a myth, fewer even than sometimes is supposed (below: 168). Most of the rituals without a myth belong to the category of simple, magic rites. They will be discussed in the next chapter. The present one is primarily devoted to an enquiry into those rituals in which the relation with myth is closest, the rituals which are dramatizations or visualizations of myth. Before we discuss them in more detail, we shall introduce the subject by a few observations concerning myth and ritual in general.

A rite is a religious act, i.e. every act concerned with an unverifiable reality which is both feared and sought, a reality which, by its mystery, amply transcends the conditions of everyday life. That reality inspires awe and fear, as well as a recurrent longing for its presence and goodness. This longing is of two types. The one is connected with the simple, often daily acts performed to express an undisturbed relation between man and the supernatural, such as saying grace before meals, the libation of a few drops of newly-brewed beer, the bringing of small offerings to the house shrine on certain days and occasions. The other type is connected with the major rituals celebrated when there is a general feeling that the relations with the supernatural are disturbed or decaying, and are in serious need of repair. The two types have many intermediate forms; on the one extreme we find the big expiatory sacrifice, on the other the simple gesture like that of making a cross.

The supernatural, the other reality, is sought for; but it is also feared and this implies that it cannot be lightly approached. The two find expression in every rite.

Every ritual has two aspects; the one is turned to the realization of contact and communication with the supernatural, the other to the expression of awe by the observance of a respectful distance. Every ritual combines a transaction with the supernatural and a taboo.

A taboo is more than a mere avoidance. Like the taboos observed by tribal Australians in their interaction with affines, notably in that between a man and his mother-in-law, the religious avoidance called taboo expresses respect combined with appreciation. It expresses man's recognition of the specific place and power of the manifestations of the hidden world which, though separate and apart, has an un-mistakable effect on the visible world. The recognition of this power of the sacred constitutes part of every ritual act. Sometimes it happens that the taboos associated with ritual are so elaborate that the observance of these taboos becomes a separate ritual which, by painstakingly delimitating the sacred from the profane, creates a situation by which the sacred acquires a prominent, clearly-defined place within the reality of the everyday world and can, from this context, exert a beneficial influence on its conditions (cf. below, ch. XI 3,4).

The more usual case is that the ritual performance is concentrated less on taboo (avoidance) and more on action. Yet, action is always combined with certain taboos which express the power and otherness of the sacred. Taboos are also associated with telling a myth. A myth refers to manifestations of the other, sacred reality. It incorporates the mystery and otherness of man's universe and thus commands respect. It has the authority which, by nature, a universe has over any individual. Myth can be defined as religious truth in story form; or, more precisely, as a story which, within the framework of a given religion, was once, or still is, valid as religious truth (Van Baal 1971: 16).

This definition is too general to be handled as an instrument for delimiting myth from the religious folktale. It is not a weakness of the definition alone. Even to the members of the religious community concerned, it is difficult to decide what is merely a religious folktale – an edifying or revelatory story which need not be accepted as truth – and what a real myth, a story which, as true revelation, has authority and must be believed by all. Even civilized society has difficulties on this point. One famous case of diverging opinions is that of the Apocrypha of the Old and New Testament. The main difficulty for making the difference between myth and folktale operational, lies in the fact that a religion is not a fixed doctrine, but a living whole of practices and beliefs relating to an unverifiable world behind the visible one. A living whole is never static; it is involved in a continuous process of change and adaptation which affects the value set upon its constituent parts, myths and folktales included. The myth of today can become the folktale of tomorrow, and vice versa.

More rewarding for understanding the intrinsic character of myth is another approach. It takes its point of departure in an observation made by Lévi-Strauss: myths are always concerned with difficulties in human thought and life which they try to explain, or at least to reduce to forms which make these difficulties bearable, by attenuating the scandal they give to the mind. This is the message proper to every myth. Throughout the four volumes of *Les Mythologiques* we are confronted with

163

this etiological character of myth.

It is an important point, but it would be wrong to dwell with Lévi-Strauss and others upon this one point alone. Myth – at least primitive myth – has a second characteristic, as general and as obtrusive as its etiological nature: the fact that in every myth there always is at least one element, event, situation or phenomenon which is impossible because it is inconsistent with reality or reason, and usually with both. I cannot fathom why successive mythologists have never cared to give due attention to this particular. The ineluctable combination of an impossibility with the etiological function of myth is, really, as baffling as the fact that it has been neglected. However this may be, it confronts us with the paradox that a myth explains a difficulty by means of an impossibility. The most general and obviously the most fundamental characteristic of myth is this paradoxality, this inherent contradiction. Although, after all, it is not so surprising as it seems because all religion is paradoxical, the fact is significant enough to make it the point of departure of further enquiry.

Myth shares this characteristic with two other phenomena, the dream and the Märchen, i.e. the kind of folktale which can be religious as well as non-religious and can include legends, fairy-tales and sagas*. This makes it attractive to pay due attention to the differences between myth on the one hand, and Märchen and dreams on the other. Those between Märchen and myth do not give serious difficulties. They converge on the point that myth is a serious matter, backed up by authority and believed to be true, whereas the Märchen is alternately of a ludic or an edifying nature, not necessarily believed to be true, and told either for fun or as a moral metaphor. It has a specific charm and this charm lies precisely in its paradoxality which it shares with myth. The paradoxical event or situation is essential for the Märchen; it defines its specific style, that inimitable something which never fails to enthral children and grown-up alike. It can also be found in the few successful efforts at composing new Märchen made in modern times: Lewis Caroll's Alice in Wonderland, De Saint-Exupéry's Le petit Prince, and Tolkien's Lord of the Ring. The wonder is the Märchen's most essential ingredient as it is in myth. Only, its sense has been reversed. What is deadly earnest in myth, is ludic and charming in the Märchen.

With the dream it is different. Dreams often contain impossible elements; but they cannot be called really essential. Dreams can be and sometimes are rational. This has important implications. On the one hand, the frequency of the paradoxical element confirms that the dream is the model on which myth is based, like myth is to Märchen. On the other hand, it is evident that not every dream could be the model of a myth, but only those which contained the paradoxical element. It was the para-doxical dreams and dream-like experiences which were deemed sufficiently meaningful to become standardized as myths, a circumstance which underlines the importance of paradoxality to myth. It reflects the paradoxality of the human condition and of man's experience in and to his world: a subject opposing a universe of which he is a part, desirous to participate in a universe that is both inviting and hostile. This raises two questions: how dreams become standardized in myth, and

* The term Märchen has no equivalent in English and can best be left untranslated.

what, in this process, is the role of ritual, the religious act which is so closely associated with myth.

2. The standardization of myth and the role of ritual

When a dream experience, so impressive that the community accepts it as significant truth, is not an elaboration of an existing mythical theme, then it is provocative of action. The kind of action, however, depends upon the community's interpretation of the vision's message. It may be understood as a warning to remove the present settlement to a place at a safer distance from a nearby river or volcano, as an exhortation to make war on a neighbouring group, or as an admonition to cultivate relations with the elusive main character of the vision. If the latter is the case, some sort of a rite has to be devised in answer to the message. If the celebration of the rite is a success, either because consecutive events suggest that it has wrought some stroke of good luck, or because the celebration satisfied certain emotional needs of the community, there is a chance that the performance will be repeated, and by the institutionalization of these early experiments develop into a recurrently celebrated ritual, an institutionalization which implies the standardization of the vision's story into a myth which contains the rationale of the ritual. In other words: the action provoked can be short-lived and incidental. Even the dream which induced a ritual experiment need not last in memory. A repetition of the ritual experiment will not be contemplated unless it has given satisfaction to the participants. If it has not, repetition does not occur, and the dream will be forgotten.

If the celebration gives satisfaction, one may be sure that the dream experience which induced the performance is concerned with existential problems common to all. In such a case, it is almost certain that the initial celebration will inspire new dreams and visions which underscore the truth or validity of the original one. This is not just a theoretical possibility; as a matter of fact, this is what happens time and again. The reports of such prophetic movements as the Ghost Dance Religion or the Melanesian cargo-cults afford a rich collection of data on recurrent supplementary and affirmative dreaming by the prophet and, above all, by his followers who participated in the ensuing rites.

The analysis of myth confirms this view. The ordinary myth greatly exceeds the compass of a single dream. Besides, the myth does not simply describe a supernatural reality, very often it is simultaneously the description of a ritual process. In my analysis of Marind-anim mythology, I was struck by the coincidence of its description of symbolic, cosmic processes with that of the symbolic acts and representations of these cosmic events in the ritual process. The paraphernalia worn by the ritual performers and the ornaments decorating the mythical heroes in the founding myth are identical; identical too are the symbolic acts of these ritual performers and those of their mythical paragons. The myth reflects the ritual just as the ritual reflects the myth; the two are inseparable and must be the products of a common development, vision inspiring ritual action and ritual action new visions.

Myth and ritual validate each other in the positive effect of the celebration on the participants individually, and on the community's well-being and solidarity generally. Here, Durkheim's analysis of the latent function of ritual (Durkheim 1912) comes to mind. Each of the participants behaves in an uncommon way, each knows for certain that he is engaged in an uncanny, superhuman reality, each expresses feelings of awe and surrenders to an abandonment common to all. The participants are united in togetherness among themselves because they all serve a common purpose by behaving extraordinarily, if not like madmen. But this togetherness includes their universe which is present in the symbolic forms and characters represented by the performers. The ultimate effect of the celebration on the participants is that they go home with the certainty of having experienced the common good.

From another point of view, the progressive development of a ritual and its concomitant myth can be described as a process of institutionalization. Conscious deliberation and rationalization make their entrance. Ritual roles must be assigned, sequences be determined, ritual grounds and ceremonial paraphernalia be prepared. This implies that both the ritual and the founding myth are more and more standardized. A systematization takes place on the basis of a logic derived from the principles of classification inherent in the founding revelations. Institutions are matters of a community's deliberate efforts. The growth of the body of myths and rituals is controlled by the community's critical reflection upon the significance which new additions have within the framework of the prevailing institutions and views. This does not exclude the possibility of important changes or the introduction of new views, but it certainly implies a process of conventionalization according to basic patterns. In this development, which begins with a significant vision or dream, one cannot speak of a myth which engenders the ritual because, beginning with the first effort at ritualization of the vision's message, the two develop hand in hand, each inspiring the growth of the other. Nor is it possible to say, with Robertson Smith (1889), that the ritual engenders the myth. It may inspire the emergence of new myths but before and after the ritual depends upon a (proto)mythical message.

The close interwovenness of myth and ritual raises a problem, that of the occurrence of myths without ritual and rituals without myths. We must go deeper into this matter before we return to the early forms of ritual.

That there are myths without ritual and that they are of very common occurrence can hardly be a surprise. Existing myths and rituals easily engender new dreams and revelatory visions, and these need not always suggest new additions to the ritual to be welcomed as information which supports the existing ritual practice by extending the backdrop of mystery which envelops the universe. People are fascinated by the mysteries of their world and they do not confine themselves to listening attentively to anyone who can relate new experiences which confirm the truth of the community's mythology or add new items which suit its pattern, but they eagerly enquire after the myths and ritual experiences of neighbouring tribes. After all, new visions and dreams of a revelatory nature are not a matter of daily occurrence. If new ones emerge, they are rarely more than elaborations on already well-known themes. Really new models are always the exception. Of course they are. We noted earlier that even in dreams a certain preference for a relatively restricted number of themes and models can be observed (above: 40). The number of themes which can be derived from dreams as significant, is necessarily even more restricted. They are, naturally, a minority. It is no wonder that people listen attentively to the revelations which their neighbours accepted as significant. How often and how consistently they do this is made abundantly clear by Lévi-Strauss's *Mythologiques*; they are a continuous demonstration of all peoples' readiness to borrow mythical material from each other. Apparently, they are hungry for information on things transcendent. And yet, they are never receptive to this new information in a purely passive way. Every borrowing requires adaptation to the borrowers' own mythical and cultural heritage, and we may be sure that much of this adaptation is the result of a combination of newly-induced dreams and the conscious deliberation of the leaders of the relevant cults.

Besides, new revelations are not always borrowed or incidentally received: often they are actively sought. We argued that primitive people dislike being alone and prefer the company of others (above: 156). Nevertheless, there are always a few individuals who court silence and solitude, who retire to the wilderness to listen to spirit voices. A well-known and quite sympathetic case is that told by Lloyd Warner of the Murngin medicine-man Willidjungo (1958: 212-214). Willidjungo had two 'familiars', two little birds which he kept under his armpits. They talked to him at night or when he was in the bush. They instructed him how to act as a medicine-man. Another, different case is that of the Marind-anim medicine-man of Wendu, a notable clairvoyant; he sometimes disappeared for a couple of days which he passed in complete solitude. Father Verschueren told me about him how, one night, when they were talking pleasantly together in the presbytery of Wendu, he suddenly broke off the conversation, and without saying a word walked out into the dark night. Not before the third day did he return to the village; and no one, not even his house-mates, ever knew where he had been. Courting the grand silence of solitude in the wilderness is not a technique first developed by the religious thinkers of higher civilizations; it is practised already by the religious leaders of primitive societies. It is a technique because these mystics consciously withdraw to solitude to meet un-foreseeable experiences. Ritual, once it has been institutionalized, becomes subject to conscious considerations and even to conscious deliberation.

About primitive man's conscious deliberations on ritual and mythological matters we know comparatively little. Such deliberations are rarely held in a white man's presence; for an important part we must depend on circumstantial evidence. A good case of such evidence is that of the inconsistencies noted in the otherwise strictly consequent Marind-anim system of classification. They could be explained from the efforts at harmonization induced by the emergence of a new cult-form among the coastal Marind-anim, that of the *imo*, an originally inland variant of the coastal *mayo*-cult. There is historical evidence of close contacts between the communities which are the traditional centres of the two cult-forms, two coastal villages situated at a distance of some 90 km from each other. These contacts led to a small number of significant changes in the re-partition of subclans between the moieties and in the classification of certain forms of magic. Changes of this kind are impossible without

167

premeditated deliberation on matters of ritual and myth (Van Baal 1966: 937-948). The case illustrates the influence which conscious thought and consideration have on the development of ritual and myth when contacts with other people introduce new ideas and vistas. Something similar happens when intertribal contacts lead to the introduction of new myths or, more correctly, when impressive stories of revelations told by foreign people inspire mystical consideration of their contents. They are not just borrowed but adapted to one's own, already existing body of mythical information. In this adapted form, they extend and specify the mythical backdrop of a people's own ritual life. It may be that some new forms of ritual are borrowed with them, but it also happens (and this obviously is the more frequent case) that they are not directly connected with the current ritual and simply contribute to the extension of the local body of myths without ritual.

A more complicated problem is that of the occurrence of rituals without myth. Rituals of this kind mostly fall into the category of simple, magical rites. Such rites often are borrowed from other tribes, the relevant formula in a foreign, unintelligible language included. The formula may refer to some mythical event known to these foreign people, but the borrowers of the formula do not know that. Moreover, it is not even necessary that a formula refers to a mythical content. Many formulas simply express a wish or a metaphor. Some do this in symbolic language, others are no more than matter of fact statements. Though their number is probably smaller than reported, there is ample reason to consider the possibility that they originated in analogy with formulas referring more openly, if not to myth, to a mystery of some sort at the back of the visible world. Once the existence of such a world of mystery has been revealed by vision or myth, references to those mysteries need not remain confined to what became known about them by revelation. We shall have to say more about magical formulas in the next chapter; here, the statement suffices that, on the basis of accepted revelations about an invisible world, simple rites may develop which do not hold any definite reference to these revelations. They can be explained as more or less individual applications by analogy.

Communal rites which do not refer to myth are decidedly rare. The question arises whether they exist at all. The ethnographic literature on New Guinea, in particular that on the mountain peoples of the island, affords various cases of rituals without myth. More recent ethnographic information gives serious ground for the supposition that the relevant myths have been hushed up by the natives concerned. The ethnographic work of Father Hylkema, who worked in the Star Mountains and in the Kapauku region, gives convincing evidence that the body of myths and *Märchen* of these peoples is far more extensive than formerly guessed (Hylkema 1974, and provisional data collections still unpublished). The point is that the mythical background of a ritual is much easier kept a secret than its celebration which, if the ritual performance is not restricted to one or two households, cannot escape from being noticed by the ethnographer.

Summarizing our discussions on rituals without myths and myths without ritual, it can be concluded that both can be explained by appealing to situations in which myths and rituals are existing institutions, but that they do not explain the origin of either myth or ritual. The latter must have originated in conjunction on the basis of significant visions or dreams which inspired to action and further dreams.

By now we must return to the earliest forms of ritual. Is it possible to make a conjecture about the forms adopted by early rituals? Taboo, prayer, offering, sacrifice, divination, singing, dance, trance, and the dramatic presentation of myth are, with magic, the forms to consider. Theoretically, each of these can have played a part in primeval ritual, either alone or in combination with other forms. Yet, some are closer to the dream experience than others, and a short review is well in place, a review from which we exclude magic which, in its performance, leans heavily on other ritual forms such as prayer, offering, singing, dancing, and the dramatic presentation of myth.

Taboo is an expression of respect associated with every myth and ritual (above: 163). Taboos can become so numerous and diversified that their observance develops into an organized cult. Such a cult presupposes a development of some duration as well as a certain measure of rationalization which explains or justifies the systematization of these forms of avoidance. In other words, such a cult implies the existence of fairly elaborate notions concerning supernatural beings who demand avoidance. It must be of later date. On the other hand: taboo must almost certainly have been part of early man's reaction to visionary revelations. However, it is fairly improbable that this resulted in a cult in which avoidance is the dominant motif.

In primitive society prayer is very often combined with offering and/or sacrifice. The combination of prayer and offering stands a good chance of being one of the really early forms of ritual. Not the combination of prayer and sacrifice. The latter implies a ritual killing; and even if it is easy to slaughter a domestic animal ritually, it is very difficult to do it to game. Game must be killed in the field, not in the sacrificial grounds where, barring exceptional circumstances or provisions, it can only be offered as a food. The combination of prayer and offering is, indeed, a form of ritual which has been reported from various primitive societies, though not from Australia. This, however, cannot be accepted as a reason to contest the possibility that offering and prayer were already practised by early man. The Australian form of ritual, the dramatic presentation of myth, differs fundamentally from that of offering and prayer. It includes a certain degree of identification of the performer with the mythical being impersonated, an identification absent in prayer which expresses the performer's dependence on the supernatural being addressed. The fact that the latter is usually identified with an ancestor or a comparable father figure (we return to this point later in this book: cf. below: 199) presents a strong argument in favour of the possibility that prayer and offering figured among the earliest forms of ritual. The father symbol is old and widely spread.

Closely associated with prayer, offering and sacrifice, are the practice of divination and the observance of omens. Of these, the latter is probably very old. The interpretation of events as signs is an immediate consequence of a worldview capitalizing on intentionality shrouded in mystery. Yet, its impact on the growth and development of ritual is small. Divination is different. It is a form of discourse with supernatural agencies aiming at obtaining their assistance or, at the very least, their directives for further action. In divination the person-to-person form of communication is obvious. Equally obvious is its dependence on a fairly well developed system of representations concerning the supernatural. Divination can hardly be seen as a very early form of ritual.

The place of singing and dancing as early forms of ritual is dubious. Song and dance are forms of human expression which are not typically religious. Superficially, it is perhaps an attractive hypothesis that "savage religion is something not so much thought out as danced out" (Marett 1914: XXXI), but one should always keep in mind that man is a being who expresses himself. Self-expression is fundamental to him. Why should he not express himself in rhythmic movements of his body or in sonorous singing without any other motive than the pure need to express his mood? Such expression can be inspired by religious motives, but it can do perfectly as well without. To constitute rites, singing and dancing must express religious contents, must be the means to realize such specific forms of religious communication as prayer, trance and the dramatization of myth. They sometimes are, but not always; and there is no reason to suppose that this was different during the days of early man.

Dances in particular are often too readily interpreted as expressions of vague religious feelings. Many primitive dances are so strikingly unfamiliar to us that we are inclined to suspect some form of religious inspiration. During the nine years which I spent in New Guinea, I saw quite a variety of dances performed in their native setting. They always started me wondering what on earth moved the dancers to express themselves in such an extraordinary manner. Yet, the same thought occurred to me when, after more than three years of detention in a prison camp in Celebes, I returned to civilization and attended a dance of European people who had passed the war in a more congenial fashion than I had. Dancing is always a deviant way of expressing oneself, and it is not without significance that the one and only Papuan dance which struck me as unmistakably religious – a Marind-anim *weiko-zi* performance – was preceded by the impersonation of a small number of mythical beings. Dancing and singing are forms of expression which do not stand on themselves. They can only become cult forms by combination with other forms of ritual.

A frequent combination is that with trance, a state of possession induced by singing, dancing or music, and sometimes induced by drugs. Trance is a demonstration of divine power, a revelation of divinity in and through the medium who is swayed by it. The identity of that divinity can be known from earlier revelations, but the trance can also be an instrument by which new divinities reveal themselves. Consequently, we must include trance among those forms of ritual which may have originated early in the history of man.

Finally, there is the ritual dramatization of myth. A myth is never taken so seriously as by its dramatization; it posits the myth as true reality. It is a cult form found in an immense variety of religions, ranging from those of the early Australians to the Christian celebration of the mass. Besides, like prayer, offering and trance, it is a plausible reaction to a dream experience that is accepted as a significant revelation. It certainly reaches far back into the early history of mankind. It is to these forms of ritual celebration that the now following sections of this chapter are devoted.

170

As cases to illustrate the dramatization of myth, we shall present brief descriptions of the Aranda of Central Australia and of the Marind-anim of southern New Guinea. They have in common that the religions of both are totemistic, but they differ in this respect that the former are very simple hunters and gatherers, the latter horticulturists who are technically more advanced. The choice of the Marind-anim as our second case has the disadvantage that we have to give up the opportunity to demonstrate the role of mythical drama in non-totemistic cultures. On the other hand, the case of the Marind-anim enables us to call attention to the role which sophistication and mystic rationalization can play in primitive religious systems. Far from being crude dramatizations of savage myths, these rites bear witness to a combination of keen dialectic thought with an elaborate symbolism. This intellectual aspect of primitive religion is worth more consideration than it usually receives.

3. Aranda myth and ritual

In the extensive body of Aranda myth, one conspicuous trait is prevalent; i.e. that of the wandering clan-ancestor who, during his peregrinations, generated men and their relevant totem animals and totem plants. The ancestors gave shape to the land so that today every well, hill, or other conspicuous spot in the landscape reminds the natives of the adventures of one or other of these ancestors. In many places they left something, a ritual implement, an ornament, a footprint, etc. In these places they stored the germs of life which are capable of impregnating the women and of fertilizing the totem species (above: 141). These germs abound in places where the ancestor ultimately retired and incarnated himself in a rock or well, or dwells in a venerated sacred object (*tjurunga*).

These ancestors are life incarnate. Though dead, they persist; they can and do reincarnate by entering as germs of life into a passing woman in the shape of an invisible grain or a minute bullroarer. The woman feels it in her womb (the first stirring of the foetus) and realizes that by now she is pregnant. The child which in time will be born from her is the reincarnation of that particular ancestor whose identity is established by the old men after having heard the woman's communications about her experience. Of course, it is not always one of the great ancestors himself who impregnates a woman. It may be an anonymous son or one of the numerous germs of life deriving from one of the ancestor's ritual implements or ornaments which he left behind on his wanderings. The child is not necessarily the lesser for having been born from a more humble 'dreamtime' character though, if a male, he will never be the 'owner' of an important rite like the reincarnation of a more prominent mythical ancestor.

The germ of life stays with its new reincarnation until death. It defines its owner's identity and his or her totemic relations. At death, the germ returns to the place where it came from to go to rest there until it decides to incarnate itself anew. Thus, every living individual is indissolubly connected with a certain part of the country and the spirit-world associated with that part, the hidden essence of its permanence and virility. The bond between the individual and his 'country' is a strongly affective one. When an old man feels that death cannot be far off, he will return to his 'country' because it is there that he wishes to die. It is the place to which he belongs most intimately.

The myths are stories of the ancestors' wanderings and conflicts. Many of these conflicts are conflicts between fathers and sons. They reflect the antagonism between every two successive generations as embodied in the Central and North Australian sections system which divides each of the moieties into generations, successive generations belonging to different sections, and alternate generations (i.e. those of grandfather and grandson) to the same. These section-systems have always been interpreted as systematizations of the complicated marriage rules (such as those prescribing marriage with a mother's mother's brother's daughter's daughter) what they are not. The natives themselves explicitly state that the choice of a marriage partner is not defined by section membership but by actual relations of consanguinity. Their point of view is correct; the sections function primarily in ritual, in particular in rituals connected with initiation. Here, the fathers of one moiety present their sons for circumcision or sub-incision to the men of their own generation in the other moiety, the potential fathers-in-law of the novices. The opposition between the generations is emphatically expressed in the harsh treatment dealt out by the older generation to the younger. In the case of circumcision, its execution is the work of the older section of the opposite moiety, but in other cases the concomitant disciplining is performed by members of the older section of the boy's own moiety (e.g. showing a young man the sacred object, *tjurunga*, embodying his mythical ancestor). The interpretation of the section-system as one for the regulation of marriage is due to the fact that the big rituals are always celebrated by intermarrying groups. This implies that the order of the ritual coincides with that of intermarriage, the participating groups exchanging women as well as rites between them. In that order of the rites the sections are of specific importance.

We must return to the myths. Other stories deal with the conflicts and friendships between ancestors of different clans; they enlarge on how their tracks crossed each other, where totems and children emanated from their bodies, where they celebrated rituals and so on. Apart from the initiation-rites proper, the rituals commemorating the mythical ancestors are relatively simple. One form is that of visiting and rearranging the more important totemic sites where the sacred objects are stowed away which were left by an ancestor and added to by later generations. T. G. H. Strehlow gives an enchanting account of such a visit (1947: 1 ff.): the careful approach under the leadership of some old men, the opening up of the depository and the unwrapping of the sacred objects (*tjurunga*) by the leader, their respectful circulation among the men who, one by one, press them for a few moments to their bodies, the greasing and repacking of the *tjurunga* to the soft-voiced chanting of the myth by the elders of the group, the final rearrangement of the spot, and the leave-taking ceremony. Later, closer to home, an impersonation of the ancestor will follow. This is a more spectacular affair. It can happen on an occasion such as the one just mentioned, but usually it takes place as part of a whole series of such performances. The personifier is a man who is a reincarnation of the ancestor or of one of his descendents. Many an hour is devoted to his body decoration. His torso is decorated with tufts of down which are stuck to the body with blood supplied by some of the assisting participants. His face is painted and on his head he often bears one or more *tjurunga*, carefully packed in leaves and held together by cords made of human hair. He may also have a long, phallus-like staff tied to his back. When, after some three hours, the decoration has been completed, he enters upon the scene, marching in a certain stylized way. Then he sits down, quivering his body all over so that tufts of down are blown off and fly around, like the ancestor did on his travels, shedding around the germs of life from which new beings can arise (cf. i.a. Strehlow 1947: 88).

There is little drama in these acts. All the attention is focussed upon the correct presentation of the ancestor's attire. He must resemble the 'dreamtime' being as closely as possible. As its reincarnation or that of one of its near descendents, the personifyer may be said to be the 'dreamtime' being himself. The paraphernalia bestowed on him are the same as those recorded by myth. The representation dramatizes all that is essential in the myth: the imposing appearance of the ancestor, the emanation of life-germs by quivering, and the presentation of the sacred *tjurunga* which the ancestor carried with him.

These *tjurunga* are often presented in phallic shape: the available photographs are fairly convincing on this point. This has its reason. In various myths (and certainly so in those of the northern Aranda) the ancestor produces sons and totem animals without the intermediary of women. And even if there is question of birth by women the part taken by the male ancestor prevails. This is most singularly the case in the final rite of the great *Engwura* ritual, an initiation rite consisting of a long and complicated series of impersonations of ancestors belonging to different clans. Spencer and Gillen gave a description of one. On the last night, the great Atjilpa-ancestor appears, represented by the headman of the celebrating Atjilpa clan himself (*atjilpa* = wild cat):

"He kneels down with some great object in front of him, made of two tjurunga which are bound together and decorated in such a way as to suggest an enormous phallus (cf. the highly suggestive photograph in Spencer and Gillen 1927: fig. 106). Its lower end is held in front of the abdomen and he slowly moves it up and down. He is assisted by two men, one kneeling to the right and one to the left, who hold his arms and help him to move the phallus-like object up and down. The two men belong to the opposite moiety* and represent the two wives of the Atjilpa-ancestor. In the meantime the initiates lie down on the ground in respectful silence. A small group of old men surrounds the actors, singing softly. All night long the monotonous rising and falling of the mysterious object goes on incessantly. Its significance is unmistakable: it is the first ancestor manipulating his phallus with the assistance of his two wives. It is a symbolic copulation. And the most remarkable of all is the name given to the mysterious object: *ambilia ekura*, amnion, womb. We remember now that [the myth told that] the first ancestor sent the *kuruna*, the life-germs, into his two women from the *ambilia ekura* he had near at hand. In other words: his phallus is called amnion and emptying the amnion simply means copulating.

The real secret of the rite is the symbolic inversion of the male genital. The penis is called a womb and the womb is moved up and down like a penis, all the time ejecting the germs of life which will impregnate the two women represented invertedly by two old men" (Van Baal 1963: 211).

* In the original I wrote "to opposite moieties". This is a mistake.

173

Essentially, the rite is an act of arrogating fertility to the male sex. These same Australians deny physical fatherhood and pretend that sexual intercourse has nothing to do with procreation and is for fun only. The ritual leaves no doubt that they know better (there are other facts which corroborate this view) and what the men really wish is to claim that their ritual contribution to fertility is decisive.

Another interesting point in this context is the role played by inversion as a technique of symbolization. There are other cases, e.g. that of the python in the myth of the Kunapipi cult in Arnhem Land (Northern Territory). The giant python *Julunggul* swallows the *Wauwalak* sisters, a mythical event to which the informant of Berndt gave the following comment: "and when the *Julunggul* (i.e. the snake) swallows the *Wauwalak*, that is like a penis being swallowed by a vagina, only we put it the other way round" (Berndt 1951: 39). Inversion is a technique to indicate that the inverted phenomenon belongs to another order of reality.

This arrogation of the female share in procreation does not imply that women are excluded from every participation in these and other rituals. Of course, in the fertility rites their contribution is marginal. Yet, they are the providers of food and sex whenever these commodities are needed. And that is often. More important is their role of frightened and admiring spectators who are kept at bay. Their fright and admiration are indispensable. Without them the males would be the easy victims of the sophistication which results from too much inside knowledge. The fright of the women confirms that, however misleading and simple the means applied, the men are doing something really 'awe-full', are handling something basically uncanny. All the same, the role of the women in these rites is small. They do better, however, in other rites, notably in the funeral rites which are predominantly a female affair.

The latter is not a typically Australian phenomenon; in many parts of the world women are important functionaries in funeral rites. They always do the better part of the wailing. Excesses in the demonstration of grief are almost invariably female roles. This association of women with death has wider connotations. It is found in many systems of classification; death and the female sex are very often associated with each other, and this association might well be connected with the role of women in mourning and funeral rites. In essence, the association is logically contradictory. Women are the proper producers of life, both in nature and in society; whereas the men, who everywhere indulge in fighting and warfare, are producers of death. In ritual, however, it is just the reverse. Here, the men pose as the champions of life and fertility who do all that is humanly possible to counter the disquieting uncertainties which are incumbent upon all who live in complete dependence on the whims of nature. In Australia, one of the important functions of the clan is the ritual promotion of the totem's fertility, a function performed by the symbolic repetition of the prime ancestor's life-giving acts. Thus, they compensate for the functional insufficiences which result from an unequal division of labour between the sexes.

The main features of Aranda myth and ritual can be summarized as follows. In the first place, myth represents the total universe. There is not a single place of any importance which does not have its specific relationships with one of the ancestors, and there is not a single human individual who is not a reincarnation of one of these ancestors or of any of the germs of life which they deposited in the universe. There is a mystery common to all. The total universe and the total community of men are homologous, all descendent from or procreated by ancestors who are incarnate in man and world, the real spenders of their fertility.

In the second place, this homology is renewed and reconstituted in ritual. Here, the ancestors appear in their mythical attire which is identical with the ritual one, just as the ritual implements are the same as and identical with those used by the ancestors in myth, and the personifiers representing them are identical with the ancestors whose reincarnations they are. Even the stories told of the ancestors are influenced by the rites. The recurrent theme of the conflicts between father and son clearly reflects the antagonism between the opposing sections of fathers and sons in ritual. It is evident that the myth which engendered the ritual has, in turn, been amplified and enriched by dreams engendered by the ritual practice itself.

Finally, and most important of all, myth, ancestor, and man are one in their common participation in what is, essentially, a human phenomenon, dreaming. Mythical time is *dreamtime*, and myth and totems are *dreamings*. Everything which is mysterious in the Aranda world is as far-off and as nearby, as concrete and as intangible as the dream which gave it its shape, and was then validated by the experience wrought upon them by the impressive forms of its dramatization.

4. *Marind-anim myth and ritual*

The overt identification of myth and dreaming is an exclusively Australian feature. No other people ever expressed themselves so lucidly on the intimate relations between the forms of their experience of the mystery at the back of the universe and the phantoms of the dream as the Australians did. Yet, where myth is projected into the past, the mythical time is by no means always a time which is far-off. It is certainly not for the Marind-anim who tell their myths in a way which suggests that it all happened 'only yesterday'. To their mind, all this happened no more than a few generations ago (Van Baal 1966: 181 f.). But they do not talk of a dreamtime. Instead, they emphasize the connections between myth and ritual. All the really important myths begin with the celebration of the great *mayo*-ritual. The ritual itself is not explained; it did not originate: it simply was there as the beginning of the mythical events which gave shape to this world. Consequently, the mythical heroes (ancestors as in Australia) are not the rather solitary wanderers of Australian mythology, but, primarily (though not exclusively), participants in an interaction of cosmic significance staged by the intricacies of the *mayo*-ritual during which and following which the country obtained its present shape, and man and animals their origins. How all this came about can be ignored. Of more interest here is their system of classification.

The Marind-anim live along the southcoast of what is now called West Irian, not far from the border with Papua. Of the two moieties in which each of the numerous subtribes is divided, one, the *Geb-zé* (descendents of Geb) is associated with homosexuality, the other, the *Sami-rek* (descendents of Sami) with heterosexuality.

175

The Geb-zé are slightly superior; they are associated with the male sex, the sun, the (dry) southeast monsoon, the sandy beach, dry land, the coconut, and numerous plants and animals, the animals being predominantly peaceful ones. The Geb-zé are the leaders of the mayo-ritual. The moiety of the Sami-rek are associated with the female sex, the (rainy) northwest monsoon, the interior, the sea and the swamps, the sago, and a variety of plants and aggressive animals such as the crocodile, the pig, the dog and the shark. Furthermore they are associated with sorcery and death; they are the leaders of the headhunting raids and of the big feasts for celebrating a successful war-party. It all looks like a fairly clean-cut form of classification in which war, death, sorcery and water are associated with the female sex, and ritual, peace, sun and dry land with the male sex. Yet, it is more complicated than this. The two moieties cooperate and this has its consequences for the system of classification and for the order of the ritual. We shall begin with the latter.

The ritual cycle begins every four (or more) years with the mayo-ritual under Geb-zé leadership, but performed in a place explicitly called interior, a Sami-rek associate. The mayo-ritual is followed by a headhunt which is afterwards celebrated with a really splendid feast. The feast, like the headhunt, is a Sami-rek responsibility, but its celebration ideally takes place on the beach round about full moon. Beach and full moon are Geb-zé associates. At this feast, all the clans cooperate in staging a magnificent show, each clan impersonating one or more of its own *dema* (totem ancestors) and totems. The actors must belong (as in Australia) to the proper clan and subclan. The show itself must be interpreted as a renewal of the birth and genesis of the universe in its pristine, divine glory.

The mayo-ritual is a big initiation ritual lasting for many months. Contrary to what might be expected in this company of homosexuals, the girls too are initiated. Though the more important roles are performed by the males, the women are not ignored. The basic theme of the ritual (which has many secondary ones) is that of the coconut-dema *Waba* (who is also the sun and the father of fire) who cannot free himself from copulating with his wife, the crocodile's sister, who symbolizes the underworld. The myth informs us that, following months of uninterrupted copulation, Waba was forcibly extracted by another dema; the friction originated a big fire which broke forth from the woman's genitals. The birth of the fire was instantly followed by that of the cassowary (associated with fire and sun) and the stork, the symbol of the mayo-initiate. Analysis of the mythical material leads to the conclusion that the mayo-ritual refers to the birth of the sun as well as to that of mankind from the earth (underworld). During the ritual, the male (Waba) is in the power of the female who, at the end of the rites, is killed once Waba has been liberated and she has given birth to the fire, the cassowary and the stork. When the ritual is completed, the victorious males can set out on a headhunt which, as will be explained presently, results in the renewed triumph of the female element. First, we must dwell for a moment on the ritual expression of female dominance in the mayo.

Ritually, the mayo-mother or mayo-woman (impersonated by a male) reigns supreme. She is represented in effigy by a beautifully carved and painted wooden image which stands in the centre of the initiation grounds. The male, however, is represented by two crudely constructed puppets made of straw and rushes. They stand outside the grounds and each of them is equipped with a big, detachable penis. More rigorous still, is the symbolization of female supremacy in the *imo*-ritual, the mid-western variant of the mayo-rites. Here, the female, the Imo-mother who bears the name of Excrement Woman, a goddess of death and decay, is represented by a number of big wooden shields. They all have a small hole in the centre into which an arrow-point has been jammed, i.e. the male. We would never have guessed the meaning of these shields if such a shield with an arrow-point jammed in its centre had not been given the name *pahui*, a term properly used for the big ceremonial club which accompanies a headhunting party. The club has the shape of a long spear with a broad, beautifully carved ornamental wooden blade on top. What makes it a club is a flat stone ring slipped round the shaft where it sticks just below the ornamental blade. The sexual symbolism is unmistakable: the *pahui* is a long penis with a small vulva around it, the exact counterpart of the shield with arrow-point which has the size of the sexes reversed.

There can be hardly any doubt that this is not merely a hypothesis; it is exactly how the Marind-anim understand the pahui's symbolism. When the war-party begins to kill its victims, the ceremonial club is beaten on the ground (or on a victim's body) so that the ornamental blade is shattered. What the club-bearer says when performing this duty has never been reported, but it has been recorded from the tribe's eastern neighbours who follow the same custom, viz.: "So-and-so will copulate with you". We have good reason to hypothesize that the Marind-anim expressed themselves in the same way, because the *pahui* can be identified with the penis of *Diwa*, a dema with a penis so long that he had to carry it over his shoulder.

Diwa is the ancestor of the penis-clan which makes part of the Sami-rek moiety, a curious attribute for a moiety so firmly connected with the female sex. However, the Sami-rek are also the ritual heterosexuals and the leading headhunters, and here Diwa fits in perfectly well. According to myth, he left the primeval mayo-celebration to attend a headhunting-feast. He made a long detour which carried him far inland. At some place, he had to cross a big river. An old woman and her daughter kindly offered him a place in their canoe; Diwa accepted, but took advantage of the occasion to importune the girl with his long penis. The mother, enraged, cut it off, and wailing with pain Diwa proceeded on his way to the feast. To the innocent listener there is little sense in this story, in spite of the fact that it must make sense because it begins with the mythical mayo. And of course it makes. Diwa's penis is the *pahui* which the bearer carries over his shoulder, and after it had been shattered Diwa's continuing on his way to the feast is not surprising at all, but exactly what Diwa had to do after having killed an enemy (symbolized by the crashing of the pahui, his penis).

There is more about Diwa. He has a counterpart in the opposite moiety whose name is Dawi. He also left the primeval mayo celebration to set out on a headhunt, beating the ground with his club (a *wagané*, a dirty word for the penis). The word-play Diwa-Dawi is clear enough, but the Marind have further elaborated upon the theme. Diwa is also called Yugil and Dawi has a son Yagil. And it is consistent with current concepts of classification that it is Diwa who is called Yugil, grammatically the feminine form of Yagil (i.e. used for female persons) and a form befitting a dema of the Sami-rek moiety which, ultimately, is associated with the female sex.

To return once more to the *pahui* and the sexual implications of headhunting: The pahui represents the male sex as dominant, but it must be shattered. The penis hangs down after copulation. But copulation is necessary; it is as necessary as headhunting which promotes the growth of the coconut, an outstanding symbol of human life. The male must submit to the female for the sake of fertility. We noticed already that the homosexual males make a big sacrifice for it, and express this in the term denoting these fertilization rites, viz. *dom-bombari*, bad rites, bad taken in the sense of reprehensible (above: 142).

The paradoxes of Marind-anim ritual have a parallel in the rich dialectics of their sophisticated speculations on mythological themes, dialectics promoted by the fact that the moieties must co-operate and that each must participate actively in the rituals of which the other moiety has the leadership. Diwa and Dawi are a good instance but by no means the only one. Each of the moieties and phratries has associations which result from participation in the other moiety's activities, or reflect the fact that everyone, though belonging to one of these , has relations with the other. A notable case is that of Geb, in a way the prime ancestor of the Geb-zé moiety.

Geb is the sun and the moon, as well as the broad, sandy beach stretching all along the coast. In spite of these lofty associations, Geb is not the representative of the main characteristics and functions of his moiety: these positions fall to Waba (who is also the sun) and Aramemb, the dema who liberated the latter from permanent copulation. Geb is more typically associated with the dialectic aspects of his moiety's appurtenances, those which reflect its co-operation with (i.e. its functions under the leadership of) the opposite moiety. This is already suggested by Geb's association with the moon, a heavenly body which, in these parts, is more usually opposed to the sun, and in Marind-anim mythology (but this covertly) connected also with the Sami-rek moiety. The myths dealing with Geb confirm this. As the sun, he lives in the far west where he steals and devours red-skinned boys. It is at the place where, according to Marind-anim cosmology, the sun enters a hole in the earth to travel underground to the east to rise again. A ringworm infested boy (a moon-symbol) discovers Geb's abode and, at the instigation of the women, the men drive him underground (or cut off his head) compelling him to take the road of the sun. As the moon, Geb lives in the far east, near the place of sunrise. Here, he is a boy whose body is covered with white acorn-shell, the effect of prolonged fishing in the sea. Girls discover him but the men take hold of him, clean his body (a painful operation) and then sodomize him and rub his wounds with sperma. Then the first banana (another moon-symbol) sprouts from his neck. When they sodomize him a second time, Geb flees and, climbing to the sky, becomes the moon. As this happened in the far east on the occasion of a pig-feast, which is always celebrated when the moon is full, Geb necessarily embodies the full moon which rises in the east just about sunset. He is thus associated with the feast on the beach, a feast under the supervision of the Sami-rek, and also with sunset. Sunset associates Geb with the beginning of the ritual cycle (sunset is also a copulation of the sun with the earth), the full moon with the feast at the end of it.

We shall not elaborate further upon the theme. The mythical stories relating the adventures of Geb are just one case out of many which illustrate the dialectics characteristic of Marind-anim mythology which, in its entirety, constitutes a fairly sophisticated system of variations on two themes, that of fertility, and that of the oneness of man and his universe. The fertility theme is that of the proud and aggressive homosexual who must submit to the female in order to perform his responsible task of fertilizing her, a task to which he grudgingly applies himself. The other is that of man's relations with his universe as symbolized by the numerous dema (totem-ancestors) and their surprising adventures. In fact, these dema are a savage horde, as cruel as nature can be, but also man's ancestors and the originators of all nature's gifts and benefits. In the great rituals, these dema and their exploits revive. In these dramatizations of mythical history, every man and woman has his or her proper place, the men personifying the totem or the dema from whom they descend, the women the *dema-nakari*, the dema's wives or sisters, but also the totem's (or dema's) secondary or female aspects. These dema-nakari constitute another surprising feature of the Marind-anim spirit world. The term is confusing because *nakaru* (sing.) means husband's younger sister. A male dema's husband's younger sister obviously does not make sense, unless the term's self-contradictory contents be understood as an expression of the mystery inherent in the dema and in nature generally. Their intrinsic femininity is not, like their maleness, a dominant feature, but all the same important enough to find expression in a self-contradictory term which indicates the auxiliary functions of the second sex in daily life in which, socially speaking, "women are treated as junior members of the gang..., the men's house community" (Van Baal 1966: 170).

Thus the ritual ensures everyone's pre-ordained place and function in society as well as in nature. Even the women are not ignored; they occupy a position which corresponds with the one they have in daily social life. In ritual everyone functions as a part of an all-embracing universe.

5. *The ritual ends*

The sophisticated intricacies of Marind-anim myth and ritual are not the raw products of the reactions of their subconscious minds to their inner conflicts and problems, but the results of conscious elaboration and speculation on these products. To a certain extent, the same can be said of every myth and ritual anywhere; but it is obvious that the Marind-anim have advanced significantly in this direction, farther than, for example, the Aranda. These leanings towards conscious speculation raise an interesting question: Did the Marind-anim ever extend these speculations to the question why they spend so much toil and effort on their huge rituals?

Although the sophistication of Marind-anim myth and classification schemes gives special occasion to raise this question, it is one which can and should be raised with regard to ritual everywhere. Actually, it is one of the intriguing problems of comparative religion generally. All over the world we find people keenly aware of the specific ends served by a great variety of simple rites, often of an individual nature and, if not, rarely exceeding the co-operation of more than a very limited number of individuals, the so-called magical rites which are discussed in the next chapter. All these peoples also celebrate big, communal rites which make a much larger demand on everyone's energy and wealth than any of the magical rites. Yet, when asked why they do all this or what is the good of it, their answers are vague and evasive: they do it because such has been ordained by the ancestors, because they have been taught to do so by tradition, because negligence of the ritual would lead to all sorts of rarely-ever-specified calamities, and so on. The answers are usually neither clear nor conclusive. Even the great Australian rites, with their strong emphasis on fertility, are rarely presented as definite means to ends. What we do find are clan rites which are properly called magical, such as the *intichuma* rituals of the Aranda, performed on behalf of the multiplication of the totem animal or totem plant. The more complicated rituals, however, are more commonly announced as initiation rituals. This, of course, they are too, but is this the real reason for their celebration?

Anthropologists are too easily inclined to subscribe to this native explanation. In as far as they really believe initiation to be the ultimate explanation of all this toil and moil, they commit a logical blunder. It is impossible to initiate anyone without some secret, some specific knowledge or technique to which the candidate must acquire access before he can assume responsibilities in the tribe's social life. It is nonsense, of course, that such secrets could have been devised for the sake of disciplining the youngsters. If this were the real aim of these extensive rituals, the men would have discovered long ago that disciplining can more easily and more effectively be realized by beginning a few years earlier by imposing decent behaviour on the boys. Besides, it is a well-known fact that sometimes rituals of moderate size can also be celebrated when there are no candidates for initiation; the so-called cyclical rites attending seasonal succession are a case in point.

This leaves us with the problem of what all these peoples themselves think about the real purpose of their big rites. Apparently, they all 'feel' that it contributes to their well-being, but they all are vague when it comes to the question 'how'? If, by now, we return to the Marind-anim for a better answer, we are disappointed again. They certainly take pride in their big rituals, but they do not have a clear answer to the question why they perform them. Of course, they too expect something good out of them, but this good is never found specified beyond the vague assertion that headhunting and mayo might benefit the prosperous growth of the coconut. This does not really go much further than asserting that, in myth, the coconut and the human head are identical and that the coconut dema stands central in the mayo rites. Besides, the coconut will thrive anyhow; it is a crop which does not give problems!

The one time I heard something approaching an expectation of real effect, was on the upper Bian, far away in the Marind-anim hinterland. It happened after the cruel influensa epidemic which, toward the end of 1937, had taken a really heavy toll of human lives in this area, in some villages up to 26% of the population. One night, sitting at a fire, the men argued passionately that, now the sickness had passed, they had to celebrate their old tribal ritual. They did not and could not specify why. It had to be done because it was good and necessary. They needed it to an extent which, to them, was beyond words. Their passionate words and gestures, however, were convincing enough: what they needed was the restoration of confidence in their world.

Their point was clear but it confronted me with an awkward problem. For all I then knew, the ritual (which can be described as a simplified version of the mayo) was worse than barbarous. It is denoted as *Ezam-Uzum,* Husband and Wife. The two are symbolized by a young man and woman who, toward the end of the savage rites, are invited to copulate under a large contraption made of tree-stems, constructed under a large shed. During the act, the contraption is suddenly torn down, killing the copulating pair who are roasted and eaten. The construction of the wooden contraption being a proven fact, the relevant reports seemed altogether too true. Long afterwards, I learned that, indeed, everything was true, except the story of the copulating pair and their victimization. The real symbols of Ezam and Uzum are two coconuts, decorated as human heads. They are indeed crushed and eaten. The story of the copulating pair is the story told to the non-initiates.

What is surprising is that what is told to the uninitiated is what we would call the esoteric meaning of the rites, and that its innocent operationalization is kept a secret. The same happens among the coastal Marind-anim where the myths containing the most cruel particulars of the fate of the main characters in the ritual drama (male and female were killed and eaten in the imo, the female in the mayo) are more or less openly told, but the innocent ways by which the murderous event is operationalized are kept a guarded secret. Again, it can be concluded that the Marind-anim are well-aware of the meaning of their symbols, but also that, to them, these symbols denote a mystery which can only be approached by the subsidiary symbols operational in ritual, symbols which are known to the initiates only. Their secrecy symbolizes the mystery underlying the ritual experience.

It is here that one should look for the answer to the question of why people are unable to give an answer to the question concerning the ends of their big ritual celebrations. If it be true that, to them, it is the confrontation with the great mystery of their universe, how could they ever answer this question? This is not a matter of ends, but of an experience which is beyond words, meeting the needs of the subconscious where only shadows are at home, shadows which fade away when hit by the light of conscious thinking on concrete ends.

In Marind-anim ritual life the experience passes through three phases. The first is that of the cult proper (Mayo, Imo, or Ezam-Uzum) that realizes the believers' participation in the true mystery of their universe as active partners. The second is that of the headhunt, the experience of the world's dangers and violence and man's ultimate triumph, dangers that symbolize the dangers of the sexual act which, if courageously overcome, result in the triumph of the third phase, the final feast which dramatizes the wonder of the ensuing fecundity by acting out the rebirth of the universe in its pristine splendour.

Today, most of this is past glory. Headhunting was suppressed during the first decades of this century. In the early twenties, when an epidemic of venereal disease threatened the population with extinction, all ritual celebrations were forbidden. One thing, however, persisted in secret, albeit in a revised and mostly rigorously simplified form: the celebration of the imo-rites and ezam-uzum-rites and, in the eastern part of the mayo territory, that of the *sosom*-cult, originally a homosexual ritual which has subsequently adopted some of the basic functions of the mayo. Apparently, the need to relive the hidden mystery of the universe, embodied in the rituals of the first phase, has been strongest of all: the need to feel a partner in one's universe.

When these things are taken to mind, myth and its dramatization lose their awkward absurdity. Myth is a message which gives form and content to man's experience of his universe as a world of mystery which alternately threatens and entices, kills and gives life, thwarts and fulfils his desires. Ritual is man's answer to this message which is understood and interpreted as an invitation to participate. Impersonating the mysterious beings and symbolically reviving their exploits, he becomes like one of them: i.e. a partner in a world of mystery which he has accepted as the world which, for better or for worse, is his world. In short, by giving shape and countenance to his own, inner experience of that mystery, man confirms his participation in, and his belonging to it. The effect of such participation reaches well beyond the realization of concrete ends; all that counts is the inner certainty of partnership in spite of danger and sorrow. The alleged concrete results of such a drama-like ritual are of secondary significance, the blessings which may reward its proper performance, but not the motives for its celebration. The fact that, where great rituals are concerned, such concrete results are rarely mentioned, let alone emphasized, is enlightening. Apparently, the performers, too, are aware that the real gift of the ritual does not lie in material signs of divine benevolence.

So far our hypothesis that ritual confirms man's partnership in his universe, is well supported. Only one question remains: What about the etiological character of myth? The answer is simple: the etiology concerned is not the etiology of the laws ruling the universe, but the etiology of its wilfulness, of its non-rules or, at best, the arbitrariness of what presents itself as rules. As long as this view of nature and the universe prevails, there is nothing illogical or absurd in myth. The wonder, the impossibility in myth, adequately expresses the problem and its explanation. All this changes when the believers' worldview changes, and notions of natural law and causality get the upperhand. When this happens, the myth becomes scandalous; and, instead of explaining something, it has to be explained itself. This was the problem which the Greek (like many others after them) had to confront. They tried in vain to solve it by the ways of, alternately, allegorism, euhemerism, and priestly fraud (Van Baal 1971: 14 f.). Once the experience of the universe has changed, the old myth loses its validity. This validity depends upon the underlying experience of intentionality incorporated in the visible world.

X

Magic: The Effective Rite

1. Rite and spell

Whereas primitive people rarely associate the performance of a grand ritual dramatization of myth with actual, material achievements, they do not hesitate to ascribe such favourable results to many other (and always simpler) rites. Sometimes, these rites involve the collaboration of all the men of a clan as with the Aranda *intichuma* ceremonies for the increase of a particular totem, or the rites celebrated by a tribe or sub-tribe before the men set out on a war-expedition. More often, however, such rites require no more than the concerted efforts of a few, or are performed by a single individual, either a specialist or a layman. In such cases, the ends are clear and unambiguous. An act of sorcery is performed to kill or harm a special person, and no one can doubt that this is why the act is performed. There are rites for practically everything: for planting a garden, for making a canoe, for letting the enemy sleep, for fishing and hunting, for planting a coconut or a banana-shoot, for making and stopping rain, for an advantageous deal in trade or good luck in playing dice, for good things and bad, for important and trivial ends, in short for every need. The performance of the rites may require serious preparations such as fasting and sexual continence, their execution by a professional medicine-man or a shaman, or imply nothing more than a simple gesture and the recitation of a formula which is common knowledge. Yet, complicated or not, the belief in the effect of the rite is unwavering.

Exceptions to this rule are few; doubt is confined to such cases as trying out a newly-acquired ritual technique, the performance of a rite out of season (e.g. a rain-making ritual) or cases in which the end pursued is not taken seriously. Personally, I remember how on different occasions during my long tramps through Marind-anim country my bearers tried to conjure an approaching rain shower by whispering a few words in their open hand which they then closed in order to throw its imaginary contents at the rapidly advancing clouds. It never worked, and never did I find that the conjurer paid so much as a second thought to his failure. It was all done by way of: 'if it does not do any good, it does not do any harm either'.

In other cases, however, when more serious matters are concerned, there is no shadow of a doubt about the effectiveness of the rite. If the rite is unsuccessful, the performer will not shrug his shoulders but try to find an explanation, e.g. the interference of an ancestor or demon, the counter-magic of a hostile magician, or a mistake of his own in the performance of the rite. Explanations for failures are frequent and varied; but nobody ever tries to explain the success of a rite. Success is accepted as a matter of course.

The unshakable belief in the effectivity of magic, as found all over the world, has given rise to the view that to the people concerned the magical act is a kind of automatism, the product of a false science (Frazer 1922). One of the principal errors of such views (there are more than one) is that they put magic in a pragmatic context of rational thought and action, presenting the magical act as a technique which (in the native's 'abortive' reasoning) logically leads to the desired effect. This is what magic does not do. The ritual act is never a substitute for properly executed work. A leaking canoe cannot be repaired by magic, and a poorly cultivated garden will be a failure whatever the magic devoted to it. Also, a raindoctor will never try his hand at making rain out of season. "The natives will never try to clean the soil by magic, to erect a fence or a yam support by a rite,... magic aims at forestalling unaccountable mishaps and procuring undeserved good luck" (Malinowski 1935: I, 77). Malinowski's analysis of magic locates it in its proper context; i.e. the realm of the unaccountable and uncertain. Uncertainty is thematic in the life of primitive man, and magic is one of his answers to it, an answer consistent with his worldview because it refers directly to the mystery behind that uncertainty.

This must be elucidated. The point is that every magic act normally refers to this mystery, either by the symbolic character of the act, or (and preferably) by the formula pronounced at performing it. A formula accompanies practically every act of magic, and it is invariably the most illuminating of the two. It expresses the performer's desire and purpose. Unfortunately, the formula is also that part of the magic act about which our information is most defective. Acts can be observed, but formulas are rarely recited aloud. Very often they are secret, and informants do not easily impart this knowledge to an occasional ethnographer. Yet, this sometimes happens. There is a comparatively abundant supply of material in the case of the Marind-anim, among whom P. Wirz collected some sixty odd formulas which were since analyzed in my book *Dema* (1966: ch. XIV). Though some of these formulas are probably incomplete, on the whole a satisfactory notion of their purport can be derived from them. We shall follow the analysis in some detail.

A striking feature of these formulas is the predilection for proper names. In 52 of the 61 formulas proper names are used. In 18 formulas these names are the names of *dema* (totem-ancestors) or refer to them; in 17 they are what the Marind call *igiz-ha*, true names, i.e. the secret names used in ritual, for example the mayo-ritual where the novices are made acquainted with the mythical history of all the more important animals and plants. Finally, there are 17 names of which Wirz says that they are *spielerisch erfunden*, playful imaginations, an elucidation begging the question instead of answering it.

A second important feature (but not as frequent as the use of proper names) is the use of rather bold metaphors. Eleven of these cases were noted, among which there were 9 which combined the use of metaphor with that of a name.

184

Finally, there are the 9 formulas which do not make any use of names. Two of them make use of metaphor, seven are just matter-of-fact statements. It is probable, however, that of the latter some at least include the use of a name but that the name was suppressed when communicating the formula. The Marind-anim are very secretive about names. In one formula, the name noted by Wirz really means 'Mr. So-and-so'; it is all but certain that in some other cases the relevant name was simply withheld.

We must return to the names. In as far as they refer to the *dema* or any other known item of secret knowledge (as in the case of the 'true names'), it is evident that the names connect the objects of the rites with the non-verifiable reality of myth and religion. But what about these other names? The analysis of a few cases in which the use of such names is combined with that of metaphor, can elucidate this point. I follow here the text of the résumé given in *Symbols for Communication* (1971: 261 f.):

> "Planting a banana-shoot the planter addresses the shoot with the following words: "Gomat-oar! on this spot thou shalt bend". The hunter, goading his dogs to catch a wallaby, addresses them as follows: "Kékus-teeth! Bite into Saparim-coconut" (Van Baal 1966: 875, 871). The Gomat-oar of the first formula refers to the future banana-leaf. It is not called a leaf but it is named after something resembling a banana-leaf, viz. an oar. As if this were not enough, it is called a Gomat-oar. Nobody knows who or what Gomat is; apparently it is a personal name, but one of an utterly unknown person. The same procedure is followed in the second formula. The coconut refers to the flesh of the wallaby, tender like that of a young coconut. The name Saparim cannot be explained, it is added on, just like Kékus is added on as a personal name to the teeth, in this case the dogs' teeth. The personal name, the name of an unknown person, adds a new quality to the teeth, as it does to the coconut and the oar, viz. that of being associated with some person of unknown origin. In other words, the object of the simple rite is represented as more than it really is: the banana-leaf refers to an oar, and a very specific one, a Gomat-oar; the flesh of the wallaby to a coconut and again not to every coconut but to 'the' Saparim-coconut. Superimposed is a reference to a totally different object which because of its specific qualities shares a certain likeness with the object of the rite, and this symbol of the object is further qualified as the image or property of a mysterious personality. The additions add unknown qualities to the object, they refer to things unsuspected by the layman which nevertheless are proper to the object. Nobody would know that a banana-leaf is also a Gomat-oar, if he had not been told so. The leaf is more than it seems to be, and the formula describes the mysterious surplus of the leaf. Similarly, the formula for goading a dog describes the mysterious surplus concealed in a dog's teeth and the flesh of the wallaby she is going to catch. The Marind-anim are well aware of this. They classify the formula of the magic rite as *kuma meen,* speech which is *kuma*, i.e. secret and hidden, a kernel, that which is at the bottom of a thing, in figurative speech also the female genitals.
>
> The statement that the formula describes the mysterious surplus of the object can be further specified. It describes the hidden side, the *kuma*-aspect of the object in the state of fulfilment of the operator's wish. The formula states that this *kuma*-aspect, i.e. all that is unforseeable, refractory and arbitrary in the object, complies or is going to comply with the performer's desire".

The setting is clear: the formula is based on secret knowledge; i.e. knowledge of the secret of the object which cannot be anything else but the wilfulness and intentionality proper to it. The problem which remains is how this knowledge becomes operational. Why does the performer believe that the simple recitation of the formula has the desired effect? And why must the recitation be combined with certain symbolic acts? Besides, not all formulas are of this kind. There are also spells which resemble prayers, and for the sake of a more complete picture it seems desirable to consider these before we turn to a discussion of the logical ground of the belief in the effect of magic.

In formulas resembling prayers, the performer addresses one or more *déma* (totem-ancestors). "When sago-sprouts are set, quite a number of déma are called upon: 'Wokabu! Sangon! Harau! Elme! Come! Come hither from Imo' " (Van Baal 1966: 874). They are the dema of the sago and sago-making, and are located in mythical Imo. A woman who is on the point of working the pith of the sago-tree will, before she starts pounding the pith, call on Harau, the mythical sago-poundress, by speaking the words 'Harau, come here' into her hand, and then beckon the mythical sago-maker with her hand. The form of all these 'prayers' is more or less fixed. There is also one case, however, of a freer form. This regards the custom of addressing one's own dema, i.e. the totem-ancestor of one's own clan or sub-clan, when, in distress, a man seeks a way out from his predicament (ibid.: 866).

With prayers these formulas have in common that they address a supernatural being, and that they are phrased in the imperative, a grammatical mood which is an urge rather than a command and, for this reason, had better be called an *anhortativus*. We find the imperative also used in the second half of the Lord's Prayer, the part concerned with specifically human needs. Besides, formulas are not recited casually, but respectfully; at least when the need is taken seriously. The case of my bearers who tried to chase away a shower which they did not really expect to change its course, does not count. Of the Marind-anim, a really respectful attitude is reported by Verschueren: "I must confess in all honesty that more than once I have been edified by the devotion of the old men applying their ... spells" (personal letter, quoted in Van Baal 1966: 864).

Nevertheless, the equation of these spells with prayers raises objections. The emphasis on the use of the correct name is an indication that the success of the rite depends on other conditions that divine benevolence alone. More important is the difference between the supernatural beings invoked in these spells and the gods and spirits called upon in prayer. The supernatural powers addressed in the formulas are embodiments of the things desired rather than authorities who direct the course of events as gods and spirits do. Among the Marind-anim spells, there is only one exception to this rule; i.e. the appeal made in distress to one's own, personal dema. And even in this case there is question of an exceptionally close tie between the supernatural being and the object of his care: he is a direct ancestor, connected by close ties of actual blood-relationship.

The close relationship, near-identity even, between supernatural being and the object of the spell, is combined with an equally remarkable confidence in the spell's effectiveness. The belief in the effect of a formula is, overtly at least, more uncon-ditional than that in the effect of a prayer. The pious Christian who confesses that he relies without hesitation on such divine promises as "Ask, and it shall be given to you" (St. Math. 7:7) and "If ye shall ask anything in my name, I will do it" (St. John 14: 14) will always make allowance for the possibility that the Lord may think better of it and fail to grant his desire. Disappointment does not shake his belief in God's goodness, because the Lord's ways are higher than those of man. He may trust that his needs are better served by non-fulfilment of his desires than by the realization of his own altogether too human and short-sighted wishes. But all these considerations do not alter the fact that he cannot be – and actually is not – certain that his prayer leads to wish-fulfilment. And this is what the magician claims to be the unfailing effect of his spell.

The magician claims it, but does he believe it? There is a subtle difference between the one and the other, and its significance should not be underrated. The belief in the effect of magic is not really unconditional. In fact, there are always conditions. It has already been noted that a spell will not work if, technically, the work itself has not been properly executed. It was also pointed out that the rainmaker will not try to summon the rains before the season is so far advanced that rain can be expected. "Magic aims at forestalling unaccountable mishaps and procuring undeserved good luck" (above: 184). Besides, there are gradations in the belief in the effect of magic. Among the Marind-anim, the magic of a member of the coconut clan is more effective for the prosperous growth of a newly planted nut than that of members of others clans. A clan member has a personal relation with 'his' dema. Similarly, a medicine-man's magic is stronger than that of ordinary people. His initiation has equipped him with special knowledge and power. Moreover, some medicine-men are better than others. Apparently, the conditions for magic being really effective are manifold. Why, then, do the believers claim that magic is always effective? It is certainly not a loose claim. We noted that, in case of failure, there is astonishment; all sorts of reasons are sought to explain the miscarriage of the magic act, whereas its success never raises questions.

To understand the necessity, or even the inevitability of the claim to effectiveness, we have to return to the fact that the formula is based on secret knowledge, knowledge of the inside (*kuma*) of the visible world. Using this secret language, the magician places himself in the midst of the hidden world, the world of mystery which incorporates all that is unforseeable and unaccountable to those who have not seen through the veil of everyday events. The magician is an 'insider' in that world, so much so that sometimes he identifies himself with a mythical being. There are a few spells in which the operator states: "I am So-and-so", mentioning the name of a *dema*. The same trend toward identification can be observed in the big rituals where the descendents of a dema – and only they – impersonate him in the enactment of the myth. They almost are the dema; when, as sometimes happens, the impersonator swoons under the weight of his elaborate paraphernalia, the public cries out that the dema has taken possession of him. The close tie between the dema and his descendent is further substantiated by the fact that the magic of a member of the relevant clan is more effective than that of a non-member. This is a reason to invite a member of the coconut clan to perform the magic for planting coconuts, a member of the sago clan for planting sago sprouts, and so on. The clan member has the best knowledge of the secret of his totem. The basic fact in magic is man's participation in the secrets of his universe. The knowledge of these secrets cannot be ineffective, because these secrets relate directly to the experienced intentionality of the world. The hidden world *is* these intentions, just like the etiology of myth is the etiology of the world's wilfulness (above: 182). Whoever knows the secret of these intentions can direct or at least influence their course.

This knowledge is power, but it is not the kind of power envisaged in the theories of magic which consider magic as an act of coercion, executed as a kind of technique based on what Frazer called 'false science'. There is a world of difference between a technical act and a magical one. The latter is performed with respect and devotion, and occasionally preceded by fasting and sexual continence. The power of this act does not derive from erroneous reasoning, but from the fact that the magician acts as an insider in the hidden world, that is as a partner in the secrets of his universe. More important still, the act does not merely serve his wish to make use of this partnership for his own benefit or that of his friends or clients, but also – and often even primarily – to confirm and to strengthen this partnership. The truth is that most magical acts do not serve any real need at all, except that of confirming partnership by expressing it. This seems a bold assertion and I have to substantiate the point.

In the first place, we have to think of the more elaborate magical rites which are re-enactments of myth. The Aranda intichuma-rites are a case in point. Performed every year, they are primarily seasonal rites. It is the season which defines the time of performance, not an actually felt need. More convincing still is the case of the Marind-anim rain ritual. Its ceremonial plainly refers to the relevant myth. It is celebrated every year, often after the rains have already set in. The redundancy of the performance may be rationalized as a means to prevent the rain from stopping prematurely, but another explanation is that the ritual is an expression of the community's sympathy with the change of the season, a ritual accompaniment of nature conveying feelings of togetherness between man and his universe.

This alternative explanation is corroborated by the fact that, under normal conditions, most magical rites are virtually superfluous. There is hardly any doubt that a coconut, a banana shoot or a sago sprout, if planted in the proper way and place, will thrive anyhow. There are few problems with these crops. Actually, in Marind-anim country there is only one plant which causes real difficulties, namely *kava*. But that does not explain the rites deemed necessary for the well-being of all other crops. Of course, one can say, quoting Malinowski, that magic aims at forestalling unaccountable mishaps and procuring undeserved good luck. But even this smells of rationalization. The point is that all these crops have a mythical history of their own. One cannot plant them without remembering how they originated, without expressing one's awareness that there is more to a plant or a crop than its outward appearance. Performing the relevant simple rite, the planter and the assisting magician (if there is one) simply confirm their partnership in their universe. They know its secrets; and by paying their respects to them, they realize themselves as true insiders. There are many such rites. They are connected with all the things of daily life such as fishing and hunting, cooking or making a fish-trap, and whatever turns up to be done. These daily tasks rarely ever miscarry seriously; and, as such, the accompanying rites are a practically foolproof confirmation of the efficacy of magic. A welcome confirmation of course, but not the reason to perform them. The reason lies in the confirmation of the operator's partnership in his universe.

188

At this point, we must return to the opening paragraph of this chapter. The grand collective rites are not (at least not primarily) connected with specific results, but the small ones are. They are individual rites; private rites I called them in *Dema*. They accompany the individual's works and exertions. At the moments when he may feel uncertain of himself and of the future result of his work, the simple rite of magic is available to persuade him that he is an insider who has a partner's place in this mysterious and often frightening world, and knows his ways in it. It is a comforting feeling; but this feeling is in need of finding its truth confirmed in empirical reality. The participants in the grand collective rites find such confirmation in the splendour of the show and the feelings of awe, togetherness, and relief inspired by the communal celebration. There is no need of specific, practical results to persuade the participants that the celebration brought them in touch with a supernatural reality, the hidden background of their world. Such power of persuasion, however, is lacking in the case of the simple rites of daily magic. Persuasion of truth and validity must come from elsewhere, and this elsewhere can only be that the rite has a favourable effect on the outcome of the task which it accompanied. The simple rite must prove its worth as, usually, it does.

It is this need of confirmation which lends belief in the efficacy of magic its some-times spasmodic character. If, inadvertedly, the rite has not the desired result, an explanation must be found for its failure. A less innocent result of such failure is that it encourages the faithful to dig deeper into the secrets underlying the visible world. The need for tangible results then assumes priority and supersedes the original motive for ritual activity; i.e. the need for partnership. The need for tangible results paves the way for a new development: the appearance of religious specialists such as the shaman and the medicine-man who, by personal talents or disposition combined with a special initiation, have acquired a deeper knowledge of the secrets of the hidden world and better contacts with its powers than ordinary people. These specialists represent a curious mixture of genuine mysticism and pious meditation with the community's need for effective help in distress and misfortune. Though seriously striving for a fuller mystic partnership in their universe, these specialists simultaneously turn religion from a means to experience this partnership into an instrument to submit the course of events in that universe to their clients' desires. Here, something (and this is where the critics of magic are right) goes wrong with religion. It must serve ends which it cannot really meet. And yet, religion is not wholly powerless either, certainly not where curative magic is concerned. We shall return to this point in the following sections, which are devoted to the activities of such specialists as the medicine-man and the sorcerer.

2. The medicine-man and his initiation

Not everyone can become a good medicine-man; a certain type of personality is one of the most common prerequisites. A more than ordinary leaning towards mysticism and a susceptibility to trance-experiences are among the talents qualifying a medicine-man. A good case is that of the shaman (and not only the Siberian one) but such predilections are not confined to cultures in which shamanism prevails. One need only consult the exposition given by the Berndts (1964: 255 ff.) of the initiation rituals of Australian medicine-men for a picture of the excess of mysticism often connected with becoming a medicine-man. It is all told in symbolic language: the candidates meet Baiami and other great spirits, liquified quartz crystal is spit onto their bodies from which feathers grow enabling the candidates to fly, quartz-crystals are 'sung' into their heads and bodies, other candidates are swallowed by a snake who vomits them out in the form of a baby who regains normal size after having been laid in the centre of a ring of fires, and other kinds of unbelievable processes which, evidently, must be understood symbolically. We do not know what is behind it, but one thing is certain: like the Siberian shaman, they pass through a great deal of agony. We know that one category of Aranda medicine-men has a hole through the tongue the size of a pencil. There is not the slightest doubt about the hole; it has been photographed by Spencer and Gillen (1927: fig. 117). Among the Marind-anim, the candidate is held in seclusion; cadaverous fluid is blown into his eyes, and he must inhale this fluid through his nose. He also must swallow a sago-dish mixed with mussels and soaked in cadaverous fluid. It has no sense to enter into details. From all over the world, in the ethnography of Oceania, Asia and America, we find telling examples of the ordeals which a candidate has to pass through in order to become a man who can see what is hidden from the eyes of ordinary mortals. Going to the verge of the bearable, balancing on the narrow edge where life and death meet, the candidates become changed men.

This does not mean that all medicine-men are successful healers; some are better than others. There also are natural talents who became healers not by suffering the trials of a terrifying ordeal, but by a mystical experience. Such a man, apparently, was Willidjungo, the Murngin medicine-man who met two little birds which became his 'familiars' (above: 167). They told him to keep them under his armpits because they wanted him to become a medicine-man. Willidjungo continued his autobiographic story as follows:

"Then I came back to camp. Dorng's daughter was sick. I did nothing but look at her. She had a big hole in her chest. It had cracked open. I kept on looking. One of the old doctors tried to fix her but he couldn't do anything... [evidently W. means that the old doctor did not see the hole]. Afterwards I took the flesh and put it together and she became better rightaway" (Warner 1958: 213).

The action of the medicine-man is symbolic action, just like the hole in the young woman's chest is a symbolic hole. There is no need to give any more examples. The reader who is interested may find a couple of highly instructive cases in Lévi-Strauss, *Anthropologie Structurale I*, ch. IX and X. Among these is that of the woman in labour who, on the second day of her pains, was induced to delivery by a medicine-man who sang a myth containing a symbolic description of the process of insemination, pregnancy and birth. The really intriguing feature of this symbolism is the reification of the symbols. They are not just symbols which stand for certain aspects of reality, they are these aspects, and are presented and handled as more real than reality itself which is but the outer shell of the reality present in the symbol. The Marind-anim

190

word *kuma* (see above: 185 and Van Baal 1966: 930 f., 946) does not leave any doubt on this point. *Kuma* also means pit, kernel, what is at the heart of a thing.

This appreciation of things *kuma* as hard realities is fully confirmed by their magical practice. I once had a medicine-man in court who had badly wounded another medicine-man for having practised black magic on his young son. The accused told me that he himself had spirited a stone from his son's abdomen. My remonstrances that the stone originated from the accused's own pouch met with no response, neither from him nor from the bystanders, though they must all have known that he had had the stone with him when he began his treatment. But they denied it stubbornly; the boy became better after the accused had extracted the stone which, moreover, was blood-stained. They suggested that I could still see the stains.

My conviction that the medicine-man himself had brought the stone and that everyone must have been aware of this, was not ill-founded. Not a single pebble of the kind he showed me can be found in this alluvial land within fifty miles' distance from the village concerned. Many years later, going through the relevant literature, I came across the following little story communicated by one of the early missionaries among the Marind-anim, Father Vertenten:

> "Little Kunga was dangerously ill. Mother Maboda told me that he would soon recover. 'Just look, Sir, at what they distracted from his little tummy', and she showed me a round, hard, brown fruit. I scoffed at it. She gave me a grave look, which conveyed that I was not to give the show away. She knew it quite well herself, but if little Kunga believed that the cause of his illness had been removed from his body, he might recover rapidly. The mother herself had devised the trick and played the medicine-man. But when a real medicine-man, a professional, juggles the most ridiculous objects out of a patient's body, everybody firmly believes it" (Van Baal 1966: 900).

They know the trick and still it is all true, the symbol having taken the place of the disorder. Such facts are astounding but they are by no means rare. The current explanation is that the medicine-man cheats his public by slight of hand. Of course he plays a conjurer's trick and a fairly simple one at that; but this does not explain why the western observer is the only one who is aware of it. The trick must be played and be played well because the symbol must be persuasive. Though it must be played with dexterity, it is not too difficult because everyone wishes to be persuaded. After all, the medicine-man is manipulating things which are hidden, things which belong to another reality. Admittedly, the credulity displayed on such occasions is rather spasmodic. This reification of symbols is virtually always connected with matters of life and death in the face of which public and patient have only one wish: that it works. They cannot be blamed too much for it; because, strange as it may be, it does, indeed, work. Many cases of illness have been cured this way. One of the first things we learned about primitive people's sensitivity to psychic influences was that the knowledge of being the object of acts of sorcery or witchcraft has a lethal effect on the victims; they wither away within a few days and the symptoms of their illness resemble those of shock. We have since learned that the suggestion emanating from the medicine-man's ritual has a comparable effect for good. It is not exceptional in modern Africa that a European practitioner invokes the collaboration of a traditional healer, especially in cases where psycho-somatic disorders are presumed. The healer's

191

knowledge of physiology may be less than minimal and the somatic aspects of his treatment accordingly poor, but his approach to the patient's psychological problems is sound enough. The least one can say of it is that it is not ineffective. After all, it is not as strange as it seemed some thirty or forty years ago. Since we have learned to give up the old doctrine of the dualism of spirit and body, an approach to sickness from the psychological angle is no longer as objectionable as it seemed before. And, as far as primitive people are concerned, the effectiveness of the symbolic treatment of illness strengthens their confidence that these symbols are not mere metaphors but the embodiments of the real truth about reality.

The close connection between primitive people's willingness to put their confidence in the healer's symbolic acts to cure the distress caused by otherwise incurable ailments, can never be an argument for qualifying their belief as a make-believe, provoked by anxiety. If it were make-believe, the suggestion would not work. What happens is that the distress urges them to penetrate as deeply as is humanly possible into the mysteries of the universe surrounding them. A universe which is both evil and good must also contain forces which work to man's good.

It is this persuasion which is at the back of the prospective medicine-man's mind when he submits himself to the ordeal of his initiation. Modern anthropologists tend to emphasize his longing for status and power as the ultimate motive for his choice of the vocation. The argument overlooks the fact that primitive medicine-men who are sincere, are often mystics who court silence and solitude, not politicians trying to gain power. Yet, there are also medicine-men who do indeed become sorcerers and employ their powers for the purpose of destroying their fellow-men by evoking the mysterious powers of evil in the hidden world. This evil aspect of the hidden world is no less important than its more benign traits.

3. Sorcery

A universe ruled by hidden powers which embody the intentions which plunge the existence of primitive man into everlasting uncertainty, is necessarily, at times, a sinister universe. The conflicts and violence prevailing in myth do not leave any doubt on this point. By ritually associating himself with these mythical powers, primitive man ensures for himself a place in his universe which allows him to participate in the secrets behind the uncertainties which threaten his life and peace. The blessing of this participation is that, by now, he knows what to do in order to forestall calamities and to enjoy the blessings which, in its ambiguity, this unreliable universe, blending threat with benevolence, is willing to grant him. He is no longer the helpless victim of the whims of his universe, because he knows what is behind them and what can be done to play off these hidden movers against each other. It is certainly a blessing, but a blessing which, with equal right, can be described as a doom in disguise.

In a universe ruled by hidden powers, one has not only to do with gods, demons, and ancestors who rule the course of nature and other people's behaviour; one must also take account of the secret powers in man himself. It is not only that human beings and groups constitute part of everyone's universe and share in its mystery; but, as initiates in the secrets of that mystery, they also have mysterious powers themselves which, like the gods, they can use either way: i.e. for their fellow-men's benefit or for their destruction. Man is as unreliable as his universe. Hostility pervades the life of primitive man; we discussed this at some length in chapter IV (pp. 75, 78 ff.). And, indeed, if there are medicine-men who are able to cure the sick, why should they not be able to bring sickness to the healthy? In a world in which so much credit is given to secret intentions, even an evil thought can do damage. The ethnography of Africa abounds with cases of sickness ascribed to the evil thoughts of one's fellow-men. On the whole, however, these disorders are mild when compared to those caused by sorcery and witchcraft. The two differ from each other in that sorcery is magic deliberately performed to kill or harm other people, whereas witchcraft is the action emanating from a man or woman who is innately bad, who has something in him or her which enables their souls to leave their bodies at night to devour the souls of others in their sleep, thus causing almost incurable illness to their victims. There is not a second feature highlighting so clearly the belief in the mysterious potencies of man as that in witchcraft. The fact that there are all sorts of intermediate forms between sorcery and witchcraft which tend to obliterate the difference, need not bother us here. More important is that the belief in both sorcery and witchcraft is a self-sustaining evil, ever provoking new deeds of violence in return, magically as well as physically.

The fact that man has learned his way in the supernatural mysteries reigning his world, does not imply that he is immune from misfortune. The one thing he has learned is how to behave in case of misfortune and what to do to ward off such consequences as it is his power to overcome by ritual action. The most appalling evils are those of sickness and death, in particular when the victims are in the full vigour of life. The death of old people does not raise problems. *Mui baren*, the flesh is out, the Marind-anim say. Practically everywhere, old people face death with equanimity. They know that their time is up, and their relatives agree. The death of babies and very young children does not raise problems either. They are so frail, so vulnerable, and child mortality is so high, that people are not upset when a baby does not survive and dies before it could acquire its place in society. There is always hope that it will be replaced by another baby, a hope reflected in the often-found belief that the new baby is a reincarnation of its dead predecessor.

The death of full-grown people in the prime of their lives is different. Though most people never reach old age, premature death shocks the community every time anew. People protest against untimely death and ask why? how? Being unacquainted with microbes to find fault with, they turn to the mysterious powers which rule their world. They even do this when a man falls from a tree and dies. The disquieting fact is not that his fall resulted in his death, but that he fell. It is not 'natural' to fall from a tree. Everyone climbs trees without falling.

No harm is done if the intention behind the calamity can be explained as an act of God, the wrath of the ancestors, or the violation of a taboo; but this is not always the case. In many primitive societies, it is so that on the occasion of a death almost everyone is potentially suspect. The medicine-men and the senior members of the group are consulted. They must decide whether there are symptoms of sorcery or witchcraft and, if so, try to find out who the culprit is. This is not an easy task; accusations of witchcraft or sorcery have serious consequences. Feuds can arise because of them. It is all the better when supernatural beings can be accredited with the responsibility. Among the Marind-anim, this happens in case of an epidemic, or of the violation of a sacred place by the deceased. In all other cases, sorcery is a more probable cause and the consultants look for symptoms which can confirm their suspicions. Knowing what is at stake, they do not readily jump to conclusions. Often, they proclaim that, though sorcery cannot be excluded, the symptoms are too vague to draw a conclusion, or they point to a sorcerer who lives too far away to discover his identity. In other cases, however, they think it necessary to make further investigations to discover the identity of the murderer. A favourite method is to pass the night at the grave, hoping for a dream which will disclose who is the sorcerer. Frequently, such inquiries come to naught or result in vague indications of the village or area where the culprit must be sought. The case that an offender is identified is relatively rare. If that happens, retaliation is imminent; revenge will be taken either by killing that person straightaway or by sorcery. Still, when identification miscarries because the consultants disagree among themselves, suspicions linger on. They easily poison the relations between neighbouring villages and eventually lead to conflicts. In Marind-anim country, people are careful not to go to extremes. Conflicts between villages (sub-tribes) will in time be followed by reconciliation. The celebration of rituals may be helpful to that end.

Not all tribes have that wisdom. In many areas of New Guinea, even neighbouring settlements are in a more or less permanent state of conflict. Reconciliation is possible but it rarely lasts; every new death arouses new suspicions and can cause new conflicts to flare up. Sorcery as a source of violent conflicts between groups has also been reported from Australia. In areas with more developed political systems, such as the African continent, conflicts between villages may be held in check by the chiefs; but chiefs cannot stop the use of supernatural means by those who feel hurt and are craving for revenge, nor the frequent migrations of individuals who, accused or not, feel themselves threatened by sorcery or witchcraft. Usually, such fears are not unfounded. They believe in the effect of these supernatural means, and people who apply these means are often more numerous than an outsider, judging on the face of peaceful appearances, could guess.

Sorcerers are despised; at least, that is what people say, but it is more correct to describe them as people who are feared. Often they are respected members of their society which holds them in esteem because their presence and the certainty that they are able to retaliate foul deeds by outsiders are appreciated as a valuable protection of the group. A sorcerer who is supported by an important section of his community sometimes feels sure enough of his position to terrorize members of minor sections. Another possibility is that a sorcerer enjoys the protection of a chief who makes use of his services to strengthen his own authority. Nevertheless, a sorcerer who threatens members of his own community must be wary: he risks his life. Sorcery may also be used for the profit and the protection of the community; it may even be applied in its service, but in general sorcery is condemned and, though often resorted to in practice, this is not wholly without significance.

There is a wealth of information on sorcery but it rarely enters into details. In more recent years, much attention has been paid to witchcraft and sorcery in Africa. Although the greater part of these studies is more devoted to the sociology of conflict than to the phenomenology of magical methods, the techniques of sorcery there have not gone unheeded. It is of interest to know that, sometimes, real poison plays a part in it. On the whole, the descriptions of their proceedings and the initiation of the magicians are less colourful than those dealing with Australian and Papuan sorcerers. The important part played among the latter by symbolism, lends them specific interest.

One of the most interesting forms is that of the sorcery practised in nothern Arnhem Land about which Lloyd Warner reported in *A black Civilization* (1958: 198 ff.). The technique is of almost exactly the same kind as that of *kambara*, the most lethal form of Marind-anim sorcery. According to the reports of the sorcerers concerned, the victim is summoned, stunned by a blow on his head, then his body is opened just below the thorax, heart and lungs are taken out and the empty space filled with grass and thistles, after which the body is closed up again without leaving so much as even a trace. Then, the victim is told that he is going to die within two or three days, brought to, and sent home. On his arrival he has forgotten all that has happened to him but he feels sick; his condition rapidly deteriorates and he dies within the appointed time.

It is all symbolism but thanks to the talent and inquisitiveness of the late Father J. Verschueren, we know now what actually happens; at least what happens in the case of *kambara*, a form of sorcery described in almost identical terms.

The case into which Verschueren stumbled almost by accident, was one of *kambara* executed at the orders of the leader of the *imo*-cult who wished to punish an initiate for having given away too much of its secrets. The work is done not by an individual but by a party of some six to eleven men, selected by the medicine-man who is their leader. The assistants have sexual intercourse with the leader's wife. The semen is collected and mixed with water. The leader prepares other ingredients which are needed in the course of the process.

> "The party of sorcerers sets out during the night, taking their various ingredients with them. When they come closer to the victim's house they stop and the leader puts a charm on a magical instrument (*tang*): Suddenly the *tang* has vanished. It is said to have gone off to fetch the victim. Shortly afterwards the leader pretends that the victim has arrived. He gives a few beats on the ground with his club, then takes a bamboo knife and makes some movements as of cutting. After that, blood... which has been brought in the bladder of (an) animal... is poured out into the bamboo tubes containing the water and the sperma. The blood is the victim's blood, which the assailants now drink. Sometimes they also eat of his flesh symbolized by young coconut mixed with sperma. The leader then pronounces a second formula, upon which the victim is believed to wake up and return to his house, where he will die within a couple of days. The party see to it that some token is left on the spot, so that people know what has happened during the night" (Van Baal 1971: 260; 1966: 907).

195

If performed correctly, the ritual is absolutely lethal. There is no counter-magic or cure against *kambara* as there are against other forms of sorcery such as that of spiriting a stone or other object into the victim's body. *Kambara* works with the strongest magical means available: sperma, blood, ritual implements such as the *tang* and the *mangon**, and above all an elaborate spell in which the sorcerers identify themselves with the mythical beings who were the first performers of the rite and, according to one reading, introduced death into the world (Van Baal 1966: 905 and 249).

Another feature is the realistic description of the symbolic acts. The flesh of the victim is eaten by the sorcerers, and of the victim they say what is said of people dying for old age: *mui baren,* the flesh is out. What normally is the result of the wear and tear of old age, is effectuated by *kambara* in two or three days. When Marind-anim talk about it, no one would guess that they were talking about symbolic action. I will never forget the story of the murderer who told me, in court, how he and his associates had caught a certain young man and how, while his assistants kept the young man pressed down to the ground, holding his legs apart, he had driven a pointed stick into his victim's body, entering under the scrotum and had pressed it forward till it protruded through the throat. He told it with so much cold realism that, at the time, I believed him and, finding his story confirmed by accusers and defendants alike, sent him to jail: the latter to the full satisfaction of everyone present. It was more than thirty years afterwards that my late friend Verschueren, on hearing the story, quietly remarked that it all sounded like a story of sorcery. Of course it was.

In Marind-anim society the magic of healing and killing have one thing in common: a reification of symbols by which the symbol and the symbolized change places. It is mentioned here not as a feature common to all cultures in which magic plays an important part, which, presumably, it is not, but as a symptom of the intensification asserting itself when the believers are faced with problems of life and death, requiring an immediate, tangible result. The transformation of the symbol into the symbolized is the indisputable symptom of the spasmodic nature of their efforts at manipulating the hidden powers of their universe. In the grand, dramatic ritual they never go to that extent. In the Ezam-Uzum ritual (above: 181) the initiates pretend that they kill a copulating couple, but actually they restrict themselves to crashing two ornamented coconuts. The symbols remain symbols; there is no question of their reification. It is only when a concrete result must be enforced through these hidden powers that the roles of symbol and symbolized become reversed in an excess of faith in the veracity of these powers. Insanity? Certainly not. This faith is effective; the patient who is relieved from a stone in his stomach, recovers. The woman in childbed over whom the myth of fertilization and birth is sung, releases her constraints and smoothly gives birth to her child. And the victim of sorcery, knowing what has happened to him, dies. The results justify the efforts.

Yet, one cannot enforce the invisible powers without paying a price. Wherever

---

* The shell of a dwarf-coconut cut out in the form of a pig's head, apparently a reference to the pig-*dema* who is associated with the introduction of headhunting and the origin of thunderstorms.

people set store on the effect of magic, they also do so on witchcraft and sorcery. Both constitute part of a worldview capitalizing on secret intentions apprehended behind the outward appearances of things and events. These intentions are, alternately, as good and bad, as kind and cruel, as benevolent and treacherous as the universe itself, humanity included. Accepting this dualism as ultimate reality, magic associates itself with this duality and finds it confirmed. The belief in witchcraft and sorcery creates a vicious circle of violence, a circle which cannot be broken for as long as vice is given an equal share with goodness among the secret powers ultimately ruling the universe.

This circle can only be broken when the individual liberates his subjectivity from the fetters of a self that has identified its libido with its desires, and its universe with that mixture of good and evil which characterizes the *projet de vie* of the unfree individual. When these fetters are broken, the powers ruling the universe are no longer identified with the universe as it actually is. They necessarily assume a normative character. Certainly not all of a sudden, but gradually; so gradually, indeed, that even in Christian theology Satan's power is acknowledged until the end of time.

However, this is another matter. Of more immediate interest is the fact that an incipient awareness of the normative character of the hidden powers is apparent in the role of the father figure, a figure present in practically every religion. This role will be examined in the next chapter. Here, we can only point out that this normative character of the powers behind the visible world is not something new, suddenly appearing in the course of historical development. It is already clearly apprehended in the earliest systems of classification which invariably class black magic with the mean and the undesirable.

It could hardly be otherwise. At the end of Part II it was argued that the foundations of ethics, of the moral law, are based in the human condition. Even among peoples given to belief in magic and witchcraft, the awareness of the moral law has never been lost; though it was permitted to be overshadowed by the evils of human lust and desire. Men given to magic are still men who, as subjects, must be parts of their universe; who, as parts of their universe, must act as subjects. Where they fail to accept the moral consequences, they simply have to bear the consequences of their failure. The whole story of magic and sorcery as described in this chapter, with all the apparent abstrusities which it entails, confirms the propriety of the decision to take the dialectics of the human condition as our starting point. They give an explanation of the facts which is consistent with human nature and with the conditions under which it has to deploy itself.

XI

The Personalization of the Supernatural.
Cult-forms concerned with the Uncanny

1. Ancestors and the concept of soul

Supernatural beings derive their origins from dreamlike experiences, or from speculations based thereon. Usually, they are personal beings; if they are not, there is question of sacral power, uncanniness or *mana*, in short of situations which are taboo and must be shunned, or of magical acts by which man himself handles supernatural knowledge and power. The latter, however, either originate from a supernatural being or refer to some form of mystic revelation obtained from a supernatural world ruled by personal or person-like beings. The world of the supernatural is a world of intent, and these presumed intentions naturally take the shape of person-like beings. A complete depersonalization of the other world is the late product of advanced metaphysics, and even here depersonalization is rarely complete. The practice of Theravada Buddhism and the teachings of Plotinus testify to this.

There is sound reason to emphasize this trend towards personalization. In earlier years various students of religion hypothesized that, in the dim past, the opposite must have been true. They welcomed the discovery of concepts like mana as expressions of the first stirrings of religious feelings (i.a. Max Müller, 1878; R. R. Marett, 1914). They overlooked the more likely possibility that these concepts are rationalizations or conceptualizations of religious experience; or, as Malinowski said of mana, that it is "an early generalization of a crude metaphysical concept" (quoted in Firth 1967: 176). Even Durkheim shared this over-estimation of the impersonal element, at least to a certain extent. He defined the emblem of the clan's totem as the seat of its mana (1912). Our brief description of totemic rituals has given ample evidence that the practice of totemism hardly gives cause to such emphasis on impersonal powers. The ritual concentrates on ancestors; they are the centres of worship, just as they are in animistic religions. The difference between totemism and animism is not that the one is earlier or older than the other, but that they differ in their approach to the common object of their worship: the ancestors. The animistic approach is that of interpersonal communication in the form of prayer, offering, sacrifice and divination; that of totemism one of symbolic identification by impersonation and the dramatization of myth.

There is a second difference between the two which clearly demonstrates that the totemism of the Australians (and the Marind-anim) is not an undeveloped, early form of religion, but a typical case of advanced specialization. By a parallel classification of the social segments of the community and the various departments of nature, totemism successfully realized the integration of the composing segments of the society into a closely co-operating community. As Van Gennep pointed out, Durkheim, taking the isolated horde as his point of departure, overlooked the fact that totemism presupposes a segmented society in which each segment makes its own inalienable contributions to the society.'s ritual, both in the simple form of individual clan magic and in that of the elaborate celebrations of the total society in which each segment plays its preordained part (Van Gennep, 1920). Technically and economically, the Australians are the most primitive people in the world, but religiously they are not. When, in the preceding chapter, we drew heavily upon Australian totemic ritual, this was not because we thought it to be an older form of religion, but because its strong preference for ritual dramatization constitutes a case of specialization which convincingly illustrates the significance of myth.

It is a specialization also in this respect that Australian mythology contains elements which could have served other forms of ritual than those they have actually chosen. Although the co-operation of totemic clans of equal rank suggests equality in rank of the respective ancestors, this equality is fairly imperfect. Repeatedly, mythology makes mention of ancestors who are more prominent than the rank and file of their mythical companions because, as true culture-heroes, they introduced certain rites and customs, or function up to the present day as the invisible leaders of the initiation rites, who supervise the behaviour of the young men and their observance of tribal law and lore. Some of these ancestors have been depicted as a kind of incipient supreme beings, a qualification too far-fetched to be of great use, but all the same indicative of the powers attributed to them by the tribesmen. It is evident that these more exalted mythical beings might have given occasion to a cult of prayer and offering if the tribesmen had chosen to think that way. They did not; but whatever their reasons, it was not because their mythological repertoire held no possibilities for accommodating another type of cult.

The outstanding fact is the dominating role of ancestors. In this, there is no difference between totemism and animism. A phenomenon of such general occurrence – i.e. occurrence under widely differing cultural conditions – must have an equally general ground. Such a ground is not far to seek. Ancestors, whatever else they may symbolize – and that can be a great variety of things – are father symbols. Earlier in this book, we argued that "it is only natural that fatherhood has become a universal symbol of a combination of loving care with distance, authority and constraint" (above: 90). "On the one hand he [the father] belongs to a group in which togetherness and comradeship prevail, on the other hand he represents outside authority and command" (ibid.). Fathers everywhere represent the authority of society as it is experienced by the individual member. As such, they are destined to become the symbols of the authority of the universe in an even wider sense.

This does not imply that the father is the exclusive symbol of authority in mythology. A similar place can be allotted to the mother. We met with the power of the mothers in our discussion of Marind-anim mythology and ritual. They occupy a central position in the great ritual which, in some of its aspects, has more of a confession of male insufficiency than of male superiority, a motif which also came to the fore in the Australian myth of the Djanggawul sisters (above: 141). In a totally different context, we find the authority of the mothers expressed in the traditional opening words of the prayer to the divine ancestors on the occasion of a sacrifice in the Eastern Lesser Sunda Islands: 'Oh Mothers and Fathers', and not 'Fathers and Mothers'!

We will not try to unravel the (many) reasons why the authority of the mothers – socially inferior to the fathers – is sometimes stressed to the extent of surpassing that of the father symbols in myth and ritual. After all, the mother is a self-evident substitute. She is the first authority whom everyone meets in the course of his life. Another outstanding substitute for the father symbol is the divine king. He plays a part in some of the higher religions. His majesty stresses the distance which separates divinity from mankind by elevating the glory of the supreme being. Sometimes, however, the divine king has to share part of his power with other gods. A well-known case is that of Zeus whose authority over the Greek pantheon was at times disputed by other Olympians. But we need not enter more deeply into this because the king is so evidently a father substitute (cf. among others Roheim 1930) that he can hardly be held to be a competitor of the father symbol.

Not all supernatural beings are primarily symbols of the authority of the universe. On the contrary, most of them are primarily representatives of its various aspects such as seasonal variations, health and fertility, success and failure, life and death, and so on. With many of these, authority is only a side aspect, expressed by the supernatural being's identification as an ancestor or as a god, the latter a being of a more princely and glorious nature. There are also beings who do not seem to have any authority at all, such as ogres and demons that must be fought, or fairies and luck-bringing goblins. As the immediate reflections of the whimsicality of the surrounding universe, they are of interest. Yet, the most salient feature of the supernatural is its authority, and the father symbol is its most obtruding characteristic.

Religion has this symbol in common with many forms of neurosis. We already dwelled on this point on pp. 5 and 150 f. above, and we have little to add to what was said there about the differences between the two, except this. The father symbol can serve two opposing ends. In neurosis, this is the conflict evoked by the authority's exigencies and the sufferer's will to resist. In religion the conflict is recognized, but the symbol is used to find ways for reconciliation. The father represents the inexorable demands of the universe, but he is also the mediator who can help. It is this feature which makes the father symbol so attractive. In the following pages we shall further substantiate this by considering its indirect contributions to the concept of the soul, and its more direct ones to that of a supreme being.

The founders of anthropology took the view that religion began with the belief in the survival of the soul. For them, the soul concept provided the model for all subsequent conceptualizations of the supernatural. Spirits answered primitive man's need for explaining the vicissitudes of nature. To Tylor "spirits simply are personified causes" (1871: II, 108). The more prominent spirits became gods. Others were worshipped as ancestors and might, in the course of history, rise to the position of supreme beings, creators of the universe who supervise the actions and behaviour of mankind. Another possibility was that, among the gods, one became their supreme leader: a sovereign who, in the course of further development, became the sole god of monotheism. A competing line of development was that which led to pantheism; the more enlightened spirits in society, taking offense at the ungodly behaviour of the divinities and the contradictions of polytheism, developed the view that underlying this confusing multitude of gods there must be such a thing as an all pervading divine principle which is the essence of all things existent.

The theory depicted the continuous progress of the human mind as a result of man's innate need for causal explanation, a need which, in the early phases of history, was badly thwarted but never really suppressed by the inconsistencies of early man's presumed childlike mentality and his supposed inability to discern fortuitous associations from causal relations. Ultimately, causality and reason won. This theory satisfied the rationalistic optimism of the time but failed in its understanding of mankind's real needs and worries. Its reduction of religion to an intellectual problem, and the explanation of its forms as the subsequent elaborations of a soul-concept which originated from the deliberations of a primitive philosopher (the term is Tylor's) are constructs which have more to do with a scholar's intellectual interests than with those of primitive people who are at the mercy of an insecure world. Because the whole theory depends on the concept of the soul as the origin of all later forms of religious evolution, we must take a somewhat closer look at it. Though modern anthropologists unanimously condemn Tylor's rationalism, alternative explanations of the origin of the concept of the soul rarely question its role as the ultimate foundation of the ancestor-concept.

For this reason, we shall not confine our discussion to a refutation of Tylor's theory that the soul-concept is the outcome of our primitive philosopher's reflections on the differences between a dead body and a living one, on the apparitions of the deceased to the living in dreams, and on the adventures of the living themselves in their dreams. The theory has been refuted many times and there is hardly a scholar left today who is willing to subscribe to it. Everyone is aware that death is not an intellectual problem, but an existential one. Here, the views presented by Preusz (1930) are of interest: belief in the persistence of the soul originates from man's fundamental incapacity to imagine his own death. It is an argument which comes close to the views developed in the first part of this book where it was argued that the subject experiences itself as ever identical with itself. The argument must also appeal to those who see in the denial of death (Becker 1973; above: 62) a prime mover of cultural development. Actually, modern anthropologists tend to accept the origin of the concept of the soul as a matter of course. The belief in the persistence of souls having been general even in the western world until the beginning of the present century, why should primitive people believe otherwise?

Surprisingly, primitive people do believe otherwise. Although they believe in the persistence of souls, they do so on grounds wholly different from those imputed to them by us, grounds which make it improbable that the belief is that very early product of religious thinking for which it is held. If only anyone ever had taken the trouble of analysing thoughtfully the extensive literature on primitive people's reactions to death and the dead, it would have been common knowledge today that these ideas cannot have been inspired by reflections concerning any ego's own death, but by considerations called forth by a fellow man's recent death, by questions such as: What will the deceased do to us?

At first sight, this objection is contradictory. Does not the question: 'What will the deceased do to us'? imply that the bystanders believe in his persistence? It certainly does, but it also implies that they came to this belief along other ways than those ascribed to them by us. The latter are founded on a civilization which added substantially to the fear of death by the belief in a last judgement. It may no longer play the part in our thinking as it did in that of our parents or grandparents, but that does not alter the fact that, until recently, the belief made dying a terrible thing. To pass through a judgement on all one's works and sins is a disquieting prospect. "If thou, Lord, shouldest mark iniquities, O Lord, who shall stand?" (Ps. 130: 3). The prospect turns death into a problem to be worried about long in advance. One has to be prepared. In the western tradition, death is a personal and ever-imminent problem. The prospect of judgement has saturated our thinking on death and it is difficult for us to accept that primitive people do not worry about their own death as often as we do. But why should they? They have little to gain or lose by it; and, in fact, their notions about an after-life are often a matter of occasional speculation rather than of a keen interest or acute anxiety. The mistake we make in our appreciation of animistic beliefs and representations is that we take the native concept of the soul to be more or less identical with ours, that of an indestructible and indivisible ego. Often it is not. A recurrent theme in Australian ethnography is the belief that everyone has two or three 'souls': one identical with the ancestral life-germ which after death returns to the totem-well or whatever the place be called; another one which after some time departs to a shady country of the dead; and sometimes even a third which stays in the vicinity, roaming about at night, tricking and frightening the living (Berndt, R. M. & C. H., 1964: 412 ff.).

Such notions are not restricted to the Australian continent. They have been reported from other parts of Oceania, e.g. Indonesia (Batak, Mentawei) and Micronesia. It is not possible to explain them on the basis of the subject's alleged wish to persist or its assumed inability to conceive its transiency. There is something else behind it and what this is, is made apparent by the case of the Truk (Micronesia). Here, the natives believe that the deceased survive in two different forms, one tricky and dangerous, the other inclined to beneficence and succour. Goodenough (1963: 137-140) explained this belief as a projection of the ambivalent feelings harboured by every Trukese with regard to his parents, a consequence of the highly negligent child-treatment characteristic of early education in this island. Goodenough also pointed out that the belief does not follow from any ego's expectations about his own fate after death, but from what people think can be expected of a recently deceased relative.

That the ideas and representations concerning the survival of the soul do not derive from any ego's anxieties about his own future fate is corroborated by the widely spread custom, found in many parts of the world, of denying proper burial to people who suffered an unhappy death, such as drowning, dying in childbirth, being killed in battle, and such like. The spirits of these dead are chased away, sometimes in the hope that they shall perish, and always without eliciting any clear sign of compassion with the poor fate of the deceased. Feelings of this kind are even blatantly absent in yet another feature of rather common occurrence, the stories told about the perils of the soul on its way to the land of the dead (cf. i.a. R. M. and C. H. Berndt 1964: 412 ff.; similar stories are reported from various other areas). On their way, the dead are repeatedly in danger of being devoured, crushed, burned, or otherwise annihilated, but we never come across an indication whatsoever that the narrators take these stories as a threat to their own future.

There is sound reason, then, to accept Goodenough's view that the death of the other stands central in the belief in the survival of souls. This confronts us with the problem of how to explain the belief that the deceased lives on in some form and continues to participate in the affairs of the living. It is a problem which I discussed elsewhere (1971: 268 ff.). The main point is that man is not confronted with death by his *own* death, but by that of a relative. There, in the hut, lies a dead body. It would be reasonable to throw it away in a distant place like dirt. But, though it is dirt, it is also a dead father, or mother, or husband, one who was 'one of us', a long-time partner in 'our own life', a part of one's own and even recent past. No one can ignore this without intimating that the deceased relative meant little to him, that partnership in a community is no more than a chance accident. Indifference to the deceased even calls the negligent mourner's own partnership in his group in question. One cannot deny the emotional value of partnership without affecting one's own position as a partner. The ghost who haunts the castle, if he is not a suicide, is always a deceased who has not been properly bewailed and buried.

Obviously, something must be done to the corpse before it can be disposed of. The emaciated body must be cleaned and decorated, everyone must take a final look at him and, above all, the deceased must be bewailed. The extent and depth of the loss must be expressed in clear and unambiguous words. Mourners all over the world praise the deceased's abilities, they pity themselves and reproach the deceased for his untimely departure. The presence of the corpse, lying outstretched in the midst of the wailers, provokes the mourners irresistibly to address themselves to the deceased personally, acting as if he were still one of them and alive.

From acting as if the deceased were alive to believing that, in a deviant form, he is alive and still participating in the community's affairs may seem but one step, but it is a very long one indeed. It is easy enough to give a touching description of the mourners' afflictions, but this cannot explain why the survivors also fear the deceased, their fear often dominating their distress. It does not explain either why they wish the deceased to go away to a far-off country, lest he badger the living, at the same time hoping that the deceased will also do something good to them all. The attitude toward the deceased is ambivalent; he is a loved one who is bewailed and pitied as well as an uncanny threat. In the deceased, lying outstretched in front of his hut, all the ambivalence of the apprehended intentionality of an inscrutable universe manifests itself; but it is difficult to understand how this manifestation can engender belief in the deceased's persistence in spirit form unless the apprehended intentionality of the universe has already taken shape in fixed forms expressing its mystery. Once there is a belief in the reality of an invisible world ruling the visible universe, in the reality of mysterious powers which manifest themselves in man too, the belief in the deceased's persistence in spirit form, in the form of more than one spirit as the case may be, becomes easy enough. The corpse as such is a shocking manifestation of mystery. Logically, the thesis that the belief in ancestors originated from that in the persistence of the dead, is reversible. Once we decide to take this to heart and conclude that the soul persists because the ancestors too manifested themselves as persisting, all that is incomprehensible in primitive notions of a multiple soul is clarified. The deceased is just such a manifestation of mystery as the ancestors are; he must be in some respects like they are.

All the same, belief in the persistence of the dead must be very old. Death is one of the most cogent manifestations of the mysterious intentionality of the universe. It is also certain that this belief, in turn, supported belief in ancestors. Yet, the belief could only take conceptual shape after other manifestations of these apprehensions had already found an incipient form, that of a mysterious something recognized as an ancestor. A case of death, though not infrequent, is incidental, but the threat emanating from an unreliable universe is permanent and takes precedence.

2. Supreme Beings

A tricky problem is that of the belief in supreme beings, a category of gods usually described as creators of the universe who watch over man's moral behaviour and determine the length of his life-span. Descriptions often lean heavily upon the use of western theological terms such as creation, divine fatherhood, omnipotence and omniscience, terms which arouse suspicion of being ethnocentric reinterpretations of native utterances. All the same, there must be something behind these descriptions: something that stands for a being held to be higher and more powerful than all the other spirits and gods who, with or without his permission or will, rule or misrule the visible world; a being who also incorporates notions of benevolence and of ultimate causality of world, life and death, the death of the individual included. That this being is a father figure is, in most cases, beyond doubt. In native invocations he is very often addressed as a father. Sometimes, he is even said to herd mankind like man herds his buffaloes (a touching statement of the Ngad'a of Flores, Indonesia).

The origin of these notions is obscure. Their absence in the religions of tribal Australians, the Papuans, and the Andaman Islanders suggests that these notions are a product of more advanced civilization. That they play a role in the religions of primitive Africans, such as Pygmies and Bushmen, cannot be forwarded as proof of the validity of Fr. Wilh. Schmidt's assertion that these notions constitute part of mankind's oldest religious inheritance. Quite apart from the many objections which must be raised against Schmidt's theories of culture and cultural diffusion (cf. Van Baal 1971: 107), these assertions are invalidated by the fact that, through the ages, the African continent has been the scene of endless migrations which upset the boundaries between ethnic groups and promoted their dispersion and miscegenation. The assumption that the Pygmies, protected by the impenetrability of the forest, have lived in prolonged isolation is founded on a profound underestimation of the effect of migrations on the inhabitants of areas situated outside the main course taken by these population drifts. The forests are areas of refuge for the victims of victorious invaders. This need not necessarily lead to miscegenation, but it certainly implies contacts which are chosen opportunities for the diffusion of ideas, religious ideas included. Primitive people are more interested in the latter than is often supposed by students of diffusion who grew up in a technological civilization.

The ultimate basis of Schmidt's theory of primeval monotheism (Schmidt 1908/1910; 1930) is not the occurrence of this belief among a number of isolated ethnic groups, but his own belief in the truth of his Neothomist philosophy which taught him that man's natural reaction to his world is the rational belief in a kind father-god who created the universe and put it at the disposal of mankind (cf. Van Baal 1971: 107 f.). Of all the objections which can be raised against this product of pretended natural reason, the most important is its utter neglect of that old thorn in the flesh of all theology, the problem of theodicy. In fact, primitive people like Pygmies and Bushmen and suchlike, have not the slightest reason to believe in a kind father-god. All the evidence of their sufferings contradicts it. Undiscouraged by considerations of a more realistic nature, Schmidt did his utmost to prove that traces of this belief in a kind father-god can be found among all the world's most isolated and backward groups, Australians and Andaman Islanders included. To that end, he constructed his ingenious but untenable theory of cultural diffusion, the *Kultur-kreislehre*. It enabled him to make a reconstruction of the ethnographic facts which, to his own satisfaction and that of his followers, yielded the desired result, but elicited the harsh and well-deserved criticism by all his opponents that he violated the ethnographic evidence.

The dogmatism of the *Kulturkreislehre* adepts and their zeal to prove their favourite case do not inspire great confidence in the results of their fieldwork. As early as 1927, Fahrenfort accused both Koppers and Gusinde of tendentious ethnography (Fahrenfort 1927). Yet, in all honesty, it must be stated that Schmidt has deserved great merits for his promotion of fieldwork and the publication of its empirical results. Though the methods applied were often unsatisfactory, these results certainly increased our knowledge considerably, even our knowledge of native beliefs in so-called supreme beings. A good case is that of M. Gusinde who has just been mentioned. It is a welcome illustration of the valuable information which even the field results of a biased explorer may contain.

In 1950 and 1953, Father Gusinde visited the !Khung Bushmen to interrogate them on their belief in a supreme being. The Bushmen did not disappoint him. He

205

got all the answers he desired; they did believe in a supreme being who is a father, and they prayed and brought sacrifices to him in a really edifying manner. The information contains two facts the implications of which he failed to recognize. The first is that the supreme being is given the name of *//gaua* and that *//gaua* is also the term for soul and spirit of the dead. The second is that the soul of every child is created and installed by the great //gaua while the child is still in its mother's womb. This //gaua (soul) stays with the child until death. It then returns directly to the great //gaua above, or is commissioned by him to mediate his commands to the living. It can also happen that the soul remains on earth to roam about at night. This information he received repeatedly from a variety of informants living in different places (Gusinde 1966: 20, 27f., 35, 39, 45, 57, 59f. and 65).

The facts display a curious likeness to some Australian notions of procreation. There, the totem-ancestor (also a primeval father) impregnates a prospective mother either by reincarnating himself in her womb, or by fertilizing her by means of one of the germs of life which he or his companions produced and stowed away during their dreamtime peregrinations. At the end of the life of the individual born from this act of fertilization, the life-germ (also a kind of soul, though in this case not the only form of soul discerned by the Australians) returns to its origin, the totem-well or totem-place, more or less as the little //gaua returns to the great one in heaven. Whatever the multifarious differences between Bushmen and Australians, they have in common that they substantiate the fatherhood of both their supreme being and their totem-ancestor with a clearly physical link constituted by what can be called an act of fertilization. Yet, the Bushmen-concept is evidently the more advanced of the two. It includes the concept of a soul which, in Schmidt's theory of primeval monotheism, is a product of later development, a point of view which we can endorse, albeit on different grounds.

Taking all things together, one has to admit that there is sufficient reason to contest the prevailing opinion of today, that the belief in a supreme being is necessarily a product of later development. There is a logical possibility that the worship of a father image led to concepts of this kind even at a very early point in human history. After all, the father image is universal and it might, at any time, have given occasion to its elaboration into a father-god who extends his cares to all the members of the tribe instead of the clan, and his offices to a correspondingly more encompassing part of the universe. It is probable that at one time or other such developments did indeed take place. Supreme beings have been reported from many corners of the world, and it is all but certain that they have a long prehistory, even if that prehistory does not reach back to the times of early man.

Even so, there is no ground for hypothesizing a close resemblance between these beings and the omnipotent creator-god of the great monotheistic religions. Apart from the fact that the notion of creation indicates a fairly advanced degree of interest in matters of intellectual causality, the god of monotheism did not derive his origin directly from a simple father image but, primarily, from that of a powerful worldly sovereign. Of course, it can be argued that the powerful divine king is, ultimately, himself a product of the father image, but then this 'ultimately' must be taken in its

206

most literal sense. Historically, the biblical notion of the almighty God's fatherhood is, to all appearances, a relatively late development. In the Old Testament it is not emphasized; it is only emphasized in the New Testament. The Old Testament God is, primarily, the Lord of the Covenant: not a father but a divine sovereign who, other than the deities of the pagans, is alien to his people, connected with them by act of covenant and not by natural ties. It is a point made already by Robertson Smith in his Lectures (1889) and even today there is no reason to differ substantially with him on this point.

As a matter of fact, the supreme beings of contemporary primitive and peasant religions, so often welcomed by missionaries as prototypes of the Christian God, differ from the latter in essence. In the Christian religion, God is, in spite of his fatherhood and paternal love, a *deus absconditus* who, when all is said and done, is unattainable to man unless it pleases the Almighty to turn to him. Such distance is foreign to pagan supreme beings. An illustrative case is that of the supreme being, *Kwoth*, of the Nuer religion. More than any pagan god, he resembles the god of the Old Testament. And yet he is particularized in a multitude of lower *kwoth*, each individual having his own *kwoth* who accompanies him from birth to death (Evans-Pritchard 1956: 106).

The Nuer case is no exception. In Africa similar views are held by the Kapsiki of West Cameroon who believe that every individual and every house has its own *shala*, a particularization of *Shala*, God (Van Beek 1978: 388 ff.). In Indonesia, a more or less identical relation between god and man has been reported from the Ngad'a of Flores. They call their supreme being by the Sanskrit term *Déva*. *Déva* resides in the upperworld and they often invoke him together with *Nitu*, the underworld goddess whose name is identical with the term for spirits of the dead (*nitu*). *Déva*, in turn, has a large retinue of lower *déva* who mediate between him and his creatures, every human having his own déva tending him (Van Baal 1947: 182).

Although this belief in a supreme being who is particularized in a multitude of lower namesakes is by no means general, it illustrates a nearness of the father-god which can be considered as a first step away from the notion of the supreme being's almost physical fatherhood which still reverberates in the Bushmen's near iden-tification of the great //gaua above with the human soul. Such notions differ widely from the Christian concept of God which emphasizes distance and otherness. It is a difference which never received the attention it deserves. In fact, the notions of the sacred and the *mysterium tremendum* which make up such an important part of the 'etic kit' of the science of comparative religion, derive primarily from Christian religion (and more advanced religions generally) in which it is the distance between god and man which prevails. In primitive religion, such distance is not absent, but it takes a more mitigated form; taking fatherhood more literally than is done in the Christian eulogies of God's paternal love.

3. Offering, prayer and taboo in a context of vagueness

In the preceding sections, we surveyed some of the more general forms of super-natural beings. We must now turn to the ways by which man responds to what he considers to be their manifestations, to the rituals which express his beliefs and experiences. In later chapters we pay attention to the rituals of more advanced cultures. In the present chapter, however, we confine ourselves to the description of the cult forms of a few primitive societies. We first turn to the role of offering and prayer in two Papuan societies, and in the next section to offering, sacrifice and divination in the taboo-ridden society of the Mentawei (West Indonesia).

Prayer, offering and sacrifice are conspicuously absent in Australian ritual, which concentrates on the re-presentation of myth. Though a few cases of small offerings brought to the recently deceased, have been reported (R. M. & C. H. Berndt 1964: 395, 397) they have no real impact on the dominant pattern of Australian ritual.

In this respect, the Marind-anim are only slightly different. Here, prayers are rare, but not completely unknown; a man in distress calls upon his personal totem-ancestor for help (above: 786). Another custom expressing awareness of a more personal relationship (one which has a parallel in the care of the Australians for the *tjurunga* of their clan; above: 172) is that of decorating the so called *déma*-spots with brightly coloured plants by members of the clan whose mythical ancestor (*déma*) retired there. Wirz suggests that small offerings are sometimes deposited here. Unfortunately, no one has ever witnessed what happened on these spots and we are not entitled to conclude on such precarious grounds that the bringing of offerings to one's personal déma was ever a custom among the Marind-anim (Van Baal 1966: 183). Nevertheless, an old report mentions a man who told the missionary at Okaba that the men of this village "had to bring a young wallaby to the wallaby-déma at Wambi (10 miles west of Okaba) because of late there had been few wallabies in the hunting-grounds and the people wished to win the wallaby-déma's favours" (ibid: 187 f.). The report does not tell whether the young wallaby was offered dead or alive; but, whatever the case, the act was an isolated event and nothing resembling an established custom. For this reason, it is none the less significant because it demonstrates that the dominant trend toward imitation of the totem-ancestor does not exclude the possibility of a personal approach.

Customary, however, is the offering of food to the dead. Again, there is something exceptional in this. The dead are never called upon for help and the offering serves no other purpose than their commemoration. The same holds true of the elaborate ceremonies for the dead. The men perform, round the grave, a show in which a small number of actors personify totems or totem-ancestors; on another day, the women visit in procession the places frequented by the deceased during his lifetime; there, they put down small offerings of food and betel. The women are headed by a young woman in festive attire who personifies the mayo-mother, the mother of the great ritual. (Note that the actor is, in this ceremony, not a man but a woman!) There is no question of praying to the dead for benefits on such occasions, nor on that of the big feasts which the spirits of the dead are invited to attend. In the course of these celebrations, small food offerings are set aside for them on the graves (ibid.: 765-806). If the feast is a pig-feast, the animals are cut up on platforms erected over the graves so that the blood that drips down can be soaked by the earth covering the graves. When the feast is finished, the hardwood sticks which marked the graves are pulled up and their sites condemned to oblivion (ibid.: 846). No mention is made of praying or dedicating anything to the dead or to anyone, and we cannot call it a sacrifice. Yet, it certainly is an offering; an offering brought with no other concrete purpose in mind than simply that of loving commemoration. On these occasions, the dead are nearby and the offerings are brought in a commensal spirit.

A culture differing widely from that of the plains dwelling Marind-anim is that of the Baktaman, a small community in the western mountains of Papua, described by F. Barth in his *Ritual and Knowledge among the Baktaman of New Guinea* (1975). Among the Baktaman no totemism, no spectacular dramatizations of myth, no intellectual play with the symbols of an elaborate pantheon but, instead, a vague awareness of a mystic relation between man, cuscus and taro, a relation which extends to domestic pigs; an equally vague belief in the beneficent influence of ancestors on luck in hunting and the prosperous growth of taro; and a deep sensitivity to the risks run by man and gardens if certain taboos are neglected.

The ancestors are called upon in small cult-houses (men's houses) where they reside in the form of a skull or, more often, of a few bones which are deposited on simple shrines. Here, they receive offerings, mostly in the form of small bones deriving from the animals eaten by the men: marsupials, pigs and cassowary. These offerings are burned in the fireplace inside the men's house.

> "The most outstanding feature of all these forms" – says Barth – "is the invariable association of sacrifice and prayer: no prayer is ever said except in conjunction with an offering, and no offering is ever unaccompanied by prayer. A number of other features are also stereotypically present: the ancestors' share is invariably delivered to a concrete relic; and its burning, rather than killing, the significant act of immolation. In nearly all cases, sacrifice implies a sacramental meal, hedged with taboos so that the *whole* victim is consumed by congregation (who eat) and ancestors (for whom it is burned) and by them alone. The only exceptions are those particular sacrifices which *only* the ancestors consume, and the flesh of man and domestic pig, where each cut, rather than the whole individual, is regarded as the relevant unit for ritual purposes" (Barth 1975: 193).

Characteristic of the small size of the allocation made to the ancestors is that the one animal that is dedicated to the ancestors in its entirety, is a small marsupial mouse. Baktaman sacrifice is primarily a commensal act which gives occasion to pray to the ancestors for hunting luck and taro growth, for fertility, health and success of man. In his comment, Barth strongly emphasizes the significance of the common meal as an act of trust. An eater always exposes himself to the danger that an unknown sorcerer stealthily sneaks a fragment of his food left-overs; eating in safety is only possible in the family circle or in the company of real friends. Eating with the ancestors expresses belonging together, communion.

The mystic relations between man, cuscus, and taro are made explicit in a myth (one of the few which Barth could obtain) stating that the first ancestor dwells underground, and that he is also a cuscus which holds the taro in its 'hands'. Having emerged, the ancestor divided mankind into clans, presented the taro to them and returned to his abode underground (ibid.: 83 f.). The myth is one of the few clues to an apprehension of the mysterious relations prevailing between man, food and animals, mainly marsupials, relations which play a role in the taboo system. The latter is interconnected with that of initiation, a protracted process of seven successive grades, some of which are separated by long periods of time.

"The Baktaman clearly express the idea that things hedged by taboo are 'strong'; taboo both protects this strength and protects potential victims *from* the strength. A system of taboos thus entails an analysis of the structure of reality in terms of implicit concepts of power and damage. It can thus be used to construct a model of the world of much greater complexity than one of dualism" (ibid.: 170). In a way, these last words are an understatement. The Baktaman codes of classification are not only "a criss-crossing structure of dichotomies", they are also a system of rules and motivations that are rarely, if ever, made explicit. "The Baktaman have no exegetical tradition" (ibid.: 226). And, indeed, the various stages of initiation are not used to elucidate relations and motives for the novices, but to let them apprehend a vague but imposing vision of the true nature of the world around them: the novice "sees the ground as something that lives, like a cuscus body or the head of a man; he sees the life force that grows out as hair, fur, vegetation; he sees the ancestral power holding the taro tuber underground, and then yielding it up as a part of a covenant of descent, cult, and exogamy. At the same time, he senses this power of fertility like heat in the ground" (ibid.: 234). Little is made explicit and everything is embedded in mystery, a mystery confirmed and consolidated by a secrecy which symbolizes the unfathomability of man's universe.

The correctness of Barth's description of the haziness of Baktaman religious concepts is amply confirmed by the elaborate picture drawn by Hylkema of the religious life of the Apmisibil Nalum, a community inhabiting a valley in the North of the Star Mountains in what is now West Irian (Hylkema 1974). Culturally, the Nalum are in so many respects similar to the Baktaman that there is reason to suppose that they are fairly closely related. Among the Nalum, one finds that same apprehension of the mysterious relations connecting man, cuscus and taro, and a comparable tradition of presenting offerings to the ancestors. There are differences, of course: most offerings are small pieces of pig-fat burned in the fire of the men's house, or they take the form of rubbing the sacred pole near the fire with fat or with leaves which have been used for cooking meat and vegetables. This pole is the abode (more or less: it is more intimated than stated) of the prime ancestor. Every night outside the men's house a mysterious pair of cuscus is sleeping under its overhanging roof. Lying in permanent copulation, their presence guarantees a quiet night to the inmates of the house. The rich variety of myths collected by Hylkema does not elucidate the vagueness of Nalum religious notions, but confirms it. The people live in a world in which vague apprehensions prevail. The most telling case is that of the men's notions concerning menstruation told above (p. 86; see also Hylkema 1974: 161 f.).

In such a world of mystery, in which clear concepts are lacking, taboos are well in place. Apprehended powers are powers which, if not avoided, should never be approached without circumspection and caution. Nevertheless, the statement that taboos fit well in a religious system dominated by vague apprehensions should not be extended to the thesis that taboos are symptomatic of vagueness and lack of articulation. This may, at least up to an extent, have been the case among the Andaman Islanders, but the data collected by Radcliffe-Brown (1922) are not conclusive on this point. The information available on the taboo ridden societies of the Mentawei Islands (Indonesia) is much richer and gives evidence that taboo can be combined with a fair degree of rationalization.

4. Taboo, sacrifice and divination; the Mentawei case

The sparsely populated Mentawei Islands are situated at a distance of about 80 nautical miles West of Sumatra. The native culture is of an archaic type; until recent years weaving, pottery-making, metal-working, blow-pipes, rice-growing, betel-chewing and the drinking of palmwine were unkown*. Although fundamentally Indonesian (they speak an Indonesian language), their culture has certain traits in common with that of the Andaman Islanders on the one hand, and with that of eastern Micronesia and western Polynesia, on the other (Nooy-Palm 1968).

In a number of articles, Schefold described the religion of the inland dwelling Mentaweians of Siberut, the most northern island, one of the very few regions still pagan (Schefold 1972, 1973 a & b, 1975, 1976, 1979). They are divided in small patrilineal clans (uma) of 5-10 families each. The word uma also means house, the communal house in which each family of the clan has its living quarters. The uma are located near the river, each separated from the other by a considerable distance. The uma of one valley co-operate. They intermarry and partake in each other's celebrations, but there is very little resembling a tribal organization. Each uma is an independent unit with its own chief (rimata) who is the leader of the cult, and one or more kerei (shamans) who officiate as ritual healers and as functionaries in more encompassing rituals to which related clans are invited. The main food is taro, supplemented with other vegetables and the spoils of hunting and fishing. Domestic animals are hens, pigs, and dogs.

In their religious world, gods do not play an important part. The central concept is that of souls. Not only men have a soul; literally everything has one. Every soul can leave the body of its owner, wander about, and communicate with other souls, persuading them to do certain actions or learning from them what they intend to do in the near future. Consequently, dreams have a prognostic meaning. Unfortunately, this meaning is not always clear; souls have the habit of veiling their messages in symbolic form. More important is that all souls radiate an influence (badjou) which, in itself, is neither good nor bad but has an effect anyway. A strong badjou may hurt a weaker one and, through its soul, its owner. Anyone introduced into a foreign group, e.g. by adoption into a clan of another valley, must ritually meet the souls of the adopting group's members to make their acquaintance; otherwise either party might hurt the other. Similarly, a newly-acquired metal gong must be carefully introduced

* This does not imply that they did not use pottery or metal ware. They bartered them from coast-dwelling traders.

211

to its new home lest either the new one or one of those already owned by the house, should burst.

"Because everything has a soul everything lives, everything can be addressed. All the world's souls are accessible by spells applied by men to act upon their milieu and its conditions" (Schefold 1973a: 98; my translation). To be effective, such spells must be transmitted by mediators. Man is aware of the distance separating him and his world from the supernatural, and the wishes and intentions formulated in his spells must be mediated to the addressees by plants and sacrificial animals. Some plants have special powers and are important mediators. One of these is a plant with a spiral stem. It has the special power to repel – to spiral down as it were – all forms of bad luck. If properly addressed it will use its *badjou* (radiation) to turn away damaging influences from the person or persons involved. The *uma* (house) is protected by a voluminous bunch of herbs representing a wide variety of special powers; to this bunch the *rimata* presents small offerings on many occasions.

Other important mediators are hens and pigs, the sacrificial animals. Before they are killed, the owner explains that he has always been kind to them and that, by now, they should assist him in his endeavours and ward off all danger and misfortune from him and his uma. The animal must use its badjou to achieve this. Immediately after the killing, the animal is cut open to inspect the heart, when it is a pig, and the entrails of the animal, when it is a chicken. Certain signs (they are common knowledge) give information about whether the animal has succeeded in its mission or not. If the augury is good, everyone feels confident; if it is bad, a second hen (rarely a second pig, though even this can happen) may be killed in the hope that this second animal will have more luck in persuading resistant souls of people or things to desist from further thwarting the sacrificer's desires, or from threatening his life and safety.

Souls are imperishable and they are found everywhere. Human souls, after death, go to the grand village of the dead. Every uma has its own in a distant, uninhabited part of the island. However, the corpse remains and, like everything else, it has its own soul, the *pitto*, which stays in the vicinity of the house, occasionally ensconsing itself in the house in order to bring harm to its inmates.

In a world populated by myriads of souls, man must be kind to the souls, in the first place to his own soul, lest it leave him to associate with the ancestors in the grand village of the dead. It is equally necessary to have regard for the objects in daily use. A hunter who has persistent bad luck, may find fault with his bow; not because, technically, it is deficient, but because the bow, apparently, does not like him. Yet, he cannot throw the bow away; that would give offence to the bow's soul and its badjou might harm the disappointed owner. For this reason, he gives it away to a friend who may be more congenial for that bow.

One must be kind to the souls and this engenders a great variety of taboos, very often taboos of a symbolic nature. A man whose wife is pregnant should not make a canoe; scooping the trunk of the tree is the reverse of what is happening to his wife inside her body. And as soon as he has a new-born baby, he must refrain from every act which causes plants to wilt. The same might happen to the baby. For the time being, there is no question of weeding his garden. An extension of this taboo – induced by

212

high child mortality among recent settlers on that island – has persuaded the Mentaweians of Pagai that it is better to give their children to the custody of the mother's parents. Even more than Siberut, Pagai (South of Siberut) is a taboo-ridden society.

Yet, even the most meticulous regard for the souls of people and things cannot prevent misfortune or sickness. Often, they are preceded by bad omens, such as bad dreams, earthquakes (which are frequent on the islands) or signs observed in plants or animals. Then it is time to celebrate a feast, just as feasts are arranged when important changes in the uma (e.g. building a new house, an adoption, buying a new gong, etc.) call for celebrations which please the souls and re-establish harmony and friendship. By now, normal work is taboo. Instead, everyone exerts himself to make ornaments which will allure the spirits of the dead to come to the *uma* to participate. But first of all the *pitto*, the menacing souls of the corpses, must be chased from the house. As soon as this has been achieved, pigs are slaughtered and the meat exhibited at the entrance of the uma to invite the souls of the living and the dead to enter. Dancing begins during which the shamans (who are able to see and hear the souls) go into a trance, communicate with them and collect the souls of all the participants. When every soul has been captured, they are restored by the shamans to their respective owners by touching the fontanel of each. The dancing continues in an atmosphere of growing benevolence and well-being. The feast may last several days.

Of particular interest are the great feasts for the dead when the invited spirits of the dead join in the dance. One after another the shamans go into a trance; after a time the excitement becomes unbearable and *rimata* (chief) and shamans request the spirits now to return. Tears run down their cheeks when they take leave of them. They 'see' the spirits and ancestors, many of them their own deceased parents and siblings, when at last the spirit-guests depart from the uma to return to their abode in the grand village.

The professional mediators between man and the world of souls and spirits are the shamans. If anyone falls ill because his soul has left him, it is the task of the shaman to conjure the soul back to the patient. If the patient's soul has been captured by a sorcerer, it is the shaman who must try to set it free. Shamans are said to be seers, though not all of them are. One cannot say that they are abnormal persons, at least not as a generalization. In a society in which everyone knows himself to be surrounded by souls and spirits, the shaman is a well-adapted person. Laymen sometimes follow similar pursuits as the shamans. If a patient's condition declines without explicable cause, every effort at improving his health having miscarried, his clanmates conclude that he has lost all interest and pleasure in his life and that his soul longs for the grand village of the ancestors. The clan then organizes a great feast. The patient is adorned as a bridegroom, neighbours bring pigs for the festive meals, everyone dances and sings, calling on the patient's soul to return and to assure itself that life is still worth living. The clansmen are kind to the patient's soul.

What prevails in all this is a deep awareness of the fact that man, every man, is part of and partner in his universe, and that this ought to be so. The souls, the taboos, the feasts, the acts of conjuring, sacrifice and divination, of dancing and trance, all convey the certainty that man and his world are one great community in which even the dead, the animals and the plants participate. It is this communion which, in sickness or misfortune, must be repaired and, in times of prosperity, respected. That respect is expressed by taboos. Taboos are not simply rules of avoidance; they give form to the faith that the visible world is ruled by secret intentions and sympathies embodied in the souls of each and everything separately. To explain this belief, one need not resort to the hypothesis of a prelogical mentality which has all things participate in each other, a hypothesis which leaves its supporters with the problem of how to explain that the same people act strictly logically in all the affairs of profane life. In fact, the belief of the Mentaweians is no more than the elaboration and rationalization of the fundamental experience that man and his universe belong together and that, in a way which ordinary people cannot fathom because the relevant knowledge is not available, all things co-operate either for prosperity or for misfortune. The two outstanding features of this culture are the extension of the moral law to the whole universe, and man's urgent need to communicate with his universe.

An intriguing illustration of this need is given by the practice of divination. Schefold has devoted a long and interesting article to it (1972) in which he emphasizes that divination is not, certainly nor primarily, a matter of sheer curiosity, but a means to communicate with the souls. Of course, the outcome of divination is, like that of the observation of omens, information, but it is always information which tells what to do about the situation in question. If the information is disappointing, one may try it a second time. When the message has been acquired by means of a sacrifice, the sacrifice may be repeated in the hope that in a second instance the soul of the sacrificial animal will be more successful in obtaining supernatural help. It is not a matter of bribing the souls concerned. They will not receive anything from the animal that is sacrificed. Its meat is divided among the participants. The only ones to receive something in the form of a small food-offering are the ancestors who taught their descendents the relevant techniques of divining.

There is nothing exceptional in this use of divination as a means of influencing the souls or the ancestors. A strictly comparable application of divination has been reported by Arndt from the Ngad'a of Flores (Arndt 1929/31) and there is good reason to presume that this use of divination as a form of discourse is fairly general. Thus, divination of the same type is found among the Kapsiki of Cameroon (Van Beek 1978). The technique of the Ngad'a differs from that of the Mentaweians in that they make use of a piece of bamboo two notches long. A hen is sacrificed and the bamboo is put into the fire. The ancestors are called upon to let the bamboo burst on the right side first if the answer is positive, on the left side if it is negative. If the relevant question was whether a certain patient shall recover from his illness and the answer is no, a second bamboo is put into the fire to enquire whether he has committed a sin which is the cause of his imminent death. If the answer is now positive, a third bamboo must decide between theft and adultery. Once the guilt is clear and the patient has confessed, new bamboos are put into the fire to learn what can be done to mend the damage, and so on. The process probably ends with a vow to sacrifice a buffalo when the patient recovers, a promise which gives substance to the

214

conspicuous custom of speaking of the sacrificed hens as buffaloes (cf. below: 226). If all goes well, the buffalo will be offered in due course. However, this is not the main point here. This is that divination can be typified as a long-drawn process of communication and even negotiation with the ancestors. Again, communication stands in the centre of the activities. The point that here, as elsewhere, the sacrificial animal is consumed by the sacrificers and their guests, whereas those to whom the sacrifice is presented, the gods, spirits or ancestors, must content themselves with no more than a symbolic trifle, is a question which will be taken up in the next chapter together with other problems such as that of the strange habit of presenting a sacrificial animal as bigger or more expensive than it actually is.

The final conclusion to be drawn from this chapter is the corroboration of the view that primitive man experiences his world as simultaneously uncanny, frightening and alluring. The ambivalence of this experience is reflected in the numerous father symbols who, in spite of the threat they inspire, invite and encourage him to seek their intermediary for acquiring a partner's place in this world's mystery.

XII

Offering and Sacrifice

Offering is an act of presenting something to a supernatural being, whilst sacrifice is an offering associated with the ritual killing of the object of the offering (Van Baal 1976b: 161). The definition, in spite of its apparent simplicity, covers a variety of widely-diverging ends and meanings. The act of presenting something can be a gift as well as a payment. As a gift, it can be an unobtrusive act of food-sharing, a commensal act as is proper among closely-related persons, but also the formal presentation of a substantial gift expressing feelings of respect and affection. As a payment, the offering can aim at striking a bargain, but can also be the fine paid to expiate a sin. The sacrificial killing of an animal need not be more than a technical necessity attendant on the wish to offer meat, but it can also have originated as or developed into a symbol of divine suffering. If this be the case, the sacrifice is the dramatization of a myth, and the act takes its meaning not from the pattern of the gift, but from imitating the divine example. A further complication is the combination of offering and sacrifice with a meal. It is not a general feature of all sacrifices but it recurs with such frequency that eating or not eating must be considered as a meaningful symptom for discerning one category of sacrifices from the other.

The variety of their forms is one problem presented by offering and sacrifice; another – and a more intractable one – is the contradiction inherent in the act as such. What can man offer to his gods that is not already theirs? And how can a gift of worldly origin be of interest to any non-worldly being or be appropriated by it? It is small wonder, then, that offering and sacrifice have been favourite topics of discussion among anthropologists and students of comparative religion since the early days of these disciplines. Unfortunately, these discussions have not resulted in a consensus, and before we try to arrive at an explanation which covers the total diversity of relevant forms, we have to pay attention to these different theories. Some of these have had a lasting influence on current ideas on the subject, and the field has to be clarified before we can proceed to a categorization of the varieties of offering and sacrifice which can lead to an elucidation of their meaning.

1. Theories on offering and sacrifice

A main source of confusion is that an offering is a gift, and that the true character of

216

the gift has been misunderstood until long after M. Mauss, in his *Essai sur le Don*, had cogently exposed its main features (1923/24). Most persistent of all was the after-effect of Tylor's theory of sacrifice (in his terminology synonymous with offering). He described 'sacrifice' as follows: "As prayer is a request made to a deity as if he were a man, so sacrifice is a gift made to a deity as if he were a man. The human types of both may be studied unchanged in social life to this day. The suppliant who bows before his chief, laying a gift at his feet and making his humble petition, displays the anthropomorphic model and origin at once of sacrifice and prayer" (1871: II, 375). What Tylor describes is, unfortunately, not a gift, but a bribe. In Tylor's description, the gift is not presented to the god or ancestor out of appreciation of the divine person (cf. above: 97 ff.) but to obtain a specific favour from him. It is a payment in advance presented in the form of a gift. Tylor's humble petitioner and his chief find their exact counterparts in modern society in the petitioner who, standing in front of the counter in the licence office, furtively encloses a banknote in the licence-form which he pushes across the desk to the clerk whom he wishes to hand him the desired licence. Tylor's theory of *do ut des* implies that an offering must be substantial; it must match the favour desired. Consequently, he felt justified in speaking of cheating when and where the sacrificers ate the better part of the victim themselves, leaving the gods no more than a trifle or the bare bones. Similarly, symbolic offerings such as a cake representing a cow and offered to the god as a real cow, had to be condemned as just another effort at faking.

Today, we know that it is the rule rather than an exception that the gods receive but a trifle and that, as far as the divine share is concerned, there is little material difference between a normal offering and a symbolic one. Tylor, in his days, could hardly know that what he called economizing on the gift to the gods, took place to such extent as to make his theory untenable. Moreover, there are indeed numerous cases in which the victim of the sacrifice is presented to the gods in its entirety, either by burning it, by leaving the carcass in the wilderness, or by setting the animal free in the desert. Holocausts dominated the Hebrew forms of sacrifice, and the fact that such forms of sacrifice occurred next to those in which the divine share was minimal, demanded an explanation anyhow. Actually, Tylor had yet another reason for emphasizing the necessity of substantial offerings. He had entered the field of anthropology as a Mexicanist, and he was deeply impressed by the importance of human sacrifice in old Mexican religion. The number of human victims may have been overdrawn, but the great significance of human sacrifice in Aztec religion is beyond doubt. It could but confirm the aptitude of the term savages for primitive people, and strengthen the readers' confidence in the reliability of the awesome stories about savage rites communicated by early visitors of the world's more backward parts. Tylor and his contemporaries never doubted their truth. In fact, what could be expected of savages other than savage behaviour? Under these circumstances, early anthropologists did not hesitate to explain certain rites, such as those of offering a pluck of hair shorn off a baby's head or the effusion of a few drops of blood, as survivals of a pristine human sacrifice. A case in point is the famous essay by Wilken, one of Tylor's followers, *Über das Haaropfer und einige andere Trauergebräuche bei den*

Völkern Indonesiens (1886/87; Translation: On the hair-sacrifice and a few other mortuary customs among the peoples of Indonesia). The 19th century reports on headhunting in Melanesia and Indonesia, the rumours about human sacrifices in these parts, and the wide publicity given to the revolting practice of *suttee* (widow-burning) in India strongly supported the view that primitives really are savages, capable of any form of offensive bloodthirstiness.

Although modern anthropologists, warned off by Mauss's theory of the gift, rarely give much credit to Tylor's views on sacrifice, many of them are still inclined to give credence to far-fetched stories of human sacrifice celebrated until a fairly recent past. They never witnessed one, but these stories are usually told with so much sincerity that it is difficult to disbelieve them. Indeed, some of these may be true. All the same, there is good reason for incredulity here. Not without purpose I reported how I have myself been duped by the men who told me how they had killed their victim by inserting a pointed stick just behind his scrotum and pushing it up until it came out at his throat (above: 196). It was not related just for the sake of a telling story, but to demonstrate how, to its performers, a symbolic act can be more 'real' than a factual one. The narrators' realism is so blatantly sincere that no normally critical hearer can guess what is behind it unless he has gone through the training of a long experience with native ways of presenting the facts of magic. An even more convincing case is that of the Marind-anim stories about endo-cannibalistic ritual. Openly giving away what – to us – is the esoteric meaning of the ritual, the initiates keep the plainly symbolic (and quite innocent) technique of its operationalization a guarded secret, exactly as they do when they describe the sorcerers' rite of lethal magic (ibid.: 195 f.), and the Australians do in their stories relating the initiation of a medicine-man (ibid.: 190). Such facts should warn everyone against taking savage stories about human sacrifice at their face value, even when they are told with a convincing show of sincerity. I am not prepared to deny that some of these stories are true; I simply hold that they do not merit the confidence so widely and easily bestowed upon them.

Most of these stories are beyond any possible verification of their truth. Almost invariably the action took place in a bygone past, and every year the relevant stories become more venerable (and thus more true) simply by recounting them over and over again. Yet, there are one or two which are palpably false and nevertheless constitute part of the unshaken credo of the learned world up to the present day. The most outstanding case is that of the bull dedicated to Dionysos. Every student knows that he was killed by savage Cretans tearing the live animal to pieces with their bare teeth. The act is physically impossible, even if the bull had been anaesthesized previously, but the story having been transmitted from generation to generation as God's truth, there is hardly a single student of antiquity who dares to admit that, in this form, it is nonsense. It is perfectly evident that the original narrator of the story has been duped by the initiates of the Dionysian mysteries in exactly the same way as Wirz was by his Marind-anim informants. They told him the esoteric truth and kept the technique of its ritual operationalization a closed secret. We shall never know that secret, but that cannot be a reason to persist in believing a cock-and-bull story. On the contrary, there is sound reason to be suspicious of so-called historical cases of human sacrifice generally.

The influence of Tylor (and Frazer) has been persistent, particularly among classicists. Once the notion had taken shape that a sacrifice had to be substantial, the custom at the great Olympian sacrifices of granting the gods nothing but the bare bones became an embarrassing problem. It could not be solved by accusing the sacrificers of premeditated deceit. The gods were well-informed on this matter; besides, the gods of the Homeric age were so human, so keen on profit and wealth, that cheating them was not a likely possibility. Karl Meuli (1946) has tried to solve the problem by explaining the custom as a survival dating back to the time when the Greeks were still living somewhere in the forests bordering the Asian plains. It is a well-known fact that Siberian hunters, i.e. hunters who depend on game for their living, occasionally honour the 'Lord of the Animals' with a sacrificial gift of bare bones, entrails and the like, because by his divine grace they are enabled to capture the animals on which they depend for their living. Meuli suggests that this custom has been retained by the hunters when they became herdsmen and eventually settled in Greece.

The erudition spent on this hypothesis is of little avail, because Meuli took for granted exactly those points which are the most dubious, to wit, the inherent improbability of unchanged survival from barbarian times onwards of a custom which, to those concerned, was of such focal interest as the great Olympian sacrifice was to the meanwhile civilized Greeks; the improbability of the hypothesis that herding originated directly from hunting; and the possibility that the Siberian hunters themselves were the borrowers who took their sacrificial rituals from neighbouring herdsmen. On the two points mentioned last something more should be said.

That herding has developed directly from hunting seems acceptable enough in the case of reindeer-herding. Unfortunately, this happens to be the one and only case of herding animals which never have been properly domesticated, as cattle, goats, sheep and pigs have been. To domesticate an animal it is necessary to capture it when it is young and still in need of care. Such care can only be given by people whose ways of life are, in the main, sedentary, not by nomads dependent on hunting and collecting. For as long as the herds or flocks are small, there is no reason for nomadic habits. This changes when they increase in numbers and there is not sufficient grassland nearby to feed them. Then it happens that people, who originally were agriculturalists, turn into herders. Professional hunters and collectors, however, have little opportunity to domesticate animals. They must move their camps too often.

Another objection against Meuli's hypothesis is that the custom of bringing sacrifices to a deity who is announced as the Lord of Animals is a mainly Siberian custom. We hear little of it among the Plains Indians of North America or the hunters of California, nothing at all among the aboriginals of Australia nor, as far as I am aware, among the hunting tribes of Central and Southern Africa. This implies that it is a local custom, not one general among hunters, whereas the custom of letting the gods have no more than a very small share of an offering is universal wherever offering and sacrifice are more or less important cult forms. There is more reason, then, to suppose that the Siberian hunters borrowed the custom of offering unprepared parts of the sacrificial victim to the deity from neighbouring herdsmen, than the reverse. The point is that hunters do not usually make such sacrifices; they confine themselves to offering titbits of prepared food to the gods. What is more, throughout Central Asia the herdsmen are respected rulers whose customs are more prone to be imitated by humble hunters than that proud herdsmen can be inclined to keep up customs which are typical of despised hunters.

It is evident that, to explain the poor size of the divine share in an offering, one must turn to Mauss's *Essai sur le Don*, in particular to the passage where he explained that it is impudent to give a substantial gift to a superior. Offerings are naturally small, and the real problem of sacrifice is not that the share allotted to the gods is usually small, but that it sometimes is big. However, there are more problems; one is that something, however small, is offered at all; another that this kind of gift-giving is combined with a request for receiving something in return. These, however, are problems to be discussed later. We first must pay attention to a few other theories which presented general explanations of offering and sacrifice.

The most attractive among these is that by Robertson Smith. He admitted that there are various forms of sacrifice and seriously tried to find room for this diversity in his theory. His main point is that an offering is an act of communion, initially an act of communion by eating the deity in the guise of the totemic animal, later by the sacrificers' feasting on the sacred animal of the flock together with the deity who received the blood. An important point of the theory is that the sacrificial animal must be sacred. Once the animal of the flock lost its initial sacredness, sacrifice deteriorated or was revived in more intense forms such as holocaust and human sacrifice, two forms of sacrifice which exclude the sacrificer from participating in the meal because the victim has become so sacred that it is utterly unfit for human consumption. This sacredness of the victim – duly emphasized in Hebrew sources – will be discussed in more detail presently. The point to be examined here is the interpretation of the sacrifice as an act of communion by means of a meal in which gods and men participate. We came across such a case in Barth's description of the offerings made by the Baktaman: Baktaman sacrifice is primarily an act of commensality; one cannot safely eat in the company of strangers: eating together is an act of confidence (above: 209).

One of the most enthralling passages in Robertson Smith's Lectures is his description of the old Hebrew sacrifice of the kind referred to in the first book of Samuel: "private householders were accustomed to reserve their offerings for the annual feast, satisfying their religious feelings in the interval by vows to be discharged when the festal season came round. Then the crowds streamed into the sanctuary from all sides, dressed in their gayest attire, marching joyfully to the sound of music, and bearing with them not only the victims appointed for sacrifice but a store of bread and wine to set forth the feast" (1889: 236). It is a picture of a sacrificial feast of the kind I attended, late in 1941, in Lombok (Indonesia): people feasting because their vows had been heard, and sacrificing goats to their 'god' who confirmed his presence and benevolence by letting the dancing women fall into a trance. An act of communion indeed; but not – as Robertson Smith thought – because the animals killed were specifically sacred, but because the god made his presence felt by entrancing the dancers. He participated.

The sacredness of the sacrifical animal is the controversial point in Robertson Smith's theory. He derived it from the sacredness of the totem animal. In his days, this was a fairly acceptable explanation; but, with our present knowledge of totemism and the insignificant role of the animal in its cult, it is no longer tenable. The combination of totemism and sacrifice is a rare exception. The totem animal is not very sacred and, besides, it is only made the object of a sacrifice if it is edible, and then, as far as we know, not because it is a totem, but because it is good for food. It is a reasonable estimate that Robertson Smith borrowed the notion of the sacrificial animal's sacredness not from his scanty knowledge of totemism, but from a historically late explanation of the essence of sacrifice: i.e. the doctrine of transsubstantiation as dictated by the 16th century council of Trent. The link between the sacrificed totem-god and the doctrine of transsubstantiation suited his view that the rite persists through time whereas dogma and explanatory myth change, a view which is basic to Robertson Smith's thought.

The sacredness of the object of sacrifice found a better, at least a more often accepted explanation in the theory presented by Hubert and Mauss (1899). The victim of the sacrificial act is not intrinsically sacred but becomes sacred through sacrifice. It is set apart because it mediates between profane man and the world of the sacred which, by definition, is separated and forbidden. The distance between the sacred and the profane is so great and the sacred so dangerous that the mediator, the sacrificial victim, necessarily perishes and thus protects the sacrificer from disaster in his effort at entering into contact with the sacred. Hubert and Mauss based their views on data borrowed from two highly-developed, purity-conscious religions, the Hebrew and the Vedantic. Their sources were not descriptions of sacrificial practice as noted by outside observers, but holy books written by members of a priestly caste who strongly emphasized the total otherness of the sacred. In less sophisticated societies, such emphasis on the danger and separateness of the sacred, which culminates in the sacredness of the sacrificial victim, is rarely found. The victims are cut up and their parts freely distributed among the participants and guests, who need not eat them within the sacred precincts of the ritual action, but may take them home for consumption. Even the share allotted to the gods is rarely protected; everyone knows that scavenging animals snatch them away and no one tries to forestall them. It often happens that, after the formal ceremony, it is condoned that the children feast on the titbits offered to the gods. The cases in which the victim is really treated as sacred and untouchable are ordinarily restricted to those of a sacrifice presented to expiate an ominous impurity or sin, or destined to ward off the powers of evil. In other words, there are indeed some kinds of sacrifice which fit into the pattern of the theory, but others deviate profoundly from it, and the deviating sacrifices are by no means a minority.

221

Mauss never retracted the views expounded in the essay which he wrote in collaboration with Hubert, but twenty years later, in his *Essay sur le Don*, he made a remark on a side-issue which should have led to a completely new approach. Commenting on the obligation of the rich always to give more than the poor and to return a small gift by a big one, he added that this explains the small size of the divine share allotted to the gods on the occasion of a sacrifice: *Car ces dieux qui donnent et rendent sont là pour donner une grande chose à la place d'une petite* (p. 169 of the 1950 reprint; translation: For these gods who give and reciprocate exist to give a large gift in return for a small one). Unfortunately, the observation was made in passing, and it never received the attention it deserved. Even Van der Leeuw, who had read the essay and referred to it, missed the point. He was more interested in Mauss's effort at explaining the duty to reciprocate from a kind of mana inherent in the gift, something deriving from the giver's personality which urges the recipient to make a return-gift lest he fall sick. We came across the argument earlier in this book, and rejected it as untenable (above: 92). To Van der Leeuw, a strong believer in prelogical thought and the mysticism of primitive mentality, Mauss's ill-timed excursions into the field of mana offered a welcome opportunity to elaborate on the magic of the gift and its mystic effect in sacrifice (Van der Leeuw 1933: § 50). The combination of offering and sacrifice with magic and mysticism added to the confusion round the problem of sacrifice rather than to its elucidation. A magical effect never explains anything but must itself be explained. And when mysticism is involved in the act of sacrifice, it is because the gods shroud themselves in mystery or because the act makes part of a ritual re-enactment of a deity's mythical achievements.

The theme of re-enactment of mythical events returns in another theory which had, and still has, a fairly strong impact on current scholarly notions of sacrifice, A. E. Jensen's interpretation of rites commemorating or dramatizing the death of a deity as *Tötungsrituale* (killing rituals; Jensen 1951). Jensen associated these rituals with what he called the *dema mythologeme*, i.e. the widely spread theme attributing the origin of the more important foodcrops to the death of a deity who made the relevant plants sprout from his corpse. The theme itself is of great interest (we return to it in the next section) but Jensen's treatment of it is controversial. To begin with, the term *dema*, borrowed from Marind-anim mythology, is ill-chosen. In Marind-anim language the term dema has other and wider implications than those which Jensen had in mind. Of the numerous dema of Marind-anim mythology no more than two fall into the pattern of a deity whose corpse changed into an important foodcrop. Far worse is that the term 'killing ritual' also covers practices such as that of headhunting. There is no denying, of course, that headhunting has its ritual aspects. Among the Marind-anim, they are even impressive. Yet, there is too much genuine aggressivity in it, often too much also of revenge and military pursuits, to qualify headhunting as primarily a ritual and not as a form of warfare, a ritualized form of warfare admittedly, but all the same warfare. It is true that the Marind-anim case raises doubts because neither revenge nor military necessity play a part of real significance, but genuine aggressivity does, and this even to a high degree. Besides, headhunting is not combined with a presentation of the victim or its head to the ancestors or the gods, neither among the

222

Marind-anim, nor among most of the other peoples who practise the custom. Although McKinley, approaching the custom of headhunting from quite another angle as Jensen, recently arrived at a similar, ritual-centered conclusion (McKinley 1976), I have not been persuaded that the ritual aspects of headhunting are so preponderant that the aggressive and military aspects can be considered as secondary. However important and often elaborate these ritual aspects be, there is more reason to consider them as forms of self-justification or symptoms of the warriors' awareness of the irrationality and even reprehensibility of their sanguinary habits, than to explain the habit as the deplorable result of the blood-lust or carelessness of their gods. After all, the gods are the creation of the Marind-anim themselves. Admitting that, in the case of McKinley's theory, there are other and more complicated aspects to consider, there is for the time being insufficient reason to extend the notion of sacrifice to phenomena so intrinsically combined with other motivations as the custom of headhunting.

2. The varieties of offering and sacrifice: a categorization

The data presented in the previous sections give ample evidence that offering and sacrifice are of many kinds, and that the first thing needed is a categorization which can elucidate this confusing variety.

To such a categorization the difference between offering and sacrifice, i.e. an offering preceded by a ritual killing, has little to contribute. The two do not stand in opposition to each other; they refer to differences in techno-economic development rather than to differences in religious motivation or form. Ritual killing depends primarily on the availability of a victim that allows itself to be brought alive to the place of the ceremony. Such victims are either domesticated animals or human beings. Human sacrifice being a rather exceptional phenomenon, this implies that sacrifice is mostly confined to societies which have domesticated animals at their disposal; in other words, to societies in which wealth has an appreciable function. In general, these are societies with a more advanced technology. Yet, this does not mean that in such societies every offering is preceded by a ritual killing. Even great ceremonial offerings composed of – among other things – meat of domesticated animals, need not be sacrifices. A good instance is that of the great Balinese offer-ceremonies. The offerings are prepared in the village where pigs, fowl and cattle are butchered without special ceremony. Then the food is prepared and arranged on beautifully ornamented dishes. This finished, the men and women decorate themselves and, in their best attire, depart in procession to the temple, the women carrying the dishes on their heads. Here, the dishes are deposited at a shrine and presented to the gods by a priest, the offerers meanwhile squatting quietly in front of the shrine. When the priest has finished his prayers and dedications, they all wait in silence for a few minutes; the gods now enjoy the *sari*, the essence, of the offerings. Then, the offerers take the dishes with what is now called the left-overs, and return to the village in as ceremonious and colourful a procession as they came. Back in the village, each household enjoys its own festive meal, usually after having deposited a few titbits of the consecrated food on their various house-shrines.

One might contest the statement that, among more primitive people, sacrifices are rare by arguing that offer-feasts are often preceded by a collective hunt which is considered to be a part of the total complex of ceremonies and activities. This is true, but does not detract from the fact that the game is not killed ritually but in such a way as the actual situation permits, that is exactly as in any ordinary hunt. Ritual killing is impossible unless the game has been caught alive with the deliberate intention of using it for a sacrifice which, in such a case, often takes place on a later occasion. This means that the animal concerned is, to a greater or lesser extent, domesticated before it is victimized. The few cases in which this does not happen are so exceptional that they do not present a suitable basis for a discussion of sacrifice generally. To that end we need another approach.

Such an approach is presented by making a definite distinction between sacrifices made in imitation of mythological events and divine acts, and offerings and sacrifices which constitute part of an act of communication of the person-to-person type. The latter can be subdivided in various kinds; but, before we proceed to this, we must first discuss the sacrifices re-enacting mythical events and divine acts.

Sacrifices of this kind refer to impressive acts of violence which are symbolically or literally dramatized. The most convincing cases of literal re-enactment are afforded by the human sacrifices performed by the Mexicans who revivified the death of the corn-goddess, or fed the sun-god with the bleeding hearts of their prisoners-of-war. The Mexican world-view as depicted by Soustelle (1955) is exceedingly gloomy. The threat of disaster hovers over their cruel universe in which the little security man can attain depends on violence. It needs a Mexicanist with a wide knowledge of Amerindian ethnology to assess the cultural conditions which inspired their fears of a violent apocalypse, fears which, in America, were not confined to Aztec civilization. Incompetent to make specific suggestions in this field, I must restrict my comment to the somewhat lame statement that the Aztec rituals give expression to a combination of strong aggressiveness and anxiety. Commonplace as it be, it is not wholly super-fluous to remind the reader of the fact that the cruelty of the Mexican rituals necessarily refers to the way they experienced their world. And such experiences of a cruel world are not as exceptional as one might think. The Mexicans had the bad luck to be overrun by a people equally warlike and equally cruel where matters of religion were at stake. The main difference between these two races of warriors was that the Mexicans believed in gods who are cruel and prepare bliss for their believers by exhorting them to cruelty to their enemies, and the Spaniards in a god who is full of love and, accepting a cruel fate for himself, encouraged his believers to deal out cruelty to the infidel.

The god who, by sacrificing himself or letting himself be sacrificed, sets an example: that of the grain of corn that falls into the ground to die in order to bring forth fruit. The parable is common to many nations and religions. Jensen's dema-mythologeme is a strong case in point (Jensen 1951). In his comment, Jensen asserts that the mythologeme derives from *die altpflanzerische Kultur*, the culture of early horticulturalists, on the face of appearances a safe conclusion based on simple logic.

Nevertheless, he also found the dema-mythologeme among the Eskimo and the Australians, two nations which do not plant. In the case of the Eskimo, the presence of the mythologeme can be explained from diffusion, but it is not clear how diffusion worked in the Australian case. But why think of borrowing? Does anyone really believe that the Australians do not know that plants grow from seeds? It is a fact that no woman in her daily digging for roots and grubs can have failed to note. They must know that life sprouts from dying seeds. The trouble with us, Westerners, is that we are so thoroughly christianized that we think that the only answer to the horrors of death is the belief in resurrection or continued existence. There is another and older answer, one deeply rooted in man's daily intercourse with living nature, namely that life springs from death. It is not only the dying grain which produces life; in nature the death of the one is always the life of another (above: 8). Death and life belong together, and the most obvious answer to the fears of death is the internalization of the truth that death engenders life. That is what myths tell us and what rituals confirm by re-enacting the mythic tragedies.

How these enactments are staged is often less certain than our sources on human and animal sacrifice pretend. They wish us to take the re-enactment to the letter. How dubious such assertions are was illustrated above by the cases of the Marind-anim sacrifice of husband and wife, and of the Greeks devouring the bull of Dionysos (181 and 218). Even the Mexican sources, with their numerous well-documented cases of human sacrifice, are not always beyond doubt. When we are told that on some occasions fire was drilled in the human victim's breast (Soustelle 1955, p. 122 of the Dutch translation) we can be certain that the man who first accepted the story as literal truth had never in his life attended an act of fire-drilling. The technique is quite simple, requiring no more than an arrow, a dry plank with a shallow little hole in it, and some perfectly dry leaves and fibre. Whoever believes that all this can be done in the breast of a freshly killed person really believes in magic. Tall stories, even those told by venerated authors of antiquity, should be read critically.

But, by now, enough has been said about the exigences of heuristic method. What counts here is that sacrifices are performed which, literally or symbolically, re-enact the events of primeval time, the mythical stories which reflect the essence of man's experiences in and with a universe characterized by a never-ending succession of life and death. How life and death are intertwined and alternate may remain unclear, a matter of incalculable chance and apparent arbitrariness, but that the two interact is a truth which cannot escape the attention of anyone living in close contact with and complete dependence upon nature. The overt purpose ascribed to sacrifices re-enacting a mythical drama can be of any kind: the promotion of fertility, the staving off of danger and death, the satisfaction of the inexorable exigences of the gods of sun and vegetation, or soothing the anxieties aroused by a disastrous epidemic, but that overt purpose never expresses the ultimate purpose of the celebrating participants. What they really do when they unite in a solemn act of sacrifice which embodies the intertwinement of life and death, is that they submit themselves to the law of their universe, accepting it as the law of their own life and death, and through the sacrifice act in unison with the mysteries of that universe which combines life and death in a manner which no one can fathom, let alone unravel. By acting in consort with his universe, the sacrificial act is an act of communion which restores the individual to perfect participation in his universe, transforming the lonely subject into a partner in its secrets.

It is evident that in sacrifices of this type the offering of the victim to the deity is necessarily a side-issue. Dependent on the content of the myth, an offering may be part of the ceremony or be lacking, just as the case may be. For this reason, these 'sacrifices' might perhaps better be called 'drama', as I suggested a few years ago (Van Baal 1976b: 177). Yet, the scenery of the act, its performance in a temple or other sacred place, the solemn attendance of an assembly, and the obviousness of its religious motivation, all concur to admit that there may be some wisdom in the traditional classification of these acts as sacrifices. For clarity's sake, we had better reconcile ourselves to current terminology and recognize them as a special category of sacrifices. Besides, the fact that it is the deity who sacrifices himself is a strong argument in favour of the current terminology.

We can now turn to those sacrifices which concentrate on offering something to a deity or spirit; in other words sacrifices which belong to the same category as offerings generally. They are of three kinds, to wit those which follow the pattern of the gift, those which obey the pattern of a punishment, and those which conform to the pattern of the bribe. Among the offerings and sacrifices subject to the pattern of the gift, three different forms must again be discerned: those which are small and resemble the unofficial gifts exchanged between participants in the give-and-take relationship pertaining to the intimacy of the small group; the more sizable offerings and sacrifices presented in official form; and finally those brought in payment of a vow.

Before we proceed, two objections must be discussed which can be raised against qualifying any offerings as gifts at all. The first of these is that giving something to a deity is a factual impossibility as well as an impropriety. The arrogance of the act may be mitigated by the circumstance that the share allotted to the god usually is small or of poor quality, but this is a lame excuse because it raises suspicions of lack of respect. All these objections disappear when it is conceded that the sacrificers see their offerings as symbolic gifts. One really need not be a scholar to understand that a gift can be symbolic! All the evidence tends to prove that this is indeed how the offerers themselves think of it. In the first place, they apparently do not mind that the food allotted to the gods is pilfered by animals or children. Once presented to the gods, they no longer take notice of these small offerings. When they find that the food has disappeared, this is taken as a sign that the deity has accepted the offering. In fact, the non-disappearance of these titbits would disquiet them more than its vanishing does! The solid knowledge of what actually happend to the food does not prevent them from explaining its disappearance as a symbolic acceptance.

In the second place, offerings are often symbolic in the fullest sense of the world. A cock is sacrificed and called a buffalo in the invocation attending the act, or a cake in the form of a cow is presented as a real ox. To think that the offerers try to cheat the

226

gods is as childish as the primitives of Tylor's imagination, and is belied by the seriousness by which the offerers proceed. They simply express that nothing could be enough to offer to the god and that it is their heart's intent to do so if they could afford it and if it would be of any use or propriety. But knowing that what is small with men is great to the gods and reversely (a saying often heard) they simply express their hearts' intents when they present their offerings as bigger and more valuable than they really are. Moreover, how could anyone approach the gods otherwise than by symbols?

Finally, the ordinary offering is one of food, and not one of ornaments or valuables. Nothing expresses nearness and friendship so patently as the sharing of food. What Barth wrote on this matter (above: 209) is illuminating. Eating together is done with reliable friends and relatives only. The offering of prepared food is a commensal act. One might ask: What then with the sacrifices which consist mainly of the distribution of meat among the participants, the gods being fobbed off with the bare bones or a small portion of heart or liver? It is just a matter of procedure. The victims are presented to the gods before they are killed. After this everyone gets his share, first the gods, then the participants. That the share of the gods is symbolic is faithful to the rules. Once the food has been prepared, the gods will again be presented with titbits of the official meal and also of the festive meals arranged on their homecoming in the households of the recipients of the meat. All this does not in the least detract from the principal fact that the offering is a symbolic gift.

The second objection against qualifying an offering as a gift is that an offering is usually combined with a prayer for all sorts of blessings. It is bad form for the donor of a gift to request anything in return, let alone to specify his desires. Nevertheless, a prayer is never omitted, and even if there is no real need, it is not confined to a mere act of praise. A good case is that of a mortuary feast among the Ngad'a of Flores. If the deceased was an important chief, scores of buffaloes will be slaughtered. Notwithstanding this demonstration of wealth and prosperity, the feastgiver still calls upon both gods and ancestors to pray them to grant him prosperity and many more things which he and the assembled merry-makers do not visibly worry about on this occasion of abundance. The moment of such a prayer seems to be ill-chosen. Is it an ideosyncrasy of simple peasants who, in view of such abundance, suddenly fear that this prosperity cannot last? But the custom to pray for something when there is no reason to request anything at all, is not confined to sacrificial feasts.

A good instance is that of saying grace before meals as, until recently, customary among Protestant Christians. In essence, it is a thanksgiving, not an occasion for asking favours. Nevertheless, the believers strongly feel that, irrespective of need or abundance, something ought to be asked anyhow, and consequently they meekly ask for a blessing. No one can say what this blessing stands for, except that it must be something good generally. But why ask it at this particular moment, with the steaming good right under their noses? Structurally, the similarity between saying grace and an offering is obvious: the meal, the assembled participants, a leader of the ceremony who, in his prayer, includes a laudation and a request, are combined in both. The one difference is that at an offering a small bit of food is set apart for the deity, but this is hardly essential. At offerings it sometimes happens that the food is arranged in such a way as to enable the deity to enjoy its essence (its *sari* as the Balinese call it) before, a few minutes after the prayer, the participants are allowed to take it away. However this may be, the offering or whatever is done instead takes place after the prayer has been said. There must be something in the situation of partaking at a meal in the presumed presence of a god which invites the participants to add a request to the thanksgivings which are self-evident in this situation. And of course there is. Vis-à-vis the deity, the utmost humility is called for; not merely in words, but also in deeds. "Requesting is both the most simple and the most decisive act of self-humiliation, the recognition at once of the requestrant's dependence and of the addressee's power. Confronting his god, asking is the most effective confession of a man's belief and worship. What cannot be done when offering a gift to a fellow-man, asking for something, must be done when offering a gift to a god" (Van Baal 1976: 170).

We can turn now to the small offerings. They are brought with great frequency in many parts of the world. Whenever a family enjoys a substantial meal, in particular with meat as an important ingredient, some of it will be deposited upon the house shrine or shrines where the ancestors or gods are supposed to find it. To a certain extent, these offerings are a matter of routine; they are brought without much ado, often without even any prayers being said. An outsider does not easily notice them. These acts are so inconspicuous that ethnographers rarely paid due attention to them, or made enquiries about details. On the whole we are poorly informed about these offerings which, because of their frequency, deserve far more of that specific attention as F. Barth paid to those of the Baktaman. It is more or less accidentally that one becomes aware of them. Once enquiries are made, it soon becomes apparent that these small offerings are found almost everywhere outside the Australian continent. They can be extremely simple, such as the spilling of a few drops of newly-brewn beer as is customary among African tribes. But not among them alone; the Greeks did the same with wine as the readers of Plato's *Phaedo* will remember. All these little acts bear testimony to the people's belief that the gods and ancestors are nearby. Sometimes they are even inmates of the house. In the traditional houses of Sumba and Flores (Indonesia), they are believed to reside in special places in the house, and there the small offerings are placed which are their share in the household's festive dish. The offering is a matter of simple courtesy. These ancestors and spirits are housemates who cannot be ignored if one wishes to live in good harmony with them. The small offerings confirm that the household lives in peace with the gods and ancestors, i.e. with the powers who are at the back of the visible world. This relation must be maintained by simple but recurrent acts of recognition and attention. They have the same function as saying grace before meals: the daily recurring affirmation of man's dependence on God and of awareness of his nearness. As gifts, these small offerings remind us of the give-and-take customary among the members of a small and closely knit group. They are always aware of each other's presence and confirm this with adequate proofs of sympathy and considerateness.

228

Other sacrifices follow the pattern of the official gift; they are formal and – to a greater or lesser extent – spectacular. The occasion can be a feast or a particular need. If it is a feast – for example a mortuary feast or the inauguration of a new house or subclan – it is an occasion for conspicuous giving. Among cattle breeding people this implies that scores of cattle must be slaughtered and their meat distributed among the guests who come flocking in from everywhere. Before the beasts are killed, the feastgiver explains the reasons for the feast and implores the gods and ancestors to come down to accept the cattle or buffaloes presented to them, and to bless the participants with health, prosperity, and everything else they may need. After the killing, the distribution of meat follows. As usual, the share allotted to the gods falls far behind that presented to the human guests. In East Flores, this unequal distribution is rationalized by the saying that what is little to mankind is much to the gods, and vice versa (Arndt 1951: 2, 18, 106). This is not hypocrisy, as little as it is hypocrisy of the neighbouring Ngad'a when, on such an occasion, they implore the invited gods and ancestors to come down to take place on the assembled people's shoulders and necks, and to surround them like a stone wall which protects the village against disasters and sickness. This is not mere oratory; it is what they actually mean. The Ngad'a always try to surround themselves with ancestors and forebears. The dead are buried in the village, they reside in the stone walls of its terrasses, in the niches of the traditional houses, and in the various ceremonial places within the village, always near at hand and always co-residents. More than anything this nearness expresses the ultimate meaning these ancestors have to the Ngad'a: they represent their universe and all that is uncanny in it. Nothing is so nearby and yet so other, so different, as a man's universe. The great feast is a chosen occasion for emphasizing this nearness and for stressing the importance of close communication between man and his gods.

Less elaborate are the sacrifices presented for a specific need. The reason can be routine such as the sacrifices made during the planting season, but it can also be an ominous dream, a protracted sickness, an impending war-raid, or whatever disquiets anyone's peace of mind. Often the sacrifice is preceded by divination to find out what the specific causes of the difficulties are and what the right measures are that should be taken. Whatever they may be, it is evident that there is something wrong in the sacrificer's relations with his fellow-men, but also something wrong in those with his ancestors or gods. The ethnographic literature on African tribes abounds with cases of sacrifices presented on behalf of a patient who has fallen ill because, in anger, a father or uncle invoked the vengeance of the ancestors upon him, or because the patient himself neglected his sacrificial duties to the ancestors, or because of some other sin discovered by divination. A sacrifice must ward off the calamity. The ceremony unites the patient and his close relatives with all those who, in one way or another, are associated with the cause of his indisposition. Beer is served, the reason for the meeting is explained and the victim, usually a goat, is dedicated to the ancestors or gods concerned, after which a communal meal reconciles all those involved. The share allotted to the supernaturals is, as usual, minimal; but, at the end of the celebration, the family and its factions are reunited among themselves and with the ancestors. Communication has been repaired and ill-feelings have been taken away. If it is a sin against gods or fellow-men which had to be made good, there is an element of atonement in the procedure, but not an atonement of the kind which constitutes part of a punishment. It is a kind of apology which smoothes over the difficulties caused by incautious behaviour. Of course, sacrifices offered on behalf of a patient are not all of this kind. They even may constitute an overwhelming display of kindness and sympathy as in the case of the Mentaweian sacrificial feast mentioned on p. 213 which was celebrated to satisfy the patient's soul. But however, or whatever, these sacrifices look like, they all focus on the offering of gifts to men and spirits or gods alike.

A special kind of sacrifice is that in payment of vows. "Vows are made in prayers sent up by a barren woman desiring a child, by a family for the recovery of a sick father or son, by a dismissed official for a new job, etc. If the prayer is heard, a sacrifice shall be presented at a certain sanctuary on the day appointed for such celebrations. The procedure followed is the same as the one described in the previous paragraphs. The beast is presented to the deity to whom thanks are brought for his benevolence. Then the victim is slaughtered, the meat divided among the guests, and a small portion set aside for the deity, at least, if the latter is local custom. The celebration is a feast, and gratitude and merriness prevail. Yet, it is also a payment. Vows must be paid and woe befalls him who fails to do so. But it is a payment of a peculiar nature. Although the vow resembles a condition in a contract, it differs from a contractual condition in that it does not oblige the other party to deliver any particular good, but only the maker of the vow. Although in making the vow a desired good is always specified, the deity remains perfectly free to hear or not to hear the suppliant. The latter binds only himself. The stage set by the vow is that the fulfilment of the prayer shall be seen as a gift, a completely free gift from the deity. If that gift be made, then, of course, the beneficiary owes the payment which now takes the form of a return-gift as stipulated in the vow. That the whole procedure is defined by the pattern of the gift is confirmed by the fact that feelings of gratitude define the spiritual atmosphere of the celebration, feelings which strengthen the sacrificer's allegiance to his deity" (Van Baal 1976b: 171 f.; slightly revised).

A sacrifice presented for the expiation of mortal sin is of a completely different nature. Mortal sin cannot be acquitted by apologies: it must be atoned, i.e. it must be combined with an accepted punishment (cf. above: 105 f.). The relevant procedure has been described and discussed by Hubert and Mauss. "The scene is well-known: the sinner puts his hand on the victim's back to express his intrinsic relation with the beast, and then, after the dedication which implies the sacrificer's confession of his sin, follows the complete destruction of the animal by fire. The victim is God's, i.e. it is sacred. It is the bearer of the sacrificer's impurity and sin which are taken away by its destruction. That the victim is the vehicle of the sinner's impurity is highlighted by the sacrifice brought on the Day of Atonement: one goat is burned, the other brought to the desert and set free. It is the goat for Azazel (Lev. 16:10), carrying the people's impurity with it, just like the bird set free for the recovered leper (Lev. 14: 5 ff.) takes the latter's impurity with it. In both cases the priest explicitly transfers the impurity to the beast by symbolic acts" (Van Baal 1976b: 172 f.).

A sacrificial victim of this kind is utterly unfit for consumption; it is impure. The celebration may be attended by many people, but it is not a feast. The most important ingredient for a feast, i.e. food, is ostensibly lacking. It is really a punishment. The sacrificer has to pay a large fine, viz. a valuable head of cattle, and he must publicly confess his guilt. If he fails to do it in words, the sacrifice itself does it for him; the assembled community is well aware of what it all means. "In East Indonesia, where holocausts are rare, the Southern Toradja will present one if a man has committed incest with his sister or a full cousin. It is a mortal sin that makes the land so hot that prolonged drought must be feared. A buffalo is dedicated to the supreme being by the priest who addresses the god with his face turned westward (the ordinary posture is eastward). The beast is then killed and cut into pieces that are subsequently burned. In one part of the area the offender himself must tether the beast and address the god while holding the rope with his hand. The act of atonement and the punishment are clear. Yet, in this case there is more to it than this alone. Just as the sin has cosmic consequences, making the land hot, so has the holocaust. The smoke-clouds that go up from the burning sacrifice will in time turn into rain-clouds that cool the earth" (ibid.: 173; oral information by Dr. Hetty Nooy-Palm).

Not all expiatory sacrifices are necessarily holocausts. In part, this may be a matter of differential evaluation of the gravity of a crime. Among the Nuer of the East African Sudan a serious case of incest must be expiated by offering an ox, but there is no holocaust. The ox, "dedicated by a priest, is killed and divided from nose to tail into two halves, one for the priests, the other for the sacrificer and his family who will consume the meat of their half. But the blood is for God and they closely observe that it runs away into the soil because it carries the delinquent's sin with it and makes for complete atonement and purification. Up to an extent, the sacrificer is identical with the victim; before it is killed he rubs its back with ashes, expressing their togetherness (Evans-Pritchard 1956: 189, 216, 298). The identification of a man and his ox is a recurrent theme in Nuer culture. In a sacrifice as here discussed it takes mystic dimensions in the identification of the sacrificer's sin with the victim's blood, and in the bisection of the carcass" (Van Baal 1976b: 174). One might call this 'magic' but then one misses the point; to wit, that it is a punishment combined with atonement, and that the symbols applied simply express what is hoped and prayed for.

Finally, there are the sacrifices which must be qualified as substantial gifts offered to a deity in the hope that he shall go out of his way and grant the sacrificer his wish. Such sacrifices are holocausts or comparable forms of annihilation meant to ensure that no one except the deity invoked can profit by the victim presented. Such sacrifices do occur, though by no means with such frequency as Tylor supposed. They are made in despair by people who are at a loss what to do to ward off an impending disaster. A good instance is that of the holocaust arranged by the Nuer when pest or murrain threaten them with eradication of their cattle. "They 'go out to meet it' (viz. the murrain). They slaughter a number of oxen in the bush where the carcasses are left behind 'as a wall'. The sacrifice is made to God, but the dead beasts are left to the evil spirits of illness. They may not be touched by anyone and the idea seems to be "that the evil has entered them through the sacrificial act" " (Evans-Pritchard 1956: 220; from Van Baal 1976b: 174).

There is a better explanation than the one given by Evans-Pritchard at the end of the preceding paragraph. The point is that the carcasses are not surrendered to God – to whom the animals were dedicated just before their death – but left to the demons which cause the disease. They must satisfy their lust for meat. The act aims at buying off the demons with a handsome ransom, and it is presented after having implored the blessing of God. The act as such is an act of despair; the Nuer are a cattle-loving people and cattle are very dear to them. But even in their despair they do not go so far as to try to 'bribe' God. They bribe the demons after an act of communication with God.

Among the divergent forms of ritual, sacrifice is one of the richest both in variegation and power of persuasion. The kind of sacrifice of most frequent occurrence is that which follows the pattern of the gift. It has the curious power of being socially meritorious; the immediate beneficiaries of the ritual are not the gods but the sacrificer's fellow-men. Consequently, it is not an act of merely symbolic communication which unites the participants with the gods in a commensal act, but also an act which efficiently re-unites the participants amongst themselves and thus has a cathartic effect on the social universe of the participants. The salutary effect of the rite is direct and persuasive.

Besides, a sacrifice has great dramatic power, in particular when several head of cattle are slaughtered. Then the sacrifice is a grand display of wealth put at the disposal of all those present. The euphoria of this celebration of tangible communality turns the participants' attention to the mediators of this effusion of well-being, the victims. Their cruel fate does not imply a lack of sympathy on the side of the participants. The latter are well-aware that they owe the victims a great deal. Among the Nuer, a man's cattle is his pride and his glory; we noted that the identification of a man and his ox is a recurrent theme in Nuer culture (above: 231). The Ngad'a go even further. Mankind are the cattle of Déva. There is one text which says that when the people on earth slaughter a buffalo, a déva dies in heaven; and when the déva above kill a buffalo a man dies on earth (Van Baal 1947: 184).

The Ngad'a have not elaborated the theme. The statement just quoted is more a matter of pious speculation than one of theology, as similar considerations generated in the religions of some more advanced cultures. The Cretans identified Dionysos with his bull. The Egyptians associated Osiris with the boar, and in Christian theology Christ is presented as the *agnus Dei*. The significance of the divine victim has been emphasized already by Hubert and Mauss (1899). It highlights a quite remarkable feature which, apart from all speculations on historical origin and development, is of specific interest. It demonstrates that the contrast between rituals of identification and rituals of a person-to-person type of communication (above: 224) is not absolute. In sacrifice the one invites the other, even to the extent that self-sacrifice in imitation of Christ has developed into an ethical ideal. Apparently, the distance inherent in the person-to-person type of communication does not fully satisfy the needs of the soul who is determined to become fully a part. The longing for mystic union is a recurrent phenomenon in all religion. Counteracted by the subject's constrasting need to be a self, mystic union remains an almost unattainable ideal, a state which can only temporarily be experienced. The subject resists complete self-surrender, a resistance sometimes rationalized in accusations of heresy directed against mystics who unduly obliterate the distance that separates man from God. The mystic's effort and the criticism it arouses have a common ground in the dialectics of man's experience of his universe which is simultaneously both nearby and far-off. We must return to the theme in the next chapter.

XIII

Distance and Nearness in Man's Contacts with the Supernatural. The Role of the Intellect and the Universality of Religion

1. Distance and nearness in trance, shamanism, and prophetism

The nearness of the gods is never so immediately and vehemently experienced as in trance, the deity taking possession not only of the medium's body but also of his spirit, so that he loses consciousness and has to be brought to. A well described case is that of Voodoo in Haiti (Métraux 1959). During the dance, the participants, all lower class people, go into a trance. Each of them has his specific deity who embodies himself so thoroughly in the dancer that, for the time being, the two can be identified. If, in his trance, the vehicle speaks, or if he returns to consciousness with a message, it is always the deity who has spoken. The experience does not last for long; when the dancer has come to he is soon his old self again. But there is this difference: he is a richer self. He has had the experience that, for a few moments, he was lifted out of the drabness of daily toil and worry to participate in a better, more powerful and, for that, more real world. He returns to his dreary routine existence with the comforting certainty that, somehow, he has a share in that better and more powerful world.

Instead of leading to a state of possession, trance can also induce visions and hallucinations. Mooney (1896) gives a lively account of the visions of the participants in the Ghost Dance who found their exertions rewarded with meeting the recent dead. Drugs, too, may be used to produce visions. A wellknown case is that of the peyote cult in the United States which, during week-end services, unites the members of the congregation in a common experience of being in contact with the divine. Going home, they take the memory with them as a comforting and reassuring thought.

A simpler form of trance is that which I observed when attending the annual ceremony at the sanctuary of Gangsa (North Lombok, Indonesia). On this festive occasion, goats were sacrificed in payment of vows. The sacrificial act being completed, dancing started. One by one the participating women went into a trance, swooned, and had to be brought round. They had no message to communicate. To the question of whether the deity of the sanctuary had entered into them or it was Allah who had taken possession of them, I received no distinct answer. The deity simply had demonstrated his satisfaction, and whether it was the deity of the sanctuary or Allah, worried no one. The trance phenomena are the sign that all is well, that God is nearby, and this suffices. A close parallel of this appreciation of trance experiences can be noted on the adjacent island of Bali. The deity who lets the young girls go into trance when they perform their beautiful temple-dances is rarely specified. It is enough that the gods have proved their presence and demonstrated their satisfaction. Those who benefit from it are not merely the performers, but the congregation as a whole. Everyone present feels comforted and strengthened by this token of divine benevolence. When we try to find out what the specific nature of this benevolence is, the only satisfactory answer is that it consists of divine nearness and the confirmation of the willingness of the gods to communicate with mankind. It is the blessing which goes with all the different forms of trance here mentioned.

Trance is specific of the shaman, the religious specialist who deliberately goes into a trance for a specific purpose, usually the healing of a sick client. Elaborate information on the shaman and his practices has been collected by Eliade in his book on shamanism (1964). It is not necessary to give a summary here of these rich materials, nor to demonstrate that shamanism is not restricted to the Siberian and East Asian field. I can confine myself to the fact, pointed out by, among others, Schröder (1955), that, in the main, the shaman follows one of two ways: that of possession which makes him the vehicle of the gods who speak through his mouth, or that of ascending to the gods in the upperworld in order to request their verdict or advice. In the first case, his trance is deeper than in the second which, accompanied by the recitation or singing of lengthy litanies, requires specific knowledge.

The training of the shaman is often a complicated one, including the learning by heart of the relevant litanies, on the one hand, and a special and often painful initiation, on the other (cf. above: 190). Like the initiated medicine-man, the shaman becomes a changed person who, through his sufferings and his knowledge, is nearer to the gods than ordinary people. Yet, in spite of this nearness there is no question of identification with the deity. The shaman is simply a vehicle or a messenger who, as a go-between, is certainly a blessed person whose supernatural relations endow him with great power, but all the same no more than the mouth-piece of the gods. It is on this point that he resembles the prophet.

The message delivered by the prophet is not a message elicited from the gods on behalf of a client, but one which the gods, themselves taking the initiative, dictated to one or other medium who must communicate the message to the people. The prophet need not have expected any experience of this kind, though it stands to reason that a shaman, seer, or medicine-man is more often chosen as a vehicle for communicating such messages than an ordinary person. Their psychological disposition makes them more receptive to visions, hallucinations and impressive dreams than anyone belonging to the rank and file of the community. Besides, they are authorities in the field of religious experiences, and messages communicated by them will be listened to with more confidence than those transmitted by a layman who has no special prestige.

235

Many more recent prophets are the bringers of new cults. We find them in America, Africa, and Melanesia. It was a prophet who, in America, introduced the Ghost Dance religion. Although his exploits and expectations caused a great commotion, they were modest when compared to those of the South American prophets who promised their followers the Country without Evil, the Land of Eternal Youth, and, dancing at the head of hundreds, sometimes thousands of followers, led the way from East to West through the continent until they perished either from exhaustion or at the hands of enemy tribes (Métraux 1967: ch. I).

In Africa the main themes of these cults are either that of restoring or establishing a social identity (Kimbangism, for instance), or that of eradicating witchcraft, the latter invariably ending in failure because these cults confirm the veracity of witchcraft instead of denying it (Van Baal 1969b: 77). Equally unsuccessful are the Melanesian cargo-cults aiming at the acquisition of wealth and modern progress (ibid.: 70 ff.; Van Baal 1960). We need not follow these cults in any detail. The main point is that they were introduced by a prophet who, through a dream or a vision, was instructed by either a deity, the ancestors, or the spirits of the dead, to initiate certain ritual activities, instructions which were confirmed in subsequent revelations to him or his followers. The prophet may or may not become the leader of the cult (sometimes this role falls to a more adroit organizer) but the message invariably comes from above. The prophet is, primarily, a go-between who is in the hand of the gods. Though he may have solicited his revelation by meditation in the wilderness, he is an elect of the gods, blessed with the task to lead his people to a new and better future.

Not everywhere is it a privilege to be elected by the gods to become a prophet, just as it is not always a privilege to become a shaman. There are shamans who feel compelled to obey the calling in order to get rid of the sufferings of their illness. With the prophet, however, the situation is more complicated. He may find himself chosen to deliver messages which go straight against the grain of his own wishes and hopes. Hebrew prophetism presents us with several instances. Jeremiah, the prophet of disaster, is the classical example of the prophet against his will. He cursed the day on which he was born and the man who announced his birth to his father: "Cursed be the day wherein I was born: let not the day wherein my mother bore me be blessed. Cursed be the man who brought tidings to my father, saying, A man child is born unto thee; making him very glad" (Jer. 20: 14 f.). Bitter were his complaints: "O Lord, thou hast deceived me, and I was deceived: thou art stronger than I, and hast prevailed: I am in derision daily, everyone mocketh me. For since I spake, I cried out, I cried violence and spoil; because the word of the Lord was made a reproach unto me, and a derision daily. Then I said, I will not make mention of him, nor speak any more in his name. But his word was in mine heart as a burning fire shut up in my bones, and I was weary with forbearing, and I could not stay" (id. 20: 7-9). And yet, shortly afterwards follow the words (vs. 13): "Sing unto the Lord, praise ye the Lord: for he hath delivered the soul of the poor from the hand of the evildoers". The dialectics of God's exactingness and goodness could not be more eloquently expressed.

Still, Jeremiah is not the Scripture's strongest case of an unwilling prophet. An even more persuasive one is that of the despised Balaam. It is not given much attention today; apparently theologians and historians of religion feel a bit embarrassed in the company of the prophet's talking donkey. Balaam is a seer, probably also a shaman; twice we are told that he fell into a trance (Num. 24:4 and 16). In the story of Numbers 22-24, however, he is above all a prophet. One cannot read it without being impressed by the overwhelming power of God who uses an unwilling seer to deliver his message and nothing but that message. Besides, there is nothing scandalous in Balaam's ass. She is the personification of her master's conscience, reminding him of what he already knows too well, namely that he is on the wrong path, setting out to abuse his uncanny powers to curse the people whom God has blessed (22: 12). Persuaded by the incident to return, Balaam is not allowed to retrace his steps. He must now carry on, and from this moment onwards the seer is a miserable and at the same time a grand instrument in the hand of God. Three times he blesses the Hebrews instead of cursing them, and finally he concludes his blessings with the prophecy of Israel's undoubted victory and glory.

The story is one of great tragedy. Three times king Balak who hired the seer, arranges a holocaust of no less than seven bullocks and seven rams, an expression of despair comparable only to that of the Nuer when rinderpest is rampant (above: 231 f.). Three times Balaam ignores the king's increasing anger; worse even, his last answer to the king is a crushing prophecy of Israel's triumph. After this, Balaam returns in disgrace.

The story describes an ideal type of prophecy. It is God who speaks, a God who does not need a willing instrument to deliver his message. It is delivered anyway by a demurring seer of great repute who is as wax in the hand of God. On the face of it, it is a primitive story. Whether it really is, must remain a matter of speculation. One thing is certain: the authors of Numbers have used it with great cunning to transmit a theological message in a really penetrating manner, the message that it is God who speaks, who takes the initiative to reveal his will to mankind, who confirms his active interest in the weal and woe of his chosen people, and proves his power by compelling his people's enemy to praise their glory and to preach their victory. The omnipotence and free will of God stand foremost. In the theology of the Old Testament, God, the Creator of the universe, is so exalted that no form of identification is imaginable. Consequently, his relation with the Hebrews does not reflect any kind of family relationship. It is one of covenant. In a covenant there are two parties; the relationship between them is not a natural one but depends upon a decision, in this case a decision taken by Jahwe. It obliges the Hebrews to obedience, Jahwe to loyalty to his promise.

Here, it is evident that there is no question of a *deus absconditus*, a God who resides in absolute unapproachability as Otto suggests (Otto 1917). In the Old Testament, God may, at times, be wrathful, but he is not distant. Besides, there is a likeness between God and man. God created man in his own image, after his likeness (Gen. 1: 26 f.). God's countenance is sought because there is a blessing in his nearness. In some 15 places in the Old Testament God is called a father, e.g. in the psalm of Moses in

Deuteronomy 32 where the relation between God and the Hebrews is elucidated as follows:

> "for the LORD's portion is his people; Jacob is the lot of his inheritance. He found them in a desert land, and in the waste howling wilderness; he led him about, he instructed him, he kept him as the apple of his eye. As an eagle stirreth up her nest, fluttereth over her young, spreadeth abroad her wings, taketh them, beareth them on her wings: So the LORD alone did lead him, and there was no strange god with him (Deut. 32: 9-12)".

A recurrent metaphor is that of finding trust under the cover of the wings of the Almighty (Ps. 17: 8; 61: 4, etc.). The ideal repeatedly voiced is that God shall dwell in the midst of his people. The prophet Zechariah expresses it as follows (2: 11):

> "And many nations shall be joined to the LORD in that day, and shall be my people; and I will dwell in the midst of thee, and thou shalt know that the Lord of hosts hath sent me unto thee".

In spite of God's transcendence and majesty, his presence is a never-ending, always recurring need. It is also a need for communication. The expression "find cover under the wings of the Almighty", does not leave any doubt on this point. Man's universe may be overwhelmingly great but it is nearby. That is what the pious, to whom God is a God of unimaginable majesty, hope and believe of their God. The demarcation line between God and man is not transgressed, but the faithful linger in its immediate vicinity. God dwells in their midst.

In the New Testament, with its strong emphasis on God's fathership and goodness, the demarcation line, separating God and man, loses some of its absolute rigidity. A good case is that of one of the words of Jesus recorded in the gospel according to St. John: "At that day ye shall know that I am in my Father, and ye in me, and I in you" (14: 20), a statement repeated in slightly revised form in 17: 21. It does not eradicate the line; it is God who crosses it by entering into the hearts of men. The same motif returns in St. Paul's epistle to the Ephesians where the Church is called the body of Christ, "the fullness of him that filleth all in all" (1: 22). And again in 4: 6: "One God and Father of all, who is above all, and through all, and in you all". The God and Father of the New Testament is more intimate to man than the Old Testament God of the covenant. This intimacy is sought in prayer.

2. Distance and nearness in prayer

Prayer is a humble or respectful address to a supernatural being. Many scholars prefer to speak of request instead of address, basing this opinion on the fact that request is the more fundamental meaning of the word pray. However, they find small support in linguistic usage. It classes eulogies to the deity with prayers, and not undeservedly so because eulogy is a part of almost every prayer. Moreover, discussing the surprising fact that offering is usually combined with praying, we had occasion to note that a request is essentially a eulogy, a recognition of the power of the deity and a confession of the agent's humbleness and dependence (above: 228). Apparently, eulogy and request should not be separated. Even the Islamologists' argument cannot persuade us to the contrary. They will point out that the Arabic language strictly distinguishes between *du'a'*, the prayer requesting something, and the *salāt*, the ritual praise-giving to Allah (Juynboll 1925: 53). Yet, in a *du'a'* the praise of Allah will not easily be omitted, whereas during every *salāt* at least one *du'a'* is said, the one contained in the opening *surah* of the Koran which must be recited at every salāt, immediately after the *takbir*, the initial eulogy (Allah is great!). It is evident that giving praise to God is an essential element in prayer. It combines the confession of distance with the belief in accessibility.

This is not to deny that prayers do occur which are either requests or eulogies exclusively. They certainly do, but it is not without interest that prayers which are requests pure and simple are not valued highly. These are the prayers said in sudden distress when need leaves no time for proper form; often they are little more than a cry. In Christendom they are classed as 'arrow'-prayers' (cf. the colloquial Dutch expression *schietgebedje*, a little prayer that is 'fired off'). Little prayers of this kind are found in many religions; we even met with a case in the description of Marind-anim magic (above: 186). They always stand more or less outside the ordinary religious practice.

In many religions, prayers always constitute part of a rite of offering or sacrifice, the part from which the bystanders can learn who the deity is to whom the offering is dedicated, and usually also the sacrificer's reasons for the celebration. As such, the prayer is the crucial part of the act of communication which every sacrifice is. As a separate religious practice all on its own, prayer plays an important part in the religions derived from Judaism, namely Christendom and Islam. A characteristic feature of this practice is that, though prayers often are obligatory at certain times and places, they can in principle be said anywhere and at any time. The practice takes the belief in God's omnipresence seriously. It suits a theology in which God, without being the universe, takes its place. Like the universe, God is always within hearing distance and, what is more, always ready to listen.

It is a comforting thought, but even this light casts its shadow. God is also omniscient and knows everything, including the hidden secret of the soul. Not even an evil thought escapes his notice. Apart from the feelings of guilt which it inspires, one would say that, under such circumstances, there is little food for conversation. Logically, the case of prayer is a weak one. God, who is so nearby, is also far off and must be called upon to listen. The dialectics of God's presence and distance are nowhere more appalling than in prayer. Praying silently, that is in the supposition that God knows the inner promptings of the soul, the soul cries out to God to hear and to listen to all the things and thoughts which it pours out to him for no rational reason at all, because God knows it already. Besides, the soul which has a request to make, is never certain that its desire will be fulfilled. In spite of the assurances that God hears every prayer and will and can meet every need, there are so many reasons to explain the fact that the fulfilment of the desire properly expressed in prayer does not follow (cf. above: 186 f.), that one wonders how people can set store on prayer as a means for acquiring something. In the modern world, this doubt has increased considerably; we know that every event has its cause and among the many causes discovered by modern science there never was a cause called God. To prove the

239

contrary, believers often point to the not really infrequent cases of healing by prayer. There is not the slightest reason to deny them; they are the effect of prayer. But none of these cases can persuade the scientist who believes in psycho-physiology rather than in God. And yet, up to the present day, there are modern people who pray. Even scientists. Why?

From early times, the practice of prayer has been defended against the criticism of the intellect by giving special emphasis to the need for praying daily for spiritual guidance and strength. It is not a special preference of modern Christendom which, wary of the dangers of scepticism inspired by scientific knowledge, entrenches itself in a position where the beneficent psychological effect of praying cannot be affected by disappointing results in the field of material success because material successes have been rejected in advance as unworthy motives for religious activity. Islam did the same long before science turned itself against religious belief. Five times a day, at each of the five obligatory *salāts,* every Muslim invokes Allah's help to set him on the path of the righteous, when reciting the opening *surah* of the Koran. The performance of the *salāt* and the attendant recitation are obligatory, but the *du'a',* the prayer for the fulfilment of a material or spiritual desire, is not. The prayer for God's help to become a good man, whether Christian or Muslim, has always and everywhere been recommended by the pious as the kind of prayer incumbent on everyone.

As a spiritual exercise, it is a sound one psychologically. Reflecting upon the right way to act and formulating the need to submit to the moral law, the agent strengthens his will to act accordingly. Besides, by communicating his sorrows and intents to a sympathetic Thou, the soul feels itself in communication and harmony with its world, experiences itself as part of its world, a partnership which is expressed as an experience of the presence of God. The psychological effect of praying is invariably described in terms of inner peace and feeling strengthened. Giving shape to its troubles and disquietude, the soul finds the strength to live with them. Having communicated it all to God, the soul is no longer alone. There is one who hears and beholds.

The implications of praying have been clarified in a penetrating manner by Heiler in his book *Das Gebet* (1923; transl.: Prayer). Prayer is always a discourse with a Thou. The bodily attitudes adopted during prayer have their origins in the gestures of greeting customary in social interaction, in particular those of greeting a superior (op. cit. 98-101). But to Heiler praying is not confined to the request for spiritual aid. Real praying – prophetic praying, Heiler calls it – does not shun to bring up all the troubles and cares that disquiet the agent's mind; he wrestles with God for enlightenment on the course he must follow. The 'pray-er' combines his confession of sin and the request for remission of his guilt with one for intercession in the world's needs and his neighbour's troubles. It is an outpouring of the soul, together with a request for divine guidance in his private and public troubles and tasks. Giving shape to all his anxieties and distress, thanking for every comfort and fortune, the pray-er speaks frankly of whatever occupies his mind and of all the secrets of his heart. No one can overhear him, and he can speak with absolute freedom, a freedom surpassing by far that of the conversations between a patient and his psychiatrist. No one can doubt

240

the cathartic value of this kind of prayer which makes a clean sweep of the agent's sorrows and shortcomings. There is only one proviso: the inner certainty that God does something about it, that he does not merely affect the pray-er's heart, but at the very least also affects the hearts of others.

This belief is threatened today. Many pray-ers shrink from imploring divine intervention, not because they do not need it, but because they doubt its possibility. They find a way out in the blessed phrase 'Thy will be done', a phrase which is no longer as pious as it used to be a few generations ago. Resigning, they accept their fate, accept the world as it is, and content themselves with the prayer to be reconciled to it all. The reconciliation is not without comfort; they too have poured out their hearts, have communicated all their complaints, and have felt a certain peace in their hearts, the peace they prayed for. But after they have said their prayers, they will not return to their world with the message: this or that is the will of God and that is what we ought to do, as the prophetic pray-er sometimes does. Modern pray-ers seek quietude and that silent contact with their God which persuades them that he is nearby. Finding cover under the wings of the Almighty, they acquiesce. Heiler denounces them as mystics which, up to an extent, they are. But is it a reason to condemn them? One might as well envy them that, in a world of uncertainty, they have succeeded in finding a way to experience their partnership in their world without becoming insincere vis-à-vis their scientific judgements. Their God may be a vague one, an impersonation of the unknowable, but all the same he is as far-off and as nearby as any god, and as such a source of comfort.

Besides – and notwithstanding Heiler – the position thus taken is by no means foreign to the traditions of Christian orthodoxy. Christendom has a deep undercurrent of mistrust in the world and in the benefit of worldly blessings. Praying for anything material that surpasses the daily bread today, has repeatedly been rejected as greed, as craving for wealth. By accepting poverty as the state befitting the pious, the faithful finds himself free of worldly fetters, free also of his own desires and lusts. Being nothing more than a child of God and just that, he has time and occasion to find the truth confirmed of the promise: "At that day ye shall know that I am in my Father, and ye in me, and I in you" (St. John 14: 20). Praising God's greatness and majesty, the pious rejoices in his nearness.

3. Distance and nearness in mysticism

Mysticism is a feature naturally common to all religion. Religion being man's means of realizing his awareness of his partnership in his refractory universe, it is obvious that religion must confirm this partnership by arousing feelings of being united with and accepted in that universe. The depth and fullness of these feelings is the one and only proof of the truth of the religious experience, and the real reward of the believer's exertions. But how far can this pursuit of mystic communion be allowed to proceed? When all is said and done, man is also a subject, naturally given to the opposite pursuit of self-realization and ever renewed distancing to the universe with which he wishes to be a partner.

One thing is certain, the mystic experience is always a temporary one. No one can remain perpetually in a state of elation. No one does. What is more, no one really needs to. The mystic experience has a long-lasting effect on memory, and easily finds itself substantiated in concepts and notions which are available at any moment to confirm the mystic that his partnership in his universe is really true. The Australian aborigine, identifying myth and totem with his dreaming, and his body and spirit with those of a mythical ancestor, 'knows' himself to be a part of his universe. Periodically, the basic experience must be renewed by elaborate ritual activity, following which he can carry on again for months on end in his struggle for life. The concepts and notions interpreting the mystic experience are strong enough to induce him when, at last, he feels that the days of his life are counted, to his pathetic return to his 'country', to die in the 'country' of his personal, mythical ancestor. He belongs to his country as much as that country belongs to him.

Other primitive religions are less emphatic on this point. Still, they maintain alive the mystic reality behind the phenomenal world by recounting myths and folktales, and by innumerable acts of routine magic and small offerings unobtrusively placed on the household shrines. The performers know themselves surrounded by spirits, and the mysterious sounds heard during the silent hours of the night rarely fail to confirm their presence. They are conceptualized as ghosts and spirits, goblins and fairies, and suchlike, each kind having its own specific qualities. We came across an outstanding case in the concept of *badjou* among the Mentaweians, the influence emanating from the spiritual essence of every animal, plant or thing. For a time, everyone can carry on with small, unobtrusive acts signifying the recognition of the presence of all these beings. When, at last, the wear and tear of routine activities has weakened the memory of more impressive religious experiences, an adverse event suffices to induce new ritual celebrations which, by their magnitude, restore the mystic union between man and the symbols of his universe.

Yet, this is not all. All these peoples have their mystics, the seers, shamans, and medicine-men who, at uncertain times, retire to the wilderness to listen to the voices of silence till a dream or vision enlightens their mind or deepens their consciousness of a frightening mystery lurking behind the universe and directing its course. These primitive seers are not regular anchorites who live on the alms of the faithful. In time they have to go back to their daily chores and the care of their families. All the same, it is these seers who keep up, renew and extend the body of myth and ritual. The universality of their occurrence (we find them also in the great religions of civilization) does not merely indicate that everywhere persons are found who are more gifted in religious expression than others, but also that everywhere these talents are allotted a role in cultural life.

The cult forms of Christendom and Islam are fairly meticulously regulated. The need for a periodic renewal of the basic religious experience has been systematized by the introduction of a fixed timetable of periodical celebrations, minor ones weekly, on Sunday and Friday respectively, bigger ones on various special days of every year. A host of professionals give guidance on the various services, study the holy books and make them accessible by comment and exegesis, or occupy themselves with the spiritual care of the flock or with works of charity. As if this were not enough, these religions also have their mystics. In the early years of Christendom, they followed the old pattern of retirement to the wilderness; later, they congregated in monasteries to spend all the days of their lives in teaching, studying, and contemplation. In the Islamic world we find a slightly parallel institution in the *madrasah*, and next to this in a widely ramified organization of mystic fraternities.

The organizatory forms are not important in this context, but the mystics are. They were no dreamers who waited in idleness for illumination or divine consolation. Many of them were learned men, given to diligent studies. Part of their spiritual exercise consisted of speculation on theological problems, studies which led them to contemplation on the dialectics of the mysterious qualities of the divine essence. The Middle Ages were a flowering period of this monastic mysticism. To the modern outsider, much of their pious meditation is idle hairsplitting. Anselm's computations of the exact number of angels make a perfect target for irony. Yet, whoever devotes more time to these sometimes astonishing speculations, discovers to his surprise behind these efforts at proving the unprovable, at fathoming the unknowable, a pious spirit in constant wonder at the indescribable qualities of God. Such contemplation ends up in adoration. In this adoration it sometimes happens that the soul discovers the nearness of God in such an impressive manner that it is as if the divine presence is filling up the whole body and spirit. In this ecstasy the soul knows itself to be in God and God in him.

Ecstasy in turn can become an object of contemplation. When this happens, there is a danger of obscuring the strict demarcation line which theology draws between God and man. Various mystics fell prey to it: Meister Eckhart and Silezius among the Christian mystics, al-Halladj among the Islamites claimed identity of their souls with God, scandalizing the Church and the congregation of the faithful respectively. Their sin was not that they had a transporting experience of the presence of God. It is a highly gratifying experience for which every believer can envy them. They sinned by extending the grace of temporal bliss into a lasting state, the essential oneness of the soul with its God, a oneness disclaimed by the temporal nature of the experience and defying the incommensurability of God and man. Apart from all the current theological arguments, orthodoxy had a good case when it protested against the claims of the mystics. There is a curious likeness between the relation of contradistinction in which God stands to the universe which he created, and the relation of opposition between being a subject and being a part in the individual. The belief that man has been made after the image and likeness of God mirrors man's belief in a God who is a subject complementary to, but never identical with his universe. To monotheistic religions, the singularity and indestructability of the subject are founding principles based on man's experience of himself and of his relation to his universe. They can appreciate the communion of the soul with God as a blessing, but only if it be an event, not as a state which, inevitably, annuls the subjectivity of the soul. The subject is fundamental both to the idea of God and to the concept of man.

There are religions which do not set great store by such distinctions. The most remarkable case is that of Buddhism. Here, prayer and sacrifice gave way to meditation and spiritual exercise, whereas the belief in gods and spirits, without being rejected, lost its relevance because of the preoccupation of the individual with the improvement of his *karma*. Karma is the constricting chain of desire which fetters man's existence, by rebirth endlessly renewed, to a world of persisting misery. The ultimate aim of Buddhist devotion is the definite annihilation of this chain by the entrance of the soul into *nirvana*. The way of salvation is one of ascetic rejection of lust and desire by a methodical training of the mind which meditates on the vanity and impurity of life and lust. This meditation leads to inner peace and awareness of oneness, a state of well-being which the monk, progressing on the way of salvation, must leave behind him by proceeding to the state of equanimity, a state devoid of all active interest and of all feelings of any kind and description. By then, he can enter the state of enlightenment, the inner vision of the four truths by which he is led to his ultimate aim, the state of nirvana in which there is neither action nor knowledge, nor feeling, nor anything but perfect peace and silence. Seemingly, nirvana is a purely negative state, an immersion in nothingness. Yet, it can also be described as a lingering with the ultimate secret behind the universe and the whole of human existence. Buddhism, abandoning every effort at personalization, symbolization or description, has consistently abandoned this secret to its utter inscrutability (Heiler 1922: ch. 10).

The way leading to the ultimate goal is a long one, requiring many consecutive lives devoted to asceticism and spiritual exercise. It is not, like the other forms of mysticism, aimed at a mystic union of the soul with the symbols of its universe, but at its total silencing. In the terms of the present study it may be called a complete dis-activation and dismantling of the subject. This implies that neither action, nor knowledge, nor feeling can persist and that, what remains, is only the universe, but a universe which, in the absence of a counterpart, has become utterly indescribable, the ultimate secret founding all and everything. The subject, source of all desire, has not won but lost itself when, at last, it dwells with the secret of the all. Stripped of every quality and design, the subject at the end of the road cannot even be described as either being or non-being. In essence, neither subject nor universe are denied. They are too fundamental ever to be denied. But in the effort at redeeming the subject from its chains, the subject is reduced to the point where both subject and universe lose their significance. Rejecting the universe as a world of misery, Buddhism capitalizes on distancing: the chain of karma, binding man to his universe, must be broken. Yet, the road ends in the complete nearness of total union. Man does not escape from being both subject and part.

4. The role of the intellect

Although, in the preceding sections, the importance of man's affective needs was repeatedly emphasized, there can be no shadow of a doubt that, in prayer and mysticism, the intellect is central. In prayer, the agent formulates his needs and desires and exposes his sorrows, hopes and doubts by wording them in fully conscious terms. Even in silent prayer, the pouring out of the soul, wording, formulating, takes an

244

important part. Its cathartic value depends upon it. A comparable activity of the intellect prevails in mysticism. Its dominant instrument is meditation, and meditation is an activity of the intellect. How much it is becomes apparent in the elaborate intellectual speculations of the scholastic mystics of the Middle Ages, and the central significance attributed to the four truths in Buddhism. Mysticism (and religion in general) may serve affective needs, but an important part of this service is rendered by the intellect.

This holds true of all forms of religion. It is evident in prophetism. In shamanism emotional states prevail; but, when all is said and done, shamanism invariably leads to a message expressed in plain words. The intellect has the last word in every shamanistic session; it formulates what has to be done. The experience of the supernatural is, eventually, translated into rational terms. It is exactly what happens to every religious experience. It is conceptualized in plain terms. The dreams and visions of early man had to be communicated to the members of the group in intelligible terms, and these members decided, on grounds provided partly, if not mostly, by the intellect, whether they should be considered as significant or not. We do not and cannot know whether many words were wasted in the deliberations concerning such a decision or in those devoted to the problem of how to act up to a vision recognized as significant. All we know is that such decisions led to the initiation of ritual. Ritual, being a communal act requiring previous planning, there must have been deliberations of some sort, that is, an activity of the intellect.

The intellect does far more. It gives form and content to every religious experience by the conceptualization of its meaning, that is of its place in the total complex of the relations between the individual and his world as apprehended by the subject. One of the most wide-spread concepts is that of the ancestor; among the most interesting ones which we noted are the Australian concept of dreaming, and the Mentaweian concept of *badjou*. Where such concepts are available, they tell how to think about certain experiences by categorizing them. Every religion includes a certain number of different categories which, together, constitute a system that brings order into the confusing multitude of heterogeneous experiences with the numinous. Connecting all things together, the intellect gives definite form to man's experiences with the awe-inspiring powers ruling his world, and provides guidelines for how to deal with them. The system of these guidelines we call a 'worldview'. It enables the members of the group to interpret their world, and to fit accidental events into a meaningful whole in which every member can find his way because the system defines his specific place in its mysteries. Besides, conceptualization gives support to memorization by allotting proper place and meaning to divergent events and experiences, thus contributing to the maintenance of the system and its development into a mainstay for life.

The value of such systems is evident. They enable man to feel at home in his world. What is surprising is that, to an important extent, they are the products of the intellect*. In our culture, we are inclined to think of the intellect as a producer of

---

* So strong is the impact of the intellect that intellectualist theories of religion never wholly die. Cf. Guthrie's recent essay: *A cognitive Theory of Religion* (1980).

doubts rather than as a defender of faith. We tend to think of the intellect as a more or less autonomous faculty geared to the critical weighing of arguments. However, this conception of the intellect is normative rather than factual. Primarily, the intellect is a tool which must enable man to survive in his struggle for life. He uses it for, among other things, the defence of all that is dear to him. To that end, he even uses his intellect to oppose the doubts which that very same intellect raises against his most cherished prejudices. In this function, we saw the intellect at work in the defence of immoral rules by means of so-called rationalizations which must elucidate their righteousness or inevitability (above: ch. VII, 3). A parallel case is that of religion where the defence of its comforting and protective graces resulted in nothing less than a scientific discipline, that of theology. The fact is of interest, because there would hardly be a science of theology if there had been no doubts. This, combined with the fact that theology can make a claim that it is the oldest of all scientific disciplines and has for many centuries attracted the keenest intellects of mankind, confirms once more that religion is closely associated with uncertainty. This was already noted in our comment on the word belief (above: 151). Religion is a matter of faith, not of firm knowledge, and consequently subject to doubts of all sorts, doubts which duly reflect man's existential uncertainty about his place in his universe. Theology assumed the task of protecting faith against the sneaking attacks of scepticism. That the intellect is called upon to defend faith against the doubts which for an important part it generated itself, is but another symptom of the dialectic nature of the human condition.

As a scientific discipline, theology is a product of advanced civilization. The circumstance that it is one of the oldest disciplines suggests that thinking about religion and about the doubts which it raises among the believers began at the dawn of civilization, at times when abstract thought came to be more systematically pursued than normally is the case in primitive culture. There are indications, however, that abstract thinking about religion begins even earlier. A famous case is that of the Dogon. Their elaborate mystic speculations bear witness to a well-developed power of abtraction, even though this abstraction remains wholly within the domain of belief in the reality of their symbolism. The fact that there is reason to suppose that this indulgence in mystic speculation has been promoted by the deliberations of the Dogon religious leaders with the ethnographers Griaule and Dieterlen, does not detract from the fact that, in more modest forms, such speculation is also found in other, even more primitive cultures. We came across such a case when dealing with the Marind-anim manipulations of the *pahui*-symbol and the dialectics of their system of classification (above: ch. IX sect. 4). Keen-witted as they are, these speculations are mystical rather than theological. In as much as they deal with concepts, these concepts are symbols of the image category, not abstractions. Besides, these speculations do not refer to any form of doubt with regard to the truth of their religious symbolism. They are symptoms of faith, evoked by delight in their faith, and not by disbelief. Thus, the question arises about whether purely intellectual doubt plays a part of any significance in the practice of primitive religion.

A fact is that, at least in the New Guinea area, one relatively often comes across expressions of doubt with regard to life after death. There is no doubt that the dead persist, but there is little certainty about the ways in which they do. These doubts, however, are more a matter of a lack of clear ideas on this point than of a critical scepticism concerning the beliefs which found expression in the cult of the dead. Primitive people have no difficulty with admitting that there are many things they do not know. It is a recognition of the impenetrability of the mystery rather than doubt of its reality.

With regard to other points of their religion, expressions of what really should be called doubt are not infrequent today, but it is difficult to evaluate their significance. Many ethnographers will, at times, have had the experience I once had, namely that an informant tells a myth, roaring with laughter because of its scurrilous contents. What is pose in it, designed to present the narrator as sophisticated, what incipient or real disbelief? The ethnographer rarely meets with people who have not been affected by influences deriving from modern civilization. My informant certainly had been and, being a village chief somewhere in the Merauke hinterland, had reason to make himself seem to me, assistant district officer at the time, as more sophisticated than he really was. His later life history supports my suspicion that he was not the sceptic he pretended. The belief in the veracity of myth goes deeper than informants care to confess.

This does not imply that primitive people are uncritical, but that they keep the use of their powers of criticism confined to the strict limits defined by their traditional belief. A good case of such criticism is a story told to me by my late friend Verschueren. Passing through Onggari, a village on the coast of the Merauke district, he found the old men discussing the experience of a woman who had seen an apparition at some place nearby. What they wished to find out was whether the apparition had been merely one of a spirit of the dead, or one of the ancestor who, according to the myth, had performed the exploits for which he was remembered in the immediate vicinity of the place where the apparition had appeared. Their doubts were concerned with the categorization of the event in their traditional system, not with its veracity.

Of a comparable nature are the doubts fostered by the Ngad'a (Flores, Indonesia) with regard to the value of their divinatory practices. Arndt reports that his informant on Ngad'a methods of divination (above: 214) concluded his description of a divination session preparatory to a war raid with the sceptic comment: although so many bamboos have been burst and so many questions been forwarded, there will always be a few men who fall in battle, who are conquered or made prisoners. For this reason a wise diviner tells the men in advance: "Don't ask me whether on your homecoming you will be alive or dead, victorious or beaten. Don't ask me for the reasons when you get wounded. What the diviner speaks comes true for many, for some not. Yet, we must follow his words, otherwise misfortune will certainly befall us" (Arndt 1931: 719 f.). There is no question of disbelief here but of doubt, either in the reliability of the gods, or in the efficacy of the ritual. The belief, as such, is strong enough to persuade the men to make the best of an uncertainty which no one can take away.

Only once I came across a case of what impressed me as possibly genuine disbelief. It was in the literature on the Toradja of Central Celebes. Albert C. Kruyt (n.d.: 46) tells us of a headman who, on more than one occasion, ridiculed the ancestors and spirits. He smartly mocked them even when addressing them in his priestly function of leader at an act of sacrifice. Outwardly adhering to custom, he clearly expressed his disbelief. How deep this disbelief went, is open to question. He certainly was not the promising candidate for conversion to Christendom the missionary (Kruyt) had hoped initially; I gather from Kruyt's account that he still adhered to some form of enlightened paganism and, as such, was more probably a victim of doubt instilled by another religion than by the oddities of his own religious heritage.

Belief in the traditional religious heritage is stronger than openly admitted. Even a systematic dissemination of doubts usually has no more than a very limited effect. No form of belief has been more vigorously attacked by missionaries and administrators alike than that in magic and sorcery, and there is no form of belief which has so tenaciously survived. Elsewhere (1979: 621) I mentioned the Ambonese Master of Law whose university education had not in the least affected his belief in the mischief of witchcraft, a belief that is strong in Ambon in spite of four centuries of Christendom and well-organized church membership. The Ambon case does not stand alone. It is of almost general occurrence. The most pernicious cases of persistence of the belief in magic and witchcraft are found in Africa where, in spite of conversion and modern education, the belief still stands unshaken in vast areas.

A beautiful illustration of the powers of traditional belief against the promptings of genuine doubt within the domain of native experience is contained in the life history of Quesalid cited by Lévi-Strauss (1958: ch. 9). Quesalid was a Kwakiutl who, as a young man, arrived at the conclusion that all medicine-men are impostors. Wishing to unmask their deceit, he decided to let himself be initiated by a medicine-man whom he found willing to impart his secret knowledge to him. Concluding his apprenticeship he had to treat his first patient. To his utter surprise his treatment was clearly successful. He soon earned himself fame as a medicine-man. His successes convinced him of the efficacy of his own methods. He remained consistent only in this respect that he rejected the methods of his fellow medicine-men as pure deceit. In spite of his doubts, he remained a captive of the beliefs and worldview of his culture.

The conclusion seems justified that religious doubts, though not unknown in primitive culture, did not grow into significance before more advanced forms of civilization had strengthened man's powers of abstraction and, with them, his abilities for critical reflection. And, even then, such budding criticism rarely aspired to more than a reform of the religion which aroused its suspicions. The Egyptian Achnaton tried to exchange one cult-form for another. Buddha went further; he rejected the existing cult but remained a captive of the notion of karma.

The Greeks went different ways. Far from rejecting their world like the Buddhists, they loved it and admired its beauties. They were traders in search of wealth. Their greed is testified by as early a witness as Homer. They were also daring sailors, and their travels brought them into close contact with various foreign civilizations, contacts which made them acquainted with numerous foreign gods and cults. How this affected their own traditional beliefs has not been recorded in any detail. We only know the result, viz. openness to a variety of foreign cults which had their adepts in a number of places all through the Mediterranean and the world of Asia Minor. The process reminds us of that observed much later in the Islamic world. Extending eastward, Islam followed the trade route. In the Malaysian and Indonesian area it was the traders – the *nakhoda* sailing their own ships – who first accepted and afterwards spread the new faith which had the eminent virtue that its God encompassed a wider universe than that of their home-bred pantheons and cults which differed from place to place.

In the case of the Greeks, the exchange of religious ideas and experiences bred a new mysticism which disentangled cosmology from crude mythological concepts, and stimulated a more intellectual contemplation on the mysteries of the universe to which, as sailors, adverse winds and weather so often confronted them. A trader like Thales (ca. 640-550 B.C.) drew inspiration from the astronomical knowledge imparted to him by some Egyptian priests. Being also a sailor, professionally used to observing the sky and the stars, the new knowledge stimulated him into closer practical observation as well as to new, mystic ideas which, later in life, he passed on to the then young Pythagoras, stimulating the latter to widen his knowledge by visiting Egypt. "Acting upon this advice, Pythagoras travelled and gained a wide experience, which stood him in good stead when at length he settled and gathered round him disciples of his own, and became even more famous than his master" (Turnbull *in* J. R. Newman I: 82). The more prominent among these disciples founded the Order of the Pythagoreans, a religious order which "made very great progress in mathematics, particularly in the theory of numbers and in the geometry of areas and solids" (id.: 83). Thus, mystic speculation on numbers and their harmony led to a steady increase of mathematical knowledge. Combining science with adoration, this new type of religion betrays the deep interest of the faithful in his universe, the same kind of interest which inspired Greek artists to their magnificent, naturalistic creations. In Pythagorean Greece, science was primarily a religious occupation. Even later, Plato's concept of the ideas is, in essence, still a religious concept.

Mathematics and science, besides inspiring new forms of religion, also bred doubt. Doubt first of all with regard to mythology, the repository of outdated religious truth. But doubt did not stop once a new creed had taken the place of the old one. Mathematics and science are matters of logic and reason; they inevitably turned thought to the art of reasoning. A new scepticism arose, suspicious of religion and truth generally. Nevertheless, the excessive radicalism of the early sophists did not carry the field. Its anti-social relativism provoked strong reactions; and, though religious scepticism persisted in certain circles, it was of the more moderate kind which respects the demands made by the moral rules. The ideal of the scientific mind was set by Socrates. He combined systematic doubt and inquisitiveness with modesty and prudence, with the wisdom that makes allowance for religion and for what we do not and cannot know. Socrates respected mystery.

To the Greeks, mystery was the heart and core of religion. When, some 400 years later, Christendom entered upon the scene, St. Paul did not hesitate to call the gospel a mystery that is revealed to the faithful. Except for the spiritual scepticism of the Stoa, the religious cults, Christendom included, had little reason to be afraid that the practice of science would do harm to religious belief. Soon after Aristotle, the rapid growth of scientific discovery had slowed down, presumably because of the lack of adequate mathematical symbols (above: 50). The one branch of science which might conflict with religious thought was cosmology, and even this only in so far as the biblical worldview of Christendom was concerned. At the time, however, such a danger was not imminent, and Christendom showed little hesitation in accepting reason as a divine gift bestowed on mankind to be used for its good. It made ample use of it in its disputes with other religions.

For early Christendom, danger lurked in philosophical scepticism and the gnostic teachings of contemporary cults rather than in science. It never eschewed a dispute. Christendom was a theological religion almost from its beginning. No reader of the epistles can be mistaken on this point. They are full of rational argument, even where they have to admit that the wisdom of God is foolishness to the Greeks. Christendom had to be firm on this point. Central to its message was the truth of a historical event: the death and resurrection of Christ. The fact and its consequence, the belief in the resurrection of the faithful, are beyond the competence of science, but not beyond scepticism and unbelief. In the fight against scepticism, the belief in these central truths became a virtue, and doubt a sin. In all other respects, *inter alia* with regard to science and mathematics, Christendom could claim in good conscience that it was a reasonable religion. It did not oppose science. During the dark ages following the migration of nations which plunged Europe into turmoil, the Church even acted as the curator of the knowledge accumulated by the classical authors. So little did the Church fear the potential claims of science that St. Thomas, the greatest among the medieval theologians and philosophers, cleared the way to its freedom. Making a sharp distinction between nature and supernature, he assigned nature to the realm of reason, and the study of nature to the ingenuity of the scientist. What the Church feared was not science but heresy, that product of theological doubt which is the inseparable companion of all theology.

It all changed when science began to make progress. The first conflicts arose in the field of astronomy, but these 17th century conflicts were small in comparison with the theological disputes of the time which broke the unity of the Church. It was with the Enlightenment that Christendom got itself into real danger. Then, a new philosophy made its entrance: that of human progress and the pursuit of secular happiness. How it affected Christian belief, and how in later times science undermined the belief in religion generally, and paved the way for the social acceptance of atheism as a respectable alternative to religion, is not our problem here. What matters is that Christendom did succeed in maintaining its prominent place in society for such a long time. In this war of defence, theology played a prominent part. It did not confine itself to defending the old religious truths against an ever more acute criticism; it also tried to adapt the Christian message to the prevailing opinions

250

of the time. This effort led to a further diversification of theology into a number of mutually incompatible schools and denominations which promised a spiritual home to those who, their unbelief in traditional dogma notwithstanding, shrank from rejecting religion as absurd or impossible. Modern theology handed them the necessary arguments. *Fides quaerit intellectum*: the intellect delivered the arguments to defend faith against the attacks of the intellect.

To a certain extent theology succeeded. Believers are still numerous, even among scientists. And where theology failed, it was not always atheism which took the place of Christendom. New creeds, most of them variations on old Indian themes, are making their entrance today. It is not at all certain that they will take root (scientifically they are not more 'probable' than Christendom anyway) but the fact as such is a serious warning against the expectation that religion will soon be a thing of the past. It certainly is not so today. The tenacity by which religion, in spite of all reasonable arguments and doubts, has maintained a position in society, is an undeniable symptom of its value as a mainstay for life-fulfilment, as a last resort against despair and uncertainty. Today it falters, but it has faltered before. It did in the days of Greek scepticism. In this uncertainty it is imperative to make sure that the pretention holds true that religion has been a universal among all mankind until the beginning of this century. If that be affirmed, then indeed religion must be more than just a symptom of perplexity. Whatever it might be, we will have to take it seriously as, at the very least, a human problem.

5. *The universality of religion*

Early writers on religion have denied religion's universality, not among the more advanced, but among primitive peoples. Later research has shown that they were wrong. There is not a single primitive people without religion. The misunderstanding that there are such peoples is mainly due to the misconception that magic is not religion. We need not waste a word on it after all that has been argued on this point.

Quite another matter is the minor part played by women in ritual. From our comment on the origins of myth and ritual, the argument may be borrowed that the women, having a full and satisfying task in their households, suffered less than the males from despondent feelings of inadequacy and forlornness, and were thus less in need of religious comfort than their consorts. One might put it this way: the women, putting themselves at the disposal of the males of their group of origin to be married out to the males of a foreign group, all for the sake of peace and security, and turning themselves into the obedient consorts of their new mates, giving them care and comfort, and acting as devoted mothers to their common offspring, obeyed the moral law and consequently must have felt themselves at ease with their universe.

This argument is edifying but quite impossible. The selflessness of letting oneself be married out (supposing that it was a matter of selflessness) may be morally gratifying, but socially it is highly frustrating and a source of uncertainty. Equally satisfying morally is devoting oneself to the care of husband and children, but materially it is a source of recurrent worry. The high incidence of infant mortality and

251

the dangers inherent in a husband's life as a hunter and warrior give more than sufficient reason for apprehension. Besides, a woman may concentrate on her family, but this does not mean that she has nothing to do with the local society. Every day she is in contact with other families, the object of other people's gossip, and subject to decisions taken by the males of the group without consulting their women. In the life of a woman uncertainty plays an even greater role than in that of a male. Her inferior social position in a group of relative strangers makes her exceedingly vulnerable. A female has not the slightest reason to feel more at ease with her universe and her position in it than a male.

That the men fill the main roles in ritual is a matter of male supremacy and leisure rather than a lack of interest on the part of the women. Even where the women are excluded from participation in the main parts of the cult, their interest in its performance is as evident as their contributions to it. These contributions are not confined to food and sex whenever these 'commodities' are needed. When it is time to be frightened, they let themselves be frightened; and when it is time to admire the achievements of the performers, the women are there to applaud. Their fright and admiration are not feigned. The ethnographic data concur in corroborating that the women are repeatedly the real, the most deeply-impressed believers in the super-natural powers of the ritual. Moreover, they are not outsiders in every ritual. Usually, they play a leading part in the rituals for the dead; certainly so in Australia where their participation in other rituals is limited. In other parts of the world, women sometimes play leading roles as healers, shamans, or prophets. But there is no sense in summing up all that is possible. The main thing is that everywhere women co-operate in the performance of ritual; and that, either as performers, spectators, or servants, they demonstrate their belief in its efficacy and truth. As a matter of fact, little would result from many of the great secret rituals of the males if the women were not there to show their fright and admiration. The role of women in ritual may seem small, but it is far from negligible. This implies that we have to accept that religion really is universal, or at the very least that it was until the beginning of the present century.

The recognition of the universality of religion implies that, normally, religion is an indispensable element in human life and culture, a hard and fast rule to which we find no exceptions outside modern civilization and, perhaps, a small circle of Helenist sceptics. At the outset of our expositions, we suggested that religion is man's reaction to the disturbing fact, that, being a subject distancing and opposing his universe of which at the same time he is and must be a part, he alternately and sometimes simultaneously experiences himself as excluded or imprisoned in a world in which he can only exist satisfactorily as a partner, a partnership that he must experience as a reality, both emotionally and intellectually. The supposition provided the key to a more satisfactory explanation of such strange phenomena as the belief in myth and magic. It was found confirmed in our analysis of the various personifications of the supernatural and the worship they receive in the many forms of prayer and taboo, divination and sacrifice in simple religions, and in the cults of more advanced civilizations. In this chapter, the examination of such divergent phenomena as trance, shamanism and prophetism, on the one hand, and those of prayer and mysticism, on the other, again called our attention to the theme of the *subject* versus the *part* as the ground of the dialectics of *nearness* and *distance* dominating these cult forms.

We conclude that the hypothesis is carried and that there is little ground to expect that a study of other cult forms and more religions can lead to any considerable emendation of these views. The study of every form of religion invariably leads us back to the contradictions of the human condition, and to man's need to surmount his alienation from his universe by means of a symbolic communication which instills in him the comforting certainty that, in spite of his opposition and distance to his universe, he can obtain a place in it as an accepted partner.

Factually, man is of course a part of his universe; a product of the planet earth he cannot fail to be. Nevertheless, man, every man, is so much a subject that the one thing he is most definitely aware of is that, to his universe, he is primarily an 'other', a stranger; whereas to him that universe is above all a field of action and a reality which is not himself. Alienation and uncertainty are inescapable, and up to the present century man found a solution for these problems either by identifying himself symbolically with the projections of the secret essence of his universe, or by assuming that he and his universe are subject to one and the same supreme power who brings the two together as the reward for acts of worship. The two solutions differ considerably, but they agree in assuming the actuality of a non-verifiable reality as the real ground and essence of the visible world. To modern man this assumption is offensive either way. Yet, he is confronted with exactly the same problems as any religious believer, ancient or modern. The question arises whether he can solve these problems in a more rational way than that of hypothesizing a non-falsifiable reality. He does not deny these problems; he simply has difficulties with what he rejects as an irrational solution, the obsolete product of the lack of knowledge characteristic of the cultural life and abilities of past generations.

This ground for rejection is not a strong one. Lack of knowledge plays an important part in every form of religion, from the most primitive to the most advanced ones. However, as an argument to declare religion null and void, it is self-destructive. There is no scientific knowledge which can ever answer the profound problems of ultimate concern to the human heart. In fact, our universe is as mysterious to us as it was to primitive man. It is very interesting to know that our universe is an expanding universe which originated by an explosion of primeval matter. It is equally interesting that matter can – at least up to a very great extent – be identified with energy. But all this knowledge does not say anything about the origin of matter or energy, nor about the causes of its explosion, nor about the grounds of the causality to which it obeys.

Similarly, science opened up new vistas when it discovered that once, under exceptionally favourable circumstances, protein molecules originated which had that curious property that we call life. It is also highly instructive that, again favoured by chance conditions which prolonged time produced, these protein molecules agglomerated into organized forms, some of which were so well adapted to prevailing conditions that they could thrive and in time produce new forms, ever more perfectly organized and ever better adapted forms from which, finally, *homo sapiens* originated. Yet, no one ever found a convincing answer to dispose of the wry remark once made by (if my memory does not deceive me) Von Üxküll, that the theory of evolution contends that a house of a certain style can be built by arbitrarily throwing stones on a heap.

Another triumph of science is the discovery of the mechanism of the nerve-cell. The transmission of messages by the osmosis of kalium and natrium ions through the cell-wall is a real wonder of simplicity and ingenuity. Nevertheless, how the co-operation of some 10 to 15 billion of such cells produces consciousness and rational thought is an unsolved and probably unsolvable mystery. Science solved many problems but never without generating new problems instead.

Science is a challenge; but modern man, accepting this challenge, invariably discovers at the end of the road a gap which, considered more seriously, presents itself as a nauseating hole. Man's universe remains a mystery and the contemplation of this mystery has equal power of disquieting his mind as it had over primitive man. To the intellect the unknowable unwaveringly stands (to express it in Lévi-Straussian terms) as a signifyer for which he has no signified. The intellectual uncertainty intensifies the existential uncertainty of the subject which knows itself alien to a universe of which it is part. What comes to mind here is the existentialist Heidegger's definition of man as a *grundsuchende Ungegrundheit*, an unfoundedness craving for foundation. The rejection of the religious answer to the existential problem as inadequate or even contradictory (Sartre) urges the quest for another solution. One of our main tasks in the final part of this book is to find out what modern man's deeper incentives are to reject religion, what his alternative solutions are to answer his existential problems, and to what extent they must be accepted as satisfactory.

Part Four

*Ethics and Religion
in Confrontation
with the Pursuit of Happiness*

About the beginning of the present century, a new type of civilization presented itself, one which pretends that it can do without religion. The claim has been – and still is – vehemently contested, but even the most fervent defenders of the cause of religion do not deny that modern civilization is highly secularized, nor that exactly secularization is one of its most conspicuous characteristics. This secularization, rather a unique phenomenon in the history of culture, is attended with, on the one hand, an equally unique growth of the extent of society, and an unprecedented wealth and prosperity, on the other. The co-terminality of these phenomena makes a study of their historical correlations an inviting task. If we refrain from it, this is primarily because it is quite uncertain that such a study would result in more than the mere confirmation of their simultaneity and apparent correlation, without clarifying the motivations which induced this curious development. For this and other reasons to be elucidated presently, we decided to take another course.

In ch. XIV a comparison of western and non-western spontaneous reactions to identical situations will lead us to the discovery that an active interest in things and their manipulation and construction is a significant characteristic of western civilization. We take stock of its rapid growth since the end of the 15th, and more particularly since the end of the 16th century; and of the contributions which it made to the recognition of reason as man's most effective talent, and as his ultimate yardstick for evaluating all secular and religious opinions. Next to being man's means for the acquisition of knowledge, reason becomes his (often failing) guide in social and political affairs, and the unfailing instrument to satisfy his craving for wealth (a heritage of the medieval struggle for power and property) and for personal freedom (a drive which originated in the Reformation's resolute willingness to bear personal responsibility in matters of religion).

These trends converge in the philosophy of the Enlightenment, and in the frank recognition of human happiness as the ultimate aim of mankind's exertions. A historical outline of these developments is necessary, because they laid the foundations for the consecutive socio-economic and intellectual growth which resulted in the grandeur and the problems of our modern civilization. Its achievements in wealth, prosperity and welfare, the predominance of the appliance of minimal ethics over that of the moral law, and its failure to produce a valid substitute for religion are the subject matter of ch. XV, and the object of a final discussion in the concluding chapter (XVI).

XIV

The Unfolding of Western Civilization

1. Specific incentives to the development of western civilization

The coincidence of the appearance of such a unique phenomenon as secularization with an unprecedented growth of the extent of society and the increase of its wealth and technical equipment, justifies the supposition that they have a common ground in a complex of inner motivations which is specific to our civilization. Unfortunately, to define this complex is a matter of serious difficulty. The methods of cultural analysis developed in anthropology are inapplicable here. They demand that, first of all, a comprehensive and well-ordered description of the culture concerned be drawn up, a demand which, in the case of western civilization, is unanswerable. It is so overwhelmingly rich that no student can master more than a tiny part of its contents. Though the descriptive task could be fulfilled by the co-operation of scores of scholars, that of ordering these part-descriptions into a coherent whole remains as an unsurmountable stumbling block. There are other obstacles besides; analysing one's own culture is a tricky assignment requiring a rigid alertness against the most diverse forms of subjectivism and prejudice. The hope that anthropological methods can lead to a neat description and analysis of our own culture which meets the normal standards of objectivity and completeness, is a vain one. If we wish to discover what the incentives are of the curious developments here in discussion, we shall have to try other ways, ways which do not promise that neat and systematic description of a complex of motivations which is the reward of a fully-fledged anthropological analysis (at least in theory: in practice it has never been fully realized) but which, as a second best, may be expected to throw some new light on the processes of western cultural development and the inner coherence of their main trends.

Our problem has the advantage that it can also be approached via comparative studies. It can be formulated as a problem of comparison: What made our civilization go such strikingly different ways than those trod by other cultures? In this field, important preparatory spadework has been done by scholars engaged in development problems: What should the peoples of the third world do to become equally prosperous as we are, more in particular, what are the attitudes that they should adopt to meet the exigencies of modern development? The disappointing results achieved by technical assistance and financial aid to the third world lent these studies a great

257

actuality. To us they are of interest because a study of the differences between western and non-western attitudes may pave the way to the discovery of the incentives which define these attitudes. A short review of a few of these studies is well worth a place here.

The answers these scholars gave to the question of what the productive causes are of western progress are various, and of divergent value. Charles J. Erasmus (1961), for instance, did not think it necessary to dig deeply. A partisan of classical economical theory, he concluded that the main impetus for economic progress is the invidious emulation by middle class individuals of their more successful fellow-men. Fortunately, others gave more consistent thought to the problem. The economist E. E. Hagen (1962), less confident in the virtues of vice, sought the founding force of human progress and development in what he called the 'creative personality', to him the product of a considerate education which protects the growing personality from fear and anxiety, and encourages the development of such valuable and productive needs as those of achievement, autonomy, and order, together with those of 'succurance' and 'nurturance'. However, the mechanism which produces this creative personality remains rather a mystery. The author scolds authoritarianism as the source of all evil, but one of the important paradigms of a creative personality presented by Hagen is Martin Luther, a man who suffered severely under the rule of an authoritarian father. Besides, authoritarianism was by no means foreign to the methods of education current in 18th and 19th century Europe, centuries of great progress and rapid development. Whereas education in primitive and peasant societies is more than once of the permissive rather than of the authoritarian type!

More convincing is McClelland's study (1961) of the significance of the need for achievement as a driving force to progress. He makes his point true in a methodically highly satisfying manner. He suggests means how to stimulate this need, and he notes significant correlations between a high need-achievement and other psychological preferences, in particular other-directedness. Unfortunately, McClelland did not differentiate between ego-directed and matter-directed need-achievement, an omission which seriously affects the validity of his results. It must be evident that for the progress of civilization an ego-directed need-achievement is as obnoxious as a matter-directed one is productive. The former produces generals and politicians of the Napoleon and the Hitler type, the latter personalities like Edison, Einstein, and Mme. Curie.

A more encompassing approach is made in the study by Kluckhohn and Strodtbeck on *Variations in Value Orientations* (1961). As orientations specific of western civilization, they mention that toward mastery over nature instead of harmony with or submission to nature; that favouring the prevalence of future over present and past; that for doing over being; and that for individualism over collaterality and lineality. The results are valuable and well documented. They confirm that modern man's approach to his world differs significantly from that of the peasants of the third world. They even specify these differences. One question, however, is not answered; and this is *why* Westerners cherish these specific value orientations, what motivates them to prefer mastery over nature to harmony with it, to give preference to the future over present and past, etc. Although the outcome of their study of value orientations confirms the desirability of our search for a complex of inner motivations as the driving force behind the growth of our civilization (a civilization characterized by a number of typical attitudes!) it does not tell us what these inner motivations are. Other authors such as Hagen and McClelland (one might also include L. Doob whose work has not been discussed here) have tried to answer this question by referring to quantitative differences in the strength of certain needs; but by presenting these needs as elementary psychological forces they failed to establish a clear relation between these needs and the relevant culture. It is not enough to know that people need achievement, autonomy and order, we should also know what kind of achievement, autonomy and order they prefer. Needs are not blind; they have an aim and this aim is not merely psychological in the sense of emotional, it also has intellectual contents defined by ends and interests. Is it possible to say something about western man's intuitive interests as the ends which define his needs?

To answer this question we should know more about western man's intuitive reactions to chance situations and this is a field which these studies have not covered. All our authors derive their data from work situations or from the artificial situations conditioned by psychological tests. These situations have in common that they impose a role on the participants in the work or the experiment; in a work situation the role imposed by either the labourer's culture or his employer, in an experiment that imposed by the psychologist. The behaviour of the observed person may be culturally specific, but it is not spontaneous. He behaves as he is (or thinks he is) expected to do. If we wish to know what a person's real incentives to action or non-action are, we should observe that person under conditions which guarantee a perfectly free, spontaneous reaction.

This is an extremely hard condition for research that must be relevant to our problem. It is not enough to observe one person in such a situation, there must be more persons and their reactions must, if they belong to the same culture, be identical and, in a later, identical situation, repetitive. To make it more difficult, Westerners should be placed in exactly these same situations and, like the Non-Westerners, react all in the same way every time they face that situation. Besides, the reactions of the Westerners should differ significantly from those of Non-Westerners to be accepted as symptomatic of (unconscious) cultural difference. And even when all these conditions are fulfilled, it is far from certain that the differences thus observed are so significant that they hold a clue to the solution of our problem, the incentives which in our culture led to the coincidence of rapid progress, vast social extension, and secularism.

These conditions must seem forbidding, as situations inviting spontaneous reactions cannot be created purposively. They must be met with by chance and it is hardly to be expected that such a chance will return and give occasion to repeated observation. Nevertheless, such chances do occur, and even though they need not give a straight answer to the questions we are after, they can be significant enough to give us a lead to detect at least one incentive which has played a prominent role in the development of western civilization. We already came across a case of repeated observations of culturally divergent spontaneous behaviour in the course of this book, i.e. my repeated observations of child behaviour on board small ships. They have been described and commented upon on pp. 157, 158 above. At the time I made these observations I had not the slightest notion of their significance. This came to me later, at the time that I got interested in the cultural diversity of child education. It then dawned upon me that I had witnessed a series of spontaneous reactions by children of different cultures to identical chance situations, those of travelling on board a small ship, and that the reactions of western children differed significantly from those reared in other cultures.

Further consideration of these differences led to the discovery – a discovery though everyone knows it! – how immensely important things, objects, and the manipulation of things are in the western infant's life. Playthings (things!) are handed out to the baby in the cradle at an age when it can hardly grasp them. Later, the infant is induced not only to grasp things, but to play with them. The child must do something, and its world is filled with manipulable objects. This is only the beginning. Objects accompany the child all throughout its life. They are of equal interest to the adult. Like children the adults feel that they must do something, even if it be only to pass the time. This doing almost invariably implies the handling of things. This handling of things is so important that it plays a favoured part in psycho-therapy. To people in distress or confusion the manipulation of objects, the fulfilment of manual tasks, is a redeeming activity, a fact which corroborates our earlier observation in quite another context: "The surest way to lay the disturbing effect of silence is, without doubt, doing things which demand the individual's close and uninterrupted attention. When actively engaged, silence is not noticed" (above: 157).

All this would be hardly important if it were just a habit. But how could a mere habit become so general without an incentive which provokes it? And of course there is such an incentive. The whole early education of the child is geared to inspire it to take an interest in things. The child is encouraged to play with his things, to take them to pieces, to reconstruct them, to build houses and cars with them, to be proud of the result and of his dexterity in handling them. Once interest has been aroused, playing goes by itself, and the satisfaction found in handling ever new objects stimulates the interest in things generally. It endures throughout life. Adults too find satisfaction in it. Having tasted the pleasure of being engaged with something or other, they wish to be engaged again and again. If they have nothing to do they feel bored, and to be bored is awkward. Later we shall have occasion to point out that the notion of boredom is a fairly recent acquisition of modern civilization (below: 298). Here, another point is more important: the fact that this interest in things is implanted at a very early age. "Mom, what shall I do now?", complains the five year old child who, educated in the company of things, fails to find something that interests him. This early implementation gives ground for the supposition that this interest in things is far more than just one ideosyncrasy among many, that it is a real incentive in our culture which directs the individual's orientation towards his world. If this be so, then this interest might well be one of the powerful impulses behind that curious leaning toward activity by which modern man distinguishes himself from man in peasant and primitive society. It might even be one of the major incentives to our industrial development.

The supposition is not as daring as it may seem to be. We find it confirmed when we turn to the one and only case of really successful adaptation to western civilization of modern history, the case of the Japanese. The present author belongs to a generation who, in their youth, looked with some contempt at the Japanese efforts to participate in modern industrialization. We readily admitted that the 'Japs' were commendably industrious, but we refused to believe that their almost hectic activity was guided by that true spirit of scientific inquisitiveness and philosophic depth which, until then, seemed the monopoly of western civilization. Actually, we held them to be adroit counterfeiters, imitating the fine products of western industry with only this difference: that the copies they made were a bit smaller in size, a bit less solid, and a lot cheaper in price. We failed to appreciate that exactly these small variations in size and design implied a thorough internalization of the technical principles applied in their production, just as we failed to realize that their thorough study of the western paradigms implied a deep interest in the construction of things and objects.

When we ask whence the Japanese borrowed this interest, the obvious answer is that it was inherent in their original culture. The refinement of their paintings of living nature, in particular their paintings of flowers, testifies to a deep and genuine interest in nature. Another indication is the interest which, during the second half of the Tokugawa period, the Japanese took in books imported from the Netherlands, at the time the only western nation that maintained (limited) contacts with the island empire. Their special preference was for books dealing with human anatomy and works on techniques and chemistry useful for the production of gunnery (Dore 1965: 160 ff.). The interest taken in anatomy (earlier than in medicine) is a significant detail in this context. My personal knowledge of Japan is limited; besides, my contacts with Japanese during the war were discouraging. In later years, however, travelling the countryside of Honshu, I became impressed by the inventiveness of the Japanese farmer and his readiness to accept simple technical perfections. Apparently, we find a similar interest here as in the western world, and this interest is, so it seems, connected with industrial development.

There is ample reason, then, to follow the track of this interest back into European history. Can we really say that it played such an important part in our cultural history as we suggested? We certainly can. One of the amazing facts of European history is that it abounds with convincing instances of men who devoted all their life to the satisfaction of that one sweeping interest in things and their construction, in things man-made, and in things of nature.

It all begins with the Renaissance period. The sketchbooks left by Leonardo da Vinci (1452-1519), painter, sculptor, architect and engineer, contain a baffling account of his multifarious interests. He meticulously measured the proportions of the human body, studied perspective, occupied himself with the power of steam, was interested in projects of canalization, and contrived machinery for the improvement of locomotion. He even experimented with flying. The restricted technical facilities of his time did not allow him to put his bolder ideas into practice, but the sketches he left depict him as the prototype of the modern engineer and researcher, a keen observer bent on turning his observations to some practical use.

Leonardo was the first in a long series of scientists who spent all their time and energy on the pursuit of knowledge by observation. One among these was Christiaan Huygens (1629-1695), mathematician and astronomer, who (*inter alia*) discovered the ring of Saturnus, formulated the undulatory theory of light, and constructed a highly accurate pendulum clock. He was a perfect instrument maker who made his own telescope, ground and polished the lenses he needed, and, at the age of 14, surprised his family by constructing in their aristocratic mansion a big lathe which he needed for making his instruments.

Huygens was a man of fairly ample means, but his compatriot Anthonie van Leeuwenhoek (1632-1723) had to make his living as an usher to the court of sheriffs of Delft. He spent all his leisure time and money on microscopic research, examining such curious things as a drop of dirty water in which he discovered the infusoria. Among his other discoveries are the asexual procreation of plant-lice, the circulation of blood in the capillaries, and the transversal lining of the muscles.

A more practical-minded man of research was the American Benjamin Franklin whose biographer, Carl van Doren, pictures him as a man of unfailing energy, as a hard working printer a successful man of affairs, as a politician a wise statesman and diplomat, and as a scientist an accurate observer who won fame by his experiments with electricity, but was equally interested in such complicated problems as the origin of hurricanes and the course of the Gulf-stream, and such homely ones as the circulation of air in an oven.

The four mentioned are but a very few, all but the first arbitrarily selected out of the immense list of men who, driven by an insatiable curiosity, spent all their leisure hours on the pursuit of their passion, the discovery of the true construction of nature. To describe this passion as an interest in things is rather an understatement. In the context of the present work, it should rather be called an interest in their universe, an interest moreover which inspired a very fruitful participation in that universe. These men must have found a deep satisfaction in their investigations. Their need-achievement was really matter-directed. This does not mean that they were insensible to praise, but worldly honours were not their incentive. Some of them became martyrs for scientific truth; Giordano Bruno and Galileo for instance. Others never saw their main works printed; e.g. Spinoza's *Ethica*. The tireless investigations of one generation after another of such men have contributed more than anything to that body of science and technical know-how which lent western civilization its superiority. And yet, we do not derogate from their merits when we describe their passion for scientific truth as simply an interest in things. After all, they have their prototype as well as a distant follower in the boy who takes his parents' alarm-clock apart to see how it works.

The interest in things is, of course, only one among various incentives which, together, constitute the complex that motivates the course and growth of western civilization. Among these other incentives, such motives come to mind as the lust for power and the craving for wealth which the new era inherited from medieval society, and the individualism of which we find the first marks in the Reformation. There may be other incentives as well, but there is no sense in trying to track them down in a haphazard way. We noted already that there is little hope of ever getting a full overview of the hidden motives behind the complex of features coinciding with the increase of secularization. Probably we do not even need it too badly. What we want is insight in the incentives leading to the growth of some specific trends in our culture, and it might well be that a study of the history of the interest in things in western civilization opens up new vistas on the motivations which induced its development. The point is that this interest in things has all the traits of a dominant motive which all through modern history has grown in force and impact. The first time we come across it is in the case of a single individual, Leonardo. There are only a few people like him in the 15th and 16th century, but in the 17th century their number rapidly increases. In the 18th century the interest becomes a fashion, it is generalized in the course of the 19th century, and in the present age we find it integrated in the current patterns of child education. It is significant that these forms of education do not consciously aim at arousing the child's interest in things; parents simple wish to activate the child because to be active is a virtue. They rarely realize that arousing the child's interest is the means to that end; the interest is taken as more or less a matter of course, so fully has it been integrated in our life-style.

To follow the growth of this interest historically must be rewarding anyhow, and this expectation is confirmed when we turn to its influence on a competing incentive in the history of our civilization, on its insatiable lust for power and its craving for wealth. They played a tremendous role in the colonial expansion which began in the 15th century and persisted until Mussolini's conquest of Ethiopia. It is worth a second thought that even the early originators of overseas conquests and adventures never omitted to consult the scientists of their times to acquire all such information as was then available, before they decided to finance and equip an expedition. As early as the late middle ages, those in power begin to seek the support of scientists and experts, and this not only for information, but also for such practical matters as the construction of fortifications (Leonardo da Vinci was one of the first fortress-engineers!) and the improvement of gun-foundry, the building of better ships and the perfection of the available instruments for navigation. It is evident that, even at that time, science and technology had become recognized as useful instruments for the acquisition of power and wealth.

Yet, even in those early days, the appreciation of science and technology is not confined to its usefulness. Princes and wealthy merchants often took an active interest in the advancement of science; they gave their support to universities and, on different occasions, encouraged research. In leading circles, science had a respected status, a status more generally accepted than in earlier times. It rapidly became an occupation in which noblemen could participate such as, in the 16th century, Tycho Brahé and John Napier. They did not pursue their studies for the sake of money or power, but simply because they were interested and could afford to follow that interest. So did others. Some of them were clergymen; but from the 17th century onwards we find also a great number of gentlemen of ample means who do not use their wealth for the accumulation of more wealth or for the acquisition of power positions, but spend it on their favourite studies. Huygens did it, Descartes too, and later men like Montesqieu, the Von Humboldts and Darwin. Others were less fortunate and had to solicit the protection of princes and great lords, or to accept a position at a university or otherwise for a living. But whatever they did, whether they pursued science for its own sake or used their talents in the service of the commercial and political ends of the rich and the powerful, their dedication to their task is amazing anyhow. The scientists's life is a monk's life. He works longer hours than anyone, and his rewards are, materially, moderate. The satisfaction for his toils he finds, not in their remuneration, but in the pleasure of scientific detection. In fact, an amazing ideosyncrasy, but all the same an ideosyncrasy which has more than anything contributed to the great successes of our civilization.

At this point, a problem arises which must be discussed before we proceed to a more detailed discussion of the effects of this passion for knowledge. There is a standing theory of considerable repute which says that the great impetus to the economic (and this includes technological) development of our culture was given not by science, but by religion, and more specifically by Calvinism. According to Weber and Troeltsch, capitalism originated from the inner-worldly asceticism preached by Calvin. Turning hard work into a duty and the pleasures which wealth can afford into a sin, Calvinism induced its adepts to use the returns of their work as investments for new forms of enterprise.

The theory is attractive because it is one of the few which give a place to virtue as a major incentive for human exertion and cultural development. Unfortunately, it is also a weak theory because the argument is conversible. Weber holds the view that Calvinism made men frugal and industrious and thus inspired them to continuous economic activity. On the same grounds it may be contended that men who are industrious and frugal felt attracted to Calvinism because it turned their personal inclinations into a virtue and permitted them to pursue their business in good conscience. There is every reason to give ample consideration to this view. Calvinism found great favour in commercial circles, i.e. among people who, professionally, *are* frugal and industrious. They must make savings to be prepared for bad years as well as to make investments for the production of new goods. They run greater risks than the agriculturalist who may rely on the expectation that his land, if properly tilled, will year after year yield its returns, one year a bit more or a bit less than another, but always enough to keep him and his family alive. The commercialist must do without such securities and if, by his thrift and industry, he manages to 'make it' and to prosper, he has to bear the blame of avarice, a blame easily earned in medieval and post-medieval society which looked askance at the trader as a man who made profit out of other people's toil. Would not such a man be attracted to Calvinism, a form of religion which raised his this-worldly occupations and zeal to the dignified level of the service of God? To God-fearing commercialists, troubled by St. Paul's warning to set their "affections on things above, not on things of the earth, for ye are dead, and your life is hid with Christ in God" (Col. 3: 2, 3), the recognition of their daily toil as a task that could be performed to the glory of God must have sounded as a redemption. Is it not a blessing to find your preferences sanctified?

This was certainly not what Calvin had in mind. He was a pious man and his Institution, in spite of all what has been said against it – but few people read it today – is an intrinsically pious book. But the history of later Calvinism or, more correctly, of the descendents of many who accepted Calvin's teachings in the early days of the Reformation, justifies the supposition that to these post-Calvinists the service of the glory of God was little more than an alibi for the persecution of their private preferences. The so-called Calvinists who inititiated the industrial revolution had strayed far away from Calvin's piety. How poor, how empty is the piety of Adam Smith (we shall have to say more about it hereafter) when compared to that of the Genevan master! It is secularism excusing itself.

When, by now, we return to the history of science, it is good to remember how easily a fundamentally pious movement can fall a prey to this-worldly interests. The scientist has in common with the commercialist – and more in particular with the industrialist who made his entry during the industrial revolution – that he is deeply interested in things. There is no doubt that the early scientists could in all sincerity subscribe to the view that all their work was to the glory of God. As a matter of fact, they knew more of His works than any industrialist. They beheld their glory, and yet, where did it lead them? How little, writes Tawney, "do those who shoot the arrows of the spirit know where they will light" (Tawney 1938: 226). We have to follow this in the next sections of this chapter.

2. The pursuit of the knowledge of things

To take an interest in things is something perfectly natural to man. Whether primitive or modern, a hunter or a clerk, man is turned to his world, his field of action and the ever-present framework of his existence. The distinctive feature of the Westerner's interest in things is exaggeration. Western man is always busy with things; he needs them even for his relaxation. Besides, his curiosity is insatiable, and he spares neither cost nor pains to satisfy it. It sometimes goes to incredible lengths. What on earth moved a man like Anthonie van Leeuwenhoek to spend months of work and all the little money he had on the construction and improvement of his microscope for the silly purpose of studying the contents of a drop of ditch-water, instead of quietly talking with his friends over a glass of wine? Puzzling is not the interest as such, but its excess. What turned simple, genuine curiosity into a sweeping passion dominating the life and work of a whole civilization?

We really do not know. All one can say with some certainty is that a hypothetic Chinese visitor who, in 1452, the year of Leonardo da Vinci's birth, travelled in Europe, might have observed much that amazed and even interested him, but very little that could shock his belief in the superiority of Chinese civilization. Wherever he went he would have found himself confronted by war or the traces of the devastations of war. He would have concluded that these red barbarians were highly aggressive, ever eager for power, and that they might be expected to carry on fighting and killing each other as they had done for over a thousand years, since the days that the Germanic tribes crossed the Rhine and the Danube. He would have brought home impressions which are more or less of the kind filling the mind of the modern reader who just finished Norbert Elias' *Über den Prozesz der Zivilisation,* the book we quoted in our analysis of power (above: 118).

Still, there are some features in medieval culture and history which might have escaped our Chinese visitor's scrutiny, features which, in part, were also disregarded by Elias in his splendid analysis of the political turmoil of the times, but all the same worth noting. One of these is the surprising fact that, in spite of the total splintering of what had once constituted the Roman Empire, and of the eternal fighting which had torn it to pieces, the Roman Empire still persisted, both in the Church and in the ideology of the German emperors and princes. Thanks to the Church, international relations between widely distant areas persisted, and the awareness of some form of ultimate unity never wholly disappeared. Even where the bishops had become the pawns of emperors and princes, and the unity of the Church seemingly had dissolved into thin air, international relations found themselves firmly substantiated in the activities of monastic orders and fraternities, genuine international bodies preaching the unity of all mankind in Christ.

Church and monasteries represented a unity which the warring overlords denied or broke down; and they acted as the custodians of a classical learning which the knights held in contempt. Nevertheless, the two orders lived in a remarkable symbiosis. The enormous extent of the landed property of Church and monasteries gives undeniable evidence of the esteem which the clergy enjoyed from the side of those in power. Their message of peace and modesty might be widely ignored, but the harbingers of the message were respected. Whether this respect bestowed on them can be explained as just another case of the effect of a bad conscience (above: 143 f.), is a question well beyond our competence. The one thing which is certain is that Church and monasteries were provided with more and better means by the secular lords than, on the basis of the latter's violence and greed, could be expected. From the 13th century onwards the great lords were even willing to extend their beneficence to the founding of universities in one or more of the towns in their realm, a first token of respect for science.

A second point worth consideration is the fact that the monks kept the lines of communication open throughout Europe. When, early in the 13th century (a remarkable century anyhow), the works of Arab philosophers like Ibn Sina and Ibn Roshd became known in Italy and Spain, this knowledge spread fairly rapidly through the rest of Europe. Thomas Aquinas brought it to Paris, and something of the spirit of the early Renaissance even reached England where Roger Bacon pleaded for the significance of experiment for the increase of knowledge. It is true that he ended his days in jail; but as an early symptom of a changing spirit – and that at the outskirts of the western realm – his work is worth remembering. Though it failed to break the biased pursuit of book learning and traditional knowledge, it certainly is an indication of a growing interest in learning anyhow, an interest to which the vehement disputes between nominalists and realists bear testimony. Without a significant breakthrough of a really scientific spirit, the 13th century marks the beginning of a process of slowly increasing knowledge and a renewed appreciation of learning.

It has a parallel in the continuous technological progress during the middle ages. It was a slow one, but it started early and never stopped. The 9th century already brought the harnessing of the horse, a device which made horse-power available for ploughing. Economically it was an important improvement, as the horse is more enduring, more manageable and stronger than the ox. During the same period the iron horse-shoe came into use which facilitated the use of the horse for transport (Slicher van Bath 1960: 72 f., 81). Windmills (probably a result of the crusades) came into use toward the end of the 12th century (ibid.: 206 and ftn. 159). More or less at the same time another, pre-existent element in medieval society began to play a more independent role in other fields of the economy. The towns became centres of trade and industry. Those of Flanders were flourishing hives of industry as early as the 13th century, and the burghers demonstrated the potential of their military power and political will in the Battle of the Spurs (1302).

In spite of warfare and turmoil, interregional trade developed, with the towns as its centres. It resulted in a substantial progress in the technology of ship-building, both in England and northern Germany. The first *kogge* (cock-boat) sailed the Hanseatic waters at the beginning of the 13th century, a sturdy sailing-boat which carried from one to three masts and measured some 29 meters in length, 7 in width and had a draught of about 3 meters. In the 14th century the Mediterraneans further improved on the type and constructed the caravel, the type of ship later to be used by Columbus (Brockhaus Enzyklopaedia). Another indication of the importance of overseas traffic is the use of the compass. It is first mentioned in a 12th century manuscript and may have been in common use since the 13th century.

Inventions, then, certainly played a role in medieval life. One of these was the 14th century discovery of the use of gunpowder for propelling missiles from an iron barrel. It initiated the art of gun-foundry and a change in war tactics, though it took some hundred to two hundred years before this became really effective. The technical innovations of the middle ages did not revolutionize society. They were effective, certainly, but only in the long run. There is one exception. Again, it is an invention which is not spectacular, one which had been made by the Chinese quite a number of centuries earlier. It is the invention of the art of book-printing. It was made round about the middle of the 15th century, the time of our hypothetical Chinese traveller's visit to Europe. The response which this invention provoked was far more spectacular than the innovation itself. Almost everywhere people began to read books. It is evident that the availability of books met a real need. The public was willing to pay for them and this willingness rapidly made book printing profitable.

The eagerness of a public sufficiently numerous to read and buy so many books that printing became a profitable business can be seen as an early symptom of that increased interest in things discussed in the previous section; but on this point a prudent reticence is well in place. The age teemed with religious ideas of many sorts,

267

and in book purchase religious interest probably played a much larger part than that in things. Even so, the demand for religious books is a symptom of change, foreshadowing forms of religion to which church membership and the participation in its sacraments is of slight value when compared with personal faith and inner certainty of salvation. What counts is not the social quality of church membership, but the spiritual quality of being and knowing oneself a child of God. Personally responsible for his own salvation, the individual is induced to personal study of the Scripture and of all that can enlighten his mind.

Such views were expounded in the teachings of the great Reformers. The echo these teachings found in the hearts of many people is more surprising than is often thought. Current beliefs concerning the fate of the soul in after-life were frightening. The paintings by Jheronimus Bosch, who died in 1516, give irrefutable testimony to the terrible prospects threatening the souls of those who had failed to match their sins by good works during their lifetime, not to speak of the gruesome fate of the soul who departed this life in a state of sin. The Reformers did nothing to assuage such fears. On the contrary, they insisted that everyone should "work his own salvation in fear and trembling" (Phil. 2: 13). That, under such circumstances, so many people were found willing to reject the means of grace mediated by the Church through the sacred sacraments cannot, as is often suggested, be explained from the discredit which the Church had incurred by the unworthy behaviour of its servants. The discredit was true enough, but it called for a severe purge among these unworthy servants rather than for the rejection of the sacraments which could shorten the sufferings of the soul. The message of the Reformers had wider implications than that of a protest which earned them the name of Protestants. It made an appeal to the duty and responsibility of the individual, and it is this appeal which found response in the hearts of many. Most curious of all, it found this response not only among those who, by birth or education, had internalized what it means to be responsible, but also among simple, dependent people who, from early youth, had been wont to rely on the guidance of patron and priest. The Reformation found a willing ear among the members of all the various classes of society, peasants and artisans included.

The willingness to accept responsibility for one's own life and beliefs can be interpreted as a sign of increased individualism. Unfortunately, this contributes little to our understanding of the process. Individualism is of many kinds. We speak of the individualism current among Papuan highlanders, of the individualism of the Guatemalese petty trader (Sol Tax 1941), of the individualism of the African migrants to South African towns, as well as of that of the modern urbanite. Each time the term must derive its proper contents from the symptoms exhibited and from the situation in which they are observed.

The origin of the 16th century willingness to accept responsibility for one's religious opinions and way of life is unclear. Even if allowance be made for the oratory of the early reformers, the impact of their preaching can only be explained if its contents gave expression to something which, in a confused and shadowy form, brooded already in the hearts of many. Where this came from, and why it was stronger among people living in the West and the North of Europe than among those of its South, are questions which it is difficult to answer conclusively. Those of Italy, where in 1498 Savonarola had been burned, seemed intellectually better prepared for receiving the reformers' message than those of Germany or Scotland. Nevertheless, Italy remained true to the Church, and afterwards lagged behind in the cultural development which, in the 17th century, had its centre in England, France, and the Low Countries. But historical causality is a difficult problem anyway, and we must acquiesce in the fact that, for unexplained reasons, quite a number of people belonging to every caste or class of West and North European society showed an unexpected willingness to stand for their own religious opinions, a willingness which, in retrospect, must be acknowledged as the incipient form of what in time would become a significant cultural incentive.

During the 16th century the wider implications of religious individualism did not yet show themselves. The movement was strictly confined to matters of dogma and faith. Not culture or economy were at stake, but man's salvation. One may argue with Tawney (1938) that Luther was more inclined towards a mild form of mysticism which turned away from the world and its amenities, whereas Calvin gave more leeway to the needs of urban tradesmen in matters of interest on business loans, but there was no question that Calvin showed himself more secularly minded than Luther. His ethics do not condone the later Puritan who, accusing the poor of laziness and ignoring their needs, applied his profits to new investments and the extension of his trade. The relation between Calvinism and Puritanism is one of a historical nature, not of affinity in substance. It also would be wrong to associate Calvinism with an incipient interest in things and their construction. All one can say – and that holds equally true of Lutheranism – is that the Reformers encouraged independent thinking. And with regard to Calvinism, one may add that, by its greater openness to the needs of a town economy and the perils of political life in a small republic, it was more attractive than Lutheranism to people who combined a solicitude about salvation with more worldly interests.

A more outspoken interest in things seems to announce itself in that other achievement of the late 15th century, the daring ocean voyages made by the Portuguese who sailed the West coast of Africa until, in 1498, they rounded the Cape of Good Hope; by Columbus who discovered the Antilles in 1492; and by Cabot who crossed the Atlantic to Labrador and then reconnoitred the American East coast as far South as Florida in 1497 and 1498. However, the interest of these sailors was not, at least not primarily, concerned with the construction of things or the true nature of this world, but rather inspired by the desire to take possession of its wealth. The aim which they had set themselves was India (or whatever it was called), and this not for the country but for the fabulous riches which were there expected. It was, more concretely, gold and silver that they were seeking, and the successes made by Columbus increased their lust. There is more than enough in the history of discovery to give ground to the opinion that colonialism is the child of greed. The gold and silver which, since Columbus, year after year poured into the Spanish harbours, had an electrifying effect on the economy, not only in Spain, but throughout Europe. The steadily increasing availability of bullion favoured the growth of a money economy which stimulated trade and industry in all the various parts of the European continent. It thus unleashed a search for wealth which, in little more than a century, carried European merchants all over the seven seas.

However, it was not all as simple as this alone. Greed is the mortal sin of avarice, and the awareness of this weighed heavily on the medieval minds of these seafarers. They could not face the perils of the big ocean in good conscience if their endeavours did not serve a better purpose than their material wealth, and they confidently combined them with the task incumbent on every Christian (since the crusades also a warrior's plight) to bring the heathen the message of Christ by extending the realm of the Church. Truly a strange combination, but, in spite of this inner contrariety, an obvious one to their contemporaries. They had little difficulty in obtaining the Pope's blessings. The papal bulls of 1455, 1456, and 1493 bear clear testimony to the Pope's almost excessive co-operation. Whatever the motivations of the Holy See, it was certainly not the first time that the Church acted as the heir of the Roman Empire. Besides, the early conquerers gave no reason for disappointment; they took their missionary task seriously. Their exploits bore all the curious traits of an old-fashioned crusade, combining the service of the glory of Christ with that of his earthly knights. Their mission inspired them to really Quixotic deeds of bravery. One need only read Prescott (enthralling reading even today) to realize that men like Cortez and Pizarro drew on deeper resources than greed alone. Apart from being the fortune-hunters they were, they were soldiers of God, and it is this firm conviction that made them persevere and win all the battles they, humanly speaking, should have lost.

They were serious also in this respect that they always took missionaries with them and gave them every opportunity to do their work, even though some of these missionaries were discouragingly critical, or displayed an interest in native culture that baffled the colonizers. In turn, these missionaries were baffled too, scandalized by the greed of the colonists. Their alarm also perturbed their colleagues at home. Much to the dismay of the emperor Charles V, the pious and learned professor of Salamanca University, Francisco de Vitoria, delivered in 1539 a course of lectures to his students in which he developed seven grounds to condemn colonialism and seven to justify it (Böhm 1936). I shall not comment on the fact that in Vitoria's discourse the seven lean kine ate the seven fat ones and then disappeared into thin air, nor on the surprising detail that his (rather papist) 20th century commentator failed to notice this. The one point of interest is the perplexity of the time at the contrariety of the motivations which inspired its actions. It was a perplexity which, in the course of colonial history, emerged time and again, and more than once had a beneficial effect.

All the same, it is evident that colonial expansion began with greed and the lust for power rather than with a passionate curiosity to find out what the world looked like. And yet, a scientific interest in things and their nature was not foreign to it either. We find this interest in the case of a number of the early missionaries. It is also found among the seafarers and colonizers themselves. Columbus and Cabot were learned experts who had given ample thought to their objectives before they set out. Daring voyages had been made earlier in the middle ages. The Vikings had discovered (and occupied) Iceland, and they had visited Greenland and the American East coast, but they left no reports which contributed to the knowledge of the public. The 15th century voyagers did, and so did those of the 16th and 17th century. I do not know who were the first to keep log-books, but one thing is certain: in the 16th century the art of navigation began to develop into a science. Moreover, if these captains did not do so by their own initiative, their backers, the princes and merchants who equipped their vessels, instructed them to bring home all the information they could gather. These backers were eager for knowledge, primarily as an instrument for the acquisition of more and other forms of wealth, but this interest in knowledge had the merit that it carried the recognition of knowledge as something that is socially and economically useful. Yet, their curiosity would never have been satisfied if, in this same period, there had not arisen men who really were interested in things and the true nature of the cosmos, the astronomers who laid the foundations for better navigation, the physicists who constructed better instruments, and the mathematicians who could solve the more complicated problems presented by number and measure. In the 16th century, some such men came forward. One of the first of them was Copernicus. They were the men who would change the image of the world and revolutionize man's concepts of himself and of his universe. It started slowly, because they were only a few; but their numbers rapidly increased.

The mathematicians are of particular interest. In the thirteenth century, Leonardo of Pisa (he died ca. 1250) became acquainted with the great discovery of the Indian mathematicians, the decimal system and the annotation going with it. It might, at the time, have started a new development of mathematical science, in particular of arithmetics, but it did not. It is only in the 16th century that the threads are picked up where a thousand and more years earlier Diophantus had left them. Turnbull, in *The great Mathematicians*, mentions the names of Ferro as the initiator of the revival, and of Fontana, Cardan, Dürer, Copernicus, Stevin, and Galileo after him. The most outstanding, however, was the Scot Napier, Baron of Merchiston (1550-1617). In 1590 he struck upon a new thing: logarithms. "So clearly did he foresee the practical benefit of logarithms... that he deliberately turned aside from his speculations in algebra, and quietly set himself to the lifelong task of producing the requisite tables... The first tables appeared in 1614, and immediately attracted the attention of the mathematicians in England and on the continent – notably Briggs and Keppler" (Turnbull in Newman I: 123). At the time the mathematical world was already in full motion. Less than 25 years later Descartes' *Discourse on Method* appeared which laid the foundation of analytical geometry and "consolidated a position which made the differential calculus the inevitable discovery of Newton and Leibniz" (ibid.: 129).

It is a story of rapid and continuous growth, the result of a passionate devotion to their self-appointed task by a relatively small number of scholars fascinated by the charms of their science. A similar story could be told about the development in astronomy and physics. But the growth of mathematics was of decisive significance. Mathematics afforded the adequate means to express observations in terms of measure and number, and to compute the relations between quantities measured. A milestone in this development was the publication, in 1687, of Newton's *Principia*. Here "Newton demonstrated that, if [the] rule of gravitation is universally granted, it becomes the key to all celestial motions" (ibid.: 145). What is more, Newton could calculate the movements of these celestial bodies. Though problems remained – the moon in particular had some peculiarities of its own – Newton had produced definite proof that the logics of human reason were valid even where such august and distant objects were concerned as the celestial bodies. It was evident now that man could rely on his reason. And so it was understood by the leading spirits of the age.

The political conditions of the time gave additional ground for putting confidence in reason. In 1648 peace descended upon Europe. It was not an undivided peace; there were the Anglo-Dutch and the French wars to think of, but they had not that deep impact on civilian life as had the wars of religion, not to speak of those of the feudal lords. Prosperity increased, and with it the confidence grew that the interest of humanity would be greatly served if mankind would become willing to listen to the lessons of reason and accept reasonableness and rationality as its guidelines for action. All that was needed were enlightened leaders and thinkers. The time was nearby that the light of reason threatened to outshine that of the glory of God.

Yet, this was a development which men like Napier and Newton (and many others with them) could hardly have foreseen. They were religious men who never doubted that the Bible is the Word of God. Dr. Staples kindly called my attention to the fact that Napier was a millenarian who expected that his logarithmic tables could speed up his calculations in the field of Biblical numerology. And he added that Newton's theological work took him unto the same area! Nevertheless, once it had been demonstrated that both the universe and nature are founded on rational principles which human reason can discover by investigating their effects, reason necessarily took the place of theological speculation in all matters accessible to experiment and observation. Apparently, God had based all his work upon reason, and it was from reason that subsequent generations of scientists and philosophers expected guidance and progress.

3. The age of reason

Newton's computations confirmed that, in the conflict between the Church and the astronomers, Copernicus and Keppler had been right. The traditional, biblical worldview was, on this point, untenable. In itself, this encroachment on a thesis of traditional theology did not give cause for alarm. It did not affect religion on a point of specific importance to the salvation of the faithful. It was possible to agree with Copernicus and still to be a good Christian. Yet, the conflict on the biblical worldview also affected the infallibility of the Bible as the Word of God, and this might, in time, lead to serious consequences. No one who had read the works of Hobbes could ignore this.

Thomas Hobbes, scandalized by the woes unleashed by the wars of religion over Europe, had in his turn in his *Leviathan* (1651) scandalized his contemporaries by a grievous lack of respect for the Bible as the revelation of undoubted truth. He had not restricted himself to the remark, made more or less in passing, that the greater part of the Old Testament is of post-exilian origin. He had openly paid greater respect to reason than to revelation.

Opposing God's revelation in nature ("the Naturall Word of God") to that in the Scripture ("the Propheticall Word"), he argues that "we are not to renounce our Senses and Experiences nor (that which is the undoubted Word of God) our naturall Reason. For they are the talents which he hath put into our hands to negotiate, till the coming of our blessed Saviour" (1952: 286). The pious but fairly dysfunctional reference to "the coming of our blessed Saviour" poorly conceals that the ground of the author's ultimate concern lies not with Holy Writ, but with reason: to him the undoubted word of God. This in contrast to the "Propheticall Word of God", the Scripture. He makes no secret of his doubts of its validity:

> "How God speaketh to a man immediately, may be understood by those well enough, to whom he hath spoken; but how the same should be understood by another, is hard, if not impossible to know. For if a man pretend to me that God hath spoken to him supernaturally, and immediately, and I doubt of it, I cannot perceive what argument he can produce, to oblige me to believe it (ibid.: 287). And to drive the point home, he adds on the next page: "To say that he hath spoken to him in a Dream, is no more than to say that he dreamed that God spake to him".

The criticism was as outrageous as it was devastating. For his contemporaries, raised in unbounded respect of the Scripture as the source of all wisdom and truth, it was too much. Hobbes was decried as an atheist (which he was not) and a materialist (what, philosophically, could not be denied). When, some forty years later, Locke disputed Hobbes's political views, he did not even dare to mention the gentleman's name, so much had his challenging views become anathema to late 17th century Englishmen (Ashley 1958: 240).

Yet, the seed had been sown and it had fallen into fertile soil. The philosophers of the 18th century could no longer believe in a God who let the sun stand still upon Gibeon and the moon in the valley of Ajalon (Josh. 10: 12), a God who punishes unbelievers in hell and counts belief for righteousness. For many of them, belief in the living God of Israel made place for that in the God of Deism, a God who was Reason itself and had created this universe so wisely that it further could take care of itself. The eroding effects of this belief upon the old Christian tradition can best be illustrated by a few quotations from Adam Smith, mainly from his *Theory of Moral Sentiments* (1759). We begin with his comment on the nature of society.

> "Human society, when we contemplate it in a certain abstracted and philosophical light, appears like a great, an immense machine whose regular and harmonious movements produce a thousand agreeable effects. As in any other beautiful and noble machine that was the production of human art, whatever tended to render its movements more smooth and easy would derive a beauty from this effect, and, on the contrary, whatever tended to obstruct them would displease on that account; so virtue, which is, as it were, the fine polish to the wheels of society, necessarily pleases; while vice, like the vile rust which makes them jar and grate upon one another, is as necessarily offensive" (1948: 52).

In this fine machine everything has its proper place, and even the terrors of death and religion contribute to its perfection:

"the dread of death, the great poison to the happiness, but the great restraint upon the unjustice of mankind,... while it affects and mortifies the individual, guards and protects the society" (ibid.: 78). "That the terrors of religion should thus enforce the natural sense of duty was of too much importance to the happiness of mankind for nature to leave it dependent upon the slowness and uncertainties of philosophical researches" (ibid.: 192).

He then turns to the difference between the rules of nature and those of man.

"Thus man is by nature directed to correct in some measure that distribution of things which she herself would otherwise have made. She bestows upon every virtue and upon every vice that precise reward or punishment which is best befitted to encourage the one or to restrain the other. She... pays little regard to the different degrees of merit which they may seem to possess in the sentiments and passions of man. Man, on the contrary, pays regard to this only... The rules which [nature] follows are fit for her; those which [man] follows for him; but both are calculated to prompt the same great end – the order of the world and the perfection and happiness of human nature" (196/97).

The sequal to this laudatory passage makes it increasingly evident that to Smith the rules of man are, in the main, little more than a special category of those of nature.

"The produce of the soil maintains at all times nearly that number of inhabitants which it is capable of maintaining. The rich only select from the heap what is most precious and agreeable. They consume little more than the poor, and in spite of their natural selfishness and rapacity, though they mean only their own convenience, though the sole end which they propose from the labours of all the thousands whom they employ be the gratification of their own vain and insatiable desires, they divide with the poor the products of all their improvements. *They are led by an invisible hand* (italics mine) to make nearly the same distribution of the necessaries of life which would have been made had the earth been divided into equal portions among all its inhabitants, and thus, without intending it, without knowing it, advance the interest of the society, and afford means to the multiplication of the species. When Providence divided the earth among a few lordly masters, it forgot nor abandoned those who seem to have been left out of the partition. These last too enjoy their share of all its produces. In what constitutes the real happiness of human life, they are in no respect inferior to those who would seem so much above them. In ease of body and peace of mind, all the different ranks of life are nearly upon a level, and the beggar who suns himself by the side of the highway possesses that security which kings and knights are fighting for" (215).

"Nature has wisely judged that the distribution of ranks, the peace and order of society, would rest more securely upon the plain and palpable differences of birth and fortune than upon the invisible and often uncertain differences of wisdom and virtue... In the order of all those recommendations, the benevolent wisdom of nature is equally evident" (238).

This wisdom of nature fills the author's heart with adoration:

"This universal benevolence, how noble and general soever, can be the source of no solid happiness to any man who is not thoroughly convinced that all the inhabitants of the universe, the meanest as well as the greatest, are under the immediate care and protection of that great, benevolent and all-wise Being, who directs the movements of nature, and who is determined by his own unalterable perfections, to maintain in it at all times the greatest possible quantity of happiness" (248).

And to the consolation of the man in distress, our author adds the following counsel:

provided that he be convinced "that this benevolent and all-wise Being can admit into the system of his government no partial evil which is not necessary for the universal good, he must consider all the misfortunes which may befall himself, his friends, his society, or his country, as necessary for the prosperity of the universe, and therefore, as what he ought not only to submit himself to with resignation, but as what he himself, if he had known all the connexions and dependencies of things, would sincerely and devoutly to have wished for" (249).

It is highly probable that the reader who has gone through all these quotations feels more impressed by the author's self-righteousness than by his arguments; they seem more fit to explain Karl Marx's passionate atheism than anything. Nevertheless, in *Das Kapital*, a work for two thirds devoted to the abuses of capitalism and the injustice which the poor suffered from the hands of so many outwardly pious employers, Marx always speaks with respect of Adam Smith. Though it is true that this respect is shown primarily to the author of the *Wealth of Nations* (1776), it is equally true that the *Moral Sentiments* laid the philosophical foundations of the work which made Smith world-famous. The same ideas return, and the main difference is that Smith pays specific attention here to the factor labour. A man's labour, "the original foundation of all property", is here called his most sacred and inviolable right. "The patrimony of a poor man lies in the strength and dexterity of his hands; and to hinder him from employing this strength and dexterity in what manner he thinks proper without injury to his neighbour, is a plain violation of the most sacred property" (Smith 1948: 366). Such violations occur because labour has two prices, a natural price and a market price, and if the latter is to the detriment of the worker, it is only nature which can intervene by making labour supply scarcer. And the ways of nature are hard: if wages fall beneath a certain minimum, the death rate rises and the birth rate falls.

It is a theme to be taken up later by Malthus and Riccardo. To Adam Smith, this hardness of nature was the price to be paid for its benefits which, in his philosophy, prevail. A merit? Certainly not. As a matter of fact, the merits of *The Theory of Moral Sentiments* are small; we already said something about it on p. 126. Why, then, did we pay such elaborate attention to it? Simply, because in its very mediocrity it so marvellously mirrors the notions and sentiments of a period of critical significance in the history of our civilization, notions and sentiments which had a decisive influence on its later development. Four of these deserve further consideration: the admiration of the wisdom of nature and the aesthetic sentimentalism associated with it because they reflect the growth of the interest taken in things; the emphasis on human happiness, and the firm belief in individual freedom as the only workable panacea for all evils because of their enduring impact on the spiritual and social life of the western world.

The wisdom of nature is, of course, a perfectly unscientific concept. It is theological rather than philosophical; and theologically it is just shallow. One wonders what can be the origin of this pious admiration of an allwise nature directed by the kind cares of a benevolent Grandpa called God. Though inspired by reason and critical observation, this admiration cannot possibly be ascribed to the mere fact of the rationality of nature and universe. Rationality has no truck at all with benevolence and little more with wisdom. Besides, admiration is an affect, not a rational concept. And here lies, indeed, the explanation of this rather unscientific attitude: the delight 18th century people took in science and in the observation of living nature was not a purely intellectual delight but also – and very markedly so – an aesthetic delight. The 18th century is the period of the private collections of curiosities. Their owners never tired

275

of beholding their tropical shells, their crystals, their dried flowers, nuts and skeletons, and revelled at every new addition to their collection. The term curiosities is revealing. They were curious, these people, devoted readers of travel stories and deeply interested in the voyages of exploration which, in this century, were undertaken: the first, poorly equipped, by Roggeveen who discovered Easter Island; and later the so much better prepared expeditions by Cook and De Bougainville who brought back the most exciting news about the Pacific.

At the time, the science of biology had made its entry, and opened the eyes of many to the inexhaustible richness of nature's multiformity. More important still, biology also taught that in nature every form and organ has its particular function, and every new discovery opened up new vistas. People interested in the construction of things and the causality directing the phenomena of nature, saw their efforts rewarded by a rapidly increasing mass of data confirming that the universe is not ruled by blind chance or despotism, but by law and inner consistency. The functionality of it all, and of the organs of the living body in particular, persuaded them that some invisible hand, directed by wisdom, must be behind it, the hand of a Creator who was Reason incarnate. The marvels they beheld brought them to the adoration of an all-wise Supreme Being, whose cult concentrated on scientific activity more than on prayer. The second half of the 18th century sees an immense growth of the number of local learned societies, salons, and cercles des beaux arts whose members ardently discuss all the new discoveries in an atmosphere of honest admiration.

For their admiration of nature, Smith and his contemporaries had sound reason. We still have it today. But why sing the praise of nature's benevolence or – what comes to exactly the same – its Creator? Had they not really noticed that nature is cruel and heartless? If Smith had not, Malthus and Riccardo certainly did. True enough, it was some thirty years later that the former described the frightful consequences of overpopulation and the latter the iron law of wages, but the founding ideas of their expositions can be traced back to Smith's writings. He knew that the market-price of labour can fall well below its natural price, and plunge labourers into the barest poverty and even hunger. A deplorable development, certainly, but one which could only be remedied by the fall of the birth rate and a corresponding increase of the death rate, the inescapable consequences of dearth. Nature would take care of this. There is no denying it. Nature certainly would; not, however, because it is benevolent but because it is cold and cruel. Smith's eulogies of his Creator's supreme benevolence have a harsh overtone of insincerity. Yet, he believed in this benevolence. How could he? How could his contemporaries?

There is an alluring explanation for this in the structure of 18th century society. It was a stratified society which offered prospective members of the upper ten thousand an opportunity – to the minds of the successful a fair opportunity – for upward mobility. Was not James Cook the son of a gardener, Rousseau just a genial tramp? The élite of this society was for a not unimportant part a bourgeois élite, satisfied because it had achieved the realization of its ambitions, a place at the top of society in the company of nobility. They had earned themselves this place by self-discipline and the ardent use of their natural talents. Experience had taught them that study and discovery lead to honours, and the use of new knowledge to prosperity. To them, nature had certainly proved itself benevolent and they felt sure that anyone who followed their example of self-discipline and hard work might expect similar benefits.

The culture of the élite was a court culture. The elegance of the rococo style (still surviving in the music by Mozart and Telemann) as well as the specific sentimentality of the time, testify to this orientation towards court culture. The feelings the time invariably honoured were noble feelings. Benevolence, too, is such a noble feeling. Actually, benevolence is a royal prerogative. Only a king can be really benevolent. The members of the élite followed the royal example when they welcomed talented newcomers of humble origin into their circle. They felt themselves in tune with nature into which they had projected the benevolence in which they revelled. But, all the same, this act of projection impresses us as an act of *mauvaise foi*, of insincerity, the product of a bad conscience. They knew quite well that nature is cruel or, at the very least, indifferent to human happiness. Were they indifferent because they wished to be happy? Was not happiness to them the aim and destiny of all mankind? The analysis of these expectations can throw some light upon what looks like hypocrisy.

The theme of human happiness plays a remarkable and by no means unimportant part in the thought and life of the philosophers of the Enlightenment. On the face of it, their concern about happiness is a heritage of the past. The Christian religion had promised it in the form of eternal bliss as a reward to the faithful who had persevered to the end. For earthly life, however, Christendom held little in stock but suffering. The doctrine of salvation by faith alone and that of the vicarious suffering of Christ are solidly misunderstood when it is assumed that they are a safeguard against suffering. Even such strong defenders of the principle of *sola fide* as Luther and Calvin never thought like this. It is the Christian's plight to follow his redeemer in his suffering too, to bear his cross after him and to follow him in all humility and meekness of heart. It is the Christian's accepted part that he suffer in this world, and that what happiness he enjoys in it, is a pure grace that he has to receive in gratitude as an undeserved blessing. When the great theologians speak of happiness as man's ultimate destination, it is the happiness of eternal life they have in mind, not that on earth in which "ye shall have tribulation" (St. John 16: 33). And the happiness which man is allowed to pursue in this world is primarily that of knowing oneself to be at peace with God and men, far less that of prosperity which can only lead to temptation. It is good to keep this in mind when one comes across such remarkable statements as the one by St. Thomas that, by nature, man desires to be happy, and cannot desire not to be happy (quoted by Pieper, 1972: 110 f.).

Until the 17th century, Christendom has been deeply suspicious of prosperity and wealth. In the 18th century, however, this changes, first of all in circles affected by the philosophy of the Enlightenment. They do not deny that there is happiness in piety or in the expectation of eternal bliss, but when they speak of happiness it is of another kind: a happiness that is more limited, and in that limitation quantifiable. Thus Adam Smith in his eulogy of that "all-wise Being... who is determined by his own unalterable perfections, to maintain... at all times the greatest possible *quantity* of happiness" (above: 274). Without saying it in so many words – which would belie his unctuous eloquence – the kind of happiness he has in mind is primarily that of prosperity. Again, it is not said in so many words, but here is the place where the accent lies, just as it does in the American Declaration of Independence when it declares the pursuit of happiness the inalienable right of everyone.

The causes of this change in fundamental orientation are evident. The discoveries made by scientists and explorers had revealed a world full of marvel and promise. Besides, the improvements which they had wrought on tools and techniques had contributed substantially to economic progress and the increase of wealth. The expectation was justified that further exploration and research, combined with a rational approach to the difficulties which adversely affected the state of society, would afford the means to prosperity and continuous progress. It had become worth while to pay proper attention to the needs and affairs of this world, more than to those of after-life. Almost automatically the scientist's concern about the knowledge of things and their nature became associated with the search for wealth, on the one hand, with the idealism of those who insisted on the realizability of a better world, on the other. In the leading circles of society the secular interest in prosperity had gradually but consistently outrivaled that in salvation.

The philosophers of the age were wise enough not to define prosperity as a *summum bonum*. They knew that it is not. But they were well aware of its urgent desirability. Europe had lived through ages of war, misery and poverty. The 18th century brought signs of betterment in Britain, like the 17th had done in Holland. The philosophers had no doubts about the effective cause of this improvement: viz. the liberty which the members of the third estate had acquired to further their own interests. The rich fruits borne by the tree of civic freedom were convincingly evident. They were not the discovery made by Smith; everyone knew about it. On the pictures lavishly produced by the age, the tree of liberty is always represented as a tree laden with fruit. The bourgeois élite was exceedingly conscious that it was civic liberty that had brought her prosperity. She was deeply convinced that liberty, and liberty only, could mend the world's woes and increase its prosperity. What, in Smith's eulogies of the benevolence of nature, impresses us as hypocrisy, is, in truth, his considered persuasion that liberty is the law of nature which, if properly respected, will bring prosperity to that maximum of people that nature can feed. It is equally evident, however, that the individualism which finds its consummation in liberty, differs profoundly from that which emphasized the individual's responsibility to God. It is of a purely secular kind, just like the happiness which is pursued. The psychological attitude which first manifested itself with the Reformation had persisted, but under the cover of happiness its orientation had drastically changed from salvation to prosperity.

The belief in the happy prospects of liberty was not a persuasion of the better situated classes, it was shared with equal intensity by the less privileged groups of society, at least for as far as their members could afford to have an opinion on this point. One of those less privileged was Jean-Jacques Rousseau who became the great prophet of

278

freedom in France, and far beyond it. It can hardly be by chance that he was native of Geneva, the town where the responsibility of the individual had more ardently been preached than anywhere, the town also where Calvin's successor, Théodore de Bèze, had revived the old and in his time forgotten doctrine of the social contract (above: 117; Halbwachs 1943: Introduction). What Rousseau had kept of this heritage and brought with him to France was a thoroughly secularized form of the religious individualism of the Reformation, and a radicalized version of the social contract.

He had the same, supreme confidence in nature as the British philosophers of the time. In his *Discours sur l'Origine et les Fondements de l'Inégalité parmi les Hommes* (1755) Rousseau argued that in their primeval, savage state all men had been equal, all free to follow their natural inclinations. Trouble started once they associated in a society. Social differences progressively took the place of those innocent natural differences in strength, sex, and age which of old had existed. The first differences which originated were those by merit, followed by those in power, and finally by those by birth and wealth. With the growth of society freedom withered away with, as its final result, the situation bluntly formulated in the opening sentence of *Le Contrat social* (1762): *l'Homme est né libre, et partout il est dans les fers*: Man is born free and everywhere he is in chains.

In this later work, he stated that this adverse development had not been necessary. The original social contract did not consist of a transfer of individual rights to one chosen person, like Hobbes had taught, but of the voluntary submission of everyone's person and power under the lead of the *volonté générale,* the will of the people as expressed and defined in the public meeting attended by all the members of the society concerned, none excluded. In this meeting, matters of principle were discussed, and the administration of the regulations agreed upon in the meeting commissioned to elected executives. The public meeting, expressing the general will, is the true sovereign and legislator, and only a return to the sovereignty of the people can restore freedom and the happiness of that peace and order which are man's natural heritage.

Rousseau rejected the idea of a parliament composed of elected representatives. Election necessarily led to the creation of new inequalities and would encroach once again upon the people's rights and sovereignty. It was a public duty and every man's personal responsibility to attend the people's public meetings. Only thus could the *volonté générale* be adequately realized. He granted that in the society of his days not everyone was sufficiently prepared to bear the responsibilities of his active participation, and in this context he pleaded the necessity that education should be geared to this end, a subject to which he devoted his *Émile, ou de l'Éducation*, which appeared in the same year.

Rousseau's ideas were bright, but they were anything but practical. A public meeting of his design might be realizable in a Swiss canton (from where the idea originated) but it is hard to see how the *volonté générale* could be realized in a country of the extent of France. Surprisingly, no one seemed to mind. Even the fact that, in the *Discourse*, Rousseau had marked down private property as one of the causes of inequality did not damage the popularity of the ideas developed in the *Social Contract*.

279

Its outstanding merit was that it had given flesh and bones to the view that social life did not exclude freedom and equality, but could thrive on them.

What appealed to the readers was the promise of freedom. To the merchant and industrial class it meant freedom from government restrictions and obsolete guild regulations, the freedom to pursue their business under no other economic laws than those of nature. To the gentry, it implied freedom from the obligations ensuing from traditional patron-client relations which had lost their original meaning because the relation between patron and client had lost its character of a person-to-person relation. The landed gentry, if sufficiently wealthy to be of any use as patrons, had their main residence in town. They had not, like their grandparents, grown up with their tenants. In as far as they knew them personally, their acquaintance lacked intimacy. Something similar had happened in town with the relations between employer and employees. The new industrial factories attracted personnel from everywhere. They were newcomers to town and had no personal relations whatsoever with their employer. What the employers, the merchants, the gentry wished was to pursue their proper ends without being impeded by regulations or personal obligations which they experienced as irrelevant to their purpose.

What this freedom meant to the working classes is less certain. They had not the opportunity nor the learning to express themselves in writing. They had, without doubt, an interest in more security, but they had experienced that the old securities were less and less expedient. They were increasingly willing to change the poverty of life in the country for an uncertain future in town or anywhere else. I am not so sure that we can call it a longing for more freedom as prevailed among the members of the better situated classes. The fact, however, that they had become relative strangers to their employers and patrons could not escape them; they could no longer rely on them. Labour relations had turned from personal relations into business relations in which no other rules are valid than those of minimal ethics (above: VII.2, in particular p. 138 f.). Consequently, the labour relation is presented as a sales contract by which the labourer sells "the dexterity and the strength of his hands" (Smith) to his employer. According to this conception, an employee is no longer a servant but the seller of a certain amount of strength and dexterity in payment of the wages offered to him. The Dutch terms for employer and employee are illuminating: work-giver and work-taker. On the labour market they meet like traders do, as equals who negotiate the price to be paid for their wares.

That the market mechanism worked against the interests of the unorganized labourers in the 18th and 19th century is not at issue here. The labourers' organization in unions and their successful struggle for economic power are achievements of the 19th and 20th century. What is at issue here is the freedom which the rules of minimal ethics allow the contracting parties. They are free to do whatever they like, provided the terms of the contract are duly met. It was this freedom that the leading classes of the age were craving for. New knowledge had opened ever-widening vistas of new opportunities for self-realization in the discovery of the world, the appliance and improvement of new techniques, and in the accumulation of wealth and the increase of personal comfort. But freedom is a tricky concept. Rousseau had already pointed out that freedom lays a responsibility on the citizen. Immanuel Kant, the last of the philosophers of the Enlightenment, gave substance to the implications of freedom.

In his *Kritik der praktischen Vernunft* (1788), Kant argued that freedom is pre-eminently a moral concept. Freedom imposes the duty to fulfil voluntarily the obligations of the categorical imperative. This is the law of freedom, *das Gesetz der Freiheit*. With Kant, the reality of the human conscience brought – via the dialectics of freedom – the European form of individualism back home to its point of departure: i.e. the knowledge about personal responsibility and the willingness to bear it. There is one difference when compared with the past. This responsibility is no longer a responsibility of the individual to his God. It has become autonomous, a responsibility to one's personal conscience, and only in second place one to society or mankind. God is no longer the ever present participant in the discussion of the soul with its conscience. He has been relegated to the background as the founding idea of Reason and Universe as such. He can be invoked, but this is not a necessity. It is the individual who decides after having consulted his conscience.

Two revolutions marked the birth of the new civilization, the American and the French. Whereas the latter confined itself to summarizing its leading ideas in a sweeping battlecry, that of Liberty, Equality, Fraternity, the American revolution gave a more considered formulation of its motivations in the Declaration of In-dependence: "We hold these truths to be self-evident, that all men are created equal, that they are endowed by their Creator with inherent and unalienable rights, that among these are life, liberty, and the pursuit of Happiness".

I can hardly assume that the writer of the text from which I quoted had a special intention in writing happiness with an initial capital letter, thus honouring happiness above life and liberty. Yet, it certainly is symbolic of the hopes that warmed the hearts of the leaders of the revolution. Progress was to remain the American ideal throughout the two centuries which have since elapsed. And not just the American; though in Europe, where liberty was more in danger than in the United States, the emphasis was primarily upon freedom.

Not all the leading motivations of the new civilization were made explicit by the leaders of these revolutions. We miss every reference to that great hobby of the leading classes of the late 18th century: the search for knowledge. It was destined to become generalized among all strata of society. But they were explicit on the rights of the individual: his freedom, his right to life (which implies the recognition of the individual's person) and the equality of all individuals amongst themselves. The French revolution added fraternity as an ideal, but fraternity soon fell victim to the violence of the revolution itself. And the Creator, so emphatically mentioned in the Declaration of Independence, remained aloof. Uncertainty about God entered upon the scene with the first philosopher of the Enlightenment, and this uncertainty persists until the present day. The legacy which modern times owe the period of Enlightenment are, next to a passionate interest in things, the secularization of the expectation of happiness, a strong belief in the individual's liberty to define his own ends, and the conviction that all men are equals. Wirh these things in mind we now must turn to the present day and the problems which development, progress and prosperity brought upon us.

XV

A Market Society

Enlightenment and the revolutions it inspired laid the groundwork for modern civilization. How it grew on this foundation and the difficulties its participants had to overcome before it reached its present grandeur, is not our concern. We are interested in the results, in the individual's place in his society and his relations with his fellow-men, in the basic facts of modern man's way of life, and in the existential problems which threaten the happiness so avidly pursued during these two hundred years. What are the characteristics of modern man's ethics and the contributions of his morality to human well-being? And what does modern civilization offer man in exchange for the spiritual security afforded by religion, his one-time mainstay which has subsequently been continuously undermined by science and philosophy, if not by the joys of the good life itself?

1. Human relations in a society of relative strangers

Hobbes, contemplating the state, summarized his fears and hopes, his distrust and his reliance, in the ambiguous statement that the commonwealth is "that great Leviathan or rather (to speak more reverently)... that mortall God in which we owe under the Immortall God, our peace and defence" (1952: 132). But for the unctuous phrasing, the words could have been written today: the modern welfare state is frighteningly powerful, watching over every corner of the realm and controlling every form of activity. A monstrous leviathan indeed, but also a mortal god who provides relief, medical care, housing facilities and food for the poor and the infirm, and offers security to all in a way which induces them to praise the freedom they enjoy under its mighty wings. Why, of all things, do they associate freedom with the modern state, that incurable busy-body which interferes in every form of public life, and even compels all the members of the society to report annually on the exact amount of their income and the cash value of their property?

When they commend the freedom they enjoy in the modern welfare state, they apparently do not think of the freedom granted them by the state vis-à-vis this 'mortal god' – which gives small cause for psalmody – but of the freedom the state guarantees the individual in his relations with other individuals and bodies. The state safeguards the observance of the rules of minimal ethics, the rules incumbent on the social traffic between relative strangers. Like traders, relative strangers interact as equals, always free to break off negotiations, and subject to no other obligations than those of being honest in their dealings, and truthful in fulfilling their contractual obligations. These are the hard obligations which, if their disregard causes financial loss, can be enforced under the authority of the state by a court decision. Next to these there is a third obligation, the one which prescribes decency of behaviour in interaction. It is a soft obligation; disregard simply disrupts the interaction. It has no further consequences, unless the disregard of good manners constitutes a punishable offence, but this is not at stake here.

The implications of minimal ethics were discussed in section 2 of Ch. VII where it was pointed out that they are founded on respect for the other's person, and ultimately on that for the universe. This respect implies that the 'other' must be allowed to be himself for as long and to the extent that he does not infringe on other persons' rights. The opportunity to be oneself is a great good. We found (above: 129) that it is one of the two basic components of the beneficent experience of feeling oneself at home. That the second component, that of knowing oneself welcome, can be woefully lacking in the market place of modern life, is another matter which will occupy us later on. What counts is, in the present context, the freedom to be oneself. This freedom must be respected by the other. It is also an important principle of legislation. Freedom of speech and press are guaranteed by the law. Other liberties are safeguarded by the absence or the non-appliance of legal prescriptions. Modern man's freedom to go where he likes, and the sexual freedom he enjoys are relevant cases. All these different kinds of freedom modern man owes to the fact that he constitutes part of a society of relative strangers which is supervised by a state which has the will and power to safeguard the observance of the basic rules of minimal ethics. It has been the state's task since its first beginnings and it has greatly promoted the development of society. The institution of a good and sufficiently powerful judiciary made an important contribution to the increase of trade by the protection of credit obligations (cf. above: 95, 133 f.).

Quite another question is to what extent modern society is really a society of relative strangers and what this implies for the extent and intensity of man's social relations. In the field of economics there can be little doubt on this point. Modern economic relations are, by nature, contractual relations. This also holds true of that socially important sector of economic life, i.e. labour relations. The contents of a labour relationship are determined by contracts which are the results of negotiations between the representatives of the workers and their employers. The negotiations give substance to the view that labour relations are founded on the market principle. It is common usage to speak of a labour market. Here the labourer sells the use of his ability and power for a stipulated number of hours a week to the highest bidder or to the otherwise, to him, most convenient employer. In the theory behind this view, a theory on which Marx sided with Adam Smith, labour is presented as a commodity which is for sale. The sociologist, however, necessarily questions to what extent this reduction of labour from a personal involvement to a market commodity presents a true picture of reality.

An argument that pleads against it is the fact that linguistic usage – which so often mirrors reality with greater acuity than political or theoretical dogma – invariably describes a labourer's acceptance of a labour contract as his entering into the *service* of a certain firm. The word service implies more than the performance of a fixed amount of specified work. It suggests a certain amount of personal involvement and dedication to work. And, indeed, in the practice of labour performance they are rarely wholly absent, often even given to a considerable degree. Nevertheless, this same linguistic usage has one peculiarity that is noteworthy. It never or hardly ever speaks of the service of any specified person, but of the service of an (impersonal) firm. Even a private secretary does not usually say that she is private secretary to Mr. So-and-So, but private secretary to the directorate of that-and-that firm or department. The difference may seem minute, but it is symptomatic of the trend to avoid personal service. If service is rendered, it is to a business or interest, not to a person. The service of an affair is anyone's free choice, a dedication inspired by his own will and interest. The service of a person is either a matter of love or of bondage.

Personal service for other than personal reasons is taboo in western Europe since the French revolution. It constitutes part of a patron-client relation which is rejected. Social scientists are allergic on this point (above: 121). Nevertheless, personal service did not disappear all at once in 1789. It even survives today in what we now call 'home help'. The term is indicative of the change that has taken place. The home help is not called a servant but a help or aid, and the relation – originally an authority relation – is wrapped up in courtesy. The authority relation has given way to one of (relative) equality ruled by respect for the other one's person. Employer and employee are equally respected.

We can see the same thing in industry. The modern employee not only expects that he will be treated humanely and that, where possible, his personal interests will be taken into account, he also demands that he will be consulted on matters concerned with the performance of his tasks. He may have entered the service of the firm, but this does not make him a servant. He is a fellow-worker whose relation with the firm is as much a business relation as that of the director. If difficulties arise, these difficulties must be settled not by a personal decision of the director, but by an impersonal regulation drafted after good, common consultation, and binding on all those concerned and not on any person in particular. Impersonal regulations more and more take the place of personal decisions. They indicate the substitution of authority relations by contractual obligations between equals, obligations which are subject to the rules of minimal ethics. All that remains of personal elements in the labour relation is the (soft) obligation to observe kindness and decency in interpersonal contacts. They are important today in a manager's relations with his employees, and they are symptomatic of the depersonalization of a labour relation which broke away from the bondage of an authority relation.

The bondage of the employee to the firm in which he works has been loosened in many ways. Important is his liberation from spatial limitations. Until the present century, employees (and directors!) had a standing interest in living close to their place of work. Modern means of communication have changed this. Today, two miles is nearby, and even five miles is still a short distance. Many members of the personnel are commuters who live at a distance of between ten and fifty miles from their work. This implies that anyone who wishes to change his job is less inhibited than formerly by the distance between house and work. He has to travel anyway. Labour mobility has become easier. More important socially is the fact that a worker has few contacts with his fellow-workers outside his place of work. He may have one or two personal friends among them, but he can afford to be a relative stranger, if not an *anonymus*, to most of them. The work has become a more or less isolated part of anyone's social life. Home-life and business-life are strictly separated, and this not only materially but also spatially. Most workers live in two different worlds alternately.

An interesting feature is the worker's partial anonymity among his fellow-workers. Anonymity is typical of life in a big city. It is not merely a natural consequence of overcrowding, it is cultivated. One only has to look at the people sitting in front of a pavement café to ascertain that the visitors prefer to remain strangers to one another. Personal contacts are carefully avoided. There may be one or two who wish otherwise, but they rarely get a chance. They have to follow the general pattern of keeping aloof. It is a pattern of behaviour common to most pleasure seekers. They do not go out to meet other people but to amuse themselves either alone or in the company of those whom they selected for that purpose. Quite a number of establishments offering entertainment are adapted to it. A movie theatre guarantees anonymity almost automatically. Many restaurants are so dimly lighted that it is impossible to recognize the occupants of more distant tables. When going out, it is good form to keep to oneself.

It is the same with travelling. People travel a great deal today, preferably abroad; but they make few contacts on their perigrinations. They may have a couple of satisfactory encounters with compatriots on a campsite, but that is about all. Even when there is no language barrier they hardly ever meet any of the inhabitants of the towns or the villages which they visit. They do not travel to meet people, but for sightseeing or to visit musea. In the hotels where they stay their anonymity is respected; the visitor can have all the information he asks for, but in principle he is left to himself. He is expected to appreciate this as, indeed, he usually does. Modern travellers are lonely wanderers. They differ widely from the travellers of the 17th and 18th century who never eschewed contacts with other guests in the inns where they passed the nights. The *table d'hôte* is a thing of the past.

Modern man may appreciate his privacy and often even his anonymity, but he is as much in need of social contacts as anyone. He finds these, primarily, in the town or village of his residence, unless his work is of the kind that makes elaborate contacts with others a necessity as happens to be the case with the newspaper reporter, the politician, the clergyman, and the sales agent. However, these are a minority, and their ways of life cannot give the right answer to the question of how the average man manages to satisfy his need for social contacts. If he were inclined to settle in the neighbourhood of the place where he was born, there would hardly be a problem. But he often is not, at least in this country. This implies that those who stay see many old friends leave. This need not be the end of the friendship. Distance can be easily bridged by car. The fact, however, that friendships thus get scattered over a wide area corrodes their functionality.

The combination of the European custom of neolocal marriage with increased mobility and the love of travel, induces many young couples to look for lodgings in another town or suburb than that of either of their parents. Sometimes they must find them at the place of their work, a must for shopkeepers and some of the members of the professions. More often they choose a place at some distance from their work (young people do not mind distance so much), a place that is new to both, as if they wish to express that, by now, they start a new life of their own. They enter the town or suburb as strangers. There is no one to welcome them although, when they are fixing up their home, a kind neighbour may occasionally offer them a cup of coffee.

For newcomers who have their work elsewhere it takes quite some time before they can feel themselves members of the local community. Contacts develop slowly and during the first years they themselves do fairly little to further them. The weekends are often passed with parents or old friends. They also consider the possibility of removing to another place. Why bother about making friends when you have not decided to stay? Similar considerations induce the local people to be rather reluctant to welcome the newcomers. More recent settlers in the locality may be more complaisant than the members of the local establishment (cf. Elias and Scotson's study *The Established and the Outsiders*) but this does not alter the fact that the newcomers are strangers, and as such have to prove their worth. The best opportunities are the membership of local sporting clubs, of a church, a political party, or regular visits to a popular pub. Once there are children and the wife stops working, the process accelerates. Children create ever new opportunities for contacts. As soon as they go to school and become members of their own junior clubs, they force their parents to stay at home during the weekends and pay more continuous attention to the affairs of the local community. By then there is no longer a question of leaving the place. The couple has become fully integrated in the life of the local community.

However, one should not think too highly of this integration, nor of that of the community as such. Most members of the community have their work and concomitant loyalties elsewhere. A fairly large number are newcomers, not wholly decided about staying or going. Even those born locally, members of the establishment, have part of their loyalties outside the local community. Everyone has his social and family relations spread out over a fairly large area. The economic interests of the members are divergent and for the better part not connected with the local community. It is a living community, and as a political unit it is interested in housing, parks development, entertainment and living commodities rather than in economic development. The social life of the group is a matter of overlapping circles, some based on religious or political enrolment, others on interest in certain arts or sports; an important binding element is that of approximately equal age. Each may have personal friends in more than one or two of these circles, friends with whom they share common social interests but not interests in business. They often meet, celebrate one another's birthday and look after one another's children when the parents are away on a short holiday. Also, when a housewife is sick, a nearby friend may step in to assist in the household and keep an eye on the children. It is all very comfortable and friendly, but the relations are not too stable. The interests they have in common are not really binding, and may change after a time. Besides, when the children grow up and leave their parental home, their parents, too, may think of departing. The house is too big and a flat somewhere in town, or rooms in a service flat may become more attractive. They will, in time, find new friends there whom they like, with whom they exchange visits, and all this without committing themselves too much. The living community is to those who are socially active and know how to participate in its life, a fairly comforting and pleasant society, but it is not enduring. In difficulties one may expect sympathy and some first aid from fellow residents, but no solutions to the real problems which arose. To that end the common interests are of a too superficial nature. The universe of the one differs too much from that of the other to make the welcome to one's own universe, how cordially offered, very effective. Differences and distance are quite real.

The one enduring unit is the nuclear family. Though it can be disbanded by divorce, it tends to be a fairly lasting and also a very close community. If there are difficulties within the family these are taken seriously, certainly if there are children. Often the expert advice of a marriage counsellor or a psychologist or psychiatrist is sought. The family tie is appreciated as essential to happiness. Its members share one another's lives. Spatially they are close together for many hours of the day, well separated from others by a solid door with a safety lock. No one has entrance except by ringing the bell. Besides, it is good form to let this be preceded by a telephone call to enquire whether a visit is welcome. The telephone is an ideal means of communication. It bridges distance without removing it. The introductory call also has the merit that it enables the receiving family to be met in the condition in which it prefers to be seen by others, a few very intimate friends excepted. With regard to all others, a mild aloofness is cultivated. The family is often alone, by itself. This does not mean that the outside world is ignored. It is allowed to enter via the television. They peep at it from a distance, from the well sheltered niche called home where each is allowed to be himself.

The family is also an enduring unit. More distant relatives may be fairly neglected, but the ties between parents and children, between brothers and sisters persist. Everyone can rely on them. It is not only that, in case of sickness, a mother or mother-in-law may come over to assist in the household. The family is also a mainstay when real troubles crop up. A son or daughter who gets into difficulties, who loses his or her job, is widowed, or returns from somewhere without having a place to stay, knows that there is still a welcome with his or her parents or siblings and expects to find a bed ready there. This does not mean that the family can give more than temporary assistance or is able to provide a definite solution to the difficulties. It means that there is a place of belonging on which to fall back in distress. The socially more or less successful, of whom we have spoken so far, rarely need turn to their

288

family of origin for such comfort. They can find it at home. There are many others, however, who are socially less well-off, who have few friends, a broken family life, or no family at all, and they pass most of their days in loneliness. There is the lonely crowd of the big cities to think of, as well as the numerous mentally sick who, by definition, are maladjusted. All they have is – if they have them at all, that is – these few family members who can give them some sense of belonging, of being part of a world which, to them, appears both far and hostile.

It is not that these unlucky people are not cared for. Everyone is cared for in a welfare society. If he is unemployed, sick, mentally disturbed or the victim of some sort of accident or calamity, he has a right to assistance, either financial or personal. The humiliation of charity is spared him. Moreover, the assistance given is always professional and, as such, many times more efficient than anything good-willing relatives or friends could possibly do for the sufferer. There is only one thing amiss with this assistance, and this is exactly that it is professional. To the professional, however kind his demeanour and however thoughtful his treatment, the applicant or patient is primarily a case. There is no tie of belonging between him and the aided person, whatever his devotion to his work. The inmate of a ward, the patient in an asylum can be frightfully lonely in spite of all the kindness devoted to him by the personnel. When it is visiting hour they hope that a friend or relative will come to see them. The same applies to the patient in a hospital. They are all longing for someone who belongs to them.

The professionalization of all sorts of personal care is a technical and economic necessity today. Yet, it weighs on our consciences. It is not so much because we are unwilling to bear the burdens which, in earlier days, were part of every man's life. Technically, the patient is better off in professional hands. The trouble is that it makes our own ways of life so much more comfortable. Often (not always!) the time spent on visiting the patient is a trifle when compared to the trouble of having to care for him day and night at home. We know this and go cheerfully to the hospital whenever we manage to break away. For the same reason we pay occasional visits to a hospitalized friend. Yet, there are altogether too many people in wards and hospitals who hardly ever receive visits. We all know this, but there are only a few kind-hearted women and men who find the time and the courage to pay visits to the utterly lonely. Most of us agree that a pastor (again a professional) does it better. We are willing to give more of less liberal grants to charitable institutions for such and similar purposes. Yet, what volunteer visitors do is admitting pitiable people to their own universe, whereas our charity serves to keep them apart from us. Our money is conscience money, a matter of minimal ethics.

Thus the practice of natural ethics remains mostly confined to the small circle of family and more intimate friends. It is of some interest to compare our social interaction with friends and relatives with that typical of primitive culture. They have much in common. We too give small presents to our friends; when we pay them a visit we bring flowers or sweets, more or less in exchange for the food and the drinks we expect. On birthdays, too, we give small presents. Yet, there is one remarkable difference. We already hinted at it on p. 102. In primitive society valuable presents are exhanged between related but distant family groups exclusively, small presents between friends and befriended relatives who do not make part of the small family unit, whereas between members of the small family unit every kind of formal gift-giving is blatantly absent. In modern society gift-exchange is confined to friends and close relatives. But note the difference: most gifts are small but if valuable gifts are presented it is to members of one's own small family unit. Moreover, it is not done informally, but formally and openly. There are fixed occasions when gift-giving is due: a birthday, a marriage, and the celebration of Christmas or Santa Claus. On birthdays and wedding ceremonies the exchange is indirect (with postponed return) and personal. At Christmas and Santa Claus it is direct and combined with folkloristic usage which affords a limited degree of anonymity. The rule that the rich (the parents) give more than the poor (the children) is well observed.

The difference between primitive and modern society raises a problem. Why can the former afford to abstain from formal gift-exchange within the small family-unit and why does the family-unit in modern society indulge in it, sparing neither cost nor trouble to turn the exchange into a really festive occasion? There can be only one answer. In primitive society there is no worry about the family. It is always there and always sufficiently great and powerful to see its members through all their troubles. In modern society, the family unit is the last stronghold of unquestioned solidarity, the one enduring unit upon which one can rely. All other social units are transitory or unobliging. Modern man's social life is often widely ramified, but always diffuse and crumbled. The family is the one exception. There is a clear need to strenghten its coherence and solidarity by emphazing its firmness and constancy: 'Let us not forget that we belong together, we against all the others. The outside world, even when it seems kind, is never to be trusted'.

2. A competitive society

The American and the French revolution were emphatic on the point of legal and social equality. How this equality had to be implemented has constituted a never ending bone of contention once the prerogatives derived from noble birth had been abrogated. The dispute rages up to the present day. On one point, however, there is a fair degree of unanimity, at least so far as the principle is concerned. It is that equality aims first and foremost at equality of chances and opportunities: equal chances for everyone to develop his personality and talents to the full, and equal opportunities for everyone to compete for the highest positions in society. The reference to the highest positions in society is of interest. It makes clear that modern egalitarianism, accepting the existence of certain social differences, is something of a compromise. It no longer denies the necessity or inevitability of such differences, but contents itself with insisting on making every position – and it is always the highest which are explicitly mentioned – accessible to everyone. Full social mobility is the best safeguard for the free and complete development of talents and personality.

The full development of talents and personality is a noble aim. It is the best thing one can do for the individual. It is also to the benefit of society. The development of all talents necessarily results in rapid progress. It opens up new fields of discovery and economic enterprise, it favours the growth of civilization and creates new opportunities for greater material well-being and happiness. Equal chances for everyone is a most powerful means for a rich and rapid development of culture and society. Yet, a more philosophically minded egalitarian might have difficulty in accepting this. The development of talents and personality must enable everyone to compete for the highest positions in society, that is to become unequal to others! Does not this turn equal chances for all into an instrument of inequality? Of course it does. Actually, the use of equality to attain inequality is one of the basic contradictions of modern civilization. It pervades all our cultural activities. In the following pages this point will be elucidated with the help of a concise analysis of our games and of our systems of education.

The space which the daily newspaper devotes to sports and games is an unmistakable sign of the interest attached to these by the general public. Matches are public events, and the great eye-catchers of our television programs. Millions and millions of people pass hours and hours watching matches, either on the field or in an armchair in front of the television screen. Most of them also participate as performers in one or two lines of sports themselves. Besides, practically everyone takes part in the more homely games played with children and friends. Games and sports take up a large part of modern man's leisure hours. They are of such vital interest to him that everywhere governments have accepted the organization of public provisions for sports and matches as a duty incumbent on national as well as local authorities.

The interest in sports and games is one of the most conspicuous traits of modern civilization. It has been steadily on the increase since World War II, a further development of a process that began roundabout the beginning of the present century. Huizinga, writing at the end of the thirties, notes that the practice of sports has increased considerably since the final quarter of the 19th century (1938; *in* V.W.: V 228), but complains that sports are taken too seriously nowadays. The complaint is surprising; Huizinga himself had always insisted that a game must be played seriously, a combination of contrasts which had enabled him to demonstrate that elements of play pervade the whole cultural history of mankind (1933). He found these dialectics in many cultural forms, in primitive ritual as well as in some aspects of modern economy. It is these dialectics which make his *Homo Ludens* such a fascinating book. They are also its fundamental weakness; the borderline between earnest and play time and again evaporates in the mist, and with it a definite answer to the question what to understand by the terms 'game' and 'play'. On this point we need a definite answer, an answer which enables us to differentiate between a game and a ritual, a match and a war, between playing and gambling on the stock-market, phenomena which are confounded rather than distinguished in Huizinga's line of thought. It is evident that we shall never come to a clear understanding of these differences unless we first introduce the notion of 'intent'. To what intent do we, does mankind play? Why do we play games?

It is not a difficult question; everyone knows the answer: games are for recreation.

The game serves the refreshment of body and mind. The word is illuminating: to re-create, to make anew, actually to make a new man of us. Equally outspoken is the Dutch term *vermaak*, from *vermaken*, to remake. *Zich vermaken* means to amuse oneself, litt. to remake oneself. But *vermaken* is also said of the trousers of an older son, which an economizing mother 'remakes' to fit her younger son. It is a reshaping. This is exactly what a game does to the minds of the participants in a game, as well as to those of the onlookers at an interesting match. The game re-places them all in another world, the world of the game. A game, then, is like a holiday, an occasion to visit another world than that of everyday life.

By now the characteristics of the game can be fitted into a meaningful context. The game creates another world, one which the imagination has staked off from the real world. It can be a tennis court, a football field, or a board, as in playing the royal game of 'goose'. Furthermore, a task is set: to kick the ball into the goal, to be the first to pass the finish, or whatever. But, above all, there are rules which must be strictly observed. The rules of a game are its essence. A 'foul' must be immediately punished or, at the very least, corrected. Whoever cheats is out. There is no place for pity in a game. If one party is decidedly stronger than the other, the stronger can be submitted to a handicap, an additional rule, but the rules must be observed anyway. Games are of many kinds: board games, field games, card games, etc. Winning the game can be a matter of dexterity and stamina as in sports, of chance as in games at dice, of superior cleverness as in chess, or of a combination of chance and cleverness as in bridge. But whatever the rules and techniques, every game is so arranged that at the outset all the participants have equal chances. Besides, they are all subject to the same, i.e. equal, rules which can neither be ignored nor changed. At the end of the game, however, equality is definitely superseded. There are only losers and winners, sometimes as many losers as winners, at other times one winner and all the others losers, but there are no games with more winners than losers. On this point games are as hard as their rules.

Solo games are only seemingly an exception. Playing patience, certain rules must be followed. Sometimes it works and the game comes out, more often it does not. Of course, the patience player has ample opportunity to cheat. However, there is no satisfaction in coming out by cheating. The fun is in winning by observing the rules honestly. The rules of a game do not come from outside, but from inside. The game *is* the rules, and it loses its interest when the rules are neglected.

There is a perplexing likeness between a game and an individual's relations to his world. The game imposes a task and it prescribes a number of inexorable rules which must be followed by all the participants. One might object that in the real world it is sometimes quite different. In the real world we always have to do with cheaters. In the game they are immediately ruled out. It is in fact an ideal world, and this in more than one respect: all the participants have equal chances and are subject to equal rules. It is a world as the world should be. But it also is a world which is like the real world: at the end of the game there are only losers and winners, often more losers than winners. There are even games which make the likeness between the game and the world specific. A good case is that of the unholy game of monopoly. It presents a shocking picture of high capitalism but, whatever the participants' political credo, they all indulge passionately in the hard practice of buying, selling and extortion which the rules provoke.

Every game must be played seriously, if not passionately. Though a game is by definition not serious, not real, it must be played both seriously and realistically, just as if there were no 'as if'. The game must be played with a dedication equal to that which we devote to our tasks in the real world. Yet, there is one difference. The difficulties we are up to in a game are exciting or even thrilling, those which confront us in the real world can be and often are worse, namely agonizing and frightening. At the moment a game turns from being thrilling into being agonizing or frightening, it forfeits its character of being a true game. This happens with gambling for big money. The gambler is an immoral character who abuses the innocence of the game for improper gain. Though little can be done against it, it is rejected as immoral. Losing may be experienced as painful, but must be kept within limits which do not affect the 'as if' character of the game which is the basis of its recreational value.

Before we try to define that recreational value somewhat more exactly we must dwell for a moment on a category of players who are not gamblers, and yet suffer more severely than the amateur players when they lose. These are the professionals for whom game-playing is a business. They are not true players but the servants of the recreation of the public who pay them. We might have omitted them from our considerations altogether, if mention had not been made of a category of really true players who have comparable difficulties with bearing their loss as a professional necessarily has. These are the young children. They are encouraged to participate in all sorts of games in order to keep them busy and actively engaged, but also to teach them sportiveness, in particular to behave with honesty and to bear their loss in good humour. It is very hard on a child. In a way, every child is a professional. The world in which he lives is not (yet) the real world. He is still protected against it. The child's real world is that of play and games. How could he be expected to be a good loser? He will learn it in time. The more he becomes engaged in the real world, the more he learns to appreciate the innocuous character of his games. And he will play with as much gusto as before.

We all play with gusto, but why? Why do we feel re-created by it? The symbolism of the game is evident. We act out our relation with our world under the condition that that world is as it should be. Every time we begin as equals, act as equals, and end as winners or losers. What we hope of the game is what we do hope of our world: that we shall win, that we shall defeat the others. The game expresses what is essential in our social life: competition. It cannot be by chance that competition is essential in sport, that anyone who joins a tennis or hockey club just for fun, has to participate in one competition after another between his own club and various other ones. And it cannot be by chance either that competition is exactly what traders do on the market, which they enter as one another's competitors. The rules of the market are as inexorable as the rules of the game. They stood and stand as the paradigmatic model for minimal ethics, the ethics of a society of relative strangers. The fact that the competitive game is our chosen means of re-creation, the means that makes us feel happier, is as significant as it is alarming. It implies that we have swallowed the whole system, hook, line and sinker. Its essentials amuse us more than anything. Intuitively we refuse to accept this. Is this how we are? And is this our goal when we educate our children? We must have a closer look at this.

The picture we have of ourselves and of our ways of educating children is more benign. When a baby is born its parents surround it with every possible care. At a very early age they take out an education policy to safeguard the child's future. The baby is really positively welcomed. Only, it is not like a savage baby laid naked into its mother's arms to enjoy the soft warmth of her equally naked body and to be fed from her breast every time that it whines, but put aside into a cradle which stands, preferably, in a room apart. It is a good room and a good cradle of course, with everything soft and of the right temperature, but all the same the baby is alone till the clock tells the mother that it is time to feed it. Repeatedly the baby protests, protests which a wise mother does not ignore. A few occasional adaptations of the schedule suffice to find it adopted by the baby. Within a few weeks the clock's regularity is well accommodated in the baby's system. It is improbable that the after effects of some four months of fairly rigid isolation remain confined to this benevolent adaptation to a time scheduled household. On the other hand, at this stage of its development the baby's faculties for interaction are poor. When these increase, a change announced by signs that the baby recognizes its mother, the régime changes too. On a rug, placed either inside or outside a playpen, the baby is admitted to the living room and to a gradually intensifying participation in the life of the family.

From now on the baby receives the attention it needs. Earlier in this book it has been pointed out that the whole family co-operates to interest the baby in handling its playthings and to encourage it through the whole period of infancy to play with all sorts of objects and to develop its manual dexterity (above: 157 f., 260). About the time that the child enters nursery school, the first efforts are made to initiate it in the attractions of games and sports.

The great event in the child's life is going to school, the entrance upon a long lasting period of daily mental training which, for the less successful, will last to the age of sixteen, and for the more gifted students until they have reached an age of somewhere between 18 and 27. At least, this was more or less the situation round about 1970. Today, the opinion is gaining ground that education should be life-long. Our civilization has set great hopes on education. Its expectations are voiced in a famous Unesco report that appeared under the names of a number of well-known experts, and was drawn up in that exalted language by which the Unesco secretariate has, from its early days, enchanted the politicians and exasperated the wise. The report in question charges the education systems with the task "to help their clients – whether they be youngsters or adults – to discover themselves, to understand the components of their conscious and unconscious personalities, the mechanism of the brain, the operating of the intelligence, the laws governing their physical develop-ment, the meaning of their dreams and aspirations, the nature of their relations with one another and with the community at large", a moral task which the authors summarize in the words: "teaching men the art of living, loving and working in a society which they must create as an embodiment of their ideal" (Faure et al. 1972: 66). After this balderdash let us try to find out what the real effect is of the school system on its numerous "clients" who, for as long as they are under the coercion of parents or law to continue their schooling, could more realistically be called 'captives'. There are not a few children who see it that way, in spite of everything that is done to make the school attractive.

The first task of the school is to offer equal chances to all. It must give substance to the saying that every American boy can become a president of the United States. It is not an easy task. Some of the pupils are less equal than others. Children who grew up in a socially backward milieu are handicapped by various difficulties, among others by language problems. Studies made of these difficulties in various countries have led to more or less satisfactory measures to give such children better opportunities to reap full profit of their schoolyears. But there are many other difficulties besides. All children are different, different also in intelligence. The etiology of these differences can be social (a broken family life for instance), personal (the interest which the child takes in its lessons) or innate (some are more naturally gifted than others). Even a good teacher cannot solve all the difficulties which arise from these differences. Some of the definitely poorly gifted children will have to be sent to a special school, for others it leads inevitably to repeating the class. If at all possible, the child must at least finish elementary education. The period lasts long enough to make the children keenly aware that some have better chances than others.

Further education brings new problems. The foundations have been laid and it is now time to develop the special talents. It is not easy to foresee what a child of twelve's special talents are, and the safest decision is to let those who are poor in academic subjects go to a vocational training course, and the others go in for further general education, a division of the sheep from the goats which may be repeated three years later when the high school phase has been reached. In these decisions the preferences of the students (and those of their parents!) tend to be more decisive than their supposed talents. Perhaps rightly so. A first condition for successful studies is the student's personal interest, a second the support and encouragement given by the student's parents. The higher the grade the more strenuous the student's tasks, and nothing comes of it without dedication and ambition. It is the student's personal interest which is decisive more than anything. We speak a lot about talents, but we have no exact knowledge of them. It seems probable that talents are more often the product of interest, than interest of talents.

The student's way on high is a painful way. When his adviser tells the boy that his special talents are manual rather than academic, this sounds very pleasant to the boy who is fed up with academics and wants to earn his own living as quickly as possible, but it is crushing to a boy who has the ambition to go higher up, who dreams of becoming an officer or a politician, or whatever promises a higher status. Kind words cannot conceal the fact that manual trades are classified lower than the intellectual and that, in the competition for higher status, the manual worker has lost in advance. All students know it and if they try to repress their consciousness of this knowledge, their parents will remind them of it. Every term the secondary school student receives a report stating the progress he made. He must show it to his parent or guardian who, if progress falls below standards, will tell him that it is his own fault when he fails. It is highly probable that he concludes his exhortations with the words: 'boy, think about your future'. Well, there stands the boy, thinking about his future! It is the longest time anyone can possibly think about; no one ever survived it.

It is the student's job to fight for his future. He knows this well enough without his father telling him. If, later, he wishes to make progress in society, he has to make good progress in class. To all but a few exceptionally gifted students this implies hard work and recurrent disappointment. The exigencies of higher learning are hard, and they make themselves felt already at a rather early stage of school-life. Modern educationalists have done a lot to make schools more attractive. Arts, sports and handicraft give opportunities to reach a certain measure of perfection in one or two fields to students who never attain any in the more academic subjects. The educationalists also abolished the once popular system of ranking the students with number one at the top and number n as the dullest boy of the class. I have still seen it applied, of all places, in the mildly socialist Republic of Tanzania. The numbers one to about five could be pretty sure of later being admitted to higher studies, the lowest knew at a very early date that they had failed, and those in the middle group were stimulated to compete with all their might to acquire a better place on the list. Competition made itself bitterly felt in the classroom (CESO: 1969).

There is one thing educationalists cannot do: they cannot conceal the fact that every system of school education is basically a hierarchical structure, counting as many grades as an army, from private to five-star general. Nor can they conceal that, whatever they do to obscure differences, every class has its own ranking. For every turn and for every task every student receives a mark, at secondary school up to three or five a day, at the university at greater intervals but with no lesser precision. Every achievement is weighed and marked. The student does not need a ranking system to know fairly exactly at what level he stands in his class. At the end of every school year he finds his premonitions about himself and his comrades confirmed. Some drop out to continue their training at a lower level type of school or to try to find themselves a job; others must repeat the class, and the more successful are promoted to the next grade. At the end of the sixth grade of the secondary school there are not too many left of those with whom a student set out in the first. The school, from elementary school up to university, is an unfailing instrument for continuous selection which allows only the better students to enter the next higher grade. When, at the end of twenty years of training and studies, the successful student looks back upon his past, he cannot fail to note that an educational system recognizes even less winners than any match or game. The equal chances for everyone have been used to select the most talented. It is a truth which necessarily has its effects, effects which cannot be undone by whatever moral education the school imparted to its students. That truth is that competition is as much the essence of social reality as it is of the games by which modern man finds relaxation.

After all this we can forgo a discussion of the various forms of competition in the

296

social life of the adult. Two remarks, however, should be made. The first is that those members of society who suffer least from competition because they fulfil their functions adequately, are exactly those whom we call competent. The second pertains to the ideal, inspired by the craving for social justice, that everyone should have access to the highest functions in society. These highest functions are political functions. How little do these well-wishers of mankind know their world! There is no harder life than that of the politician. Politics knows neither pity nor mercy. It is more relentless than market competition.

Opting for equality and freedom western man opted for a market society: all men are functionally equal and free to compete. It is more than is humanly bearable. Young people complain that our society is cold, as cold as the stock-exchange as the Dutch saying goes. It is exactly what can be expected of a market society with no other obligations than those of minimal ethics.

Yet, the victims of the system, the losers of the race, cry all the louder for more equality and for more radical equalization of their chances. So, in the end, they co-operate to keep up the system that kept them down.

3. *Components of modern man's cultural personality; a case of defective partnership*

In the course of our explorations we came across four features so general that they may be regarded as constituents of modern man's cultural personality. The four are, in the order of our discussion, modern man's interest in things, his almost restless activity, his spirit of competition, and his inclination to practise anonymity. We have to consider their interrelatedness and their effects on man's problem how, as a subject, he can be part of and partner to his universe. In passing we shall also have to pay attention to what came of two features discussed at some length in Ch. XIV, western man's greed for wealth and power (above: 263, 269 ff.) and his readiness to accept responsibility (id.: 268 f., 281).

Of the four components of modern personality just mentioned, the first can be traced far back into history, beginning not as a general trait common to all contemporary Westerners, but as the specific interest of a small élite which, early in the 16th century, had ventured on the way of scientific discovery. Their attempts inspired successive generations in ever increasing numbers to follow their footsteps and, in the course of the 19th century, to devise means and methods of instilling a similar interest into children generally. So successful were their attempts that 20th century parents everywhere in the western world see it as their duty to animate their offspring's interest in things from a very early age, thus generalizing it into a typical characteristic of western personality. In our comment on this sometimes passionate interest we pointed out that it leads to an active and quite satisfactory participation of the subject in his universe, enabling him to feel himself a partner in it (id.: 262).

Another question is whether the restless activity which we mentioned as a second conspicuous trait of modern man's personality is the direct result of this interest, and of nothing else. Certain is that parents do not see it that way. To them activity is an end in itself. The child must be encouraged to be active, to do things whatever they are. Not the things are their aim, but the activity, and this activity need not always be devoted to the manipulation of things. Games, too, are encouraged and much of the activity displayed by children as well as by their parents, might with at least equal right be called the product of that spirit of competition which we discussed in the preceding section. This supposition finds strong support in a peculiar detail of the outcomes of McClelland's explorations of the relative strength of need-achievement among the character traits of managers. Managers generally score high in need-achievement, but there is one group of managers which scores significantly higher than all the others in the four countries where reliable tests could be procured: that is the group of sales managers (McClelland 1961: 267). If this need-achievement (which is the motivation underlying great activity) were the product of the interest in things the production managers and the construction engineers should score higher. They are the people who concentrate their attention far more exclusively on things than the salesman who hardly need be interested in them at all. His interests are concerned with a high turnover and the profits he can make. One need not subscribe to the medieval depreciation of the tradesman as an individual who reaps the profits of other people's industry, to concede that there is an element of truth in it. When all is said and done, the salesman is more self-centered, a more active individualist with his own profit in mind, than any producer of things.

That of all people it is precisely the salesman who appears as the prototype of hectic activity confirms the correctness of our view that trade stood and stands model for modern man's social relations and activities. In both, competition and activity play a conspicuous role. That of competition hardly needs further comment after what has been said about it in section 2 of this chapter. An exception must be made on one point, and this is that behind this drive for competition we recognize the greed for wealth and power which played such a conspicuous role in the history of the 16th and 17th century. In modern society, no longer held in check by the old, religious prejudice against avarice, greed became generalized and individualized under the civilized mask of competition.

Activity is a feature which demands more elaborate comment. The drive for activity has had a number of curious side-effects which should not pass unnoticed. First among these is the fact that, though modern man has shorter working hours than many generations before him, and thus has a considerable amount of leisure time, he does not know leisure, at least not the leisure of which Pieper speaks in his essay *Musze und Kult* (1958), nor that which the more or less primitive peasant enjoys who, squatting in front of his hut, ponders on nothing in particular while he surrenders himself to the quiet voices of nature like the murmur of a nearby brook (above: 157). People of our generation and culture who have nothing to do get bored. We hate boredom. Boredom is a fairly recent phenomenon, a feature proper to our civilization. In his study *Die Psychologie der Langeweile* (The Psychology of Boredom; 1949) Revers pointed out that Greek and Latin had no word for it. Even the neo-Latin term *acedia* cannot properly be translated by boredom. The first in history who wrote about it was, according to our author, Blaise Pascal. It was in his lifetime (1623-1662) that boredom began to play a role in western social life.

298

Leisure time, then, must be filled, not filled by leisure which is boring (and often disquieting, an aspect to which we return later on) but by activities which engage the mind such as games and sports or hobbies. But no one can run or play forever, the body too needs some relaxation. Yet, simply sitting involves boredom. The problem has been solved by the entertainment industry which brings everyone his relaxation at home, primarily in the form of radio and television. The mass media have unchained the most decisive revolution in human life of the last hundred years. As social institutes, their influence dates back to 1925 and 1960 successively. Only yesterday. The radio in particular is always with us for music and information, the television as the unfailing companion who entertains us when we do not wish to do anything in particular. They have a far-reaching impact on modern life and thought.

One of the positive consequences of radio and television is that they keep us well informed of anything happening in the world, not only the world around us, but also of what is going on on the other side of the globe. Where formerly we passed our lives in a village or town and kept the great world at the horizon of our existence, we now live our life in the world of 'everywhere' with, at the horizon, the appurtenances of the events about town. This may seem somewhat overdrawn – and I would not like to deny this – but it is certainly true that events on another continent often keep us more occupied or worried than a local strike which disturbs the economy of our town. Our world has widened immensely. We participate in all the world's great tragedies, we see the fighting in the streets of an Asian town, the dying victims of drought in the Sahel, the Russian army in Czechoslovakia or Afghanistan, and the installation of a new president of the U.S.A. on the screen in our living-room. The daily news turns us into world citizens. Citizens, however, who are utterly powerless; spectators, secretly peeping from a hidden corner at a world which is for a great part strange to them, attending events that are not their business and yet can influence their life and happiness. That big world reveals itself on modern man's television screen in a similar way as nature does itself to primitive man, as a superior power which has no concern for the onlooker's vital interests, a power unpredictable and unreliable in its actions which sometimes are beneficent and then again damaging and threatening. To that world modern man knows himself an inmate as well as a stranger who must see how to make the best of it, how to carry on to preserve his own little life and interests.

This confrontation by an immense, unpredictable and unreliable world has a curiously twofold effect. On the one hand, the onlooker repeatedly feels that something ought to be done about it, a feeling that inspires him to participation in all sorts of social and political action, action in which he is hurt time and again by that big world's immutability and apparent insensitivity to equity and human rights. His powerlessness enrages him: he articulates his disillusionment in terms of being manipulated, not manipulated by anyone in particular, but by the repressive tolerance of an anonymous system. More than once, listening to the passionate exhortations of rebellious students, I was struck by the likeness between the images of The Establishment, The International Monopoly Capital, The Multinationals, or simply The System as accused by them, and the dragons and ogres of primitive mythology. I do not mean that their complaints were wholly unjustified. What impressed me was the aggressiveness evoked by these anonymous monsters. It was not the mild aggressiveness which is an inescapable component of behaviour modelled on the competition of the market; it was rage, the rage which carries away young people who are proud of their freedom and their right to be themselves when they discover that the contents of that freedom are void, that their willingness to sacrifice that freedom to a social ideal leads to nothing, that they are running into a blank wall.

The other effect of man's confrontation with an all encompassing and for by far the greater part strange world is the recurring acceptance of the onlooker's role. It is a role which favours anonymity, the anonymity of the traveller and the pleasure seeker. He goes out in his own self-chosen company. His anonymity outside that company is ensured by his avoidance of making contacts with others. He is the perfect stranger who enjoys a maximum of freedom, the perfect individual who is engaged with no other interests than his own and those of the few whom he selected for his company. The trend to seek partial anonymity is conducive to greater personal freedom by giving a person the opportunity to do as he likes (i.e. always within the limits set by public law) without being held responsible for his doings by co-members of any of the social groups in which he participates. Such co-members know nothing about it. This implies a limitation of the person's responsibilities. It is a limitation which is pursued in various ways, the most conspicuous form being that of the privileged type of economic organization, the limited liability company. In other words, the readiness to accept responsibility which we discussed in the previous chapter (cf. on this point pp. 268 f., 281) has become reduced. After all, a relative stranger cannot bear full responsibility. He prefers to carry along in his world as a potential purchaser on the market of life, moving at leisure from stall to stall, nosing about for something that is to his liking.

On that market everything is for sale, all that can contribute to the pursuit and increase of human happiness. The entertainment industry has grown into one of the world's biggest industries, more or less on a par with war (or 'defense' as it is euphemistically called) and education. It is not only games and sports, travel and comfortable housing, entertainment parks, theatres and restaurants: we are entertained from morning to night. And if the entertainment presented by radio or television does not satisfy our mood we can make a choice from our collection of records and tapes to have just the music that satisfies. There are endless means to protect us from boredom, and these means are available to everyone. Even sex is easier to get than at any time before. In view of our present wealth everyone ought to be happy. And yet, after two hundred years of unabated pursuit, no one is.

The complaint most frequently heard is that about loneliness. In a society possessing such perfect means for entertainment and communication complaints of this kind must seem unreasonable, and yet they are not. The modern world is a noisy world, filled with music. Sometimes this music is listened to when, at leisure hours, there is time for art-enjoyment. However, more often than not the music is only heard. It is background music. Many people assert that they need it to concentrate on their work. There is no reason to doubt the truth of these assertions. There is music, today, in every workshop and in every motor-car. The fact, however, that music stimulates the worker's concentration, is significant. It implies that music helps him to occupy himself with his work and with this alone, in other words, to keep to himself. Would the effect of radio-music be different when it resounds in a living room? Perhaps there is one who listens, whilst another is reading the newspaper or a book, and a third is knitting. There are households where the radio (or the television) is never silent, keeping conversation down to a minimum. It functions as a noisy tranquillizer rather than as a means for communication. And if really listened to, it still keeps the listener concentrated on his own art-enjoyment, communicating with the outside world in a way which is strictly individual. Damping the opportunities for communication with others, the everlasting noise aggravates the individual's loneliness by making it bearable whilst preventing him from surmounting it through interhuman contacts.

A quick review of the principal components of modern man's cultural personality pattern suffices to locate some of the main causes of the difficulties engendered by a defective partnership in his world. It is certainly not his interest in things. We argued that it makes for a happy participation in one's universe, a participation which encourages activity. The real source of his agonies is in competition and the trend toward anonymity, both products of a society which patterned its forms of interaction on the model of trade: all individuals equal, all competitors, all relative strangers to one another, all subject to minimal ethics. And all in pursuit of happiness, the ultimate object of the social trade.

The happiness our society is after, necessarily is individual happiness. All its members are competitors on the market of life. Yet, in trade as in games there are winners and losers. The equality that stands at the outset, is inevitably broken by competition and changed into inequality. Because equality is the founding condition the consequences of losing must, at the very least, be attenuated by awarding the loser a consolation prize. The contradictions between equality and competition lead directly to the contradictions of our economy. Everyone must gain something by it. Though we know that we cannot go on *ad infinitum* with increasing our production – a palliative synonym of increasing our consumption – the model of an expanding economy still reigns supreme. Every year a little bit more. Even in times of economic regression the purchasing power of income, at least of the lower incomes, must be maintained. For equity's sake we try to cut down the higher incomes, but the effect is restricted because competition must be maintained. The one viable compromise is higher production and consumption to ensure that the less privileged also get a share in the ever increasing wealth. A contraction of the economy would be fatal to the more vulnerable classes. They have equal rights to work and food and so many other things as the well-to-do, and these rights have to be respected as much as the right to compete.

Competition means strife. A market society is an aggressive society, not aggressive in the sense that its members indulge in physical fighting, but in claiming an ever stricter observance of their rights. The rule of balanced reciprocity prevails; and, as in trade, the balance must be found by negotiations. There is no place for informal procedures of give-and-take between individuals who are not partners but parties to one another. There is not really place for authority either. Authority can only be attributed to the rule which has been agreed upon, and the executive has, in principle, no other authority than that bestowed on him by the rule upon which agreement has been reached. Authorities everywhere have suffered from the aggressive attacks of the partisans of basic equality who, rejecting the polite manners current in more traditional circles, forcefully claimed the recognition of their rights to be consulted on everything that regards them as students, as victims of housing problems or as inhabitants of a residential area. In the fight for perfect openness manners have become considerably ruder these last fifteen years (cf. Van Baal 1974).

Still, these fighters for radical equality cannot be described as champions of individualism. The contrary is true. They fight for greater solidarity and they deeply pity the poor and the underprivileged. On this point they represent ideals which are general in our affluent society. The underdog is its pet animal, whether he live in one's own country (where the genus is comparatively rare) or in Cambodja, the Sahel, or the Amazone forests. In their fight for human happiness and rights they are deadly serious and well prepared to sacrifice time and money for it. They are also in their fight against individualism in our own society. They know that it is a social evil, and they are genuinely disconcerted about the growing number of suicides, about the many who are lonely and alienated; they visit them and try to console them, they endeavour to create new forms of sociality in communes and the like. The young and rebellious generation fights for greater interhuman communication, for more genuine love and togetherness. And when they feel themselves the captives of what they call The System, they are tragically right. It is the system of the model of trade in which all are equals. Fighting the system, they give support to the pillars which bear it because it is exactly from more equality that they expect happiness.

There is hardly a right so confidently vindicated as that of the pursuit of happiness. To modern man's mind it is not only the pursuit, but happiness itself which everyone may claim as a right. Happiness has been the ground for one reform after another. One of these is that of our sexual conventions. It did away with the sexual taboos that inhibited and sometimes even ruined the lives of earlier generations. From the anthropologist's point of view the disappearance of premarital chastity is a purely rational development. The wish of modern young people to cohabit without going through a marriage ceremony is not irrational either. Why should they bind themselves as long as there are no children? A marriage in modern society is not an alliance between two families, but one between two persons. If a child is on the way, the two will probably marry because a child has a right to a father. That he should also have a mother's brother is out of date. Why should he? A marriage is a matter between two individuals; the one thing which is important is that they are happy together. They know that this happiness need not last. Even if there are children it need not, though they may agree that up to a certain age it is important to a child to grow up in a harmonious family. And for the children's sake they will try to have it that way.

All the same, motherhood – and whatever changed, motherhood counts for more than fatherhood – is not a necessity. To modern women it is but an option, and as an option no more than a temporary affair. It is improper to have more than three children, decent to have only two. Of course it is. Infant mortality having been reduced to an absolute minimum, it is a social duty to keep the exuberance of life within limits. Neither pope nor synod can ignore this without taking responsibility for a future catastrophe, the consequences of which they altogether too easily relegate to the Almighty. Fortunately, young people see farther ahead. And with this knowledge in mind, why should marriage be more to them than a temporary affair? Why should parents not separate once the children have grown up? Haven't they a right to happiness, each of them, and why should they not take another partner, to start a new life all over again?

To start a new life all over again, and all for happiness! Those who more or less successfully tried it, assert that it works. It never works wholly successfully. The trouble is that a man or a woman does not *have* a past, but *is* his or her past. It is their dowry to a new union. That dowry need not spoil their happiness. The one, pertinent trouble is that such happiness depends on the presence and availability of exactly one person, and if he is taken away little remains. It is the one risk against which there is no insurance. This happiness is a matter of all or nothing, purely personal. It is not embedded in society. It is not partnership within a universe, but partnership with one other, the poorest, tiniest universe imaginable. Although the isolation of the marriage institution need not be as thorough as here suggested and can be compensated for by the availability of a network of friendships, one drawback is permanent, i.e. the lack of institutionalization from which all personal ties suffer in consequence. They are to a large extent temporary and dissolvable. What is lacking is the existence of sufficiently stable mini-universes that offer an unfailing refuge to their members. The increased mobility of mankind has deeply affected man's social relations.

Another problem is what the effect will be of the declining significance of motherhood. There is uncertainty on this point; not because there is any fear that motherhood will disappear, but because of the shortening of the period spent by a woman on effective care-giving to her family. In the past this period lasted some 30 years. The restricted size of the planned family has reduced it to at most 20 years. Less than before a woman is a mother who is always there. Motherhood has always been mankind's paradigm of merciful care, and the reduction of its duration is necessarily a loss to society. It is impossible to foresee what the extent of this loss will be. The one thing certain is that modern society, with its professionalization of care-giving, is already very deficient in personal care, i.e. care that expresses affective togetherness. It is not that our society ignores or wilfully neglects the demands of personal, natural ethics but that, in spite of many individual efforts to practise such ethics, the opportunities for effective partnership have become scarce. The causes of this untoward development have been briefly discussed in this and in the preceding sections. As a final comment the following may be added.

In this development, an important role has been played by man's right to the pursuit of happiness. It is a right almost thoughtlessly espoused as a self-evident ideal by everyone. Even Immanuel Kant fell for it. Earlier in this book I have expressed my doubts on this point, not any doubts on the significance of the ideal for the development of modern civilization, but on its significance for what is for the good of mankind (above: 130, 144 f., 277 f.). Happiness is of two kinds; it can be found in effective partnership, but also in successful self-realization. In our age of entertainment the emphasis on the indidvidual's right to full development and deployment of his personality, has turned the pursuit of his happiness almost by necessity into a licence to indulge in joy-riding. It is for this reason that, here again, I wish to express my doubts on the legitimacy of this ideal and its pretended self-evidence.

4. Religion and non-religion in an age of entertainment

The crushing criticism which the Enlightenment launched upon revealed religion halted at the threshold of the belief in a Creator-God and in the survival of the human soul. These were the founding truths of what the Encyclopaedists called natural religion, a religion dictated by reason. The belief in God was rationalized into a primeval cause, or into a postulate of practical reason. The certainty of survival after death was derived from Cartesian dualism which opposed the indestructability of the spirit to the instability of matter. The 'natural religion' of the Encyclopaedists did not last for long. Later philosophers had little difficulty in demonstrating that the idea of God is not the necessary postulate of reason as Kant had contended, and that agnosticism is a both simpler and a more honest answer to the problem of first causes.

The belief in after-life proved itself equally untenable. The dependence of the mind on its material substrate became ever more obvious. Though this does not imply that mind and matter can be wholly identified, a viewpoint still under discussion (cf. Ornstein 1972), the dependence of the mind on the brain is too evident to maintain a belief in the mind's or the spirit's persistence after death. Altogether too often the mind has already disintegrated well before death because of the onset of senility. In religious circles, belief in the survival of the soul has mostly given way to that in its resurrection by a divine deed of re-creation. Besides, to a great many people the idea of survival has lost much of the comfort it had to generations who had to face the probability of early death. Those of our generation have seen too many cases of men and women who lived until they were old and full of days, too tired even for desire, to be quite certain about the desirability of after-life.

With the rapid development of the sciences, in particular with that of comparative religion, the defence of traditional Christendom became more and more difficult. All the support the defenders of Christendom could borrow from the results of scientific enquiry was the argument that religion meets a human need, is a normal phenomenon. Christendom, however, had never insisted upon the utility of its creed but upon its truth; actually, its historical truth. What had always constituted its pride appeared more and more to be its weakness: the historical truth of the resurrection of Christ, the seal and foundation of the expectation of eternal bliss. Whereas the death of Jesus is a well-established historical fact, his resurrection depends on the meagre testimony of a small collection of stories in which a score of simple people relate their apparently visionary experiences. They do not persuade the modern reader of their truth.

Still, the mordent criticism of this and many other points of so-called revealed truth is not the main cause of the weakened position of Christendom (and religion generally) in the modern world. This lies in the coincidence of modern man's quest for truth with his struggle with authority. Modern man is every inch an egalitarian, disinclined to recognize anyone as his superior. Modern labour relations leave no doubt on this point (above: 284, 285). This is not to say that he rejects every form of authority. He knows quite well that no society can do without it. The one thing on which he insists is that authority should be founded upon reason. This is what made the doctrine of the social contract so attractive to him. It supplied a rational and reasonable ground for accepting the authority of society, one of the same nature as that for respecting the binding force of a contract based on agreement reached by open negotiations.

In itself this reluctance to bow down before authority is nothing intrinsically new. Mankind has always had difficulties on this point. Although part of his universe and desirous to function as a partner in it, every individual is also a subject and inclined to make his universe the object of his self-realization and to submit it to his will. The fact that one's universe (and society) are so overwhelmingly powerful that, in the end, the individual always has to submit to that power does not imply that he automatically acknowledges that power as authority. Therefore universe and society are too evidently other to the subject that ever distances them, even when it acts as a part. If the subject recognizes their power as authority it is always on the ground of some sort of rationalization, of an obligation imposed by a power which has authority over both subject and universe. We found this demonstrated by the fact that the ultimate ground for the recognition of worldly authority is always attributed to something supernatural inherent in power (above: 113, 114). The doctrine of the social contract has substituted this irrational ground for the recognition of worldly authority by a rational one, but such a solution is not possible with regard to the problems of man's place in his universe and the ultimate ground for his relations with it. These problems arouse questions which human reason cannot answer, which confront rational thought with its proper limitations. We discussed this at the end of Part III. Reason cannot explain the universe, and yet man needs something to support him in his confrontation with his universe. All he can do is to try to wrench a meaning from the unknowable, an interpretation that gives sense and significance to his existence in his universe.

We shall have more to say about meaning in the next chapter. All that is relevant here is that a meaning which gives sense and significance to man's existence, is a concept that is closely related to that of religion. Decisive on this point is not that religion, having become more civilized, has cleared away the more appalling irrationalities which it inherited from myth, but that a meaning of this kind has to be authoritative and therefore needs a metaphysical foundation which cannot be derived from the knowable alone. It inevitably refers to something hypothesized behind it. By this appeal to the unknowable, however reluctantly formulated, the authoritative meaning crosses the threshold of religion as here defined, and becomes subject to the criticism that it has overstepped the strict limits of reason, the one and only ground of his universe about which modern man has no doubts. He holds the view that the only thing which, in reason, he is justified in doing, is to confess his impotence to solve the problem of meaning, and to acquiesce in agnosticism as the one and only rational and honest attitude vis-à-vis problems of ultimate concern.

Keeping all this in mind it is evident that, after two hundred years of attack and ridicule, Christendom ought to have disappeared. And yet, it still remains, battered perhaps and shaken, but still the hope and expectation of millions of believers, millions in the western world, millions even in the Soviet Union. What is more, these believers are found in all strata of society. Among members of the intellectual classes there may be a leaning towards more modern forms of Christendom, forms in which the sacraments and the belief in eternal life have lost the dominant significance they once had, but this leaning towards modernism is not a hard and fast rule. Though old-fashioned fundamentalists are fairly rare among intellectuals, many of them must be reckoned among the followers of one of the various intermediate forms. They are aware that religious truth is no longer as obvious as it used to be but they do not wish to give it up; either because it gives meaning to their life, or because of the weak excuse that it works and makes people better, or happier. All the same, they persevere in participating in common worship, and their support to their church is not confined to a financial contribution to its maintenance. They are often active in various kinds of community work. In recent times these middle groups are characterized by a distinct trend towards the deprofessionalization of church-work. Laymen and -women claim functions in it; an interesting development which runs counter to the now normal professionalization of personal care. Church membership today is a matter of conscious choice, far more than it used to be, and this choice leads to activities of ethical value such as visiting the sick and the lonely. It is by no means a mass movement, but it is not without significance that there are young people too who participate in this kind of work; that adolescents volunteer in care for the aged is not such an exception today as it was fifty years ago.

These youth activities are not always church inspired. The desire to contribute to welfare activities that give emotional satisfaction is widespread among young people. We noted already that they condemn present-day society as cold (above: 297), and experiment with new forms of social units which promise greater togetherness, such as communes (ibid.: 302). When they have given up Christendom as hopelessly obsolete this does not mean that they have lost all interest in religion. The contrary is true. There is a new interest in mysticism, notably in mysticism of Indian origin. Even magic may be included. Already in the mid-sixties the book-displays in the windows of the bookshops in the Quartier Latin in Paris and around the British Museum in London gave testimony to this changing interest of a new generation of students. Books which no student would have deigned to look at in previous years were suddenly en vogue. The students did not confine themselves to mere reading. Glock and Bellah (1976) have published a substantial collection of descriptions of new religions which recruited their membership largely amongst students. They emphasize community life, yoga, meditation and suchlike, and excel in readiness to believe teachings which are in no way more probable or credible than those of the Christendom which they rejected.

These new religions are found all over the world. Their adherents are mostly young people and they all concentrate on meditation and mystic experience. They do not always shun the use of drugs to promote the experience of mystic union. However it is reached, they all sing the praise of the euphoria and comfort found in it. The effects are important and real enough to induce a critical rationalist like Frits Staal to an elaborate and well-founded plea for the desirability of exploring mysticism (1975). Among young people, religion is not dead. That in some cases their religious experience can be described as a 'spiritual ego-trip' does not alter the fact.

It is evident, then, that in spite of his agnosticism western man finds it difficult to live without religion. Some people openly admit that they would be only too happy to believe in religion if they only knew how. Amongst these are the armchair philosophers who have their private thoughts on the metaphysics of world and universe, but never disclose their secret thoughts because they think them too vague or too intimate to be communicated. Far more numerous, however, are those who simply acquiesce in the fact that religion has to be given up as illusory. Sometimes they will grant that everything would be much easier if God existed (Sartre 1946); but this does not affect their conviction that man has to pull himself together to face the facts. Rejecting the vain efforts at giving meaning to the unknowable they conclude that man must create his own life and find realistic ways for the realization of a more satisfactory existence and world. In the anxiety that this existence inspires, he cannot hope for any other support than that which he finds in himself, and in his relations to his fellow-men. When he feels emotionally dissatisfied, forlorn in a world which he experiences as distant and repelling, the alienated individual can always find his way back to his world by surrendering himself to that supreme product of humanity, the arts, and recognize his own fate and longing in the expression given by great artists to the experience of their relation to their world. There is peace in the arts. Windelband already spoke of it, concluding his comment on the unsolvable problems that worry man's mind with the words: *Bis wir das problembekümmerte Haupt zu seliger Ruhe niederlegen in den Schosz der Kunst*, until we lay down the problem-troubled head in blissful peace to the bosom of art (Windelband 1919: II 345).

And, indeed, the enjoyment of art is a highly rewarding experience. Art is consummated in a quite peculiar way, namely in perfect silence, not a silence that comes from outside, but the silence which the beholder or listener himself makes from within (Van Baal 1972: 81 ff.). Approaching an object of visual art the spectator becomes silent; in this silence the contemplated object turns into a subject that projects its message into him to pervade his inner mind with its beauty, that undescribable quality which reconciles the spectator with his world as it meets him in the contemplated object. Whatever the object represents, it lends the represented a new lustre by presenting it as seen from a very peculiar angle. Beholding an object of art is like losing oneself in the contemplation of a panorama. From on high, the landscape gains new qualities, reveals a surprising harmony which below, seeing it all from nearby, the spectator had not expected. Seen through the perspective of art, the world is overshone by a lustre of goodness, or clad in the twilight of resignation. Beauty has the uncommon power to make us aware of our partnership in our universe.

Music has a similar effect. More alien to the world of everyday, as elusive as sound itself, it ushers us, as Lévi-Strauss said, into a world of timelessness which confronts us to virtual objects of which only the shades are actual, to conscious approximations of truths ineluctably inconscient and yet present (Lévi-Strauss 1964: 25 f.). Music reveals to us a way of being in and unto our world in which the subject succumbs to the embrace of another world which pervades him with its melody and sound. In music this other world speaks and the subject becomes silent or, rather, swings on the waves of its sound.

The enjoyment of art leads the subject back to its universe to be incorporated in it. The same holds true of reading poetry or enjoying the products of verbal art generally. Yet, there is one complication here. In a poem or novel it is not only the beauty of expression which counts, but also its intellectual message, which may range from a romantic revelling in the beauties of nature to an explosion of political indignation or disgust. In an effort at estimating the effect of art-enjoyment the products of the verbal arts can better be left out of consideration. This makes it possible to concentrate on the main point, the fact that the function of art-enjoyment has close similarities to that of religion. In one way or another art reconciles the listener or beholder with his universe. And it is of particular interest in this context that the modern means of reproduction and communication have given access to the products of art on a scale as never before. In a previous section we spoke somewhat slightingly of the entertainment industry. Yet, it has the great merit that it made art available to everyone in unsurpassed quantities, and often of perfect quality besides. Everyone can make his choice in accordance with his specific needs and preferences. No longer a privilege of the well-to-do, art has acquired the important social function of taking the place of religion as a comforter of the lonely who is at odds with his place in his universe. Art has even the power of bringing a person to ecstasy.

Another question is whether art-enjoyment is a really adequate substitute for religion. On three points the religious experience differs substantially from that of art-enjoyment, to wit that of its social implications, that of its intellectual components, and that of the after-effects which it engenders. Each of these three points has to be considered in some detail before a conclusion can be drawn.

The religious and the aesthetic experience have in common that they are strictly individual. They must be consummated in inner silence, which makes the soul receptive to the voice of the gods and of beauty respectively. Yet, there is a difference. The gods represent the essence of man's universe, beauty a certain aspect of it that must be actualized. In communicating with the essence of his universe, man's relations with his fellow-men are implied, relations which rarely play a role in the aesthetic experience. As a matter of fact, the aesthetic experience is well-adapted to modern man's style of life, that of the individual who goes his own way. In attending

308

a concert the presence of others has no influence on the quality of the listener's enjoyment of the music; but for the effect of a ritual such attendance is essential. In art-enjoyment the individual is strictly receptive. Communal action (community-singing for instance) is an exception. A ritual, however, requires the active co-operation of the community, and in this action its members realize a certain togetherness. In other words, the religious experience – often a ritual experience in the company of others – has a social component which is usually lacking in the aesthetic experience.

In the second place, religion has an intellectual component of a kind which is conspicuously absent in the aesthetic experience. The role of the intellect has already been the subject of discussion in section 4 of chapter XIII. Here, it is important to emphasize that religion is the embodiment of a worldview which assigns every man and woman his or her proper place. This implies that each of them stands in a specific relation to all the others and to his or her universe generally, a relation which can be specified as a meaning. The religious experience is an emotional experience which affirms the truth and validity of that meaning. Suchlike cannot be said of the aesthetic experience. It is, of course, a wonderful experience which fulfils one's heart with peace and admiration. Yet, no one can properly say what it is, or specify how the experience determines or changes one's place in one's universe. It is the experience that, for the time of its duration, everything is good; but this experience cannot help anyone who is assailed by intellectual doubts concerning his place in his universe and the meaning of his existence.

This leads more or less automatically to the third point, the after-effect of the religious and the aesthetic experience respectively. The former has a conceptual component. The experience enables the believer who participated in an important ritual to return to everyday life with the certainty that between him and his gods everything is alright, that he is a partner in his universe. For a long time afterwards simple rites suffice to maintain this certainty. The aesthetic experience can be as impressive as a great religious experience, but it cannot be conceptualized. All that is available to memory afterwards is a tune or an image. The memory can be comforting, but its power of persuading anyone that he lives in harmony with his universe is weak. Anyone who went through an experience of aesthetic delight, is soon afterwards looking forward to a new experience. To a certain extent the aestheticist's longing for new experiences is insatiable. He is less easily satisfied than the religious believer.

On the score of these three points the aesthetic experience is the lesser of the religious experience. However, when art-enjoyment is combined with art-performance, the effect of the aesthetic experience is considerably greater. Participating as a performer in a band or a chamber orchestra implies both the socialization and the frequent repetition of the aesthetic experience. Nevertheless, apart from the fact that active performers are almost by necessity a minority, art performance has not the capacity of giving meaning to human life and existence as religion has. It is even uncertain whether art-creation (always an exceptional gift!) has that power. It is on the point of meaning that art-enjoyment and art-performance are inferior to religion.

Art is not really an adequate substitute for religion. It is a last resort in case the possibility that life and existence can have a meaning at all must be rejected as a utopian dream.

The denial of the possibility that the human existence can have a meaning is a decision of the intellect which should not be taken light-heartedly. It has serious consequences. It leaves mankind no other choice than that between the consolations of art which are never wholly satisfactory, and that of forgetting oneself in action or in the trivialities of games and entertainment. Although of the two the pursuit of art is the more promising, it suffers from the same deficiency as that of games and diversion: viz. that it gives no answer to man's problems about his place in his universe. The results of modern man's uncertainty on this point are revealed by the rapid growth of the number of people who are in need of psychological guidance and psychiatric treatment. Medical practitioners complain that almost half of their time is spent on pastoral counseling. The facts are sufficiently alarming to justify a renewed consideration of the limitations set to the contents of the concept of meaning. It might well be that the demands made on these contents are too far-fetched, and that here the reason lies why the possibility of meaning has been denied.

There is a sound reason for this supposition because 'meaning', and more specifically 'ultimate meaning', has repeatedly been confounded with (ultimate) 'explanation'. Yet, there is an important difference between the two. The term 'meaning' denotes a relation of interdependence, primarily one of purpose and action, whereas 'explanation' implies a relation of causality. The intellectualist – whose mind is always in search of causality – cannot feel satisfied with a meaning unless it has a certain explanatory value. In the case of ultimate meaning this dissatisfaction has had serious consequences. Pondering on 'ultimate meaning', thought inevitably approaches its proper limitations, to be confronted with the unknowable. In search of a meaning which has explanatory value successive generations of thinkers have been unable to resist the temptation to interpret their confrontation with the unknowable as a sign inviting them to fill the hole with pseudo-knowledge. Nevertheless, all that in reason can be derived from the discovery that at the end of all thought there is an unknowable, is the fact that behind the universe there is a mystery to which man has no access. At the end of his search for the ultimate 'why' of his universe and existence, man has to accept that such knowledge is denied to him. What can be concluded from it is either that questions concerning the ultimate 'why' of his universe and existence are illegitimate because there is neither ultimate meaning nor explanation, or to concede that such ultimate meaning is kept concealed from man in and by an inscrutable unknowable, which invites him to respect its inscrutability, and to recognize the unknowable as the ground of all things and thus as the ultimate authority which ordained that the knowable is as it is.

The first answer, that of denying the possibility of ultimate meaning is, essentially, a presumptuous act, as presumptuous as that of ascribing the unknowable certain qualities which are, after all, not more than the projections of man's own hopes and fears and which, for this reason, must be rejected as pseudo-knowledge. The rejection of a meaning based on pseudo-knowledge is justified, but that of the possibility of a

310

hidden meaning not. The latter implies that the unknowable is void and empty, a pronouncement which oversteps the limits of the unknowable as definitely as pronouncements which ascribe certain qualities to it.

There is only one consequence which can be drawn with some confidence because it does not conflict with the dictates of reason. This is that the inscrutable mystery behind the universe is the ultimate authority which allotted the knowable to man as the field for his actions, the field also from which he has to wrench a meaning which leads to the fulfilment of his existence as a partner in and of his universe. One might object that a meaning derived from the knowable can never be 'ultimate'. However, this objection is not valid, at least not in every respect. If the unknowable is accepted as the ultimate authority behind our universe and existence, a meaning derived from the knowable can certainly have ultimate value as an interpretation of what has been ordained on grounds which man cannot fathom. Besides, the assumption that the unknowable has ultimate authority does not impinge upon its inscrutability. As a matter of fact, the assumption that ultimate authority should be located in the unknowable is a confession of man's limitations, the only means available to man to express his awareness that the ultimate ground of all things must be behind the knowable. And what can, to man, the ultimate ground of all things be otherwise than ultimate authority?

A more valid objection against the ultimate value of a meaning derived from the knowable is, that it is necessarily as limited in power of truth as every human opinion. We will return to this in the next chapter where the further implications of a more humble concept of ultimate meaning must be discussed.

XVI

Conclusion

Man's world has widened, and the horizons of his knowledge border on infinity. The rapid growth of his world has been attended by a serious lag in the concomitant development of the institutional forms of modern man's social life and by a violent crisis in his religious faith which confronted him with the task of either finding an adequate substitute for religion, or creating religious forms which meet the exigencies of his altered worldview. It is evident that the first solution, that of finding an adequate substitute for religion, has failed. In this chapter we must try to arrive at a definite conclusion about the opportunities for overcoming the obstacles which prevent religion from functioning adequately in modern society. Before we set about this task, however, we shall have to reconsider the difficulties besetting the ethics of modern man's social life. They are more tangible than the religious problems and may help us to fathom the impact of the latter.

Our explorations of ethics confirmed the view that the contradictions arising out of the fact that man is simultaneously a part of his universe and a subject confronting it, find their ultimate solution in active partnership. To effectuate such partnership man has to fulfil three duties. The first and most general of these is that he respect his fellow-men, whether they are strangers or not. As parts of one's universe they share in the respect due to the universe. Respect implies the obligation to observe reciprocity, honesty, and decency, an obligation binding on all social interaction concerned with the pursuit of non-personal interests. If these interests have a business character, the business obligations implied are sanctioned (protected) by authority. The second duty is the obligation to welcome the other as part of one's universe. We called it the moral law. It applies to all interaction concerned with personal interests. The exact contents of the obligations implied in the moral law are co-determined by the variations of social distance within a given universe. Fulfilment of the moral law creates partnership. It has its reward in itself and does not require protection by authority or law. The third duty, though its observance is more rewarding than any, is also the hardest of all, viz. the liberation of the subject from the fetters of the self which restrain the subject from acquiring the faculty to realize complete partnership.

In modern society the relevance of the first of these duties, that of respect, has taken almost absolute precedence. Various factors have co-operated to that effect. The growth of the extent of society has increased the number of strangers and half-strangers in anyone's personal universe to excess. The concomitant growth of wealth and facilities has multiplied the number of desirable business relations, the specialists whom everyone needs for the fulfilment of his material, technical, social and personal needs. The generalization of highly-perfected means of transport has resulted in an accelerated geographical mobility which has contributed to an increased temporariness and instability of personal relations with, in their train, a progressive reduction of stable social forms conducive to the integration of interpersonal relations. Another result of increased spatial mobility is, apart from its contribution to the widening of the spatial extension of society, the creation of a multitude of opportunities for going about in anonymity.

All this has greatly favoured the freedom of the self to pursue its self-chosen ends, many of which have come within easy reach by increasing affluence and wealth. This freedom of the self impinges in a negative sense on the subject's faculty to liberate itself from the fetters of the desires forged by the self (above: 144). Simultaneously, the destabilization and reduction of the institutional forms conducive to the integration and persistence of interpersonal relations has had a restrictive effect on the opportunities for the realization of real partnership. It is not so much that the will to welcome another to one's universe has slackened, but that there is no form of universe to which to welcome anyone. In our immense social universe there is a frustrating deficiency of mini-universes such as were available in the past in extended family, clan and village community. They have been superseded by voluntary societies of all sorts, but all these voluntary societies are concerned with a specific aim and their membership is both optional and temporary. They are not communities, but stalls on the market-place of life. The complaint that our society suffers from a lack of warmth is well founded; but, in spite of such complaints, the process of the depersonalization of social relations progresses. The desire for greater freedom and more equality sustains the steady ascendancy of the trade model. The one institution which has retained its function as a social haven is the nuclear family, and even this suffers from a reduction in size and from the impact of temporariness on all social relations.

Still, we also came across efforts at founding new communities which meet the need for personal security and support. The most viable, and also the most stable among these, are the many religious communities of relatively small size. They stimulate their members to mutual, personal care-giving and to look after one another's worries. Of particular interest is the accompanying trend towards the deprofessionalization of religious functions, in particular where local congregations are concerned. Deprofessionalization also plays a role in the main-line, established churches; but, here, it often takes the form of a protest against authority and establishment, protests which are symptoms of the trade-model rather than of an incipient deviance from this model. On the whole, the main-stream churches impress us more by their interventions in world-wide problems and world politics than by their pastoral care of the local flock. Nevertheless, it is locally that the social problems lie: in the need for mini-universes willing and capable of giving support to the lonely and a spiritual home to the alienated. As there is no way back to the stable social

313

forms of the past such as extended family and such like, these local religious communities might be a proper and promising answer to the coldness of modern society. There is only one proviso to make: the religion there practised must give a credible answer to the existential problems besetting the life and thought of modern man. Everything hinges on the feasibility of such an answer.

Whereas modern man's means to feel at home in his social universe as a real partner are restricted and adversely affected by temporariness and geographical mobility, his uncertainty about his place in his universe at large is even greater. That universe has become altogether too big and remote to offer him a support to go by. He feels himself a stranger who belongs to that universe by pure chance, *geworfen* as Heidegger called it, thrown into it for no proper reason at all. In comparison to a Marind or an Aranda who, in their rituals, give colour and content to their undoubted partnership in their universe, modern man is a beggar, roaming through his universe without any goal except the realization of his aimless self. Factually, he cannot deny that he is a part of his world, but he misses the means to make this true to himself as a felt and consolidated partnership. All he can make available to that end are the elusive comforts of his aesthetic experience, but these comforts fail to arouse a lasting certainty of his inner belonging to his world. The reconciliation effectuated by the aesthetic experience cannot last because it is insufficiently supported by the intellect and does not give his world a more definite meaning for him. And it is exactly meaning that he needs.

Man's quest for meaning has been a source of recurrent difficulties to him. One of the worst is the one mentioned at the end of the previous chapter. Ultimate meaning must have authority over man, assigning him his place in his universe. From where must this authority be derived? From anything he observed in his universe? This is impossible, because his universe has no ultimate authority over man. It is his field of action, and it is essential to the subject to distance its universe and to decide for itself whether it shall oppose or submit to its exigencies. Confining himself to the observable universe, the 'knowable', man may try to find a way out by attibuting authority to reason. It is of no avail; for the foundation of its authority, reason itself has to refer to certain founding hypotheses which, whether openly located in the unknowable or not, necessarily overstep the limits of the knowable. Besides, however founded, the hypotheses must all derive their authority from its recognition by man. And this is, in fact, the worst of it.

Religion suggests a way out of the dilemma by offering the possibility of divine revelation. Theoretically, the possibility cannot be denied but, unfortunately, there are no compelling grounds to believe the truth of anyone's assertion that he did receive a divine revelation. The critique by Hobbes on this point is irrefutable (above: 273). Besides, through the ages, so many mutually contradictory revelations have been presented as God's truth! All there is upon which to decide that one revelation is true (or, at least, contains truth) and the other revelation not, is the inner conviction that that one revelation is, indeed, a meaningful message. And here we are confronted yet again with exactly the same difficulty: i.e. that authoritative meaning,

314

wherever located and to whom or to what it is ascribed, ultimately depends upon man's assent.

The concept of authority is, basically, a contradictory one. Authority depends upon its recognition by those who are subject to it. It is not based on any objective quality or power which compels to submission. And yet it has power! The contradictions of the concept of authority are of the same kind as those characteristic of the human condition; viz. of being part of one's universe and yet a subject distancing and even judging it. It is this contradiction which drives man out on his quest for meaning. To find meaning is not just a need; it is a must which has all the characteristics of a duty. Just as it is man's duty to realize himself as a (meaningful) partner in his social universe, so it is also his duty to realize himself as a partner in his universe at large by ascribing a meaning to it. Obviously, even modern man still feels that way. His efforts to derive meaning from philosophies of various brands confirm this as convincingly as the fact that, in spite of bitter criticism and ridicule, millions and millions of people still give credence to forms of traditional religion or, instead, embrace a new one which arouses similar criticism as the old forms they rejected. Apparently, finding a meaning is not merely a must because it is a need, but rather a need because it is a must, an obligation imposed by the human condition as such. The inner necessity to realize his partnership in his universe compels man to ascribe a meaning to his universe and his existence in it to which he can wholeheartedly submit himself because an inner conviction persuades him of its authority. Rephrasing all this in the language of formal logic: Meaning is the form by which the subject defines its partnership with its universe.

Why does modern man fail to discover such a meaning whereas previous generations succeeded? How could these contrive a meaning which, in their cultural and intellectual condition, satisfied them? And why is this impossible to modern man who, on solid grounds, rejected these previous solutions? Is it because of his superior knowledge and his more critical methods of thinking? This is the opinion which is often heard, and yet it is false. A meaning to which credence can be given, must reflect reality, must give sense and significance to man's life and conditions as he experiences them from day to day. But modern man does not wish to have it this way. He is in pursuit of happiness, and he innerly rejects every 'meaning' which does not acknowledge his right to happiness. It is a worldview which is fundamentally unrealistic. Man exists unto death, and suffering is an essential part of everyone's life. In nature, we wrote on p. 8, the death of the one is the life of another. No one escapes from suffering. Even those blessed with a long life do not do so. They suffer from arthropathy, cataract, deafness, or dementia, if they do not get cancer or a heart disease. Any effort at attributing meaning to man's existence which ignores suffering, or tries to minimize it by interpreting it with Adam Smith as an inevitable means to the ultimate good, miscarries and founders in contradictions. They create unsolvable problems of theodicy, and end in utter disappointment in the goodness of God and men.

The craving for happiness and the supposition that it could be anyone's right are an insurmountable obstacle on the way to finding a meaning in life, just as they are on the way to finding a religion to which credence can be given. Here comes to mind what Geertz said about religion: "A system of symbols which acts to establish powerful, pervasive, and long-lasting moods and motivations in men by formulating conceptions of a general order of existence and clothing these conceptions with such an aura of factuality that the moods and motivations seem uniquely realistic" (Geertz 1966: 4; above: 151). Religion cannot ignore the factuality of suffering. Actually, the acceptance of suffering and death are basic themes, not only in an important number of primitive religions, but also in such great religions as Buddhism and Christendom as well.

No one in search of meaning can ignore suffering and death as basic themes in human life. One cannot ignore the good things of life either. They belong to life as much as the bad things. The problem is how to combine them in a meaningful whole. Myth has no problems here; it is contradictory by nature (above: 164). However, a mythological solution is unacceptable to modern man. If he fell for it, he would again be unrealistic. There is no reason for it either. In modern man's life suffering and the bad things of life are often more than balanced by the good ones, and he should have no difficulty in seeing his life as a gift which, ultimately, he owes to the mystery behind his universe.

Perhaps there are other ways to give meaning to life and existence than that of considering it as a gift. However that be, the acceptance of life as a gift can hardly be called too far-fetched. In fact, it is an infallible means for giving meaning to life. It creates a relation between man, his universe, and the mystery behind it in which man, as the receiver of a gift, is called to present a return-gift, that of the service which he renders to his fellow-men. On this basis religion, too, can again acquire form and content; viz. in symbolic acts which confirm man's relations with his universe as forms of partnership, and those with the unknowable behind his existence as that of a child with his father. Is not the unknowable the ultimate ground of all that exists? And thus the ultimate source of all the good things of life and all man's sufferings? The age-old father symbol is still the most effective form for expressing the experience of apprehending a power which dispenses both suffering and the good things of life upon man.

There are, of course, various ways to give religious form to this type of meaning, both within Christendom and outside it. It would be preposterous to specify these in a work devoted to an analysis of the foundations of man's moral and religious behaviour. Here, comment must be confined to what is essential. And it certainly is essential that an ultimate meaning based upon the idea that life is a gift, refers directly to the human condition as described and analysed in all the previous chapters. The gift is a phenomenon of basic importance in human life, and its implications are so rich and variegated that there is sound reason to recognize the gift as a sign referring to the ultimate meaning of the human existence.

The one thing which remains to be done here, is to point out some of the consequences which the acceptance of a meaning of this kind may have for modern man's social life. One of these is that the acceptance of suffering, as implied in the acceptance of life as a gift, enables the 'believer' to share the suffering of others in real com-passion, in *Mitleid*, co-suffering in true togetherness. More important, however, is the fact that this view of man's place and duties in this world can inspire to social forms which function as mini-universes in our mass-society of relative strangers. The need for such mini-universes is obvious, and it has been pointed out that the small, religious congregation is one of the opportunities to answer this need (above: 313 f.). To the members of a religious group which accepts suffering as an intrinsic part of human life and the good things of life as a divine gift, it is almost a matter of course that they should shoulder the task of extending a welcome to each other as well as to outsiders who are in search of a spiritual home. Such small congregations have two things in common with a primitive society. The one is that they cultivate personal relations and togetherness. It is an important point because we noted earlier in this work that the essence of the moral law devolves upon the give-and-take and the informal exchange between the members of small groups (above: 128-130). The second point which the small congregation has in common with a primitive society is that, by common ritual acts, it leads its members back to participation in the mystery which is the essence of their universe. It is here that they find that peace with God and men which accompanies true partnership in the acceptance of life as a gift.

There is deep truth in Schumacher's assertion that *Small is beautiful* (1973). Man's real and effective home is, of old, not on the market but in the small group, socially as well as spiritually. Whether mankind will listen to the call of its own, human condition, is quite another matter. There is so much for sale on the market of mass-society that satisfies the desires of the self, and so much entertainment that suppresses the whispering voice of conscience, that it has become uncommonly difficult to exchange the pursuit of happiness for that of partnership. Yet, it is in the latter that the fulfilment of the human existence lies. The quest for partnership comes to an end where ethics and religion meet, i.e. in the acceptance of life as a gift. It comes to an end because the subject, voluntarily accepting the authority of a self-chosen meaning, has realized partnership as its destination. And it is worth a second thought that this acceptance of an ultimate authority is as much a free act of the subject as, in the field of ethics, its decision to liberate itself from the fetters of the past which constitute the self. The ultimate call of the human condition is the call to freedom: the freedom to be good.

Bibliography

ADAMS, PARVEEN (ed.)
1972   Language in Thinking. Hammondsworh, Penguin Books.

ARDREY, ROBERT
1972   The social Contract. Fontana Library.

ARIÈS, PHILIPPE
1977   L'Homme devant la Mort. Paris, Seuil.

ARNDT, P.
1929/1931 Die Religion der Nad'a. *In*: Anthropos 24 and 26.
1951   Religion auf Ost Flores, Adonare und Solor. Studia Instituti Anthropos I, Wien, Mödling, Missionsdruckerei Sr. Gabriel.

ASHLEY, MAURICE
1958   England in the seventeenth Century. Hammondsworth, Penguin Books.

BAAL, J. VAN
1941   Het Aliip-Feest te Bajan. *In*: Mededeelingen Kirtya Liefrinck-van der Tuuk 16.
1947   Over Wegen en Drijfveren der Religie. Amsterdam, Noord-Hollandsche.
1960   Erring Acculturation. *In*: American Anthropologist 62.
1963   The Cult of the Bull-roarer in Australia and Southern New Guinea. *In*: Bijdragen tot de Taal-, Land- en Volkenkunde 119.
1966   Dema. Description and Analysis of Marind-anim Culture. The Hague, Nijhoff.
1967   Mensen in Verandering. Amsterdam, Arbeiderspers.
1969a   The modern School: an imported Institution. *In*: C.E.S.O. 1969b.
1969b   The political Impact of prophetic Movements. *In*: International Yearbook for the Sociology of Religion V.
1971   Symbols for Communication. Assen, Van Gorcum.
1972a   Past Perfect. *In*: S. T. Kimball and J. B. Watson (eds.), Crossing cultural Boundaries. San Francisco, Chandler.
1972b   De Boodschap der drie Illusies. Assen, Van Gorcum.
1974   De Agressie der Gelijken. Assen, Van Gorcum.
1975   Reciprocity and the Position of Women. Assen, Van Gorcum.
1976a   Tussen Kolonie en nationale Staat: de koloniale Staat. *In*: Claessen, Kaayk en Lambregts, Dekolonisatie en Vrijheid. Assen, Van Gorcum.
1976b   Offering, Sacrifice and Gift. *In*: Numen 23.
1977   Geschiedenis en Groei van de Theorie der Culturele Anthropologie. Leiden, Kon. Instituut voor Taal-, Land- en Volkenkunde.
1979   The Role of Truth and Meaning in changing religious Systems. *In*: Vrijhof and Waardenburg (eds.), Official and Popular Religion. The Hague, Mouton.

BAIRD, ROBERT D.
1971   Category Formation and the History of Religions. The Hague, Mouton.

318

BALANDIER, GEORGES
1969   Anthropologie Politique. Paris, Presses Univ. de France.
1972   English translation: Political Anthropology, Hammondworth, Penguin.

BANTON, MICHAEL (ed.)
1965   The Relevance of Models for Social Anthropology; A.S.A. Monographs I; London, Tavistock.

BARTH, FREDRIK
1975   Ritual and Knowledge among the Baktaman of New Guinea. Oslo, Universitätsforlaget.

BATESON, GREGORY and MEAD, MARGARET
1942   Balinese Character. New York Academy of Sciences, Special Publications.

BECKER, ERNEST
1973   The Denial of Death. New York, Free Press.

BEEK, W. E. A. VAN
1973   Alternative Solutions in componential Analysis. In: Bijdragen tot de Taal-, Land- en Volkenkunde
        129: 57.
1978   Bierbrouwers in de Bergen. Mededelingen Inst. v. Cult. Antropologie Utrecht 12.

BENEDICT, RUTH
1934   Patterns of Culture. London, Routledge.

BERGSON, HENRI
1932   Les deux Sources de la Morale et de la Religion. Paris, Alcan.

BERNDT, R. M.
1947   Wuradjeri Magic and 'Clever Men'. In: Oceania 17, 18.
1951   Kunapipi. Melbourne, Cheshire.
1952   Djanggawul. London, Routledge & Kegan Paul.

BERNDT, R. M. and C. H.
1964   The World of the first Australians. Sydney, Ure Smith.

BIDNEY, DAVID
1953   Theoretical Anthropology. New York, Columbia University Press.

BÖHM, A. H.
1936   Het Recht van Kolonisatie. Utrecht, Oosthoek.

BOLTON, NEIL
1972   The Psychology of Thinking. London, Methuen.

BRINK, J. H. VAN DEN
1974   The Haida Indians. Leiden, Brill.

BRUINESSEN, M. M. VAN
1978   Agha, Sheikh and State. Doct. diss., Utrecht.

BURLING, R.
1964   Cognition and componential Analysis. God's Truth or Hocus-Pocus? In: American Anthropol-
        ogist 66: 20.

BURRIDGE, K. O. L.
1969   Tangu Traditions. Oxford, Clarendon Press.

BUYTENDIJK, F. J. J.
1972   Mens en Dier. Utrecht, Spectrum (Dutch Translation of Mensch und Tier, Hamburg, Rowohlt
        1958).

CASSIRER, ERNST
1944   An Essay on Man. Garden City, N. Y., Doubleday.
1953   The Philosophy of Symbolic Forms. 3 vols. New Haven, Yale Univ. Press (Original German edition, 1923/31).

C.E.S.O.
1969a   Primary Education in Sukumaland, Tanzania. Groningen, Wolters-Noordhoff.
1969b   Educational Problems in Developing Countries. Groningen, Wolters-Noordhoff.

CONKLIN, HAROLD C.
1954   The Relation of Hanunóo Culture to the Plant World. Doct. diss., Yale Univ.

DIETERLEN, GERMAINE see: GRIAULE

DIJK, IS. VAN
1949   Socrates. Haarlem, Bohn (2nd. ed.).

DOOB, LEONARD
1960   Becoming more civilized. A psychological Exploration. New Haven, Yale Univ. Press.

DOORN, J. A. A. VAN en LAMMERS, J. C.
1964   Moderne Sociologie. Utrecht, Spectrum.

DORE, R. P.
1965   Education in Tokugawa Japan. Berkeley, Univ. of California Press.

DOREN, CARL VAN
1938   Benjamin Franklin. Abr. ed. New York, Overseas Editions Inc.

DURKHEIM, ÉMILE
1893   De la Division du Travail Social. Paris, Alcan.
1912   Les Formes élémentaires de la Vie religieuse. Paris, Alcan.

DURKHEIM, ÉMILE et MAUSS, MARCEL
1901/02   De quelques Formes primitives de Classification. Année Sociologique VI.

EDEL, MAY(MANDELBAUM) and ABRAHAM
1959   Anthropology and Ethics. Springfield (Ill.), Thomas.

ELIADE, MIRCEA
1948   Traité d'Histoire des Religions. Paris, Payot.
1961   Images and Symbols. London, Harvill.
1964   Shamanism. London, Routledge & Kegan Paul.

ELIAS, NORBERT
1969a   Über den Prozesz der Zivilisation. 2 vols. 2nd. ed., Bern, Francke. Quotations from reprint by Suhrkamp, Taschenbuch Verlag.
1969b   Die höfische Gesellschaft. Neuwied, Luchterhand.

ELIAS, NORBERT and SCOTSON, JOHN L.
1965   The Established and the Outsiders. London, Cass.

ELKIN, A. P.
1954   The Australian Aborigines. Sydney, Angus & Robertson.

ERASMUS, CHARLES J.
1961   Man takes Control. Minneapolis, Univ. of Minnesota Press.

ESCHER, M. C.
1971   De Werelden van M. C. Escher. Ed. J. L. Locher. Amsterdam, Meulenhof.

320

EVANS-PRITCHARD, E. E.
1940   The Nuer. Oxford, Clarendon Press.
1956   Nuer Religion. Oxford, Clarendon Press.

FAHRENFORT, J. J.
1927   Het Hoogste Wezen der Primitieven. Groningen, Wolters.

FAURE, EDGAR et al.
1972   Learning to be. Unesco. London, Harrap.

FIRTH, R.
1967   Tikopia Ritual and Belief. London, Allen and Unwin.

FRAZER, J. G.
1922   The golden Bough. Abr. ed. London, MacMillan.

FREUD, SIGMUND
1901   Zur Psychopathologie des Alltagslebens. In: Monatschrift für Psychiatrie und Neurologie X.
1913   Totem und Tabu. Leipzig/Wien, Holler.
1930   Die Traumdeutung. 8e Aufl. Leipzig, Deuticke.
1940/68 Gesammelte Werke, chronologisch geordnet; 18 vols. Vol. 1-17: London, Imago Publ. Cy.; vol.
        18: Frankfurt am Main, Fischer.

GEERTZ, CLIFFORD
1966   Religion as a cultural System. In: Anthropological Approaches to the Study of Religion, A.S.A.
        Monographs 3 (ed. M. Banton). London, Tavistock.

GEERTZ, HILDRED
1961   The Javanese Family. Glencoe, Free Press.

GEHLEN, ARNOLD
1961   Anthropologische Forschung. München, Rowohlt.

GENNEP, A. VAN
1920   L'État actuel du Problème totémique. Paris, Leroux.

GLOCK, CH. Y. and BELLAH, R. N.
1976   The new religious Consciousness. Berkeley, Univ. of Calif. Press.

GOODENOUGH, WARD H.
1963   Cooperation in Change. New York, Russell Sage Foundation.

GRIAULE, M.
1947   Entretiens avec Ogotemméli. Paris, Duchêne.

GRIAULE, M. et DIETERLEN, GERMAINE
1965   Le Renard pâle. Travaux et mémoires de l'Institut d'Ethnologie 72.

GUSINDE, MARTIN
1966   Von gelben und schwarzen Buschmännern. Graz, Akad. Druck- und Verlagsanstalt.

GUTHRIE, STEWART
1980   A cognitive Theory of Religion. In: Current Anthropology vol. 21, no. 2.

HAGEN, E. E.
1962   On the Theory of social Change. Homewood, Ill., Irwin.

HALBWACHS, M. see: ROUSSEAU, 1943.

HEIDEGGER, MARTIN
1927   Sein und Zeit. Halle, Niermeyer.

HEILER, FRIEDRICH
1922   Die buddhistische Versenkung, 2d. ed. München, Reinhardt.
1923   Das Gebet, 5th ed. München, Reinhardt.

HERSKOVITS, M. J.
1948   Man and his Works. New York, Knopf.
1958   Some further Comments on cultural Relativism. In: American Anthropologist 60: 266.

HOBBES, THOMAS
1952   Leviathan. Reprinted from the edition of 1651. 5th imprint. W. G. Pogson Smith, ed. Oxford, Clarendon Press.

HOCART, A. M.
1941   Kingship (abr. ed.). London, Watts.

HOEBEL, E. ADAMSON
1954   The Law of Primitive Man. Cambridge (Mass.), Harvard Univ. Press.

HOOFF, J. A. R. A. M. VAN
1967   The facial Displays of catarrhine Monkeys and Apes. In: Primate Ethology, D. Morris ed. Weidenfield and Nicholson, London.
1971   Aspects of the social Behaviour and Communication in human and higher Non-primates. Rotterdam, Bronder-Offset.

HOOGERBRUGGE, JAC. and KOOIJMAN, SIMON
1976   Seventy Years of Asmat Woodcarving. In: Asmat Art, Rijksmuseum voor Volkenkunde, Breda.

HUBERT, H. et MAUSS, MARCEL
1899   Étude sur la Nature et la Fonction du Sacrifice. Année Sociologique II. Reprinted in: Sociologie et Anthropologie par M. Mauss, 1950 (Lévi-Strauss ed.).

HUIZINGA, J.
1933   Over de Grenzen van Spel en Ernst in de Cultuur. Haarlem, Tjeenk Willink.
1938   Homo Ludens. Haarlem, Tjeenk Willink.
1948/53 Verzamelde Werken: 9 vols. Haarlem, Tjeenk Willink.

HYLKEMA, S.
1974   Mannen in het Draagnet. Verhandelingen Koninklijk Instituut voor de Taal-, Land- en Volkenkunde 67. 's-Gravenhage, Nijhoff.
n.d.   Unpublished Fieldnotes.

JAMES, WILLIAM
1912   Memories and Studies. London, Longmans & Green.

JENSEN, A. E.
1951   Mythos und Kult bei Naturvölkern. Wiesbaden, Steiner.

JOLLY, ALISON
1972   The Evolution of Primate Behaviour. London, MacMillan.

JONES, RICHARD M.
1970   The new Psychology of Dreaming. New York/London, Grune and Stratton.

JOUVET, MICHEL
1967   The States of Sleep. In: Scientific American. Reprinted in Thompson 1976.

JUNG, C. G.
1928   Die Beziehungen zwischen dem Ich und dem Unbewussten. Darmstadt, Reich.
1952   Symbole der Wandlung. Zürich, Rascher.

322

JUYNBOLL, Th. W.
1925   Handleiding tot de kennis van de Mohammedaanse Wet, 3d. ed. Leiden, Brill.

KANT, IMMANUEL
1920   Kritik der praktischen Vernunft. Ed. Karl Vorländer, 7th ed. Leipzig, Meiner.

KARDINER, ABRAM
1939   The Individual and his Society. New York, Columbia Univ. Press.

KLUCKHOHN, F. R. and STRODTBECK, F. L.
1961   Variations in Value Orientations. New York, Row, Peterson & Co.

KORN, V. E.
1932   Het Adatrecht van Bali, 2nd. ed. 's-Gravenhage, Naeff.

KRETSCHMER, ERNST
1926   Medizinische Psychologie, 3d. ed. Leipzig, Thieme.

KRUYT, ALB. C.
n.d.   Van Heiden tot Christen. Oegstgeest, Zendingsbureau.

KUPER, ADAM
1979   A structural Approach to Dreams. In: Man (N.S.) 14.

LANGER, SUSANNE K.
1951   Philosophy in a new Key. New York, Mentor Books.

LEACH, EDMUND
1976   Culture and Communication. Cambridge, Univ. Press.

LEEUW, G. VAN DER
1933   Phaenomenologie der Religion. Tübingen, Mohr.

LÉVI-STRAUSS, CLAUDE
1945   L'Analyse structurale en Linguistique et en Anthropologie. In: Word I. Reprinted in Lévi-
        Strauss 1958.
1950   Introduction à l'Oeuvre de Marcel Mauss. In: Sociologie et Anthropologie par Marcel Mauss.
        Paris, Presses Univ. de France.
1958   Anthropologie structurale (I). Paris, Plon.
1962a   Le Totémisme aujourd'hui. Paris, Presses Univ. de France.
1962b   La Pensée sauvage. Paris, Plon.
1967   Les Structures élémentaires de la Parenté, 2me éd. Paris/La Haye, Mouton.
1964/71 Les Mythologiques I-IV. Paris, Plon.
1964   I. Le Cru et le Cuit.
1966   II. Du Miel aux Cendres.
1968   III. L'Origine des Manières de Table.
1971   IV. L'Homme nu.

LÉVY-BRUHL, LUCIEN
1910   Les Fonctions mentales dans les Sociétés inférieures. Paris, Alcan.
1922   La Mentalité primitive. Paris, Alcan.

LOWIE, ROBERT H.
1924   Primitive Religion. New York, Boni & Liveright.

MACBEATH, A.
1952   Experiments in Living. London, MacMillan.

MALINOWSKI, BRONISLAW
1922   The Argonauts of the Western Pacific. London, Routledge.

1926   Crime and Custom in savage Society. New York, Harcourt Brace.
1927   Sex and Repression in savage Society. London, Kegan Paul, Trench, Trubner.
1929   The sexual Life of Savages. London, Routledge.
1935   Coral Gardens and their Magic. 2 vols. London, Allen & Unwin.
1948   Magic, Science and Religion, and other Essays by Malinowski. Redfield ed.; Boston, Beacon Press.

MARETT, R. R.
1914   The Threshold of Religion. London, Methuen.

MARX, KARL
1961   Das Kapital. 3 vols. Berlin, Dietz. (First published in 1867).

MAUSS, MARCEL
1923/24   Essai sur le Don. In: Année Sociologique, Nouv. Série I; reprinted in Mauss 1950.
1950   Sociologie et Anthropologie par Marcel Mauss. Lévi-Strauss ed. Paris, Presses Univ. de France.

MAYBURY-LEWIS, DAVID
1969   Akwě-Shavante Society. Oxford, Univ. Press.

McCLELLAND, DAVID C.
1961   The achieving Society. Princeton N. J., Nostrand.

McGAUGH, JAMES L; WEINBERGER, NORMAN M.; WHALEN, RICHARD E. (eds.)
1966   Psychobiology, the psychological Basis of Behaviour. Readings from Scientific American. San Francisco, Freeman.

McKINLEY, ROBERT
1976   Human and proud of it: A structural Treatment of headhunting Rites and the social Definition of Enemies. In: G. N. Appell, Studies in Borneo Societies. Center for Southeast Asian Studies. Northern Illinois Univ., report no. 12.

MEAD, MARGARET
1928   Coming of Age in Samoa. New York, Morrow.
1930   Growing up in New Guinea. New York, Morrow.
1935   Sex and Temperament in three primitive Societies. New York, Morrow.
1936/49   The Mountain Arapesh. In: Anthropological Papers American Museum of Natural History 26, 27, 40, 41.
1949   Male and Female. London, Gollancz.

MEGGITT, M. J.
1957   Notes on the vegetable Foods of the Walbiri of Central Australia. In: Oceania 28: 143.
1962   Desert People. Sydney, Angus & Robertson. Reprint 1965, Univ. of Chicago Press.

MERLEAU-PONTY, M.
1945   Phénoménologie de la Perception; 7me éd. Paris, Gallimard.

MÉTRAUX, ALFRED
1959   Voodoo in Haiti. London, Oxford Univ. Press.
1967   Religions et Magies Indiennes. Paris, Gallimard.

MEULI, K.
1946   Griechische Opferbräuche. In: Phyllobolia für Peter von der Mühl. Basel, Schwabe.

MOONEY, J.
1896   The Ghost-Dance Religion and the Sioux Outbreak of 1890. 14th Annual Report of the American Bureau of Ethnology.

MORRIS, DESMOND
1967   The naked Ape. New York, McGraw-Hill.

324

MOUNTFORD, C. P. (ed.)
1960   Records of the American-Australian Scientific Expedition to Arnhem Land, Vol. 2, Anthropology and Nutrition. Melbourne, Univ. Press.

MURDOCK, G. P.
1949   Social Structure. New York, MacMillan.

MÜLLER, F. Max
1878   Lectures on the Origin and Growth of Religion as illustrated by the Religions of India. London, Longman, Green, Williams and Norgate.

NADEL, S. F.
1942   A black Byzantium. London, Oxford Univ. Press.

NEEDHAM, RODNEY
1972   Belief, Language and Experience. Oxford, Blackwell.

NEWMAN, JAMES R. (ed.)
1956   The World of Mathematics; 4 vols. New York, Simon and Schuster.

NOOY-PALM, HETTY
1968   The Culture of the Pagai-Islands and Sipora; Mentawei. In: Tropical Man I.

ORNSTEIN, JACK H.
1972   The Mind and the Brain. The Hague, Nijhoff.

OTTO, RUDOLF
1917   Das Heilige. Breslau, Trewendt & Granier.

PEURSEN, C. A. VAN
1966   Body, Soul, Spirit. London, Oxford Univ. Press.

PIAGET, JEAN
1962   Play, Dreams and Imitation in Childhood. New York, Norton.

PIEPER, JOSEPH
1958   Musze und Kult, 5th ed. München, Kösel.
1972   Über die Liebe. München, Kösel.

POSPISIL, LEONARD
1956   The Nature of Law. In: Transactions New York Acad. of Sciences, Ser. II, vol. 18 no. 8.
1967   Legal Levels and Multiplicity of legal Systems in human Societies. In: Journal of Conflict Resolution, vol. 11.
1971   The Anthropology of Law. New York, Harper & Row.

PRESCOTT, W. H.
1843   History of the Conquest of Mexico. And later editions.
1847   History of the Conquest of Peru. And later editions.

PREUSZ, K. Th.
1914   Die geistige Kultur der Naturvölker. Leipzig/Berlin, Teubner.
1926   Glauben und Mystik im Schatten des höchsten Wesens. Leipzig, Hirschfeld.
1930   Tod und Unsterblichkeit im Glauben der Naturvölker. Tübingen, Mohr.

RADCLIFFE-BROWN, A. R.
1922   The Andaman Islanders. Cambridge, Univ. Press.
1924   The Mother's Brother in South Africa. In: South African Journal of Science 21. Reprinted in Radcliffe-Brown 1952.
1952   Structure and Function in primitive Society. London, Cohen & West.

RADIN, PAUL
1938   Primitive Religion. London, Hamish Hamilton.
1951   Die religiöse Erfahrung der Naturvölker. Zürich, Rhein Verlag.

RAPAPORT, DAVID
1971   Emotions and Memory; 3d ed. New York, International Universities Press.

READ, K. E.
1955   Morality and the Concept of the Person among the Gahuku-Gama. In: Oceania 25: 233.

REDFIELD, ROBERT
1953   The primitive World and its Transformations. Ithaca, N. Y., Cornell Univ. Press.

REVERS, WILH. J.
1949   Die Psychologie der Langeweile. Meisenheim a. Glan, Hain.

RIJKSEN, H. D.
1978   A Field Study on Sumatran Orang Utans. Wageningen, Veenman.

ROBERTSON SMITH, W.
1889   Lectures on the Religion of the Semites. Edinburgh, Black.

ROHEIM, GEZA
1930   Animism, Magic and the Divine King. London, Kegan Paul, Trench, Trubner.

ROUSSEAU, JEAN-JACQUES
1943   Du Contrat Social; Texte original publié avec Introduction par Maurice Halbwachs. Aubier, Ed. Montaignes.
1959/69 Oeuvres Complètes. Paris, Gallimard.

SAHLINS, MARSHALL D.
1965   On the Sociology of Primitive Exchange. In: Banton 1965.
1968   Philosophie politique de l'Essai sur le Don. In: Cahiers de l'Homme VIII (4).

SAPIR, EDWARD
1932   Cultural Anthropology and Psychiatry. In: Journal of Abnormal and Social Psychology 27. Reprint in Selected Writings, Sapir 1949.
1934   The Emergence of the Concept of Personality in a Study of Culture. In: Journal of Social Psychology 5. Reprint in Sapir 1949.
1949   Selected Writings of Edward Sapir. David Mandelbaum ed. Berkeley/Los Angeles, Univ. of California Press.

SARTRE, JEAN-PAUL
1943   L'Être et le Néant. Paris, Gallimard.
1946   L'Existentialisme est un Humanisme. Paris, Nagel.

SCHEFOLD, REIMAR
1972   Divination in Mentawei. In: Tropical Man I.
1973a   Religiöse Vorstellungen auf Siberut, Mentawei. In: Anthropos 68.
1973b   Schlitztrommeln und Trommelsprache in Mentawei. Zeitschrift für Ethnologie 98.
1975   Das bewirkende Symbol. Stencilled ms., Amsterdam, Free University.
1976   Religious Involution. In: Tropical Man 5.
1979   Speelgoed voor de Zielen. Catalogue Exhibition Nusantara Museum, Delft, and Rietberg Museum, Zürich.

SCHMIDT, WILHELM
1908/10 L'Origine de l'Idée de Dieu. In: Anthropos 1, 2, 3.
1930   Handbuch der vergleichenden Religionsgeschichte. Münster, Asschendorf.
1926/55 Der Ursprung der Gottesidee; 12 vols. Münster, Asschendorf.

SCHRÖDER, D.
1955   Zur Struktur des Schamanismus. *In*: Anthropos 55. Reprinted in C. Schmitz, Religions-Ethno-
        logie. Frankfurt, Akad. Verlagsgesellschaft, 1964.

SCHULTZE-WESTRUM, THOMAS
1965   Innerartliche Verständigung durch Düfte beim Gleitbeutlern *Petaurus Breviceps Papuanus Thomas.*
        In: Zeitschrift für vergleichende Physiologie 50.

SCHUMACHER, E. F.
1973   Small is beautiful. A Study of Economics as if people mattered. London, Blond & Briggs.

SLICHER VAN BATH, B. H.
1960   De agrarische Geschiedenis van West-Europa (500-1850). Utrecht, Aula.

SMITH, ADAM
1948   Moral and Political Philosophy. Ed. Herb. W. Schneider. New York, Hafner. Containing the
        slightly abridged text of Theory of Moral Sentiments, and selections from the Lectures and from
        The Wealth of Nations.

SNYDER, FREDERICK
1966   Toward an evolutionary Theory of Dreaming. *In*: American Journal of Psychiatry 123 (2): 121.

SOUSTELLE, JACQUES
1955   La Vie quotidienne des Aztèques à la veille de la Conquête Espagnole. Paris, Hachette.

SPENCER, B. and GILLEN, F. J.
1927   The Arunta; 2 vols. London, Macmillan.

STAAL, FRITS
1975   Exploring Mysticism. Hammondsworth, Penguin Books.

STRATHERN, A. J.
1970   The female and male Spirit Cults in Mount Hagen. *In*: Man (n.s.) 5: 571.

STRATHERN, MARILYN
1972   Women in Between. London/New York, Seminar Press.

STREHLOW, C. und LEONHARDI, M. VON
1907/21 Die Aranda- und Loritja Stämme in Zentral Australien. Veröffentlichungen des Frankfurter
        Museums für Völkerkunde, Frankfurt.

STREHLOW, T. G. H.
1947   Aranda Traditions. Melbourne, University Press.

TAWNEY, R. H.
1938   Religion and the Rise of Capitalism. Pelican Books A 23.

TAX, SOL
1941   World View and social Relations in Guatemala. *In*: American Anthrpologist 43.

TENNEKES, J.
1971   Anthropology, Relativism and Method. Assen, Van Gorcum.

THOMPSON, RICHARD F. (ed)
1976   Progress in Psychobiology. Readings from Scientific American. San Francisco, Freeman.

TIGER, L. and FOX, R.
1972   The Imperial Animal. New York, Dell (Delta Books).

TINBERGEN, N.
1952   The curious Behaviour of the Stickleback. *In*: Scientific American; reprinted in McGaugh et al.
        1966.

1958   Curious Naturalists. London, Country Life Ltd.
1960   Spieden en Speuren. Amsterdam, Ploegsma. (Enlarged Dutch edition of Tinbergen 1958; quotations refer to 2nd. ed., 1971).

TROELTSCH, ERNST
1912   Die Soziallehren der Christlichen Kirchen. Mohr, Tübingen.

TURNBULL, H. W.
1956   The great Mathematicians. *In*: Newman 1956.

TURNER, VICTOR W.
1969   The ritual Process. Structure and Anti-Structure. Aldine Publ. Cy., Chicago.

TYLOR, EDWARD B.
1871   Primitive Culture. 2 vols. London, Murray. (Ref. to 4th ed.).
1889   On a Method of Investigating the Development of Institutions; applied to Laws of Marriage and Descent. *In*: Journal Anthropological Institute 18.

UBEROI, J. P. SINGH
1962   Politics of the Kula Ring. Manchester, Univ. Press.

UMBGROVE, J. H. F.
1946   Leven en Materie. 3d ed. 's-Gravenhage, Nijhoff.

VERMASEREN, M. J.
1970   Matrem in Leone sedentem. Leiden, Brill.

VYGOTSKY, L. S.
1962   Thought and Language. Selected fragments *in* Parveen Adams, 1972.

WALTER, W. GREY
1961   The living Brain. Hammondsworth, Penguin Books.

WARNER, W. LLOYD
1958   A black Civilization. Rev. ed. New York, Harper.

WASHBURN, SHERWOOD L.
1960   Tools and Human Evolution. *In*: Scientific American. Reprinted in Thompson 1976.

WEBER, MAX
1904/05 Die protestantische Ethik und der Geist des Kapitalismus. *In:* Archiv für Sozialwissenschaft und Sozialpolitik 20, 21. Re-edited in Gesammelte Aufsätze zur Religionssoziologie; Tübingen, Mohr, 1920.

WESTERMARCK, E.
1906/08 The Origin and Development of the Moral Ideas. 2 vols. London, MacMillan.
1932   Ethical Relativity. New York, Harcourt.

WHITING, BEATRICE (ed.)
1963   Six Cultures. New York, Wiley.

WHITING, JOHN W. M.
1941   Becoming a Kwoma. New Haven, Yale Univ. Press.

WHITING, J. W. M. and CHILD, I. L.
1953   Child Training and Personality Development. New Haven, Yale Univ. Press.

WHORF, B.
1941   The Relation of habitual Thought and Behaviour to Language. *In*: Essays in Memory of Edward Sapir. Reprinted in Parveen Adams, 1972.

WILKEN, G. A.
1886/87   Über das Haaropfer und einige andere Trauergebräuche bei den Völkern Indonesiens. Revue
          Coloniale Internationale. Reprinted in Verspreide Geschriften, edited by F. D. E. van Ossen-
          bruggen. 4 vols. Semarang, Van Dorp, 1912.

WINDELBAND, WILHELM
1919   Präludien; 2 vols. 6th ed. Tübingen, Mohr.

WIRZ, PAUL
1922/25   Die Marind-anim von Holländisch-Süd-Neu-Guinea I-IV; 2 vols. Hamburgische Universität,
          Abhandlungen aus dem Gebiete der Auslandskunde Bd. 10 und 16. Hamburg.

ZANTWIJK, R. A. M. VAN
1967   Servants of the Saints. Assen, Van Gorcum.

Index of Names

Adams, P., 29
Ardrey, R., 8
Ariès, P., 62
Aristotle, 51, 92
Arndt, P., 214, 229, 247
Ashley, M., 273

Baal, J. v., 24, 34f., 62, 75f., 83, 91f., 113, 137,
141f., 154, 163, 168, 173, 175, 179, 182, 185f.,
191, 195f., 205, 207f., 216, 226, 228, 230ff.,
236, 302, 307
Bach, J.S., 36
Baird, R.D., 151
Balaam, 237
Balandier, G., 113f., 117
Barth, F., 209f., 220, 227f.
Becker, E., 62, 201
Beek, W.E.A.v., 57, 207, 214
Bellah, R.N., 306
Benedict, R., 54, 121
Bergson, H., 153
Berndt, R.M., 62, 105, 141, 174, 190, 202f., 208
Berndt, C.H., 62, 105, 190, 202f., 208
Beth, 92
Bèze, Th. de, 117, 279
Bidney, D., 126
Boas, F., 100
Böhm, A.H., 270
Bolton, N., 29f.
Bray, G. de, 130
Brink, J.H. v.d., 100
Bruinessen, M.M. v., 80, 123
Burling, R., 57
Burridge, K.O.L., 84
Buijtendijk, F.J.J., 10, 13

Cabot, J., 269f.
Calvin, J., 117, 264f., 269, 277, 279
Carrel, A., 9

Cassirer, E., 19, 26, 31
C.E.S.O., 296
Clairvaux, B. de, 130
Columbus, C., 267, 269f.
Conklin, H.C., 31
Copernicus, 271f.

Descartes, R., 264, 271
Dieterlen, G., 246
Dijk, I. v., 56
Doob, L., 259
Doorn, J.A.A. v., 108
Dore, R.P., 261
Doren, C. v., 262
Durkheim, E., 46, 91, 125, 166, 198f.

Edel, M & A., 127
Eliade, M., 40, 235
Elias, N., 116, 118, 266, 287
Erasmus, C.J., 258
Escher, M.C., 34
Evans-Pritchard, E.E., 207, 231f.
Eysink, 10

Faure, E., 295
Fox, R., 69
Franklin, B., 262
Frazer, J.G., 184, 188, 219
Freud, S., 22f., 32, 45, 54, 126

Gardner, R., 79
Geertz, C., 151, 316
Geertz, H., 54
Gehlen, A., 59
Gennep, A. v., 199
Gillen, F.J., 105, 173, 190
Glock, C.Y., 306
Goodenough, W.H., 202f.
Griaule, M., 246

330

Subject Index

Aesthetic, 39f., 275, 308f., 314
Affect(ive), 4, 6, 23f., 26ff., 33f., 36, 40, 44, 47f.,
    51, 80f., 118, 129, 131, 171, 244f., 273, 303
After-life, 202, 268, 278, 304
Aggression(ive), 4, 15, 74f., 77ff., 81, 95, 119f.,
    176, 179, 222ff., 266, 300ff.
Agriculture, 47, 85, 96, 264
Alienation, 61ff., 253, 302, 313
Alliance, 61ff., 253, 302, 313
Alliance, 82f., 85, 97, 99, 302
Amnesia, 54
Ancestor, 40, 67, 70, 113, 141f., 169, 171-176,
    178ff., 184, 186, 192f., 198-201, 204, 206,
    208ff., 213ff., 217, 222, 227ff., 236, 242, 245,
    247f.
Animism, 161, 198f., 202
Anonymous, 37f., 286, 290, 297, 299ff., 313
Aranda, 40f., 161, 171, 173ff., 180, 183, 188, 314
Archetype, 40f.
Art, 21, 24f., 33ff., 37f., 41, 44, 49, 61, 154f., 300f.,
    307-310
Atone(ment), 105ff., 131, 230f.
Attitude, 258f., 278
Authority, 41, 66, 85, 88, 90, 104, 106, 123, 125,
    127, 131, 137, 139, 142, 164, 199f., 284f., 291,
    302, 305, 310-315, 317
Autonomy, 7, 281
Avarice, 264, 270, 298
Avunculate, 83ff.
Avunculocal, 85

Baby, 48, 52, 71, 75f., 103, 152, 190, 193, 212, 217,
    294
Baktaman, 132, 209f., 220, 228
Bali, 37, 39, 88, 122f., 235
Ballet, 21, 37f.
Beauty, 24f., 307f.
Behaviourist, 10
Belief(ve), 38, 61, 163, 187, 192, 194f., 200,
202-206, 208, 214, 227f., 238, 240f., 243, 246ff.,
    250, 252f., 287, 306, 309, 316
Bore(dom), 28, 260, 298ff.
Brain, 13f., 45f., 49, 52
Bribe, 97, 101, 214, 217, 226, 232
Brideprice, 97
Brother, 83ff., 87, 89, 102, 110, 141, 288
Buddhism, 198, 243ff., 248, 316
Bushmen, 152, 204-207

Capitalism, 115, 275, 293
Capital punishment, 18, 106
Caste, 125, 140, 143, 221, 269
Cattle, 122, 219, 223, 229, 231f.
Central nervous system, 7, 10f.
Chant, 48, 172
Chimpanzee, 20, 71f.
Choice, 13f., 25, 37, 52, 54, 57f., 63, 80, 85, 92,
    144, 192, 285, 287, 300, 306, 310
Classification, 28, 49, 92, 109, 166f., 175ff., 179,
    197, 199, 210, 226, 246
Collecting, 69-72, 76f., 80f., 88f., 119, 141, 152,
    219
Commensal(ity), 128, 209, 216, 220, 227, 232
Communication, 16, 20, 25f., 29-32, 42, 55, 59f.,
    130, 135, 159, 161, 163, 170, 211, 213ff., 224,
    229, 232f., 238, 240, 253, 300ff., 308
Competition, 16, 74, 78f., 90, 96, 115f., 134, 160,
    290, 293, 295-298, 300f.
Congener, 13, 16, 53, 59, 74f., 93, 132
Conscience, 56, 66, 109, 117, 140, 143ff., 237, 264,
    266, 270, 277, 281, 289, 317
Contract (social), 91, 117f., 134, 136f., 230, 280,
    284f., 305
Credit, 97, 133f.
Crime, 93, 104-107, 111, 131
Culprit, 18, 104-107, 111, 131
Cultural personality, 54, 56, 297, 301
Culture hero, 141, 199

333

Cure(ative), 156, 189, 191ff., 196

Dance, 21, 25, 37-41, 79, 142, 169f., 213, 221, 234ff.
Daughter, 76, 86, 99, 177, 288
Dead, Death, 8f., 25, 45, 62, 72, 86, 106, 110, 152, 156, 159, 171, 174, 176f., 190, 193f., 200-204, 206-209, 212ff., 222, 224f., 229, 232, 234, 236, 247, 250, 252, 273f., 315f.
Deafmute, 21, 29
Deity, 142, 207, 217, 219f., 222, 226, 228, 230f., 234ff., 238
Desire, 18, 26, 51, 54, 56ff., 60, 81, 89, 95, 97, 100, 109, 144, 160, 182, 184f., 197, 227, 230, 239ff., 244, 269, 274, 313, 317
Die, dying, 48, 103, 172, 196, 202f., 224f.
Diet, 8, 68ff., 74, 76
Divination, 41, 169f., 198, 208, 211, 213ff., 229, 247, 252
Drama(tization), 21, 25, 33, 38, 40f., 161f., 169ff., 173, 175, 179, 181ff., 196, 198f., 209, 216, 222, 224ff.
Dream, 14, 21-24, 34f., 40, 45, 54, 159ff., 164-167, 169f., 175, 194, 198, 201, 211, 213, 229, 235f., 242, 245, 273, 294, 310
Dreamtime, 171, 173, 175, 206
Drive, 27, 32, 42, 51-54, 60, 74, 298

Ecstasy, 25, 308
Education, 18, 54, 58, 76, 79, 87, 140, 143f., 157f., 202, 248, 258, 260, 263, 268, 279, 291, 294ff., 300
Employer, 280, 284f.
Enemy, 13, 16f., 78, 82, 106, 132, 153, 177, 224, 236
Enlightenment, 250, 256, 277, 281, 304
Entertainment, 37f., 44, 156, 286f., 299f., 304, 308, 310, 317
Equal(ity), 88, 90f., 94f., 98, 100, 104, 107, 117, 133, 135f., 199, 279-282, 284f., 290-293, 295ff., 301f., 313
Ethology(ist), 10, 15f., 52, 67, 74f.
Exchange, 77, 80, 91f., 94, 96-101, 103, 106f., 115, 131-135, 139, 172, 288ff., 317
Existential(ism), 46, 165, 201, 246, 254, 283, 314
Exogamy, 82, 85, 110
Expiate, 143, 162, 216, 221, 231
Ezam-uzum, 181f., 196

Falsify, s. non-falsifiable
Family, 16, 53, 72, 76f., 80, 82f., 85, 87-91, 97, 101-104, 111f., 121, 129, 131, 152, 158, 211, 229ff., 237, 252, 264, 288ff., 294, 302ff.

Father, 41, 73, 77, 83ff., 89f., 100, 103, 108, 110, 122, 158, 169, 172, 175f., 197, 199f., 203-207, 215, 229f., 236, 238, 241, 258, 296, 302f., 316
Feeling, 23-28, 33, 36, 61f., 78, 92, 99, 103, 105ff., 154, 156, 161f., 198, 216, 220, 239, 241, 244, 251, 299
Fertility, 8, 77, 89, 141ff., 161, 171, 174f., 178f., 200, 209, 225
Folktale, 163f., 242
Free(dom), 3, 7, 10f., 14, 57f., 60, 62, 85f., 95f., 104, 129, 134, 144f., 250, 259, 275, 278-281, 283ff., 287, 300, 313, 317
Funeral, 25, 98, 174

Games, 291-294, 296, 298-301, 310
Garden(ing), 59, 78, 81, 87ff., 115, 128, 184, 209, 212, 276
Genetic, 7ff., 40f., 45, 69
Gift, 58, 91f., 94, 96-101, 107, 131ff., 145, 216f., 220, 222, 226-232, 290, 316f.
Give-and-take, 91, 93f., 97, 101, 103, 107, 131, 226, 228, 302
Grace, 162, 227f., 268, 277
Greek, 180, 200, 219, 225, 228, 248-251
Guilt, 142f., 145, 214, 239f.

Happiness, 17, 59ff., 63, 82, 86f., 130, 144, 250, 256, 274f., 277f., 281, 283, 288, 291, 294, 299-304, 306, 315, 317
Headhunting, 38, 74, 142, 176ff., 180f., 218, 222f.
Hierarchy, 72, 112, 115
Homo sapiens, 15, 67, 69, 72
Horticulture, 81, 83, 153, 171
Human condition, VII, 4ff., 44, 51, 63, 66, 80, 98, 128f., 140, 149, 164, 197, 246, 253, 315ff.
Hunter, 21, 68-74, 76ff., 80ff., 87, 99f., 115, 119, 152, 160, 171, 183, 185, 188, 208f., 211f., 219f., 224, 252, 265

Image, 23, 38, 40, 44, 56, 61, 93, 185, 206, 243, 246, 309
Imagination, 17, 128, 154ff., 159, 184
Imo, 167, 177, 181f., 186, 195
Impersonation, 40, 170, 172f., 176, 182, 187, 198, 241
Impurity, 125, 140, 221, 230f., 244
Incarnation, 88, 175
Incest, 84, 231
Individuation, 7, 9
Inferior, 91, 96, 107f., 200, 274, 309
Initiation, 46, 142, 172f., 176, 180, 189f., 192, 195, 199, 210, 218, 235
Injury, 103ff., 120, 125

334

335

251, 259, 266, 268, 313